Inconclusive Theologies

Sor Juana Inés de la Cruz, Kierkegaard, and Theological Discourse

MERCER
UNIVERSITY PRESS

Endowed by
TOM WATSON BROWN
and
THE WATSON-BROWN FOUNDATION, INC.

Inconclusive Theologies

Sor Juana Inés de la Cruz, Kierkegaard,

and Theological Discourse

Lisa D. Powell

Mercer University Press
Macon, Georgia

MUP/ P475

1400 Coleman Avenue
Macon, Georgia 31207

First Edition

Books published by Mercer University Press are printed on acid-free paper that meets the requirements of the American National Standard for Information Sciences—Permanence of Paper for Printed Library Materials.

Mercer University Press is a member of Green Press Initiative (greenpressinitiative.org), a nonprofit organization working to help publishers and printers increase their use of recycled paper and decrease their use of fiber derived from endangered forests. This book is printed on recycled paper.

Chapter 2 was previously published in a slightly different version in *Journal of Feminist Studies in Religion* 27:2 (Fall 2011).

Library of Congress Cataloging-in-Publication Data

Powell, Lisa D., 1975-
Inconclusive theologies : sor Juana Inés de la Cruz, Kierkegaard, and theological discourse / Lisa D. Powell. -- First Edition.
pages cm
Includes bibliographical references and index.
ISBN 978-0-88146-463-4 (pbk. : alk. paper) -- ISBN 0-88146-463-5 (pbk. : alk. paper)
1. Juana Inés de la Cruz, sor, 1481-1534. 2. Kierkegaard, Søren, 1813-1855. I. Title.
BX4705.J726P69 2013
230.01--dc23

2013036286

Contents

For David,

my brother in blood and the struggle

"O you dig and I dig, and I dig through to you."

—Paul Celan

Acknowledgments

Philosopher and theologian Franz Rosenzweig said he could no longer write a book, as everything turns into a letter, and in a highly philosophical letter to his friend, said he had written the ideas there recorded "looking at you." There are a number of people I wrote this "looking at" (and not all of them can be recognized here): my friend and colleague at Princeton Seminary, Erin Kesterson Bowers, who was my constant theological conversation partner throughout our M.Div. and Ph.D. programs and with whom I met regularly to discuss how the things we learned applied to our Christian lives; Christy Barker, with whom I have maintained a correspondence through handwritten letters for over twenty years—I continue to learn about communication and the life of faith through our exchange.

I am grateful to Mark Taylor for his willingness to advise me in this project from its most nascent stages; he continues to be an example for me of one whose thought is embodied in action, or rather whose commitment and activism are also reflected in scholarship. Luis Rivera-Pagán not only served on my dissertation committee and endured my labored translations but also regularly asked me about my life, my family, and all of those topics that press upon one in all stages of life and education but are rarely considered in institutional settings. I hope I model such humanizing interaction with my students. I am also grateful to Wentzel van Huyssteen who first taught me about epistemic humility, and Yolanda Martínez-San Miguel, who gave me invaluable suggestions and guidance in this project; I am greatly indebted to her.

Many colleagues at Princeton were excellent conversation partners throughout this process and continue to be: Alice Yafeh, Sarah Zhang, Rosanna Suh, Stina Busman, James Logan, Eduard Iricinschi, Elias Ortega, Laura Thelander, Kevin Hector, Scott Jones, Eric Gregory, and Ken Reynhout. In our exchanges they challenge me to expand my understanding and consider alternative perspectives, and I am better for it.

Sor Juana wrote that "had Aristotle cooked, he would have written a great deal more." Thanks to Jennifer Thweatt-Bates and Jennifer Bayne, who not only both read portions of this manuscript, but cooked together with me as we shared culinary secrets, theological musings, and life experiences. Some of the best theological dialogue happens in the kitchen and the women's restroom.

I am grateful to my colleagues at St. Ambrose University for many reasons: to Corinne Winter for her unflagging support since my first day on campus and for her helpful comments on various drafts of chapter 2; to Mara Adams for her encouragement to keep pressing on in research; and to an interdisciplinary group of scholars at Ambrose who are significant partners in dialogue about pedagogy, activism, faith, and gender: Jessica Gosnell, Katy Strzepek, Micah Kiel, Regina Matheson, Matthew Coomber, Bill Parsons, and Tadd Ruetenik.

I must acknowledge my indebtedness to the literature department at Point Loma Nazarene University in San Diego, California, where I was first introduced to Sor Juana Inés de la Cruz and first encouraged by a table full of female faculty to pursue theological study. I owe much to the education I received at that institution and department. I am also forever indebted to the Las Cruces First Church of the Nazarene, where I first learned what the Church can be and have never forgotten. My commitment to the Church of Christ owes much to this community.

My family deserves recognition for the completion of this study. I owe much of this project to my mother, Mary Bryson, who wisely encouraged me to write what interested me and not to worry so much about what interested "the academy." Thus, I greatly enjoyed this project from start to finish. I attribute my love of reading, as do my siblings, to our father, Reverend Larry Powell, from whose library I began to steal at a young age and continue to do so. My stepfather, Allen Bryson, has also been an invaluable support throughout this and all my pursuits; he has always endeavored to read what I write—from high-school term papers to college essays to this book when it was still a long dissertation. I am grateful to my sister Kathy, who came home from a women's studies class in college and talked about it around the dinner table. And thanks to my parents for encouraging us to think and talk about our ideas. I save a special thanks for my brother, to whom I dedicate this book. Neither this book, nor I as a person, would be the same without his influence.

And finally, I am grateful to my husband and true partner, John Arnold. He also brought with him an incredible family, who have become as supportive of me and my work as my own blood; I am thankful for them. John is my greatest support and encouragement; he is my calm in the storm. I hope my work will always reflect his peaceful influence and hopeful perspective.

I received the proofs for this book the week I gave birth to our daughter, Marigold Inez. May she share Sor Juana's courage, passion, creativity, and faith.

Introduction

Toward an Inconclusive Theology

"System and conclusiveness correspond to each other, but existence is the very opposite."—Søren Kierkegaard's Johannes Climacus

Statement of the Argument

This book investigates what it means for Christianity, and specifically for Christian discourse, that existence resists "system and conclusiveness." Following Søren Kierkegaard's argument that Christianity pertains to existence, to be detailed in chapter 1, I consider how the nature of human existence influences the Christian faith and the way in which this should be communicated theologically. The discipline of Christian theology has long been dominated by propositional and systematic forms of discourse, a reality Kierkegaard scorned. However, as Christian faith pertains to people in specific socio-temporal locations, I claim along with Kierkegaard that it is not conclusive, and thus does not accommodate a system. In fact, to the extent that Christianity concerns persons in existence, it is by nature *inconclusive*; therefore, forms of communicating it should correspond to this reality of Christian revelation from the human side of the God-human relationship. This book considers the ways this subjective side of Christianity—as it pertains to subjects in ongoing existence—should influence forms of communicating it.

Approximation, speculation, interpretation, and precommitments—all activities of any Christian subjects—have always influenced conceptions of God and of God's involvement with the world. Such interpretive elements are known to impact conclusions in fields of study like history, for example, and recent work asserts that even scientific disciplines, once considered pure and objective, involve interpretation and pre-commitments to particular scientific theories that impact the evaluation of the final outcome. Few, if any, fields of knowledge remain unaffected by interpretation, or the influence of the subject herself in the act of knowing. So, too, in the field of dogmatics: interpretation, priorities, and commitments are inevitably involved. Thus, theology is clearly not the objective expression of fact, and perhaps more importantly the purpose of it is not simply to communicate a constructed set of beliefs from one person to another. Rather, Christian teaching from its inception has been about conversion: conversion of life, or transformation. If one desires to communicate that Christianity includes making Christian knowledge one's own in faith, one needs to invite the other to appr opriate it.

Certainly the Church has not always retained this view, and has at various points in its history taken theology to be the legislation of acceptable beliefs, controlled by the church and imposed upon the laity and clergy alike. The church began establishing acceptable boundaries for Christian discourse centuries ago, when the church first held binding councils to determine acceptable teachings. From the First Ecumenical Council, convened by Emperor Constantine in 325, and for centuries thereafter, the most powerful and influential leaders of the church gathered under the summons of the top political authority in the empire to establish official church doctrine by which the orthodox and the heretic could be measured.[1] Since then Christian dogma has primarily been written in the language and style of the elite and educated—in Latin, for example, instead of the vernacular. And although less is written in Latin today, certainly the languages, schools, and styles of European universities dominate.

Christian dogma has thus proceeded according to an established set of rules, setting up its own hierarchy and canon. Those discourses that abide by this system of rules are considered acceptable transmitters of truth. This traditional Christian theology looks at revelation as a completed event to which we have access through scripture and tends to take the form of an objective and propositional account so as to avoid ambiguity, unresolved tensions, or room for alternative understandings. Unfortunately, the desire to safeguard correct teaching has become the primary function of the theological discipline, and at times has become a matter of protecting words and ideas to the point that punishment and death were imposed upon those who considered things outside of it.[2] Theology in this view appears more as entrenchment, a retreat to protect

---

[1] H. A. Drake, *Constantine and the Bishops: The Politics of Intolerance* (Baltimore: The Johns Hopkins University Press, 2000). See also Joerg Rieger, *Christ and Empire: From Paul to Postcolonial Times* (Minneapolis: Augsburg Fortress Press, 2007).

[2] An obvious example of when this was the case is the Inquisition, when a powerful ecclesiastical body, the Holy Office, functioned primarily to protect the Church's teaching, conducting trials, tortures, and executions of those whose ideas and/or activities were in question. This was not the case only during the Middle Ages, however. Maximus the Confessor (580–662) was tried in Constantinople in 661/662 for his views on Christ and condemned to mutilation for his refusal to stay silent even after

and conserve, rather than an open form of discourse in which the person finds herself an active subject in its meaning.

Rather than a closed form of theology that is imposed upon a person from outside sources of authority, I am here explicating a form of theology that remains open, that welcomes dialogue, and is non-coercive. I am not denying that one function of theology is doctrinal and that some level of preservation of teaching is a valid practice. However, if we agree with the impetus of Kierkegaard's pseudonymous authorship, then we would affirm that this cannot be the primary function of theology, because this closed form of authoritative dogmatism cannot express an important aspect of religious truth, which is subjective, inextricably tied to faith.

This book explores the character of faith as it pertains to the human subject or subjectivities, and its system-resistant qualities, but not simply by developing a contemporary attack on systematicity; instead, believing that the history of theology has always deployed genres that defy systemic closure, we can turn to the Christian tradition itself to find faith developed through theological discourses that respect and express the inchoate, interpretive aspects of Christian faith. If one looks at the diversity within Christian scripture, for example, one finds a plurality of voices and of genres (narrative, poetry, philosophical discourse, epistle, etc.), and interpretations of God's relationship to the world and humanity. One may interpret this diversity as a call for theological discourse to take a variety of forms in openness and a variety of perspectives as well, in accordance with scripture.

Accordingly, this book examines the theological contribution of Sor Juana Inés de la Cruz (c. 1648–1695) utilizing Kierkegaard's theory of indirect communication. Sor Juana may not have employed genres with the same sort of intentionality as Kierkegaard, since as a woman she was forbidden to write in forms generally considered legitimate for theology—sermon, treatise, or summa. However, the content of her work clearly addresses theological themes,

---

he had been banished years before. The eighty-two-year-old monk had his right hand cut off (for refusing to sign a doctrinal statement with which he did not agree) and had his tongue cut out (for continuing to confess the then heretical doctrine of two wills in Christ), before he was again sent off to exile, where he never recovered from the torture and soon died. During the Third Council of Constantinople, the Sixth Ecumenical Council (680–681), Maximus's teaching on the distinct natures of Christ, including distinct wills, divine and human, became the orthodox belief, and he was declared innocent of heresy and named a saint.

and she utilizes literary forms to enter the epistemological debates of her day and to question the prevailing ways of acquiring and communicating knowledge. In the pages that follow I examine letters, dramas, and poetry by Sor Juana, finding in her discourse an instructive example of the communication of Christianity that conveys the subjective aspect of Christian knowledge. Further, Sor Juana's use of these genres in discourse about God highlights the inconclusive nature of theological construction, and actually functions to resist the totalizing tendencies of traditional systematic theology.

Sor Juana's discourse contrasts those that come from an authoritarian position, imposed from above and insistent on the absolute acceptance of its original articulation. She achieves this in part through epistemic humility and her conception of the ongoing process of the Christian life, which includes a conviction that its ideas and growth in knowledge never reach conclusion in time. I interpret Sor Juana's contribution through the concerns of theology in postmodernity, particularly as her work resists the enforced boundaries of a closed system of thought.[3] The unique contribution of this book lies in its examination of her work as a methodological challenge and opportunity for contemporary constructive theology. Overall, then, this project argues that Sor Juana's thought provides an example, from within the history of theology, of theological genres that respect the inconclusiveness of existence, display a resistance to closure, and foreground the subjectivity and interpretive variety of Christian faith.

Sor Juana's Context

The Baroque period to which Sor Juana dates experienced a reaction against the stronghold the church had over centers of learning, knowledge, and notions of truth. The church tightened its grip over these domains in response to the crisis of the Reformation, and conflict developed further during the seventeenth century as modern ideas began to emerge and question these authorities.[4] In

---

[3] This interpretation is not unfounded as she was writing during the Inquisition in New Spain, when scholasticism still ruled the field in Catholic theology, and orthodoxy was monitored closely. Sor Juana's confessor, Núñez de Miranda, for much of her convent life was, in fact, a censor for the Holy Office. The theological assertions she makes in light of this context, then, serve as reasonable support for such a reading.

[4] See José Antonio Marvall, "From the Renaissance to the Baroque: The Diphasic Schema of a Social Crisis," in *Literature Among Discourses: The Spanish Golden Age*, ed. Wlad Godzich and Nicholas Spadaccini (Minneapolis: University of Minnesota Press, 1986) 3–40.

time the ideas of modernity would also become so rigid and authoritative, dictating what can be known and how that knowledge can be gained and disseminated, that a further movement would emerge to release its hold—this time of transition we call postmodernity.[5] The world is now witnessing a reaction to the grip that judges truth by its single standard of objectivity.[6]

The seventeenth century was characterized by struggle for and against change, and a challenge to the centers of power, be it their control over fields of knowledge and truth in church and academy or over political entities in the form of empire; today we find a similar challenge to the academy, as it is dominated by principles of the Enlightenment, and also against modern-day empires; the challenge comes from postcolonial criticism, feminist theory, and others. The seventeenth century witnessed a battle over these domains and the attempt of those governing these centers to preserve their position and their established standards of meaning, knowledge, truth, and organization.[7] It was a time of

---

[5] By "postmodern," I refer to a late twentieth and twenty-first-century critique of the Enlightenment and modernity through the recognition and affirmation of the multiple, fragmentary, contextual, and fluid character of knowledge, life, and culture. See Jean-Francois Lyotard, *The Postmodern Condition: A Report on Knowledge*, trans. Geoff Bennington and Brian Massumi (Minneapolis: University of Minnesota Press, 1984).

[6] Tracing a line from the seventeenth century to postmodernity is not a particularly unusual step. Elena Feder sees similarities between what Sor Juana was arguing in her *Respuesta* and *Primero sueño* and postmodern thinkers like Derrida. See "Sor Juana Inés de la Cruz; or, The Snares of (Con)(tra)di(c)tion," in *Amerindian Images and the Legacy of Columbus*, ed. René Jara and Nicholas Spadaccini (Minneapolis: University of Minnesota Press, 1992) 473–529. Leah S. Marcus in *Redrawing the Boundaries: The Transformation of English and American Literary Studies* has also noted that scholars "are coming to view the period more in terms of elements repeated thereafter, those features of the age that appear to us as precursors of our own twentieth century, the modern, the postmodern" (41). Leah S. Marcus, "Renaissance/Early Modern Studies," in *Redrawing the Boundaries: The Transformation of English and American Literary Studies,* ed. Stephen Greenblatt and Giles Gun (New York: Modern Language Association of America, 1992). Quoted by Stephanie Merrim in *Early Modern Women's Writing and Sor Juana Inés de la Cruz* (Nashville: Vanderbilt University Press, 1999). Merrim also notes recent scholarship that considers the seventeenth century part of the early modern period, as she does in her work.

[7] Or, as Antonio Maravall says: "It was the spectacular and problematic breakdown of a society within which forces driving it to change struggle with other…forces whose object was preservation." José Antonio Maravall, *Culture of the Baroque: Analysis of a*

instability and uncertainty, summarized well by John Donne who wrote of the time: "Tis all in pieces, all coherence gone;/All just supply, and all Relation."[8]

The postmodern state may be described similarly: the academy is challenged to consider other ways of knowing, to recognize the subjective nature of the acquisition of knowledge; the ideals of capitalism and the effects of globalization are being questioned particularly by those on the underside of this "advancement," or "progress." Postmodernity is known as a time of pluralism, and uncertainty prevails. The sciences are no longer viewed as achieving the sort of objective certainty once believed possible, as interpretive elements in the process of investigation are recognized. The awareness of a multitude of valid religions grows, along with the recognition that the Christian church has proven miserably fallible, corrupt, and violent. These understandings have shaken Christianity's position in the Western world where the ideas of postmodernism are most prominent. This cultural shift and its impact on theology are not unlike what Luis Harss wrote of the seventeenth century:

> But with the breakdown of the Scholastic system the poetic word began to reclaim earlier powers that implicitly challenged Christian doctrine, even while relying on its symbols, but as increasingly hollow conventions spiraling into other forms of insight, particularly the syncretic thinking of Neoplatonism, which on the one hand subverted dogma by seeing all cultures and mythologies as related allegories and on the other revived the old Gnostic faith in the inner path to individual enlightenment open to those—poets and mystics—in touch with the occult sources that reveal the language of reality. In all this was potential heresy that had to be disguised in pedantry, obscurity: the convoluted extravagance—or exuberance—of what appeared to be nothing but a poetry of surfaces, caught in its own mirrors. So it was a "coded" poetry of emblems, myths, riddles, puns, cabalistic erudition, and geometric patterns leading, apparently, only into its own maze of words. Except that in the "sphere of verse," as it was called, words wanted to be more than words: the figures in the stars caught in the figures of speech.[9]

Historical Structure, trans. Terry Cochran (Minneapolis: University of Minneapolis Press, 1986) 26.

[8] Quoted in Theodore K. Rabb, *The Struggle for Stability in Early Modern Europe* (New York: Oxford University Press, 1975) 47.

[9] Luis Harss, "Introduction," in *Sor Juana's Dream*, trans. Luis Harss (New York: Lumen Books, 1986) 9. Harss does well here to describe the way the particularly elaborate and decorative style of the Baroque may be used to disguise some ideas that would be condemned in the strict Catholic Reformation and Inquisition.

Centuries after Sor Juana, subaltern thinkers pushed these concerns to the forefront of Western philosophy: an awareness in these fields of the complexities of pluralism, the existence of "the Other," the instability of knowledge, the lack of a universal objective perspective, and the inacceptable ignorance in Western academies of the ideas and ways of knowing of other cultures, orientations, races, and sexes. Sor Juana's themes and the impulse behind her work correspond with many of the themes of postmodernity, such as opening epistemological and theological discourses and creating space for dialogue with the other, because she herself was the outsider struggling to speak to the debates. She attempted to enter the discussion, and among her boldest moves was the positioning of a woman at the center of the epistemological debates of her day.[10]

The Problem of Totalizing Discourse in Theology

The key to the significance of the argument developed here arises as it addresses the problem of totalizing discourse. While systematic theologies often aid in providing a needed holistic perspective and vision of creation, humanity, redemption, God, and so on, this holistic viewpoint becomes a problematic "totalizing" when the theologies fail to maintain a form of expression that conveys its incomplete nature. Systematic theologies through the centuries, while possibly mentioning incomplete knowledge of God, have generally constructed linguistic forms that present the illusion of having comprehension of God and God's dealing with the world and humanity. The inadequacies of totalization have been highlighted especially in the postmodern critiques of modernity, as systems of modernity have often suggested complete knowledge in some form of "meta-narrative." Although some modernist system-builders admit their incomplete status, they still assume a systematic form, which as Kierkegaard points out, is a contradiction:

> The dialectician is indeed amazed to hear the same systematician say that the system is not yet completed. Oh yes, in the end everything will become clear, but the end is not here yet...for it is indeed ludicrous to treat everything as completed and then to say at the end that the conclusion is lacking. In other words, if the conclusion is lacking at the end, it is also lacking at the beginning. This should therefore have been said at the beginning. But if the conclusion is

[10] See Yolanda Martínez-San Miguel, *Saberes Americanos: Subalternidad y Epistemología en los Escritos de Sor Juana* (Pittsburgh: Instituto Internacional de Literatura Iberoamericana, University of Pittsburgh, 1999) 82.

> lacking at the beginning, this means that there is no system. A house can indeed be finished even though a bell pull is lacking, but in a scholarly construction the lack of a conclusion has retroactive power to make the beginning doubtful and hypothetical, that is, unsystematic.[11]

Systematic theologies often force an artificial coherence between doctrines. To accommodate the rigid structure of a totalizing theological system, one must decide which doctrine will determine the way in which the rest can be conceived. One doctrine tends to predominate, from which the others are derived, but oftentimes this logic forces a coherence of ideas that are not unitary in scripture, the Christian tradition, or Christian experience. Thus, the theologian's precommitment, or initial decision and commitment to a particular conception or articulation of a doctrine, is a cornerstone for the construction of a totality that is supposed to communicate the truth across the entire range of Christian belief and life. According to this view the goal becomes the creation of a perfectly consistent system; but is a theology to be valued primarily because it is wholly consistent, regardless of what aspects it must leave out because the system cannot accommodate them? This view of the purpose seems to prefer a fabricated and imposed ordering and structure to that which better reflects the complex nature of Christianity as it relates not only to scripture and tradition, but also the person and community. A systematic structure cannot accommodate the many tensions, differences, and diversity of the Christian message. Imposing an artificial and static structure on an ongoing process of salvation and Christian life, and forcing the movement of relationship and development into an "*eins, zwei, drei*" structure, distort the message being communicated and obliterate its multiplicity.[12]

The totalizing and systematizing that dominate theology also warrant critique because recent developments in other fields have reinforced postmodern suspicions of systems, particularly in linguistics, developmental psychology, literary criticism, rhetorical philosophy, and cultural anthropology, each of which in various ways uncover the probability that different cultures

---

[11] Søren Kieirkegaard [Johannes Climacus] *Concluding Unscientific Postscript to Philosophical Fragments*. trans. Howard and Edna Hong (Princeton: Princeton University Press, 1992) 13.

[12] "The systematic *eins, zwei, drei* is an abstract form that also must inevitably run into trouble whenever it is to be applied to the concrete" (Kierkegaard, *Concluding Unscientific Postscript*, 357).

and genders construct and express ideas differently.[13] However, there seems to be only one form of acceptable theological expression, the form determined by those in power in the church for centuries.[14] I maintain that other rhetorical forms and constructions should be accepted in the theological discipline, because barring them undermines the influence on the field of female theologians and those of non-Western cultures, and thus deprives the church of other facets of Christian witness.[15] The shift in contemporary culture will no longer allow a responsible theology to assume a place of dominance for Euro-American masculine modes of thought and meaning.

It is hardly a secret that theology's form has mirrored that of philosophy, so a discussion of the form theology takes could be expected to relate to the changes taking place in the form of philosophy. Yet let me again reiterate, this is not a proposal for a change in theological form based upon these shifts in philosophy, but because of the nature of Christianity itself, which relates to a person in existence, a person who is greatly affected by temporality, processes of development, changes in culture, conceptions of knowledge, time, and the

---

[13] For a work on cultural anthropology see George Marcus, *Anthropology as Cultural Critique: An Experimental Moment in the Human Sciences* (Chicago: University of Chicago Press, 1986). For a work in developmental psychology see Carol Gilligan, *In a Different Voice: Psychological Theory and Women's Development* (Cambridge MA: Harvard University Press, 1982).

[14] This is also true of philosophy generally. For examples of this argument made in and of philosophy, see Hélène Cixous, "The Laugh of the Medusa," in *The Critical Tradition: Classic Texts and Contemporary Trends*, ed. David H. Richter (New York. St. Martin's Press, 1989). Also Julia Kristeva, *Powers of Horror: An Essay on Abjection*, trans. Leon S. Roudiez (New York: Columbia University Press, 1982); Julia Kristeva, *Time and Sense: Proust and the Experience of Literature*, trans. Ross Guberman (New York: Columbia University Press, 1996); and Martha C. Nussbaum, *Love's Knowledge: Essays on Philosophy and Literature* (New York: Oxford University Press, 1990).

[15] Of course there are those writers who have assumed a masculine Western discourse as a result of a cultural and social system that encourages this particular sort of expression, and this has resulted, according to Cixous, in artificial expressions: "It is well known that the number of women writers (while having increased very slightly from the nineteenth century on) has always been ridiculously small. This is a useless and deceptive fact unless from their species of female writers we do not first deduct the immense majority whose workmanship is in no way different from male writing, and which either obscures women or reproduces the classic representations of women (as sensitive—intuitive—dreamy, etc.)" (Cixous, 1092).

like. Because Christianity relates to a person in existence and is a religion about the transformation of the person and community because of an encounter and relationship with the living Christ, forms that express that nature are more appropriate to the communication of the Christian religion. I maintain this shift in forms of discourse should occur not simply because this is the trend in acceptable postmodern thought, and Christianity must speak to culture, but because the nature of the Christian faith itself, as I understand it and will describe it, relates to and includes persons in specific socio-temporal locations and histories, and because these unique and unconcluded factors play a significant role in the faith. Forms of speaking theologically must accommodate this difference, inherent within Christianity itself, to be honest and truthful. Systematic, propositional forms largely misrepresent the nature of Christianity, giving the impression that it is a religion of propositional statements rather than one lived out in the course of one's life, where it is embodied and not simply held in the mind as an established set of beliefs.

Postmodernity and associated contemporary research have brought into question the very norm of objectivity which gave foundation to modern systematics, that is the notion that one could assume the universal perspective of "reason" and therefore be "objective."[16] They have rejected the assumption that an absolute, bird's-eye perspective, with a comprehensive vision, is at all possible. These thinkers assert that the transcendental generalizations typical of totalities are actually based on the view of particular cultures, genders, worldviews and persons.[17] Such universalizing has been shown to have dangerous implications for the marginalized as the dominant discourse assumes the place of Truth to the exclusion of other viewpoints and often lends itself to enforcement in an oppressive manner.[18] Feminists and other postmodern critics also oppose the a-historical perspective such systems assume. Feminists insist

---

[16] See Richard J. Bernstein, *Beyond Objectivism and Relativism: Science, Hermeneutics, and Praxis* (Philadelphia: University of Pennsylvania Press, 1983).

[17] See Donna Haraway, "Situated Knowledge: The Science Question in Feminism as a Site of Discourse on the Privilege of Partial Perspective," *Feminist Studies* 14.3 (1988): 575–99.

[18] This is certainly true of the Inquisition, where people's ideas and publications were scrutinized based upon a predetermined set of standards and doctrines set down by the ecclesiastical authorities. For more recent examples and studies see these studies in feminist thought from a variety of disciplines: Linda Nicholson, Dale Spender, Héléne Cixous, Elaine Showalter, Deborah Cameron, and Carol Gilligan.

that constructive thought be "rooted in concerns of the present,"[19] and they reject the modernist "view from nowhere."[20] This is a critique, for example, that feminists have directed toward non-narrative forms of philosophy. Feminists are not alone, however, as one of the first spokespersons for postmodernity, Jean Francois Lyotard, has declared "war on totality," and proclaims: "Let us attest to the unpresentable."[21] Postmodernity rejects grand totalizing narratives that once were thought to invest meaning in things by incorporating all under its massive sense-giving umbrella. Postmodernity instead views life "as an assemblage of intersecting narratives."[22]

Some of the characteristics of postmodernism include a distribution of power or the "multiplication of centers of power," the desire to dissolve totalizing narratives, [23] an emphasis upon diversity of various kinds (stylistic, ethnic, religious), and a resistance to the power modernity "invested in institutions and canonical traditions."[24] Postmodern thinkers "focus on contingency and temporality, implicitly denying the modern ideal of an atemporal, universal truth."[25] They also emphasize the temporal "in order to dislodge the reader from his or her attempt to view the world from a vantage point outside time."[26] Postmodern writers seek to drain the world of the idea that "eternal essences are

---

[19] Linda J. Nicholson, "Introduction," in *Feminism/Postmodernism*, ed. Linda J. Nicholson (New York: Routledge, 1990).

[20] Ibid., 9.

[21] Jean Francois Lyotard, *Postmodernism Explained*, trans. Don Barry, Bernadette Maher, Julian Pefanis, Virginia Spate, and Morgan Thomas (Minneapolis: University of Minnesota Press, 1992) 16.

[22] Stanley J. Grenz, *A Primer on Postmodernism* (Grand Rapids: William B. Eerdmans Publishing Company, 1996) 26.

[23] Steven Connor, *Postmodernist Culture: An Introduction to Theories of the Contemporary,* 2nd ed. (Cambridge MA: Blackwell, 1997) 9. "The postmodern condition, we are told repeatedly, manifests itself in the multiplication of centers of power and activity and the dissolution of every kind of totalizing narrative which claims to govern the whole complex field of social activity and representation. The waning of the cultural authority of the West and its political and intellectual traditions, along with the opening up of the world political scene to cultural and ethnic differences, is another symptom of the modulation of hierarchy into hierarchy" (Connor, 9).

[24] Grenz, 26.

[25] Ibid.

[26] Ibid.

unaffected by the flow of time and the contingencies of temporal context."[27] Postmodernity does not only tolerate diversity and difference, it strives for it. It prefers dissensus, seeing consensus as something forced or imposed. Postmoderns deny that an objective body of knowledge is accessible and assert that, even if it were attainable, it would not be value-free or neutral; postmodernity likewise rejects the modern ideal of the disinterested knower. Postmodernity also denies "the belief that truth is a claim to knowledge that can be validated by procedures devised by the appropriate scholarly community."[28]

Feminists have also exposed the political power located in the academy and denounced its claims of neutrality and objectivity. They argue "that what had most frequently been presented as objective because supposedly devoid of the influence of values, such as those related to gender, actually had reflected such values."[29] Further, they assert that "such biases were inevitable" and that "all scholarship reflected the perspectives and ideals of its creators." They conclude that it is only possible to avoid "narrowness in the academy" to the extent that "the inclusion of a multitude of points of view" could be ensured.[30]

Academic disciplines are cordoned off with their own technical vocabulary and rules that govern what may be an accepted expression of the "truth" for that field. The perspective of one group establishes the criteria on which all other discourse is measured, and so preserves its power. Moreover, as feminists argue, "the very development and use of such criteria, as well as their extension to ever wider domains," must be "described as representing the growth and development of specific 'regimes of power.'"[31] In this way, the view of one group, often a minority with the power of formal education, position, and command of the discipline's jargon, controls what is accepted as valid discourse in the field at large. These systems consolidate their influence, creating a tight circle of power. In these ways totalizing systems often hamper true dialogue, squelching the perspectives of those outside the dominant view or those without the power.

---

[27] Ibid., 29.

[28] Grenz, 131. See Foucault: "There is no power relation without the correlative constitution of a field of knowledge, nor any knowledge that does not presuppose and constitute at the same time power relations" [Foucault, *Discipline and Punish: The Birth of the Prison*, trans. Alan Sheridan (New York: Vintage Books, 1977) 27–28].

[29] Nicholson, 3.

[30] Ibid.

[31] Ibid., 4.

Totality systems in their rigidity and closed structure, and as they generally have the power of authority behind them, quash those fragmented discourses that lack powerful backing but which honestly reflect the inconclusive nature of theological constructions. "Unofficial" discourses, in contrast, do not tend to construct totalities, and do not determine the criteria of what is recognized as "true" or affirmed to be reality or considered an authentic expression of it. Feminist and postmodern thinkers actually seek the fragmenting of massive closed structures of thought and the decentralizing of the voice of the elite group of those educated to think in correspondence with the totality, or of those in power whose systems of thought preserve their power and their centrality in the discussion.

An assemblage of narratives, ideas, or values is a characteristic of postmodernism that shows itself in a variety of fields. The form of communication possibly most representative of the postmodern perspective is the collage, whose inherent heterogeneity and juxtaposition of images ensure "that the meaning it elicits can be neither univocal nor stable."[32] The pastiche is another example of a form of postmodern communication, which is a relevant form for musical, visual, or literary arts, and is composed primarily or entirely of motifs, images, or materials from a variety of different sources. Such an incongruous composition, incorporating "even clashing images," calls "into question any sense of objective meaning."[33]

I am not arguing that diverse forms of discourse from these subaltern voices should be included simply because we should compromise with some pervasive cultural concern to be "multicultural." Defenders of Western, totalizing theology often resist diversification in the name of not compromising with trendy multiculturalism. My approach, however, is not based on any such alleged "compromise," but on the view that these fragmented, non-dominant discourses often communicate the inherent connection of the Christian faith to inconclusive human existence. In communicating this, these discourses are both an invitation to an encounter with Christ and to an appropriation of Christ's benefits. They more honestly represent the inconclusive nature of theological claims as they relate to subjectivities. Totality systems in theology, however, assume a form that does not present the invitation to appropriation but often hands Christianity over as a completed, decided package in a rigid authoritative

[32] Grenz, 25.
[33] Ibid., 26.

text of direct propositions.[34] This is problematic theologically because Christianity includes the life of each; it is myriad in its manifestations across the globe, and multiform based on the very richness of Christ. A single holistic view is not possible theologically. This is so because that which pertains to existence is not concluded, and therefore it cannot be honestly systematized, nor is it "one," because it involves each person in her history and her temporal embeddedness.

Sor Juana Inés de la Cruz: A *Criolla* Resisting Totalizing Closure

Although this book is not itself in a form deploying creative genres like those we will discover in Sor Juana, the inclusion of this *criolla* is a step toward heteroglossia, polyvocality, and the breaking open of the closed discourse of traditional theology. Sor Juana Inés de la Cruz has not gained the attention of the dominant schools of theology, though she has received that in Women's Studies, Latin American Studies, and Literature. It is likely that the reasons for this neglect among theologians include her status as a woman from Latin America, who wrote in Spanish and in diverse literary genres. Additionally, when she recorded her theological ideas in these literary forms, she did not do so from a position of authority since she was a colonial subject and a cloistered nun in the patriarchal context of seventeenth-century New Spain.[35] Admittedly, as she was a *criolla*, and not an *india, negra,* or *mestiza*, her position was not

[34] According to David Griffin, modernity posed two choices for belief: "*either* let experience and reason be decisive for the content of one's faith," where experience is understood as empirical, sensory experience and reason largely means "thinking that conformed to the modern worldview;" or to "maintain a robust faith by basing it upon the authority of scripture and tradition, allowing experience and reason a merely subservient role" (6–7). "In this context, a reassertion of the authority of scriptures (and perhaps tradition) appeared to be the only way to maintain 'a faith worth having.' A significant theology seemed to require a conservative method" (7). Griffin goes on to argue that in postmodernity one is able to have a "significant theology" without adopting this "authoritarian method" (7). David Ray Griffin, *God and Religion in Postmodern Theology: Essays in Postmodern Theology* (Albany: State University of New York Press, 1989).

[35] Sor Juana took vows with the Hieronimite order in 1669, after which she never left the confines of the convent. During Sor Juana's lifetime Mexico suffered the colonial rule of the Spanish Empire and was known as New Spain.

only one of the oppressed and powerless.[36] With allies among the Spanish viceroyalty and a slave serving her in the convent, she was not innocent of the complex power relations of her time.[37] Nonetheless, the inclusion of Sor Juana's insights in contemporary theological construction supports the goal among feminist and postcolonial theologians of breaking opening the canon; she stands outside the dominant voices and forms of theology as a subaltern woman from colonial Mexico, writing in diverse genres.[38] Further still, the method she employed, as will be highlighted here, called those wielding power within the ecclesial hierarchy, and all who engaged in God-talk, to approach theology with epistemic humility and an openness to the Other. She invited theologians to abandon the combative and competitive postures often characteristic of the discipline, favoring theological discourse that is inclusive and tolerant of difference.

Sor Juana's work is rich ground for such an investigation, as she wrote from a complex sociopolitical context at a time when the church explicitly exerted its power to control religious discourse. Authority was used as a force of coercion, and the relationship between the church's control over religious discourse and its use of violence was easily visible in the Inquisition. Despite writing at a time when religion was often imposed upon individuals, communities, and even nations, Sor Juana promoted a different form of religious conversation, one that invites dialogue and insists upon epistemic humility. Writing on the heels of late scholasticism and the authoritarian revival of the Catholic Reformation and the ongoing Inquisition, Sor Juana advanced a type of theology that does not make bold claims regarding objective knowledge

[36] The hierarchy of Sor Juana's day gave ruling power primarily to the Spanish born; the viceroyalty all came from and returned to Spain after their terms. *Criollo/as*, those born in the Americas of European lineage, were subject to the Spanish, but still had significant privilege over the *indio/as, negro/as, mestizo/as*, a term which refers to those of "mixed" descent, be it a blending of any European, *indio/a*, and/or African lineages. Mulatto/a referes specifically to a person of African and European descent.

[37] Even entering the convent took some privilege in the form of a dowry. Sor Juana had a wealthy sponsor who donated the money necessary for her to join the convent of San Jeronimo in Mexico City.

[38] Sor Juana wrote numerous plays, poems, and songs of both theological and secular natures and is most known for the few of her preserved letters. Her stated position may not directly have called for the destruction of canons, but she certainly can be seen calling for a loosening up of their claims to closure.

of the divine.[39] Her work promoted the use of voices other than the authoritarian ones employed by theologians of her day, as they relied on their titles and status or on references to the "fathers" and sanctioned theologians of history in order to set their perspective in power over that of another.[40]

Her epistemic humility and employment of indirect communication are, of course, not unrelated to her position as a woman in the networks of power of her day. For centuries women were forbidden from writing theology "proper." The church, however, did let women write as mystics, with the assumption that they were not writing theology through the use of their reason but through the direct inspiration of the Holy Spirit.[41] Some women, like Sor Juana, whose writing is not primarily a description of personal spiritual experiences and therefore not traditionally classified as "mystical," were also permitted, with some difficulty, to write stories, poems, and plays.[42] Both groups of women writers were, of course, closely monitored. This book's thesis will proceed against the backdrop of a consideration of the power structures of Sor Juana's context and examine the ways in which her writing was a subversive form of resistance against the enforced boundaries of acceptable theological thought during the Mexican Inquisition. I consider the rigid boundaries enforced around acceptable theological ideas of her day to be a *de facto* closed system of thought and totality. This serves as a proposal for the way Sor Juana's thought and use of literary genres challenge contemporary theological construction to assume forms that invite encounter and appropriation and to utilize forms that resist

---

[39] The Catholic Reformation refers to the reform of the Roman Catholic Church in reaction to the Protestant Reformation sweeping across Europe.

[40] The theologian Sor Juana most openly critiqued by name is António Vieira, but as this book demonstrates, she subtly criticized this tendency in all theology, and she did so at a time when theological lines were firmly and decisively drawn, when claims of knowledge of God's inner workings were extreme, and when her interjections into the discussion at all was dangerous for her. Though Sor Juana did utilize the works of those authorized by the church, such as Thomas and Augustine, to prove that she does have this learning and knowledge, she more often uses voices and examples of those denied power in the church, such as the indigenous and women.

[41] See Grace M. Jantzen, *Power, Gender, and Christian Mysticism* (New York: Cambridge University Press, 1995); also Electa Arenal and Stacy Schlau, *Untold Sisters: Hispanic Nuns in Their Own Words* (Albuquerque: University of New Mexico Press, 1989).

[42] Sor Juana received much of her criticism because she did not abide by the expectations of a woman religious and wrote numerous "secular" pieces.

totalization and express epistemic humility. This project also provides a methodological foundation for the retrieval of marginalized views and a plurality of voices. A significant part of Sor Juana's exemplary function in this project is her strength as a *criolla* to resist the pressure for closure and totalization in theological discourse.

A Note on Method

Elaine Showalter calls for a "Feminist Poetics," and labels that which she develops "gynocritics," a form of discourse that is not determined by the standards established by the tradition of male scholars, but is developed by women according to their ways of communicating. Showalter's gynocritics would "take into account the different velocities and curves of political, social, and personal histories,"[43] and would "free ourselves from the linear absolutes of male literary history."[44] Hélène Cixous does something similar in "The Laugh of Medusa," calling for women to write feminine texts and further charging that texts produced by women are not enough, as so many women disguise their discourse to look like that of men. Cixous, Showalter, and other feminists criticize the view that the only acceptable discourse is that which proceeds according to linear models. They are right to note that the symbol for such discourse is often also a symbol of masculinity itself: the sword. As a symbol for discourse, this blade suggests the linear, the direct, and that which cuts straight to the core of the issue, not unlike the form of discourse lauded as the acceptable form of communicating in a range of academic disciplines in the Western world.[45] These feminists are not alone, however, in a push for different modes of discourse. Works in postcolonial theory often proceed in a nonlinear

---

[43] Elaine Showalter, "Toward a Feminist Poetics," in *The New Feminist Criticism: Essays on Women, Literature, and Theory* (New York: Pantheon, 1985) 132.

[44] Ibid.

[45] Showalter argues: "Too many literary abstractions which claim to be universal have in fact described only male perceptions, experiences, and options, and have falsified the social and personal contexts in which literature is produced and consumed. In women's fiction, the complacently precise and systematizing male has often been the target of satire.... What women have found hard to take in such male characters is their self-deception, their pretense to objectivity, their emotion parading as reason. As Adrienne Rich comments in *Of Woman Born*, 'the term 'rational' relegates to its opposite term all that it refuses to deal with, and thus ends by assuming itself to be purified of the nonrational, rather than searching to identify and assimilate its own surreal or nonlinear elements'" (Showalter, 127).

fashion, incorporating a surprising range of diverse topics into one text to subvert the demands of "Western Reason." Postmodern philosophers also solicit alternative modes. Deleuze calls for new forms of philosophy, suggesting the use of the history of philosophy as material in a collage:

> The time is coming when it will hardly be possible to write a book of philosophy as it has been done for so long: "Ah! the old style…". The search for new means of philosophical expression was begun by Nietzsche and must be pursued today in relation to the renewal of certain other arts, such as the theatre or the cinema. In this context, we can now raise the question of the utilization of the history of philosophy. It seems to us that the history of philosophy should play a role roughly analogous to that of *collage* in painting.[46]

One of the emphases of this project brought out of the work of Sor Juana Inés de la Cruz is a concern to avoid violent and combative forms of rhetoric in pursuit of alternative modes that are open to dialogue and difference. It should not be surprising, then, that the approach taken here does not follow the linear model of the sword. Rather, I take a cue from Showalter, seeking instead a curved discourse. Arguments develop more by way of a forward progressing spiral than an arrow to the bull's-eye. A spiral advances, but the movement is not direct; it includes retrieval, a gathering, a lifting, and an advance. This is an activity in harvesting and thus the sickle is a more accurate depiction of the function and shape of this discourse. It is still a sharp instrument, but it is curved for purposes of gathering, and it is as much a feminine image as it is a masculine one. In contrast to swords and daggers, the purpose of wielding this blade is not in a defensive stance, nor an aggressive one against another life, but the sickle is an instrument of production and growth, as well as of survival, as a tool for gathering sustenance.

Another metaphor that could be used for such a project and close to the postmodern imagination is the collage, as mentioned above by Delueze—gathering pieces from a variety of places and media and bringing them together in one fragmented image. Or it could be compared to a Kierkegaardian "repetition," which is recollecting forwards; it is not a straightforward reconstruction, but a push forward to new meanings even in the remembrance.

---

[46] Gilles Deleuze, *Difference and Repetition*, trans. Paul Patton (New York: Columbia University Press, 1994) xxi.

"Repetition" is said to involve "the abandonment of a coercive methodology in favor of an unmethodical and generous dialogue."[47]

A common metaphor in feminist theology is "weaving." Many women of my generation have taken up knitting needles, and so this image may remain relevant: bringing strands together into a colorful, purposeful piece—something that provides warmth and beauty. I, however, do not even cross-stitch. So this image is lost on me, except that it may remind me of my mother's mother, who created detailed, hand-stitched quilts we all still use in winter. I can do a little hair-braiding, however, and so I use a weaving metaphor in that sense: of lifting a stand of hair and bringing it up into the braid, twisting it into a piece and folding the pieces over each other, to then pick up another strand, combining it in, folding those over, and so on, to create one functional design. Here I braid together ideas presented by Sor Juana Inés de la Cruz through poetry, plays, and letters, with Kierkegaard's indirect communication, gathering Luther's *Anfechtungen* together with Federico Garía Lorca's *duende*, folding Heidegger's thought on poetry and the "rift" of truth together with the Hidden and Revealed God, and finally collecting Bakhtin's interest in the incarnate word with Sor Juana's final turn to silence and action.

Mapping the Chapters

Because here I utilize genres normally relegated to literary studies, I employ the work of some literary theorists to interpret these texts. When I discuss letters, I draw on Rosenzweig and a scholar of epistolary literature. When I examine Sor Juana's poem *First Dream (Primero sueño)*, I utilize Heidegger's work on poetry. And when I turn to drama, I consider the dialogical elements in Sor Juana's *loas*, using Bakhtin's work on novelization. In each chapter I make an argument for a non-systematic or indirect form of communicating Christianity; each genre allows not only for a different approach but functions specifically in the overall argument for the inconclusive nature of Christian knowledge and what this means for Christian discourse.

In chapter 1, "Kierkegaard and the Socratic Ignorance of Faith," I provide the theological introduction to the project. I examine the nature of salvation and faith, highlighting the significance of the human subject in each, both as

[47] William Spanos, "Heidegger, Kierkegaard, and the Hermeneutic Circle: Towards a Postmodern Theory of Interpretation as Dis-closure," in *Martin Heidegger and the Question of Literature*, ed. William Spanos (Bloomington: Indiana University Press, 1979) 122.

salvation was wrought through the course of Jesus' human life, death, and resurrection, and as salvation is applied to the individual through faith. My description emphasizes the elements of process and temporality, which point to the inconclusiveness of a theological construction. I proceed with a discussion of Kierkegaard's *Concluding Unscientific Postscript*, particularly as it deals with the idea of indirect communication and the development of this theory in contrast to the systemizing tendencies of theology as it stood under the influence of Hegelianism in his day. The nature of our certainty in Christianity, which Kierkegaard says is only of our uncertainty, is at the heart of faith. This also relates to Kierkegaard's lifting of Socratic ignorance, which I highlight as it relates to epistemic humility and the inconclusiveness of our claims. I conclude with a consideration of the limits on our knowledge of God, due to God's hiddenness in the dissonance between revelation and much human experience. Because of this incongruity, a complete and concluded description of the Christian faith cannot be given. I provide a description of the theological theme of the hiddenness of God, especially as it comes through Luther, arguing that it is an important theological concept to be recovered if Christian knowledge is not abstract fact or proposition but something gained in a God-relation, that is, within one's lived existence. The Hidden God should not be worked into a system, however, because there it only becomes a form of certainty instead of a way to communicate our inconclusive knowledge.

In chapter 2, "The Epistemic Humility of Faith in Sor Juana's Letters," I begin an explicit discussion of Sor Juana Inés de La Cruz. Starting with the genre of the letter, I analyze the way in which the letter, as exemplified by Sor Juana, is a form that remains true to the temporality of the Christian message and the concreteness of it applied to the individual. The letter is a discourse that remains true to the nature of human existence and the process of human life, and thus the letter is exemplary as a form that invites dialogue and communicates the nature of Christianity with a call to appropriate its message. I consider the voice of traditional theology's systemizing approaches, or the way in which its claims are often articulated, and view these in contrast to the alternative form of theological discourse utilized by Sor Juana and her arguments against the aggressive, authoritative speech used by other theologians. I analyze the rhetoric used by Sor Juana in these letters and argue that she does not feign an artificial modesty, as is often argued, but actually asserts that theology too often takes an unwarranted arrogant stance and should rather voice the fallible nature of theological opinion due to the inconclusive nature of one's perspective on the topic. Thus, I consider her stance very similar to the Socratic ignorance lauded by Kierkegaard. In this way I also introduce the theme of the relationship between discourse and violence, or of rhetorical violence, which is further developed in chapter 4.

In the third chapter, "Sor Juana's *Dream* and the Hiddenness of God," I develop a critique of the "view from nowhere" common in totality systems through Sor Juana's long poem, *Primero Sueño*. The poem depicts an attempt to disembody and decontextualize the mind as the soul lifts from the body in sleep and soars above and beyond the earth, contemplating all things. A comprehensive and complete knowledge is sought, but the mind ultimately fails, crashing back down into the historical, contextually and temporally positioned and sexed body. The poem in both form and content elaborates on the inconclusive nature of ideas in embodied human existence. The knowledge we seek is not gathered, stored, and systemically arranged so much as it is sought and limned in ways that never escape inconclusiveness. I utilize Heidegger's thought on poetry to argue for poetry's unique ability to communicate a tension like the experience of the Hidden God as Heidegger presents truth as a place of conflict between what is revealed and what is concealed and poetry as a valuable form for communicating this space, or "Open." Religious knowledge is incomplete because of its relation to the individual in process; poetry is an appropriate form for such a communication as it is a fragmented form itself.

In chapter 4, "Internal Persuasion in Sor Juana's Dramas," I examine the dramatic introductions to Sor Juana's *auto sacramentales* through a consideration of the literary criticism of Mikhail Bakhtin. These three brief plays by Sor Juana exhibit many of the qualities highlighted by Bakhtin as those which function to break open the canon and closed forms of discourse, such as: heteroglossia, presentness, and dialogue. These features also serve to persuade the reader internally rather than through external, centralizing, and authoritative force, and they exhibit the possibilities available for subjective appropriation found in unofficial discourse in contrast to that of official discourse. Unitary or authoritative discourse hampers the subjective appropriation of an idea; theologically speaking it complicates the invitation to one's own encounter and interaction with Christianity. This literary approach also gives ground for a consideration of the view of authority and persuasion in these dramas by Sor Juana and furthers my discussion of rhetorical violence in theology. Her dramas also give further evidence for her position on the inconclusive nature of theological constructions and provide an example of Sor Juana depicting herself in masculine disguise in order to get a hearing for her ideas on epistemic humility in theology and the appropriate rhetorical forms for theological debate.

In chapter 4, I push the discussion still further by considering non-canonical and non-authoritative forms of discourse—those which serve to persuade the individual internally, in accordance with Kierkegaard's (and the Christian's) concern that the person appropriate religious truth. The expectation of Christian discourse is that, transformed by it, one pursues the transformation of society toward the coming Reign of God. This very need for appropriation as an essential aspect of religious knowledge contributes to the inconclusiveness of theological claims and is something Bakhtin also affirms.

In the final chapter, "Beyond the Limits of Theological Language," I revisit the theological darkness described in chapter 2 and consider silence as a form of theological expression, looking at the controversial final year of Sor Juana's life. I offer an interpretation of her move away from writing and into action. It serves as a protest against the silencing of the subaltern in theology. It also expresses the epistemic humility for which she called in the theological discipline and leads me to conclude that the embodiment of one's thought in one's life and action is a most appropriate form for communicating Christian thought.

A Brief Biographical Introduction

Before I develop my theological exposition, however, it serves to provide a brief introduction to Sor Juana's life. A thorough study of her life can be found in the influential work of Octavio Paz, *Sor Juana, or Traps of Faith*, though his biography is highly interpretive—certainly all biographies are, especially one on an individual from centuries past with few remaining trustworthy documents on her life. There are a number of aspects of Sor Juana's history that will not be given attention in my brief treatment, such as: her relationship with her confessor and an Inquisitor, Núñez de Miranda;[48] the impact the misogynist Archbishop Aguiar y Seijas may have had upon the context in which Sor Juana worked; or a detailed look at the period in which Sor Juana lived, Baroque New Spain.[49] Nor will you find here an extended study of the historical genres in

[48] The complicated relationship between Sor Juana and this powerful religious figure in New Spain has been brought to further light with the recent discovery of the *Carta de Monterrey*, in which Sor Juana takes a strong stand against her confessor, dismissing him from his position as her spiritual advisor.

[49] For a study of Baroque New Spain, see Irving A. Leonard, *Baroque Times in Old Mexico: Seventeenth-Century Persons, Places, and Practices* (Ann Arbor: The University of Michigan Press, 1959). Also Mariano Picon-Salas, *A Cultural History of Spanish America*, trans. Irving A. Leonard (Westport CN: Greenwood Press, 1982).

which she wrote or whose work may have most influenced her own. We are looking at Sor Juana's use of literary genres from a theological, rather than chiefly a cultural or historical perspective so more attention will be given to the ways in which her particular works function theologically as an example of the use of various forms of discourse to communicate Christian teaching and what this may mean for contemporary theological construction.

Sor Juana Inés de la Cruz was born Juana Inés Ramírez de Asbaje probably in 1648 to a poor and unmarried couple.[50] Sor Juana's mother never married Sor Juana's father, with whom she had three daughters. Sor Juana's father was a small landholder at a large *hacienda* southeast of the city of Mexico, but little is known of her father and Sor Juana makes almost no reference to him beyond saying he was Basque.[51] When her father died, Sor Juana's mother, Isabel Ramírez, oversaw the farm and eventually entered into another relationship with a man, with whom she bore three additional children. Sor Juana's mother is thought to be a strong and independent *criolla* who likely served as an example for Sor Juana, though Sor Juana was sent away to live with her aunt's family at a young age, between eight and ten. In the social hierarchy of Baroque New Spain, the *criollos* were beginning to form independent identities, but were still second to the Spanish, who stood as the ruling class. The viceroyalty was all Spanish born and raised, and they came to New Spain to rule in limited terms, returning to Spain at the end of their service. The *mestizo* residents had less social power than the *criollos*, but the *indios* had the least power in New Spain.[52]

According to her own account, Sor Juana learned to read at age three by persuading her sister's tutor to teach her. She studied Latin and pursued a rigorous study schedule, disciplining herself by cutting her hair if she had not mastered the desired lessons by an established date. Becoming proficient in Latin, though not a master, Sor Juana later studied the works of Thomas Aquinas, Jerome, and other theologians. She apparently begged her mother to

[50] Her first biographer dated her birth in 1651, but a baptismal certificate for an Inés whose godparents were the siblings of Sor Juana's mother gives the year 1648.

[51] Octavio Paz makes quite a lot out of his absence in his formative study on Sor Juana. Octavio Paz, *Sor Juana or, Traps of Faith*, trans. Margaret Sayers Peden (Cambridge MA: Harvard University Press, 1988).

[52] See José Antonio Mazzotti, ed., *Agencias Ciollas. La Ambigüedad "Colonial" in Letras Hispanoamericanas* (Pittsburgh: Instituto Internactional de Literatura Iberoamericana, 2000).

dress her as a boy so she could study at the university, but being unable to receive this formal education, she instead read through her grandfather's library. Her accumulated learning even by the age of ten was so impressive that she is said to have wowed the residents of the city of Mexico upon her arrival at her aunt's family home. Sor Juana's brilliance brought her some fame, and so when the new Viceroy and Vicereine of New Spain arrived in the city when she was approximately sixteen, she was soon invited to court, and shortly went to stay there court as a lady in waiting for the Vicereine. Her earliest biographer describes a scene much like that of Jesus at the Temple astonishing the elders with his wisdom, or that of Catherine of Alexandria who at eighteen is said to have been questioned by a room of pagan philosophers, whom she astounded with her arguments, leading many to conversion.[53] Sor Juana is said to have been questioned by the gathered scholars of various disciplines from the university and to have amazed them with her learning, her responses, and her arguments.

The Viceroy and the Vicereine were great appreciators of the arts, and Sor Juana became especially close with the Vicereine, Leonor Carreto, Marquise de Mancera. Despite the support and friendship of the viceroyalty, however, Sor Juana chose to leave court after a few years and enter a convent. Hypotheses abound regarding this decision, though Sor Juana says it was because she was not inclined to marriage. Sor Juana first joined a Carmelite convent, where she lasted only three months; it is speculated that the order was more strict and rigorous in discipline than Sor Juana desired. In 1669 she took her vows in the Convent of St. Jerome, an Augustinian rule, where she lived until her death. The strong ties Sor Juana established with the viceroyalty, however, continued long after she left court for the convent, and the viceroys often visited her there after attending mass.

The Hieronymite order had communal obligations, prayer times and meals, and Sor Juana also kept the order's accounts and taught in the convent school, but the religious vocation allowed her to pursue her studies more rigorously than other life options given women at that time. The living conditions at the

---

[53] Or, in the words of Sor Juana on St. Catherine: "For with knowledge pure and holy she's convinced the learned men and has emerged victorious—with her knowledge glorious—from their arrogance profane, but which would convince and conquer her" (*The Answer/La Respuesta, Including a Selection of Poems*, trans. Electa Arenal and Amanda Powell (New York: The Feminist Press at the City University of New York, 1994) 161.

convent were not particularly severe, nor were the communal meals enforced. The nuns had private quarters including a kitchen, sleeping chambers, and a parlor of their own, as well as servants to attend them; Sor Juana had a mulatto slave given her by her mother.[54] Clearly the life of a nun was a rather privileged one, and Sor Juana would not have been able to enter it had she not been able to offer a dowry to the convent, which in her case was donated by a wealthy benefactor, thanks probably to her connections at court. Sor Juana amassed quite a library in her parlor, possibly the largest in colonial Mexico, along with some scientific instruments and music. The Viceroys and Vicereines visited her there, as did other intellectuals and religious professionals in the area, such as Carlos de Siguenza y Góngora, a renowned man of letters in New Spain. Her parlor became something of a salon, or a *tertulia*, a gathering of people for discussion. And there she not only engaged in lively debates, but carried on a prolific writing carrier. Luis Harss does a good job of cataloging the vast variety of Sor Juana's creative and intellectual work:

> But she had occasion for much else and was versatile in many genres and conventions: skits, interludes, farces; dirges, roundelays, panegyrics; verse epistles and medleys; courtly love poems, song lyrics, dedications; biting satires and epigrams; devotional exercises for the nuns at the convent; philosophical ballads; her autobiographical *Response*; a theological tract that the Bishop of Puebla ("Sister Filotea") declared and titled *Letter Worthy of Athene*; a lost music method, *El Caracol* ("The Spiral"); her prolific correspondence (also lost); perhaps a book of riddles for a parlor guessing game; comedies of manners, even some fairly raunchy burlesque sonnets that have scandalized her Catholic commentators but are, nevertheless, clearly attributable to her. Among her best works: some perfect sonnets (on themes sacred and profane); a Calderonian comedy, *The Trials of a Noble House*, with the Pirandellian twist of having the

[54] Luis Harss describes, "One should remember that convent life in the 17th century, in spite of its strict vows and the many hours of spiritual devotions and disciplines, was fairly worldly in some orders, particularly the Jeronymites, who although cloistered, found ways to participate in public festivities: concerts, plays, masques, poetic tournaments. It was an age of great pageantry, given to grand entries through ceremonial arches, majestic Te Deums with ringing church bells, allegorical floats and fireworks, dramatic mystery plays, rousing popular farces. Although the conventual ideal was still sacrificial self-denial, many nuns, like vestal courtesans, led quite luxurious lives, with slaves and servants. They dressed in finery, wore jewelry, enjoyed comfortable furniture, and collected valuable ornaments" (4).

characters address the audience from the front of the stage; and the strings of carols—an art at which she excelled, particularly in the use of popular characters, blacks, Indians speaking or singing in dialect and Nahuatl—written for the Matins that were sung on the eve of the religious festivals (Christmas, the Assumption, St. Catherine's Day, etc.), when the carols were performed in counterpoint to the psalms of the liturgy. On the whole, not much religious poetry: only sixteen strictly religious poems, according to one count. ...And, of course, *The Dream*....[55]

In 1680 a new viceregal couple, who would be very important to Sor Juana's life and career, arrived from Spain: Tomás Antonio de la Cerda, Marquis de la Laguna; and his wife, María Luisa, Countess de Paredes, Marquise de la Laguna. They were patrons of the arts and encouraged Sor Juana in her work, later getting it published in Spain. Sor Juana built a close and lasting friendship with the countess, who commissioned many works by Sor Juana and who is the subject of a number of Sor Juana's poems, verses that speak with deep affection similar to that of the courtly love tradition. The two mentioned vicereines, Leonora and María Louisa, were those who most encouraged Sor Juana to pursue her literary works and her studies, and both were memorialized in affectionate verse. They were avid supporters of her, and with their political power they were key instruments in her freedom to write without as much resistance as one might expect of a strong-willed, articulate woman with keen wit in New Spain during its Inquisition. Though she won patronage from these two vicereines, she also gained favor with five viceregal administrators.[56]

María Luisa arranged for Sor Juana's first book to be published. Two editions of Sor Juana's works were published in her life and a third soon after her death.[57] Sor Juana enjoyed years of prolific work and not a small amount of

---

[55] Harss, 6.

[56] See Frederick Luciani, *Literary Self-Fashioning in Sor Juana Inés de la Cruz* (Lewisburg: Bucknell University Press, 2004) 27.

[57] This third edition of her works is thought to be encouraged by the archbishop; it included a biography of Sor Juana that suggests she had a dramatic religious conversion late in life, followed by severe self-mortification, and humble devotion to caring for the sick. It is also suggested that, with the publication of this edition, organized by the Church, the religious authorities were attempting to control her public image. See Elías Trabulse, "El Silencio Final de Sor Juana," in *Sor Juana & Vieira, Trescientos Años Después,* ed. K. Josu Bijuesca and Pablo A. J. Brescia (Santa Barbara: Center for Portuguese Studies, Department of Spanish and Portuguese, University of California,

fame in New Spain and Spain itself where her works were published, but she did not enjoy a life without controversy. Once the countess and the viceroy left for Spain in 1688, she no longer had such strong ties with the political authorities of New Spain, and she encountered more opposition from those of the church. Still some of her most respected work comes from this time: her letter *La Respuesta* and her *villancicos* for the Feast of St. Catherine of Alexandria, both in 1691, come from these later years of her writing. However, in 1692 she sold most, if not all, of her library and her musical and scientific instruments, giving the proceeds to charity.[58] Paz calls this act: "the gesture of a terrified woman attempting to ward off calamity with the sacrifice of what she most loves."[59] In 1694 she signed a declaration of faith, repentance, and renunciation, though she never directly renounced her writing or study. She directed her attention to service and penance, and died caring for her sisters at the convent during an epidemic in 1695.

For contemporary scholars this is the most controversial period of Sor Juana's life, and a variety of interpretations of her silence abound. Some scholars view this as a sincere spiritual renewal in the life of Sor Juana and a sign of her conversion and faith. This view rests on the interpretation of her life leading up to this as being primarily concerned with the secular and suggests that she gave up secular studies, writing, and publication in order to submit herself more fully to the church.[60] Others view this as Sor Juana's final acquiescence to the pressures of the ecclesiastical authorities when she no longer had strong ties with the viceroyalty, and their power was waning in the face of a series of crises in the region.[61] Here her turn to service and "silence" is considered lamentable and rather suggests she lost the strength and

---

Santa Barbara, 1998). A similar position is taken by Marie-Cécile Bénassy, "Hipótesis Sobre la 'Conversion' Final de Sor Juana Inés de la Cruz," *Revista de la Universidad de México* 30, no. 3 (Noviembre 1975): 21–24.

[58] She began re-amassing her library almost as soon as she gave it away; however, at the time of her death, she had 180 books and fifteen bundles of writings by her. See Luciani, 153, and Elías Trabulse, *Los Años Finales de Sor Juana: Una Interpretación (1688–1695)* (Mexico City: Centro de Estudios de Historia de México Condumex, 1995).

[59] Paz, 463.

[60] Among those who hold this view, Paz names Asunción Lavrin.

[61] Dorothy Schons primarily supports this interpretation, though Schons sees the silence primarily as a response to the suffering in New Spain at the time. See also Bénassy and Trabulse.

determination of spirit evident in her *Respuesta*; it depicts her as finally giving up the fight and submitting to the clerics who took issue with the public, erudite voice of a woman. In the 1990s Elías Trabulse investigated newly found documents that led him to conclude that this period of Sor Juana's life was the result of secret ecclesiastical proceedings against her, which, in essence, forced her to renounce, "confess," and to give up her public life in order to avoid formal charges. These later documents also reveal that she began re-assembling a library and writing, suggesting she did not give away all her books and instruments on her own will and did not give up on study and writing.[62] Pamela Kirk also provided an alternative interpretation, arguing that the documents Sor Juana signed, her repentance and renunciation, and the subsequent penitence are all related to the renewal of her vows on the twenty-fifth anniversary of her commitment to the order. Kirk views the signing of the documents as the beginning of a penitential year spent in service and mortification, and notes that we cannot be certain what Sor Juana's intentions were in regard to her studies and writing at the end of this year because Sor Juana died before the year concluded.[63]

It has been noted that other factors contributed to the change in Sor Juana's support and vocation as well, leading one to conclude that many factors likely contributed to this end: a devastating flood in the city of Mexico, superstitious fears from a solar eclipse, and a plague of weevils, which ate the crops that survived the flood and left the area in crisis. The scarcity of food, firewood, and coal grew even worse through speculation and hoarding. "Rising prices touched off spontaneous protests. The viceregal palace and municipal building were set on fire. Punitive responses triggered panic, further rioting, penitent religious processions, and executions. Sor Juana's most significant supporters had returned to Spain or had fallen out of favor."[64] This controversial end of Sor Juana's life and work is something we will return to in the final, concluding chapter.

Theological Language at the Limits

---

[62] Elías Trabulse, *Los Años Finales de Sor Juana: Una Interpretación (1688–1695)* (Mexico City: Centro de Estudios de Historia de México Condumex, 1995).

[63] Pamela Kirk, "Introduction" *Sor Juana Inés de la Cruz, Selected Writings.* trans. Pamela Kirk (New York: Paulist Press, 2005) 23-24.

[64] Arenal and Powell, 12.

No direct line of influence can be drawn between Sor Juana and the theorists used here, but Luther questioned the systems of authority and power, spurring the Reformation, which drew the Catholic Reformation and Inquisition in which Sor Juana was situated, leading to the full emergence of modernity. Kierkegaard is an appropriate figure to utilize because he and Sor Juana both struggled against the organized church of their days and the church's formalized and closed discourses.[65] Bakhtin likewise dealt with issues of authority and coercion not so dissimilar to those faced and addressed by Sor Juana. In Stalin's Russia, Bakhtin's work was repressed, and he was sentenced to exile in Siberia; it also became too dangerous for him to write philosophy so he put his ideas forward through another form: in analyzing the writings of others and literary theory.[66] Heiddeger, in the lineage of existential philosophy of which Kierkegaard was an originator, emphasizes the temporality of human existence and challenges the propositional form philosophy's investigation into meaning and life takes. Sor Juana's suggestions toward a localized knowledge and the importance of body, location, and context in knowledge are not entirely dissimilar from Heidegger's moves in philosophy. Hers did not arise in the line of the existential tradition, but emerged as she was constantly aware of the limits placed upon her in her context due in part to her sexed body and her status as a colonial subject under ecclesial authority as a cloistered nun. Her epistemological position, like those of all thinkers, was influenced by her life situation, her context, and her status. Her situation was one that kept her on the margins of the debates of her day, and so her arguments were often for the expansion of the debate and of the fallibility of those philosophical and theological viewpoints considered certain or final. Her voice from the margin calls for change in the narrow field of theology she faced, and today voices echo hers from the long-marginalized groups in theology.

The rhetorical forms I discuss in the following chapters all possess a "spirit of process and inconclusiveness," which corresponds to authentic human life and the appropriation and application of Christ's benefits in said life. The

---

[65] I recognize that the situations and unique social locations of these figures make their reasons for these reactions and use of literary genres to be for particular and even unique reasons. I bring them together here because of their similar themes and their common efforts to push the boundaries of "acceptable" theological or philosophical discourse of their days.

[66] See Ruth Coates, *Christianity in Bakhtin* (Cambridge: Cambridge University Press, 1998) 22.

discourse is infused with an aspect of the concrete (of temporality, contemporaneity, contextuality, and embodiment), and with movement as it relates to the person in the present with all of its uncertainty, pointed to an open future. They break open the closed discourse and concluded dialectic of totality systems; they are non-canonical. Yet the forms discussed here are a more appropriate means for communicating the subjective nature of Christian knowledge, while they are also an effective means to resist unitary, systematic tendencies in traditional Christian discourse that work counter to the very appropriation of Christian teaching.

1

Kierkegaard and the Socratic Ignorance of Faith

Theology has long been influenced by philosophy; we could trace it back to the gospel writer of John, for example, who spoke of the *Logos*. Theologians, conscious or otherwise, are committed to a certain philosophical understanding of knowledge, truth, language, and existence, among other things. Likewise, the form theology takes has also been modeled on the philosophical forms of discourse. This is not to say Christian teaching is determined by philosophical ideas of the day, but theology has always been influenced by philosophy as it attempts to articulate Christian teaching in a way that is understandable to people shaped by such cultural influences and worldview. My conception of Christianity, salvation, and faith is not dissimilar. I emphasize themes present in Christianity that correspond to developing conceptions of these themes in contemporary philosophy. And the theologians and thinkers we turn to in the coming pages share these concerns.[1] I work from a conception of knowledge and existence that shares similarities with postmodern ideas on the subject: the concrete as privileged over the abstract; a heterogeneity of voices over the monovocal; a recognition of epistemological and linguistic limits; the temporality of human existence; and what these mean for the process of salvation. This approach, however, does not stem from a commitment to postmodernity but is a matter of emphasis when consideration is given to the relation of Christian teaching to the person to which it is applied or by whom it is appropriated. This consideration may in fact alter the content of the teaching itself, or at very least it will impact the form in which the teaching is communicated, so that the teaching includes the expression that the person's lived existence in time, history, and relationship as essential to the teaching itself, to faith and Christian knowledge.

I begin here in the first chapter by articulating the theological perspective that orients the following chapters. It is important to first provide a description of what I mean when I speak of Christianity or Christian faith, as my argument

---

[1] Rosenzweig, Kierkegaard, Heidegger, and Bakhtin all highlight the importance of temporality. Bakhtin brings in the important concept of physical locatedness as well, holding time and space together in his idea of the chronotope.

for indirect communication is dependent upon this understanding of the nature of the Christian religion. In this chapter we walk backward through the thought of a series of theologians whose work complements each other to constitute the underpinnings of the theological argument of this text. We begin with a look at Kathryn Tanner's theology, as her work proceeds in a strictly theological manner, influenced by an understanding of human existence true to the postmodern context, which then impacts her conception of the incarnation and thus the relationship of God in Christ to a truly human existence.[2] It is this focus on Christianity as reflection upon the God-human relationship, with an understanding of human existence as progressing through time in a particular spatial and embodied location, that is central to this argument.

Tanner emphasizes the lack of conclusiveness and the ongoing process in human existence as this relates to salvation and faith. She also stresses the crucial importance Christ's authentic human existence has for salvation, as well as the ongoing, inconclusive nature of faith for a person in history. She makes sense of the struggle and ongoing battle of faith throughout the course of human life, even showing the essential nature of that same struggle in the life of Christ. These are all theological themes that build a foundation for an argument for indirect communication such as we find functioning in the genres of Sor Juana. These theological themes contribute to the inconclusive nature of Christian knowledge and point toward a conception of Christianity that cannot be encapsulated in a system or expressed primarily through propositional statements. The theological positions laid out by Tanner give support to Søren Kierkegaard's argument that, because Christianity relates to time, it is not composed of objective knowledge and therefore cannot be communicated directly. She also, in emphasizing the process of salvation through Christ's life, is able to give sense in her description to the struggle of humanity in faith.

I begin by giving a brief look at a theological framework that takes human existence and Christ's human existence seriously in its conception of the ongoing nature of salvation. A theology such as the one described does not deny the inconclusive and ongoing nature of existence in history, but gives credence to this reality in its articulation of Christian teaching. We then move back to Kierkegaard, who is considered by some a father of postmodernism, and is at least a precursor to it, writing in opposition to the closed forms theology and philosophy were taking already in the eighteenth century; we consider

[2] This description of her work is based primarily on her book *Jesus, Humanity, and the Trinity: A Brief Systematic Theology* (Minneapolis: Fortress Press, 2001).

particularly his call for indirect communication and a form of epistemic humility he calls Socratic ignorance. My description is reliant upon the work of Søren Kierkegaard, as he is the thinker who first made this explicit argument for the need of indirect communication based upon a particular understanding of Christianity. It is said that he explored the "dialogic possibilities of an open, temporal, and existential form," as that opposed to the distancing of a closed form, and that he serves as a forebearer of postmodern literature by making "the 'medium' itself the 'message.'"[3] Kierkegaard is also described as withstanding "the enormous pressure of—and the security offered by—the Western metaphysical/aesthetic tradition to write author-ially (from a privileged origin) about existence, and chooses rather to write, with all the risks it entails, within the human—the temporal—situation of openness and uncertainty."[4] This will provide the bare theological bones which are then given flesh through an examination of the conclusions drawn by Kierkegaard about the form Christian communication should take based upon this conception of Christianity as it relates to a person in time. Using Kierkegaard, I develop a critique of traditional systematic forms of theology and propose the use of indirect forms of communication in keeping with the described understanding of faith.

Lastly we step back to a time pre-dating Sor Juana to consider one aspect of the work of Martin Luther, who spurred the Reformation in reaction partly to the power the church was exerting over all forms of human life, which likewise ignited the Catholic Reformation, of which Sor Juana's era is a product, a time when the Roman Catholic church, recovering from the effects of the Reformation, imposed conservative restrictions on Christian thought and life. Luther's work interests us primarily as he makes room for the hiddenness of God at those points in human life where revelation seems to run counter to human experience. By leaving this element open, Luther, who was never a systematic theologian and did not develop his thought by way of the scholastic system which later reformers did, avoids a theological framework that had all aspects of God and God's ways in the world classified and explained. And by avoiding a systematic ordering of this category of Hiddenness, he avoids making this form of unknowing just another form of knowing. He truly creates

---

[3] William Spanos, "Heidegger, Kierkegaard, and the Hermeneutic Circle: Towards a Postmodern Theory of Interpretation as Dis-closure," in *Martin Heidegger and the Question of Literature*, ed. William Spanos (Bloomington: Indiana University Press, 1979) 135.

[4] Ibid., 134.

space in his theology for authentic human existence to be reflected in the Christian articulation of the God-human relation.

Tanner's Inconclusive Theology in Temporality and Process. I presuppose that Christianity is a religion that seeks both the transformation of the individual who receives it and the formation of Christian community that pursues the transformation of society in accordance with Jesus' teaching on the Reign of God. Because this transforming process of the person and the world is central to this understanding of the Christian faith, both the temporal and spatial nature of human social existence is significant. The salvation process and the transformation of society occur throughout one's life in history and require spatial locality. Because Christianity is concerned with transformation, I examine how to communicate such a conception, that is: religious truth that seeks appropriation in the life of people such that it is lived out actively in the world. I will not be investigating the intricacies of how salvation is wrought through Christ or how it is applied to or received by the individual, but will assume the basic Christian affirmation that salvation is received by grace through faith and that redemption is wrought by Jesus Christ. Obviously many works could be devoted to a historical investigation of different conceptions of these basic tenants, but here I will only briefly offer some suggestions about these concepts in order to proceed into a consideration of ways to communicate Christianity such that the communication of it remains as true to its nature as possible.

In Kathryn Tanner's *Brief Systematic Theology*, she outlines a conception of redemption wrought in Christ that I will use as the foundation for my brief discussion of salvation and of faith.[5] Kathryn Tanner agrees with Karl Barth (and Athanasius, Gregory of Nyssa, Hilary of Poitiers, and John of Damascus), that it is crucial to affirm that the human nature assumed by the Word in the incarnation was a fallen human nature. She understands the redemption of fallen humanity to occur in time through the historical life of Jesus as he struggled with the effects of sin in the world, yet without giving in to temptation. It is through the process of his very human life that Jesus purifies the human existence in all its aspects. She writes:

> This fully human life of Jesus exhibits the usual historical conflicts and historical processes of human life as we moderns conceive it. ...As Jesus' life and death proceed, all these various happenings are made part of God's assumption of the

---

[5] Kathryn Tanner, *Jesus, Humanity, and the Trinity: A Brief Systematic Theology* (Edinburgh: T&T Clark, 2001) 26–27.

human, with purifying, healing, and perfecting effects. Each aspect of Jesus' life and death, moreover, is purified, healed and elevated over the course of time, in a process that involves conflict and struggle with the sinful conditions of its existence. The purification and elevation of the human in Christ is a historical process because the humanity assumed by the Word is historical.[6]

Her emphasis on the process of Jesus' life and the redeeming effects of it is reminiscent of Irenaeus, who writes that Jesus "did not abolish in his person the law of human growth," but instead, Irenaeus asserts, "he sanctified every age by the resemblance we have with him." Irenaeus describes the process of redemption as rooted in Jesus' life, proceeding through all stages of human growth and development. Jesus "passed through every age, and among infants was an infant, sanctifying infants; among children a child, sanctifying those who have this age," and so on, until finally in death, Jesus redeems humanity from death and into life.[7] Tanner draws on the work of Gregory of Nyssa, who like Irenaeus emphasizes the truly human nature of Jesus' existence. Nyssa describes it this way:

> By his intimate union with humanity, [Christ] shared all the marks of our nature. He was born, reared, grew up, and went so far as even to taste death.…[I]t was in keeping with his intimate union with our nature that he should be united with us in all our characteristics….That is why, in view of the fact that our life is bounded by two extremities (I mean its beginning and end), the power which amends our nature had to reach to both points. It had to touch the beginning and to extend to the end, covering all that lies in between.[8]

---

[6] I want to stress her use here of "the course of time" and "historical process" to describe the work of Christ as this processing nature of human life through time and in a physical location or embodiment in space, as this becomes a crucial concept for my sustained argument for Sor Juana's writings as appropriate forms for communicating Christianity. Tanner references along with other theologians the work of Rahner, who wrote: "The Logos did not merely become (statically) man in Christ; he assumed a human history." Karl Rahner, "Current Problems in Christology," in *Theological Investigations,* vol. 1, trans. C. Ernst (New York: Crossroads, 1982) 167.

[7] Irenaeus, *Against the Heresies*, in *Irenaeus of Lyons,* trans. Robert M. Grant (New York: Routledge, 1997) Book II 22.4, 114. It is well known that Irenaeus uses this line of reasoning to then argue that Jesus must have lived into old age, so as to sanctify all aspects of human existence from birth, through growth, aging, and finally to death.

[8] Gregory of Nyssa, "An Address on Religious Instruction," trans. C. Richardson, in *Christology of the Later* Fathers, ed. Edward Hardy (Philadelphia: Westminster Press, 1954) 304.

Tanner describes the process of Jesus' life as a "fight" with the effects of sin in human nature, "a fight whose success is assured by that very unity of the human with the Word, but a genuine fight nonetheless where success is not immediate but manifests itself only over the course of time."[9] The human nature assumed by the Word was not instantly perfected in the moment of the incarnation but in overcoming the struggle with sin across Jesus' lifetime: "the incarnation is a given but what is being assumed and the effects of that assumption vary over time."[10] She draws the conclusion that "Jesus saves therefore *as* a human being… Salvation occurs *in* a human life; that life is not incidental to salvation's achievement. Salvation is extended to us, moreover, only as the effects of incarnation come to be realized in Jesus' own life."[11] An authentic human existence is crucial to salvation on both sides: both on the "objective" side of the completeness of God's work in Christ and on the "subjective" side as salvation is received in a human life and community. This includes a human embeddedness in a context and life history and in the ongoing process of time, both in Jesus' life achieving salvation and in the human life to whom it is applied.

There is an "element of process" in redemption as Tanner describes it, "in so far as what is assumed" in the incarnation, that is a true human existence, "is in process."[12] Tanner explains that the "effects of the incarnation are universal in scope," and that "we are *all already* saved by Christ, in the sense that the saving power of Christ is already complete and does not need repeating or reenactment by any of us."[13] I take this to mean Christ has accomplished that which is required for salvation, and we do not contribute to it or need to duplicate it. To the extent, however, that this saving work is realized in the existing individual, community, and world, it is not complete, but continuing. The application of this salvation to our lives and community becomes manifest

---

[9] Tanner, 28.

[10] Ibid. Tanner further explains the course of the redemption process through the life of Christ: "Jesus does not overcome temptation until he is tempted, does not overcome fear and death until he feels it, at which time this temptation and fear are assumed by the Word. Jesus does not heal death until the Word assumes death when Jesus dies; Jesus does not conquer sin until he assumes or bears the sin of others by suffering death at their hands, the ultimate human rejection of God's beneficence offered in his person" (Tanner, 28).

[11] Ibid., 30.

[12] Ibid.

[13] Ibid., 55.

in time, in a similar sort of process of purification true of the life and ministry of Jesus. Though we are "*all already*" saved, the purification of our natures occurs in time through the work of the Spirit and our acts of obedience to the Spirit. Tanner explains that although the salvific event of Christ's life is completed, our particular salvation "occurs after the fact of our existence with an already established character," and therefore "this union with Christ requires tending in a way that humanity's assumption by the Son of God in Christ did not. Our union with Christ must be nurtured through the workings of the Spirit."[14]

Tanner describes growth in faith and the ongoing process of salvation as something that occurs in time and across the course of one's life. It is not something grasped or received in an instant. Normally this may be understood as the ongoing process of sanctification, the important second aspect of redemption conceived of as justification and sanctification. But Tanner never gives this label to the ongoing development and process of assumption into the life of Christ. In fact, on growth in "faith" across a lifetime, she references Luther, who does not articulate the doctrines under these distinct headings like later reformers. Faith itself is not static; it may be stable and secure as it rests in God, but as it is relationship, it grows, shifts, and changes in the course of life. Luther even warns that a perfect or completed faith would endanger one's mission here in the world and the present life given by God. He writes:

> [I]t is evident how difficult a thing faith is; it is not learned and grasped as easily and quickly as those sated and scornful spirits imagine who immediately exhaust everything contained in the scriptures. The weakness and struggle of the flesh with the spirit in the saints is ample testimony how weak their faith still is. For a perfect faith would soon bring a perfect contempt and scorn for this present life.[15]

As faith rests in God, it is unchanging, complete, and absolute, yet to the extent that faith relates to the humanity in the world, it is necessarily changing, developing, and dynamic. Much Christian theology understandably, as talk about God, reinforces the unchanging, eternal nature of God, and thus the form of discourse, and that which is articulated, emphasizes this stability and absolute certainty in God. However, as Christian knowledge, rather than knowledge of the Christian religion, is still subject to the process of the human in existence, it

---

[14] Ibid.

[15] Martin Luther, *Lectures on Galatians* (1535), Chapters 1–4, in *Luther's Works*, vol. 26, trans. and ed. Jaroslav Pelikan (St. Louis: Concordia Publishing House, 1963) 393.

is not itself complete or absolute. A theologian desiring to communicate the nature of Christianity would most honestly articulate it through an expression of both sides: the eternity and the faithfulness of God as well as the importance of the relation of this truth to the individual and community in transition or process through time. And as I will argue more fully in chapter 3, Christian truth actually rests on that rift between these two. Truth is not only what is completed in Christ, but his life in time which then stands in contemporary relation to the person and world now in time and in specific histories and locations. Similarly, as much as faith is about God's faithfulness to God's covenant with humanity and God's faithfulness to reconcile us to Godself in Jesus Christ, then it is complete, objective, and unchanging. But as much as this is itself a relationship, God offering Godself in Christ and through the Holy Spirit to be with us and in relationship with us as existing human beings in time, struggling over the course of existence to live into that which has already been accomplished in us or for us, as well as promised as the Reign of God, it is not concluded but is an ongoing process. In that faith is a relationship with the living Christ through the Holy Spirit, or as Kierkegaard says, a "God-relation"; it is not solely objective, and it is certainly not static.

Tanner lays out a conception of salvation wrought not in the instant of incarnation, nor in the moment of Christ's surrender on the cross, nor in the flash of the resurrection, but a redemption that spans all of this in the process of a human life in time, a true human existence assumed by the Word and purified through real struggle over the course of a lifetime with the fallen nature and the effects of sin in the world.[16] Her concept of redemption, however, does not end there, as she considers the assumption of our humanity into the life of Christ. Unlike the Word's original assumption of humanity in the incarnation, our assumption involves a human nature already in existence, already formed with habits and a character shaped by actualized sin in our own lives and by a sinful environment. Thus, a full attainment of salvation in perfect conformity to the life of Christ and his promise of the Kingdom will not be found in our lifetimes but only eschatologically.[17] Therefore our faith and our salvation continue in process throughout our existence:

---

[16] One of the defining characteristics of human existence for Tanner is this struggle. The struggle and striving involved in the Christian life are considered further in chapter 3.

[17] Tanner again expands upon the nature of the relationship between Christ's authentic humanity and our own: "Jesus' sinlessness is not a static property for our

> The force of our assumption by Christ is felt, as it was in Jesus' own life, in and through the way our lives are led, in and through what happens in them, the shape they take… The one process—Christ's dwelling in us and the effects that has—is dependent upon the other—our being assumed into Christ's own life—though (again as they were in Christ) not in a temporal sequence. Because we have been assumed into Christ's life, the changes in our lives are continuously fed by the workings of Christ in us through the power of the Spirit. The two processes, moreover, do not simply run alongside each other; the one—assumption by Christ—is, instead, the immanent motor of the other.[18]

The specificity of each person's existence in both time and space plays a role in the way in which salvation is applied to one's life. Various life factors are involved if existence is to be taken seriously in the salvation process: history, community, location, among others. As so many factors impact the person's identity and one's development, so then these clearly impact that existence that is being saved. I am not arguing that human experience itself is the foundation of theology, and this alone makes it inconclusive, but it is inconclusive because theology is reflection on the God-human relation, is reflection on a whole web of relationships: God and the human in Christ; God and creation through Christ and the Spirit; God and Israel through the covenant; God and the church; God and the human subject, who is herself constituted through a complex web of relationships and influences.

I am making no argument regarding the completeness of what God accomplished in Christ and God's revelation in Christ; however, an essential aspect of revelation is the work of the Holy Spirit in making this revelation to the individual, as revelation is never simply an abstract revelation but is always revelation to someone—it is personal. The person is very much involved, or at least should be, if it is to be true of the nature of the subject discussed—the God-human relation. Christian revelation includes the recognition of God in Christ, and it is the appropriation of, or obedient response to, what God has

---

imitation, but something that takes shape in a process of overcoming temptation as that process is empowered by the fact of Jesus' being the Word incarnate. Jesus does not have his perfection as an achieved state, short of his resurrection, and certainly neither will we, assumed by Christ and battling active sin through the Spirit of Christ that thereby indwells us. We have thus achieved perfection only eschatologically; it is ours now only as we live in Christ's own glorified humanity, and will be our very humanity's own only when its reformation according to the form of Christ is complete—something that never appears to us to be finally the case" (Tanner, 75).

[18] Ibid., 58.

done in Christ, reconciling the world to God, and the sending of the Spirit to transform the person, society, and world. And because Christianity is at its heart a living out of this relationship, ways of communicating this aspect of Christianity ought to be sought out and embraced by theology if it desires to be true to the nature of Christianity.

I have provided this discussion in order to give clear content to what I mean when I write of Christian existence, Christian knowledge, and Christian truth in the pages that follow. In them I borrow from Kierkegaard, utilizing his ideas on indirect communication especially as developed in *Concluding Unscientific Postscript* under the pseudonym Johannes Climacus.[19] Because salvation and faith involve human existence as above described, a conclusive or "direct" form of discourse such as one finds in propositional statements and systematic theologies is inappropriate for its communication. I propose the inclusion of additional forms of theology other than exclusively the propositional and systematic genres that dominate the field today.

Kierkegaard's Theology in Existence

Kierkegaard's use of pseudonyms in the first half of his authorship is one way in which he seeks to exemplify the sort of indirect discourse he proposes.[20] Kierkegaard indicates that he intended *The Concluding Unscientific Postscript*

[19] For an argument delineating which arguments in *Postscript* are in fact Kierkegaard's own, see Thomas C. Anderson, "Kierkegaard and Approximation Knowledge," in *International Kierkegaard Commentary, Vol. 12. Concluding Unscientific Postscript to "Philosophical Fragments,"* ed. Robert L. Perkins (Macon GA: Mercer University Press, 1997) 187–203. C. Stephen Evans has this to say: "This theory [indirect communication] is propounded by Johannes Climacus.... It is not Climacus' personal property, however, as K employs the concept in his own writings and in his *Journals and Papers*, not only to expound the idea itself, but to understand his pseudonymous authorship" [C. Stephen Evans, *Kierkegaard's Fragments and Postscript: The Religious Philosophy of Johannes Climacus* (Atlantic Highlands NJ: Humanities Press, 1983), 9]. Louis P. Pojman agrees: "The difficulty with Kierkegaard's disclaimer is that it contradicts what he later asserts in *Point of View*, where he embraces the pseudonymous works. Furthermore, it is clear that from Kierkegaard's journals that he believed the substance of the Climacus writings to be correct interpretations of the Christian faith." [Louis P. Pojman, *The Logic of Subjectivity: Kierkegaard's Philosophy of Religion* (University, Alabama: The University of Alabama Press, 1984) 89.]

[20] The second half of his authorship is far more direct and attributed to him specifically.

to be his last publication, and he identifies himself as the editor of the work. It is considered the "postscript" to a much shorter work, *Philosophical Fragments*, which describes the height of religion as belief in the paradox, the god-man. *Postscript* confronts closed systems of thought as it argues that anything relating to human existence, which philosophy and theology are at their core, cannot be worked into a system.[21] Kierkegaard opposes the use of dogmatic systems to communicate Christianity because it suggests Christian knowledge is a matter of garnering objective facts. He argues that Christianity is instead a matter of subjective truth which requires appropriation by, and the action of, the hearer or reader, and because this is its nature, it cannot be communicated directly. Direct propositional statements like those of math or the empirical sciences are appropriate to the form of objective knowledge of such disciplines, but such statements are not adequate for communicating something that relates to a person's existence and the way she lives her life in the world. More recent development in the philosophy of language and epistemology would suggest "intersubjective" may be a better term to use to communicate the relational aspect of Christian knowledge that Kierkegaard is getting at. Not only is the "subjective" nature of Christian knowledge dependent upon a relationship with another subject, namely Jesus Christ, but also a whole history of persons throughout the course of time, including one's relationship with others in the present.

[21] Luis Pojman notes the critique of systems in both *Postscript* and *Fragments,* and he speaks of the falsehood involved when existence is understood and communicated in abstract ideas. The falsehood of direct expression of "truth" and assumed comprehensive knowledge is something we consider again throughout the following chapters. Pojman writes: "In *Concluding Unscientific Postscript* to these *Fragments* he once again disclaims 'system'—not merely 'scientific' system, although the natural sciences are elsewhere (in the *Journals*) deflated in their pretensions—in an exposition of a central weakness in the Hegelian system, namely, that it submerges existence in abstract and pure thought, and so is enabled to present a false and unreal objectivity as truth. Against such an ideal Kierkegaard elaborates a doctrine of subjectivity as truth, a doctrine which makes sense of many spheres of experience in a manner beyond Hegel, and which opens up the possibility of understanding Christianity in a way more consonant with its own understanding of itself than the subordination to philosophy which is all that the deceptive patronage of Hegelianism can concede to the gospel." Luis P. Pojman, *The Logic of Subjectivity: Kierkegaard's Philosophy of Religion* (University, Alabama: The University of Alabama Press, 1984) 37–38.

In what follows I outline Kierkegaard's argument on the subjective nature of Christianity, meaning its essential relation to the existing subject, and the contrast he emphasizes between this understanding of Christianity and that which emphasizes Christianity as dogma, or as Kierkegaard terms it, as objectivity rather than subjectivity. Kierkegaard's stress upon the distinction between subjective and objective knowledge serves to convey the idea that when speaking of Christian knowledge, a person as subject does not simply know the object—God, religious truth, and the like—but one's "knowledge" itself is an encounter, a relation, and an ongoing transformation. And because the knowledge is not of an object, language cannot be used to communicate it as static fact, or as a proposition. I want to move away from the subject-object dualism and see knowledge of Christianity not as separable into these two forms but standing there at the tension between what has occurred and what is occurring. I will introduce Kierkegaard's notion of indirect communication through his discussion of the subjective nature of Christianity, and throughout I will highlight the way he utilizes Socrates as an example of a philosopher who lives his beliefs rather than simply holds them cognitively, whose form of indirect communication reflects this, and whose ignorance comes close to an image of Christian faith.

Integral to Kierkegaard's philosophy and the structure of his writing as a whole stands his conception of the stages of an individual's life, or spheres of existence. Generally they are: the esthetic, the ethical, and the religious. As is well known, Kierkegaard's pseudonyms often represent the personality of one living in a particular stage. Kierkegaard conceives of the life of striving to actualize one's possibilities as one in which a person progresses through these spheres, and he crafts his work in order to expose the reader to where he or she is in this process and hopefully to stir the reader into a response of decisive action; his writing serves to prompt self-knowledge. The spheres, however, should not be understood simply as phases one passes through successively, because this is not necessarily the case.

In the following brief description of Kierkegaard's project arguing for what he calls the subjective truth of religion and the indirect communication of it, I will refer primarily to Johannes Climacus as the author, who is the pseudonym Kierkegaard gave to *Fragments* and *Postscript*. An extended debate persists among Kierkegaard scholars as to which concepts from the pseudonymous authorship, if any, can be attributed directly to Kierkegaard himself. I am generally in agreement that most of the ideas presented in *Postscript* are Kierkegaard's, as he develops similar thoughts in his *Journals* and because he actually places his name on the work as editor. However, because here we are concerned simply with the ideas presented and how they will assist us in analyzing the religious contribution of Sor Juana in her use of genres as a way of indirectly communicating religious truth, the attributable name of the authorship is not of central importance.

In his development of the spheres of existence throughout the pseudonymous works, Kierkegaard attempts to draw his readers into a consideration of their existence. The idea is that they may begin to consider whether their lives reflect their thought and then to stop holding their thought and existence in separation. It concerns the "development of spirit," or of becoming a self. [22] This development of spirit is a self-activity available to everyone born into the world, according to Climacus.[23] Even more so, he argues that it is every person's "task to become a whole human being," and asserts that "everyone is born in the state of being able to become that."[24] It is not only for the elite or the educated, as everyone is capable of acting, or of "venturing the decisive thing…in utmost subjective passion."[25] This decisive action to actualize one's possibilities at its highest expression is to be religious. Religious knowledge is not like a learned skill, nor is it an accumulation of facts or cognitive learning. One does not become Christian because of extended hours of study, but through an encounter and a relationship which transforms the self. It is open for all. Selfhood and the decisive action to develop it and live one's confession are available to, and even the given task of, all humans.

Kierkegaard is attempting to foster "subjective thinkers," whom he contrasts with the "scientist-scholar." To become a subjective thinker is to become an artist for whom existence itself is the art.[26] It is to realize "that to be a human being is something other than year in and year out pinning something together into a system."[27] Kierkegaard is concerned that people take decisive

---

[22] It is interesting to note that Climacus asserts that this development of spirit persists after death—what one accomplishes through this self-activity is retained in the afterlife. See *Postscript,* 345.

[23] This may be a rather privileged assumption, as such self-reflection on one's philosophy compared to one's lived existence requires certain comforts; this may not be of primary importance, for example, if one's very existence itself is in jeopardy due to poverty, persecution, hunger, mental illness, etc.

[24] *Postscript*, 346.

[25] Ibid., 304.

[26] Ibid., 351.

[27] Ibid., 304.

action for a true existence in time: to determine what sort of person one wants to become, and then to actively pursue it, such that one's life corresponds to the idea held. He recognizes that this decision, the decision that he ultimately fleshes out in Christian terms, is one which will not give rest, but, he says, it will give a future.[28]

One aspect of this self-development is a sort of balance in the elements of the person: imagination, feeling, and thinking. Climacus recognizes that a person is not naturally perfectly balanced but leans one way or another due to a person's particular strengths; however, he asserts that "thinking," "imagination," and "feeling" are all important things to possess simultaneously. "With respect to existence, thinking is not at all superior to imagination and feeling but is coordinate."[29] He describes "the task" as not being the elevation of "one at the expense of the other," but is "equality" and "contemporaneity" among the elements held in union through the "medium" of "existing."[30] This aspect of his argument is important for our discussion because it highlights the importance of the inclusion of other elements of the self besides only the intellect when something pertaining to existence is concerned. Christianity pertains to life/existence and thus the communication of it should draw upon or confront the person in terms of these elements: imagination, feeling, and understanding. Climacus observes that the systematic and "scientific" philosophy of his day has duped the masses into believing that feeling and imagination are to fall away in favor of an elevated intellectualism.[31] He sees this as something hampering real existence, or at least promoting a very mediocre one. He writes:

> To have been young, then to have grown older, and then finally to die is a mediocre existence, for the animal also has that merit. But to unite the elements of life in contemporaneity, that is precisely the task. And just as it is a mediocre existence when the adult cuts away all communication with childhood and is a fragmentary adult, so is it a poor existence when a thinker, who is indeed also an existing person, has given up imagination and feeling, which is just as lunatic as

---

[28] Climacus states specifically: "But where everything is in a process of becoming, where only so much of the eternal is present that it can have a constraining effect in the passionate decision, where the *eternal* relates itself as the *future* to the *person in a process of becoming*—there the absolute disjunction belongs. In other words, when I join eternity and becoming, I do not gain rest but the future" (*Postscript,* 307).

[29] *Postscript*, 346–47.

[30] Ibid., 348.

[31] These are exactly the words used to describe what the *auto sacramental* speaks to; see chapter 4.

> giving up the understanding. And yet this is what people seem to want. They oust and dismiss poetry as a surmounted element because poetry corresponds most closely to imagination. In a scientific-scholarly process, it may be all right to classify it as a surmounted element, but in existence it holds true that as long as there is a human being who wants to claim a human existence, he must preserve poetry, and all his thinking must not disturb for him the enchantment of poetry but rather enhance it.[32]

Objective conceptions of Christianity, then, as they are removed from such elements of existence and strive to move the individual solely through the intellect, suggest that Christianity is an intellectual endeavor, and therefore they stunt a full human Christian existence. The emotions and imagination should be engaged in a communication pertaining to one's existence.

The religious sphere can be broken down further into two categories: Climacus labels them "Religiousness A" and "Religiousness B." The former refers generally to paganism of some sort, including the religion of Socrates, as well as those who conceive of the God-human relationship as essentially one of immanence. "Religiousness B" is specifically paradoxical religion, or Christianity as Kierkegaard understands it.[33] Highlighting the difference between Religiousness A and B, Climacus explains that Religiousness A includes "the individual's own pathos-filled transformation of existence" and assumes that all people essentially participate in eternal happiness and will eventually become eternally happy, whereas Religiousness B is directed toward "the paradoxical transformation of existence by faith through the relation to something historical," that is, the incarnation.[34] Religiousness B does not assume an essential relation to the eternal, as Religiousness A does, but requires a relation to "something historical," which is, paradoxically, the eternal in time. Thus the theological task as Kierkegaard conceives it begins in exposing the spheres of existence to provoke the reader into a recognition of his or her way of being, and to spur the reader into a decision for existence, which is a step toward becoming a Christian. Climacus writes: "one does not prepare oneself to become aware of Christianity by reading books or by world-historical surveys,

---

[32] *Postscript,* 348.

[33] Kierkegaard adds to this structure in *Concluding Unscientific Postscript* by describing what exists in transition between the stages—humor, irony, etc. See *Postscript,* 531–32. Irony lies between the esthetic and the ethical, and humor lies between the ethical and the religious.

[34] *Postscript,* 581.

but by immersing oneself in existing.... The difficulty is not to understand what Christianity is but to become and to be a Christian."[35]

One's existence in time becomes an important concept for Climacus, as it both underlies the difficulty of being a Christian because it requires that one relate to the eternal in time, and because it distinguishes paganism from Christianity. Because the immanence in Greek philosophy supposes the individual to have memory of the eternal, to have been once of the eternal and to have fallen away from it into time, it suggests that the human does not essentially belong *in* time, and thus the temporal is to be escaped and is inconsequential. For Christianity, however, time is an essential aspect of created human existence and salvation is found when the eternal entered time.[36] Climacus explains that "because the eternal has come into existence at a moment of time, the existing individual in time does not come to relate himself to the eternal or to collect himself in his relation (this is A) but in time comes to relate himself to the eternal in time. Consequently, the relation is within time, a relation that runs directly counter to all thinking, whether one reflects upon the individual or upon the god."[37] An emphasis on the importance of time keeps Climacus hammering the significance of the concrete and the particular in contrast to the abstraction and the universalizing of speculative philosophy and no small amount of theology.

Climacus, in both *Fragments* and *Postscript,* emphasizes the heart and distinctive feature of Christianity to be the paradox: that the eternal (God) came into existence in time. He underscores the qualitative distinction between God and the human in terms of sin, time, eternity, and transcendence. It is the holding of these elements together with one's own individual existence that makes a Christian existence so difficult. Climacus admits that the acceptance of Christianity as a way of living rather than as a doctrine to be affirmed is a more difficult task, for such a conception requires one to hold fast to a paradox, or to "relate oneself day in and day out to something upon which one bases one's eternal happiness, while maintaining the passion with which one understands that one cannot understand."[38] It is difficult to live in that contradiction of

---

[35] Ibid., 560.

[36] And as stated for the conception of salvation emphasized in this work, temporality on both sides of salvation are crucial—both in Jesus' existence and in its application to the human being now.

[37] *Postscript,* 570.

[38] Ibid., 558.

venturing all on an "if," or of maintaining passionately that one cannot understand when it is so "very easy to slip into the illusion that now one has understood it."[39] The belief that Christianity is not primarily a cognitive or intellectual enterprise is what makes Christianity available to all. Whereas Christianity as doctrine to be cognitively understood may be easier for those with acute intellects and more difficult for those less intellectually gifted, true Christianity is equally strenuous for all, but possible for all. Climacus says "the difficulty is absolute," not comparatively such that it is easier for one than another; "the difficulty pertains absolutely to each individual in particular and absolutely requires his absolute effort."[40]

One of Climacus's tasks is to depict this type of existence in all its difficulty, not more difficult than it is, but absolutely as difficult as it is in reality. Too often, he says, preachers and professors give their hearers the impression that it is not so difficult to be a Christian, which he says is not fair to those who leave the pews and attempt to live it. Christianity might not seem strenuous if one holds that it is simply a set of doctrines, but if it is to exist, to become fully human while clinging to the absurd, it is very difficult indeed. He says it is: "qualitatively and essentially difficult for every human being, because, viewed essentially, it is equally difficult for every human being to relinquish his understanding and his thinking and to concentrate his soul on the absurd."[41] He sees the actual merit of "religious discourse" to be "making the way difficult, because the way is the decisive thing."[42] Religious discourse is not a worthy or honest endeavor if it simply sets out to make cognitive sense of religious doctrine. Its purpose, rather, is to make clear the way, the difficult intensity of "the way" that is the religious existence. And again, it is the way that is decisive, not the set of doctrines one holds, but the directing of one's life toward that of Jesus Christ. For Christianity, Jesus is the way, not doctrines about him; it is him in life, in an authentic human existence that transforms that of the individual and society now in time through a lived relation across the course of temporal life.

Concluding Unscientific Postscript provides an extended argument for the subjective nature of religious knowledge, and for the subjectivity of Christianity over and against the objective conceptions of Christianity popular in

[39] Ibid.

[40] Ibid., 430.

[41] Ibid., 557.

[42] Ibid., 428.

Christendom. According to *Postscript,* Christianity is about existence; it is spirit, inwardness, and passion, all elements related to subjectivity.[43] Christianity is not a matter of objective knowledge, nor is it a matter of accumulated knowledge. If it were simply these, then one could expect that people of modernity would have an easier time becoming Christians because modern knowledge has advanced beyond that of the Middle Ages, but it is not truly easier to live a Christian existence in modernity, despite progress in objective knowledge. Climacus asks his reader to suppose that as "Christianity is not a matter of knowing; then much knowledge is of no benefit, except to ease a person more readily into the confusion of regarding Christianity as a matter of knowledge."[44] He explains that viewing Christianity as a form of objective knowledge is precisely un-Christian and is at best paganism.[45] He does not deny objective truth overall, however. He notes that it is appropriate for certain fields of knowledge: "In a mathematical proposition, for example, the objectivity is given, but therefore its truth is also an indifferent truth."[46] Climacus drives home his point:

> One becomes objective, one wants to consider objectively—that the god was crucified—an event that, when it occurred, did not permit even the temple to be objective, for its curtain tore, did not even permit the dead to remain objective, for they rose up from their graves. Thus what is able to make even the inanimate and the dead subjective is not considered objectively by Messrs. Objective.[47]

The objective conception Climacus finds in Christendom is one that supposed no personal encounter with Christian truth, an encounter that would include a personal transformation in relation to it. This would involve a person becoming him or herself most fully, becoming a subject, or living into his or her fullest, God-given individuality. Instead he finds the conception of Christianity popular in Christendom to be one that remains distant from the individual through the desired objectivity, because objectivity requires personal distancing. Climacus argues that in Christendom, a person considers herself Christian based

---

[43] Climacus writes: "Christianity is spirit; spirit is inwardness; inwardness is subjectivity; subjectivity is essentially passion, and at its maximum an infinite, personally interested passion for one's eternal happiness" (*Postscript,* 33).

[44] *Postscript*, 215.

[45] Climacus asserts that such "an objective acceptance…is paganism or thoughtlessness" (*Postscript,* 130).

[46] *Postscript*, 204.

[47] Ibid., 279.

on a birth in a "Christian nation," an infant baptism, or because she cognitively affirms a set of doctrines. This sort of creedal affirmation does not make one a Christian any more than one can claim to understand a concept simply through repeating the words of a teacher. Reciting something by rote memorization is not the same thing as learning the ideas themselves, nor is it proof that the ideas have been taken in, understood, and made one's own. This sort of internalization is necessary for most forms of knowledge, but especially so for Christian knowledge, because according to Climacus, Christianity is subjectivity. He explains,

> If Christianity is essentially something objective, it behooves the observer to be objective. But if Christianity is essentially subjectivity, it is a mistake if the observer is objective. In all knowing in which it holds true that the object of cognition is the inwardness of the subjective individual himself, it holds true that the knower must be in that state.[48]

Subjectivity here does not refer to utter relativism or the idea that there is no truth, but rather conceives of knowledge as something involving more than fact, and includes the person, her history, context, community, and world. Knowledge is not removed from these in a pure state of objective fact but involves complex relations to many aspects of existence. This is particularly true of Christian knowledge because it explicitly makes claims upon the person's way of living and future becoming, claims that will not fit within a conception of knowledge as an act of holding cognitively to an objective, logical, "correct" fact that is reliant on a "disinterested" universal perspective. Christianity is belief in a paradox; it is the crucifixion of the understanding, and a passionate clinging to the absurd.[49]

---

[48] Ibid., 53.

[49] Through Climacus, Kierkegaard argues: "Without risk, no faith. … If I am able to apprehend God objectively, I do not have faith; but because I cannot do this, I must have faith. If I want to keep myself in faith, I must continually see to it that I hold fast the objective uncertainty, see to it that in the objective uncertainty I am 'out on 70,000 fathoms of water' and still have faith" (*Postscript,* 204). Pojman notes that in Kierkegaard's "later journals he seems to modify his earlier absolutist and fideist position," realizing "that he had sometimes exaggerated the claims of subjectivity." However, "the concept serves as an antidote," nonetheless; it worked "as a corrective to an overly rigid and smug objectivity." In time Kierkegaard's emphasis fell on "the concept of hope," rather than "the strenuous and strained notion of believing against all evidence" (Pojman, 146).

Climacus makes a distinction between the conception of truth as an object to which the knower relates herself, and the conception of truth as the very relation itself between the knower and that which is sought to be known. According to the former, a knower is in truth if that to which she relates herself is in fact the objective, absolute truth, if it is "correct." Here the focus is exclusively on what is known, whereas in the latter, a knower is "in truth" based on *how* she relates herself to that which is sought. As Climacus states, "Being a Christian is defined not by the 'what' of Christianity but by the 'how' of the Christian."[50] Climacus distinguishes between two different types of worshippers: one who seeks objectively after God, or "the approximating truth of the God-idea," and another "who is infinitely concerned that he in truth relate himself to God with the infinite passion of need."[51] He asks where a person will find more truth: in a Christian nation where a person has "knowledge of the true idea of God" and prays in "the house of the true God," but does so in a state of untruth; or in an "idolatrous land" where, although the person prays with eyes directed to an idol, nonetheless "prays with all the passion of infinity."[52] Climacus concludes the latter "prays in truth to God although he is worshipping an idol"; the former "prays in untruth to the true God and is therefore in truth worshipping an idol."[53] As long as the "how of this relation is in truth, the individual is in truth, even if he in this way were to relate himself to untruth."[54] The "truth" is in the "how" of the relation, not in a doctrine.

Christianity is not a religion about God's internal nature or God's transcendence over and against creation. Christianity is instead the religion of God as God relates to God's creation, primarily the way God relates with humanity, and especially as God relates to humanity through the incarnation. Christian knowledge, then, is not simply some knowledge about this which Christianity affirms, but is itself a relation, a relation through the Holy Spirit to God incarnate in the time of Jesus Christ with the human now in existence. Simply put, Climacus asks the question as to where truth in religious knowledge is to be found, where truth is for the existing individual. "Objectively, what is reflected upon is that this is the true God; subjectively, that the individual relates himself to a something *in such a way* that his relation is in truth a God-

[50] *Postscript*, 611.

[51] Ibid., 201.

[52] Ibid.

[53] Ibid.

[54] Ibid., 199.

relation."[55] God can certainly have objective knowledge of Godself, but for a person in the process of becoming, true religious knowledge is found in the God-relation; this involves the subject at the core of her being.

For Kierkegaard, and expressed through Climacus, the decision to relate oneself in truth, or to appropriate religious knowledge, rests within the individual. There is no way out from the path that leads through despair in the struggle to relate to the paradox in Christianity, not in an infant baptism, a birth in a Christian nation, or a doctrine of predestination.[56] Decision is a crucial element in the process of becoming and of fully existing.[57] If one takes "subjectivity" (that is, the decisive way of relating to God) away from Christianity, decision is also removed. "At no point does an observer (and that is what the objective subject is) have an infinite need for a decision, and at no

---

[55] Ibid.

[56] Pojman notes that the doctrine of predestination "haunted" Kierkegaard, and that Kierkegaard eventually resolved the issue for himself somewhat by understanding the idea in subjective rather than objective terms. Kierkegaard wrote: "Here is the real solution to the problem of predestination. When it is said that they are chosen *Quos Vocavit*, they are chosen to salvation or are damned, for what else does the expression *quos vocavit* mean than those in whose consciousness Christianity emerged, and thus this view can be united with Schleiermacher's relative predestination, for those who have lived in this world but to whom no call came are obviously not predestined (since they are not called); nor is it enough to be able to say anyone is called but only the person in whose consciousness Christianity has emerged in relation to the rest of his life views." *Søren Kierkegaard's Journals and Papers,* vol. 3, L–R, ed. and trans. Howard V. Hong and Edna H. Hong (Bloomington and London: Indiana University Press, 1995) 625, entry no. 3547. Pojman comments: "Predestination in the sense of *quo vocavit*, being called by God and elected is thus transformed from an objective dogma (as may be seen in Calvinism or Luther's writings) into subjective awareness of God's sovereign grace in one's life, which paradoxically, does not annul the awareness of freedom. The synergistic motif dominates. It is God who acted in procuring our salvation, yet our response is vital to his activity. This is exactly the position Climacus takes in *Fragments*. Grace is the condition which makes the choice of faith possible" (Pojman, 12). Kierkegaard's reaction to the formation of an objective doctrine of predestination relates to themes developed later in this chapter where we see predestination as it could be viewed as pertaining to the hiddenness of God become so certain and objective as to become a form of knowing rather than unknowing; what was once a mystery of the Hidden God, became a doctrine of which theologian knew exactly where and how it belonged to God's nature.

[57] *Postscript,* 33.

point does he see it."[58] The decision of faith requires subjectivity and the passion of an infinite interest. And now we turn to a more detailed description of this paradox held in faith.

Faith in the Paradox. The paradox of the incarnation does not allow for removed observation or an objective relation. It requires passionate decision in faith to relate oneself to this uncertainty, to allow one's existence to be transformed by the paradox. Climacus asks what objective faith could even mean. He says: "It means a sum of tenets…. Objective faith—it is indeed as if Christianity had also been proclaimed as a little system of sorts… It is as if Christ…had been a professor, and as if the apostles had formed a little professional society of scholars."[59]

Climacus's insistence on the paradoxical nature of Christianity is not an assertion that God is a paradox within Godself or that "the eternal, essential truth" is itself a paradox, but rather "it is a paradox by being related to an existing person."[60] Nor is this paradox a direct logical contradiction as in X equals 2 and X does not equal 2, held together as if both could be true simultaneously, but this religious paradox is something of which we as humans, living in time, cannot make complete and objective sense. The paradox is the eternal God becoming human in time, and this paradox is magnified as Christianity is then the relation of a human subject embedded in a present temporal existence in relation to the incarnate Christ. Meanwhile, the individual already lives a paradoxical existence, as she is finite and temporal with yearning for the infinite and with hope for the eternal.

Uncertainty is faith's one certainty for Climacus: "Without risk, no faith. Faith is the contradiction between the infinite passion of inwardness and the objective uncertainty. If I am able to apprehend God objectively, I do not have faith; but because I cannot do this, I must have faith. If I want to keep myself in faith, I must continually see to it that I hold fast the objective uncertainty."[61] Climacus asserts that uncertainty is the "mark" and "form" of faith. When it is

[58] Ibid.

[59] Ibid., 216.

[60] Ibid., 206.

[61] Ibid., 204. This view of faith is also true of Kierkegaard in many respects: "What is it to believe? It is…, to defend oneself against the vain thought of wanting to comprehend and against the vain imagination of being able to comprehend." *Søren Kierkegaard's Journals and Papers,* vol. 2, F–K, ed. and trans. Howard V. Hong and Edna H. Hong (Bloomington and London: Indiana University Press, 1970) 14, entry no. 1130.

otherwise and we claim a certainty, we are not advancing in religion but regressing into "childish forms."[62] Christopher Simpson calls faith for Kierkegaard "a mode of knowing that can cope with the uncertainty of historical knowledge while continually recognizing the possibility of failure—of being wrong."[63] And he says "this recognition of risk stands in opposition to the quest for certainty."[64] Even claims such as: it is certain that "what pleases God succeeds for the pious" undercut true faith, because the moment this certainty is lost, so is faith.[65]

Climacus sees a correspondence between "truth as paradox" and passion, in that truth becomes a paradox "precisely in its relation to an existing subject,"[66] and for Christianity the truth is found at that relation, or one does not have Christian knowledge if one is not in that relation, which by its very nature is a paradox. When one forgets that one is an existing subject, one loses passion, and thus, in turn, truth does not become a paradox. Retaining passion becomes more difficult in the "pencil-pushing modern speculative" era, because passion is discounted—one of the handful of reasons Climacus gives as to why it may be more difficult to truly become a Christian in modernity than before.[67] He defines faith in a variety of ways in *Postscript*, one being that "faith is the objective uncertainty with the repulsion of the absurd, held fast in the passion of inwardness, which is the relation of inwardness intensified to its highest."[68] He explains that demonstrations of proof only become necessary when passion wanes. He says that at the point that faith loses passion, "faith ceases to be faith," and so a person then seeks to gain some "general esteem from unbelief" in a proof, a demonstration, or a certainty.[69] It is essential to faith that one does not "slip" into the illusion that one can have certainty and faith simultaneously, because as soon as uncertainty is not a person's one certainty, one loses authentic faith, as truth becomes like a "circular letter upon which signatures are

[62] *Postscript,* 507.

[63] Christopher Simpson, "A Way Between Freeplay and Totality: Kierkegaard on Faith and the Other," in *Søren Kierkegaard and the Word(s): Essays on Hermeneutics and Communication*, ed. Paul Houe and Gordon D. Marino (Copenhagen: C.A. Reitzel, 2003) 66.

[64] Ibid.

[65] *Postscript,* 507.

[66] Ibid., 109.

[67] Ibid., 197.

[68] Ibid., 611.

[69] Ibid., 31.

collected."[70] Or again as soon as uncertainty no longer keeps the religious person in a continual state of "hovering" so that she can instead "continually grasp certitude," or "as soon as certainty seals with lead, as it were, the religious person—well, then he is naturally about to become part of the mass."[71]

Throughout *Postscript* Climacus commends a posture he calls "Socratic ignorance," which one may assume refers simply to Socrates' claim to know nothing and a style of teaching that asks questions instead of dictating answers. However, beyond this Climacus states, "Socratic ignorance is an expression of the objective uncertainty,"[72] and thus it was "the expression, firmly maintained with all the passion of inwardness, of the relation of the eternal truth to an existing person, and there it must remain for him a paradox as long as he exists."[73] And he says, "It is possible that in the Socratic ignorance there was more truth in Socrates than in the objective truth of the entire system that flirts with the demands of the times and adapts itself to assistant professors."[74] The truth is not located in the proposition held in the mind, but in the life lived in accordance with it; thus "ignorance" serves as an expression of the philosophical principle that religious truth is about how we live rather than doctrinal statements held cognitively. Climacus even lifts up Socratic ignorance as an analogue to faith, while clarifying that there can be no direct analogy. "Socrates, whose ignorance was shown…to be a kind of analogy to faith (keeping continually in mind, however, that there are no analogies to the paradoxical-religious in its entirety), was no fool because he did not want to dally with glimpsing and knowing this and that but wanted to be absolutely ignorant."[75]

A discussion of Socratic ignorance is important to this project because it serves as an analogue to faith, when faith is belief in the paradox and includes the crucifixion of one's understanding. Socratic ignorance refers to the acknowledgment that one does not have access to objective, certain, or conclusive knowledge of God and, because it signals this wise uncertainty, it is a metaphor for authentic Christian faith.

---

[70] Ibid., 243.

[71] Ibid., 507.

[72] Ibid., 206.

[73] Ibid., 202.

[74] Ibid.

[75] Ibid., 566.

As stated, objective thinking looks for results and conclusion, but subjective thinking, as it relates to existing, is a continual striving, and thus does not end in conclusion. When existence is understood with this sort of intensity, one that involves continual action to actualize one's internal possibilities, when life is understood as always a process of becoming that requires a striving effort, life does not offer a resting peace. Climacus admits that the subjective thinker "does not derive positive, cozy joy from life."[76] And it seems for this reason that although many people may strive throughout their youth, "when they have come to a certain point in their searching," their conception of life changes:

> They marry, they enter occupations, in consequence of which they must out of decency finish something, must have results (because shame before people bids them to have results...) So they believe that they themselves actually have arrived, or they must believe it out of custom and habit, or else they sigh and complain of the many things that keep them from striving.... So off and on they also engage in a little striving, but the last is merely a skimpy marginal note to a text finished long ago. In this way, one is exempted from becoming aware, in action, of the strenuous difficulties contained in the simplest statement about existing *qua* human being, whereas in the capacity of a positive thinker, one knows all about world history and our Lord's most private thoughts.[77]

The perpetual striving exhorted by Climacus could bring a person to despair because one naturally yearns to have something completed and finished. However, Climacus considers this urge, in terms of existence, to be an evil that "must be renounced."[78] He explains that "the perpetual process of becoming is the uncertainty of earthly life, in which everything is uncertain. Every human being knows this and says so once in a while, especially on a solemn occasion and not without sweat and tears."[79] Thus, the human life in pursuit of this is characterized by a continual quest. Kierkegaard is criticized by some theologians for a view of Christianity that lifts the function of striving to reflect the truth of Christianity to such an extent that to truly be a Christian comes to resemble a work of human effort.[80] Kierkegaard does attempt to hamper this

---

[76] Ibid., 85.

[77] Ibid.

[78] Ibid., 86.

[79] Ibid.

[80] See James Brown, *Subject and Object in Modern Theology* (New York: Macmillian Company, 1955). Brown notes: "The doctrine of the absolute paradox certainly means that two incommensurables are concerned in the Christian salvation. But

emphasis, however, by insisting that this striving only signifies the process of becoming that the individual is undergoing. He explains that "the Socratic is not to be understood finitely as a continued and perpetually continued striving toward a goal without reaching it. No, but however much the subject has the infinite within himself, by existing he is in the process of becoming."[81]

Climacus finds another unlikely ally and philosophical hero of *Postscript* in eighteenth-century German philosopher Gotthold Lessing. Climacus highlights Lessing's declaration that if God offered him the choice between complete knowledge of Truth in one hand and continued striving after the truth in the other, Lessing would choose the continued striving. Lessing writes: "If God held all truth enclosed in his right hand, and in his left hand the one and only ever-striving drive for truth, even with the corollary of erring forever and ever, and if he were to say to me: Choose!—I would humbly fall down to him at his left hand and say: Father, give! Pure truth is indeed only for you alone!"[82]

Lessing is also credited with the concept of "the leap," which becomes central to Kierkegaard's understanding of Christian faith and is commended for his avoidance of systematizing, even to the point of being elusive so as not to create direct adherents. As Climacus states: "Lessing is not didactic but subjectively evasive, without wanting to obligate anyone to accept it for his sake and without wanting to help anyone attain direct continuity with the originator."[83] In a classic Climacian move, he cloaks his interpretation of Lessing's work with an abundance of "perhaps," so as not to present an absolute decided conclusion about the work to the philosopher: "Perhaps Lessing himself understood that such things cannot be expounded directly; at least his procedure can be explained this way, and perhaps the explanation is correct, perhaps."[84]

---

the emphasis on faith as passion, joins oddly with an equal emphasis on it as strenuousness, if these are both meant to cover the same point in the process of salvation. We could conceive the latter as the result of the former easily enough, the Christian works as flowing from the Christian faith, with all the more ardour from the knowledge of the love which first loved us, with all the more diligence from the combined sense of gratitude and responsibility in the adoption of the sons [and daughters] of God. But Kierkegaard makes faith itself a work, if not in the first then in the second instance, if not in its inception at least in its continuance" (Brown, 81).

[81] *Postscript,* 92–93.

[82] Ibid., 106. (Quoting Lessing—s.w., v. p. 100.)

[83] Ibid., 93.

[84] Ibid.

Existence is not something "finished" to be studied for conclusive results. Because existence is a process of becoming, there can be no static knowledge about one's existence. Climacus likens the systematician's labeling of his thought as a "system" to a person who loses a silk umbrella but advertises that the lost umbrella is cotton, so the finder would be less tempted to keep it. If one calls one's philosophy a "continued striving for the truth," who will buy or admire it? But if one claims to provide an "absolute system," everyone will be interested.[85] The problem, however, is that existence cannot be systematized for those in existence: "A system of existence cannot be given. Is there then, not such a system? ...Existence itself is a system—for God, but it cannot be a system for any existing spirit. System and conclusiveness correspond to each other, but existence is the very opposite."[86] Existence is a system for God alone, in that God has a full and complete understanding of it, but for humanity it is always an approximation, because it is always in process for us and is never conclusive while we exist. And because Christianity is a relation between an existing subject and God in time in Jesus Christ, it is not conclusive, and therefore not material for a system, and because it is this relation, it cannot be communicated directly.

Because Christianity has to do with a relationship with God in time, the communication of it involves communicating one's God-relation. This creates a contradiction, however, as one simultaneously wants to communicate this while also retaining it as one's inwardness. It is impossible "for this contradiction to become manifest in a direct form," though one can easily understand that "a subject existing in this way may want to communicate himself."[87] In a lengthy footnote, Climacus explains the relationship between the uncertainty of faith in the paradox and the inconclusiveness of Christianity as it pertains to a person in existence and the way in which this difficulty may be communicated through the illustration of a person in love. Such a person, as he is "occupied with continually acquiring the inwardness of erotic love,...has no result and is never finished, but he may nevertheless want to communicate; yet for that very reason he can never use a direct form, since that presupposes results and completion."[88] This is true also of the God-relationship: "Just because he himself is continually in the process of becoming in an inward direction,...he can never communicate

[85] Ibid., 108.
[86] Ibid., 118.
[87] Ibid., 73.
[88] Ibid.

himself directly, since the movement is here the very opposite. Direct communication requires certainty, but certainty is impossible for a person in the process of becoming, and it is indeed a deception."[89]

Continuing the metaphor of an erotic love relationship, Climacus likens the search for certainty in faith to the certainty a lover seeks when she yearns for the wedding day, because this would give her "assured certainty" in the legal security of marriage.[90] Climacus suggests that this drive and search for certainty alter the love relationship just as they actually undermine the nature of faith. As stated earlier, faith has steadfast certainty only of objective uncertainty. The very assertion that "the eternal becomes, that it comes into existence," is paradoxical for the individual.[91] Christianity is illusive also in that the human existing subject has a sense of the infinite, yet death is possible at every moment of life. "All positive dependability is thus made suspect."[92] If these contradictions are communicated directly, the illusiveness is removed, and therefore, the truth of the matter is not communicated; the form interferes. "Therefore it is important for the thinking of the existing subject to have a form in which he is able to render this."[93] He claims that "an illusive form is the only adequate one, because direct communication implies the dependability of continuity, whereas the illusiveness of existence, when I grasp it, isolates me. Whoever is aware of this...he will avoid direct utterance."[94]

Climacus says that "system and conclusiveness are just about one and the same," and his extended argument strives to convince the reader that Christianity, as it relates to the existing individual, is not, after all, conclusive. So, clearly a completed system cannot foster Christian truth. If one admits that the system is not concluded, an admission he says Hegel makes, one's "half-finished system," is "nonsense," whereas a system with a conclusion is nothing more than a hypothesis, as such a comprehensive account cannot be known, dependent as it is upon a conclusive knowledge.[95] While system and conclusiveness correspond to each other, "existence is the very opposite." Thus, "system and existence cannot be thought conjointly," because "existence is the

---

[89] Ibid., 73–74.

[90] Ibid., 74.

[91] Ibid., 82.

[92] Ibid.

[93] Ibid.

[94] Ibid., 83.

[95] Ibid., 107.

spacing that holds apart; the systematic is the conclusiveness that combines."[96] Climacus sees the system-building, scholarly tendencies that have taken over the communication of Christianity as a move that makes Christianity like a "seedy saloon keeper," trying to come up with new ways to draw customers. In accommodating itself to standards of objectivity, Christianity is altered, as well as is the way a person relates to it. He says,

> I rather think that it is ashamed of itself, like an old man who sees himself rigged out in the latest fashion. Or, more correctly, I think it focuses its wrath against people when it sees this distorted figure that is supposed to be Christianity, a perfume-saturated and systematically accommodated and soiree-participating scholarliness, whose whole secret is half measures and then truth to a certain degree—when it sees a radical cure (and only as such is it what it is) transmogrified nowadays into a vaccination, and a person's relation to it equivalent to having a certificate of vaccination.[97]

Johannes Climacus lays out a contrast between two conceptions of doctrine. On one hand, doctrine is conceived as "a philosophical theory that is to be comprehended and speculatively understood," and on the other, doctrine is simply understood to be those beliefs that one is actualizing in existence.[98] To comprehend the latter is to "understand that it is to be existed in, to understand that difficulty of existing in it."[99] If one is to consider Christianity as a doctrine of any sort, it must be understood to be a doctrine of this type, that which is to be actualized in existence, to be appropriated in the form of one's life. It is not for speculation. To speculate on Christianity is precisely to misunderstand it. In order to clearly distinguish Christianity as he understands it from the speculative doctrine commonly accepted as Christianity in modernity, Climacus defines Christianity as that which "expresses an existence-contradiction and is an existence-communication."[100] If one communicated Christianity directly, this would communicate Christianity as a form of objective knowledge rather than as intersubjective knowledge, and so would not be communicating Christianity at all. Therefore, Climacus expresses the need for an existence-communication, a form of discourse that will represent and express that which is being communicated—indirect communication.

---

[96] Ibid., 118.
[97] Ibid., 294.
[98] Ibid., 379.
[99] Ibid.
[100] Ibid., 379–80.

According to Climacus, objective thought is indifferent to the thinking subject and, in fact, encourages distance from the subject's existence in order to keep the ideas pure and unaffected by the subject herself. Climacus suggests that the tendency of speculative thought to distance the individual from that which is considered and to view all objectively is the result of the mindset of modernity and is "the orientation of the whole age."[101] Because moderns assume a high level of accumulated knowledge, they have "entirely forgotten what it means to *exist* and what *inwardness* is."[102] This is the problem as he understands it: assumed knowledge in a worldview that prizes objectivity; and he recognizes that any hope of communicating the lack of inwardness in the age would require that he do so in an indirect form. Additionally, objective thought "invests everything in the result" and encourages humanity "to cheat" by copying and rattling off the answers.[103] A direct form of communication, then, is used to offer these results directly either to be claimed as fact or truth by the other, to be memorized and repeated by rote, or to be followed identically. When a person repeats what another says verbatim, it is often assumed that they agree and understand each other. However, because the relation of thought to existence is central to true religious knowledge, such conceptions of knowledge by rote is altogether a misunderstanding. Subjective thought cannot be separated from the subjective thinker, as the thinker exists within it. Subjective thought "invests everything in the process of becoming and omits the result" because there is no conclusive result for the thinker who is in the continual process of becoming.[104] Climacus explains that as "the subjective existing thinker" is set free by thought-existence, "so the secret of communication specifically hinges on setting the other free," a task that cannot be accomplished through the direct communication of oneself to another.[105]

A direct communication is also not appropriate because it hinders a person from making the thought her own. Climacus explains:

> The reception intrinsic to inwardness is not a direct reproduction of what was communicated, since that is an echo. But the repetition of inwardness is the resonance in which what is said disappears, as with Mary when she *hid* the words in her heart. But when the relationship is between human beings, not even

---

[101] Ibid., 242.
[102] Ibid.
[103] Ibid., 73.
[104] Ibid.
[105] Ibid., 74.

> this is the true expression for the repetition of inwardness, because she *concealed* the words as a treasure in the beautiful setting of a good heart, but there is inwardness when what is said belongs to the recipient as if it were his own—and now it is indeed his own. To communicate in that way is the most beautiful triumph of resigned inwardness. Therefore no one is as resigned as God, because he communicates creatively in such a way that in creating he *gives* independence vis-à-vis himself.[106]

To receive a communication, one cannot just repeat or directly replicate what is communicated. He gives the example of Mary as one who takes the communication to her heart. However, Mary's communication was from God, so to communicate the eternal from one person to another, it is even more complex. One cannot simply conceal but must, in turn, communicate to the other such that the communication becomes truly the hearer's own. The hearer must appropriate knowledge for herself.

Because the modern era has so much information, has so much cognitive or objective knowledge about Christianity, be it either in knowledge of doctrines, systems of thought, or historical critical scholarship, Climacus argues that indirect communication will need to subtract knowledge. He compares adding knowledge to someone already full of knowledge to force-feeding someone whose mouth is so stuffed with food that she cannot actually eat and may starve. He states that instead of adding food, one must first take food away so the person can at least chew. Similarly, he asks,

> When a man is very knowledgeable but his knowledge is meaningless or virtually meaningless to him, does sensible communication consist in giving him more to know…or does it consist, instead, in taking something away from him? When a communicator takes a portion of the copious knowledge that the very knowledgeable man knows and communicates it to him in a form that makes it strange to him, the communicator is, as it were, taking away his knowledge, at least until the knower manages to assimilate the knowledge by overcoming the resistance of the form.[107]

He sees one of the obstacles of a knowledgeable person to be the traditional form of receiving knowledge, such that one becomes used to confronting knowledge only in one particular form. If the form were changed, one would not understand—like a person who can correctly solve a mathematic

---

[106] Ibid., 260.
[107] Ibid., 275.

equation "if the letters read ABC but not if they read ACB."[108] As in the example of mathematics, the person may be able to duplicate the work demonstrated by another, but being unable to solve the problem if the letters are simply changed means the person never understood the concepts to begin with. This changing of form in some sense does take knowledge away from the person, but in so doing communicates that the person does not necessarily understand the concept. A Christian, for example, may know what the church affirms about the incarnation, may be able to define hypostatic union, but not understand what the fact of the incarnation means for that person's life. Climacus observes that this subtraction may often actually involve telling the person in an unrecognizable form what he or she actually "knows" but does not understand. This is a reason why the form of discourse becomes so important. When religious thought is communicated in its standard and expected form, it is not as able to expose the reader to her life and existence as an unexpected one can. Such forms are more capable of startling and awakening the reader to consider her way of living because it places the thought itself in existence. This is true especially of narrative forms—drama, novel, and short story, but poetry also, as the most inconclusive form—as, by their very natures, they evoke an existential correspondence and serve to shake the reader through their elusive form.[109] In *Practice in Christianity* Kierkegaard places his writing on Christianity in the form of existence under the pseudonym Anti-Climacus, in which Jesus' life, works, and parables are understood as a form of indirect communication. Here God is said to be communicating in the form of existence, the best way to communicate something that essentially has to do with one's existence.[110]

As mentioned earlier, the differences between objective and subjective thought are reflected in the way their knowledge is communicated, as "objectively the emphasis is on *what* is said" and "subjectively the emphasis is on *how* it is said."[111] The "how" Climacus refers to when speaking of the communication of subjective or religious knowledge is "not to be understood as manner, modulation of voice, oral delivery, etc., but it is to be understood as the

---

[108] Ibid.

[109] Søren Kierkegaard, *Practice in Christianity,* ed. and trans. Howard V. Hong and Edna H. Hong (Princeton: Princeton University Press, 1991).

[110] See chapter 5 for a developed argument on existence as form in the life of Sor Juana.

[111] *Postscript*, 204.

relation of the existing person, in his very existence, to what is said."[112] Climacus illustrates the difference between what is said and how it is said with the example that something true can become untruth when it is spoken by particular people. There are truths that find veracity in relation to the subject involved or none at all. These are subjective truths, which include Christianity, and the "how" of their communication includes the life or subjectivity of the one communicating. Life must be shaped by the idea for it to be true knowledge. An existence-communication can be expressed only by another subjective thinker, that is, one who is herself existing in her thought, so that her life corresponds to her ideas of life. In communicating the truth of Christianity, then, as it is subjectivity or inwardness, the communicator must in some sense communicate her God-relation. However, what is to be communicated is not an objective result that this individual has found, as if the learner could just mimic the way of the speaker. In fact this is the problem he sees with many Christians who have looked for God through the *via negativa*. He says that once they have made some progress in this "way," they then turn it into something positive, as in a program they can pass on for others to follow. They find a certain amount of results and then stray from their negative way.

Socrates is a prime example of someone who communicates his thought through the embodiment of it, and Climacus lifts up Socrates' view on immortality in particular to illustrate this. Socrates not only teaches immortality as a truth of human existence, but he puts his life on the line for this "if," drinking the hemlock. Unlike those who make an argument for immortality based on logic, Socrates demonstrates his belief with his life and death, because this thought of the infinite shaped his existence. However, exemplars never serve to motivate, according to Climacus. "The fact that this person and that person actually have done this and that can just as well have a delaying as a motivating effect. The reader merely transforms the person who is being discussed (aided by his being an *actual* person) into the rare exception; he admires him and says: But I am too insignificant to do anything like that."[113] When applied to differences among persons, admiration is a fitting response, but, as discussed earlier, authentic subjectivity is available to all and difference

[112] Ibid. Climacus also states that a primary difference between ancient times and modernity is that in antiquity only a few individuals claimed to know the truth, and that in modernity everyone claims to know it, but "inwardness has an inverse relation to it" (*Postscript,* 204).

[113] Ibid., 358.

is not the basis for it. Thus, admiration for another's religious existence is a misunderstanding because it is the ethical duty of all humans; it is a universal ability and call. Climacus asserts that this should be presented, then, in the form of possibility rather than a completed actuality.

> In the form of possibility, the presentation becomes a requirement. Instead of presenting the good in the form of actuality, as is ordinarily done, that this person and that person have actually lived and have actually done this, and thus transforming the reader into an observer, an admirer, an appraiser, it should be presented in the form of possibility. Then whether or not the reader wants to exist in it is placed as close as possible to him.[114]

A person cannot take the findings of another at face value and hold them as truth, removed from one's own internalizing of them; such appropriation will not be identical for each person. Therefore the teacher, or the one communicating Christianity, must remove herself from that communicated, so as not to create a follower for herself. Climacus is therefore suggesting that a person must communicate herself, but then immediately or even simultaneously remove her personality from the learner so that the learner can deal with her own individual consciousness rather than focusing on that of the communicator. After all, "the learner essentially has himself to deal with and...the inwardness of truth is not the chummy inwardness with which two bosom friends walk arm in arm with each other but is the separation in which each person for himself is existing in what is true."[115]

But how does one communicate oneself, one's inwardness? Climacus recognizes the difficulty of this:

> The very thing that makes communication so difficult dialectically: that the receiver is an existing person, and that this is the essential. To stop a man on the street and to stand still in order to speak with him is not as difficult as having to say something to a passerby in passing, without standing still oneself or delaying the other, without wanting to induce him to go the same way, but just urging him to go on his own way—and such is the relation between an existing person and

---

[114] Ibid., 359. He asserts his point: "Never in all eternity is it true that someone has been assisted in doing the good by someone else's *actually* having done it, because if he himself actually did come to do it, it would be by understanding the other's actuality as possibility" (*Postscript,* 359). And "Ethically understood, there is nothing on which one sleeps so soundly as on admiration over an actuality" (*Postscript,* 360).

[115] Ibid., 249.

> an existing person when the communication pertains to the truth as existence-inwardness.[116]

It is to pass someone on the street and encourage her on her own path and not your own, all while not pausing on your two journeys; it is a challenge.

Communication of subjectivity and inwardness, or the religious, is also difficult because language is not adequate for the task of communicating existence; speech is "a more abstract medium than existence," to which these pertain.[117] Systematic thought is organized in abstract form, forced into a one, two, three structure and thus "must inevitably run into trouble whenever it is to be applied to the concrete."[118] Climacus argues for artistic, or indirect, forms of communication. The subjective thinker's form, however, "must be just as manifold as are the opposites that he holds together."[119] Climacus argues that the form of communication for the subjective thinker "must first and last be related to existence, and in this regard he must have at his disposal the poetic, the ethical, the dialectical, the religious."[120] Any sort of knowledge of which the subjective holds an important position and for which appropriation is the main point, the communication of it will be "a work of art."[121]

Climacus provides the Socratic method, or the "maeutic art," as one example of the communication that he proposes. Socrates emphasizes the importance of instruction in right and wrong, justice and injustice, in contrast to the Sophists, who, without concern for veracity or falsity, taught that the power of persuasion to defend oneself in court and convince the assembly was of utmost importance. The Sophists taught students how to live *successfully* rather than *morally* in their society; they have been described as giving "voice to the prevailing tone of cynical disillusionment" and of preaching "relativity of all values."[122] Socrates, however, is concerned with the student's moral development in goodness, even as it goes against accepted customs of his day.[123] "Socrates seeks to goad people into making a search to become

---

[116] Ibid., 277.

[117] Ibid., 465.

[118] Ibid., 357.

[119] Ibid.

[120] Ibid.

[121] Ibid., 79.

[122] Raphael Demos, "Introduction," in *The Dialogues of Plato,* vols. 1–2, trans. B. Jowett, M.A. (New York: Random House, 1937) ix.

[123] See Plato's dialogues: *Protagoras* and *Gorgias*.

concerned about the good of their souls—by convincing them of their ignorance, and persuading them not to be led astray by the success that the Sophists promise."[124]

One might expect a philosophy to function as a discipline like mathematics and be primarily concerned with content, a group of propositionally true statements. But for Socrates philosophy is not a group of true statements about virtue or the Good.[125] Socrates emphasizes philosophy not as a cognitive exercise, but as a way of life, such that philosophy is the searching after the Good, requiring that one's life be shaped by this Good. For Socrates philosophical knowledge is virtue and thus cannot simply be transferred from one person to the other through rote memorization or direct instruction, but is something the person must endeavor toward on her own. It can only be attained in the active search. Therefore it is the job of the philosopher to ask the questions that will evoke a sense of discovery and a response in the individual. This questioning process should draw the learner to consider her way of living and to pursue truth in such a way that she directs her life toward it, so that her life may reflect the Good that is sought philosophically. Philosopher David Burrell describes the impact of the Socratic method this way: "under the influence of 'Socrates' art' one is drawn to bend personally, as it were, in the direction of the object sought after, and (at least temporarily) to order one's own life according to the order inquired into."[126]

---

[124] Diogenes Allen, *Philosophy for Understanding Theology* (Atlanta: John Knox Press, 1973) 41.

[125] For Plato, metaphor and myth play a supplementary role by making it clear that a direct telling would be inadequate to the realities being sought after, discussed, and pondered. Plato's use of metaphor and myth suggest something of the nature of the reality sought by "inviting and invoking a fuller personal participation in the inquiry." David B. Burrell, *Analogy and Philosophical Language* (New Haven: Yale University Press, 1973) 60. Burrell describes this as "auxiliary" because although it does not contribute anything directly in terms of content, it is still cognitive in that it orients the learner to the nature of that pursued and suggests what sort of inquiry is appropriate to the nature of the object, i.e., that virtue or the Good are such that one's life must be formed in reflection of them in the very pursuit of knowledge of them. He also explains that poetic form stands somewhere between music and science, which he doesn't claim is a breakthrough concept, but states that this signifies that "poetry can play a cognitive role, especially in those areas where any scientific account is inadequate" (Burrell, 60).

[126] Burrell, 48.

The literary form points to the limits of a propositional account, and in implying that the object sought after in philosophy cannot be grasped in the direct, mathematical sort of statement, something of the nature of that object is indicated. "By eliciting a fuller participation of the inquirer, the very genre of discourse suggests that the more fully one is engaged in pursuing an object, the more adequately can one come to know it."[127] In the *Republic,* for example, a student answers a question on the nature of justice by quoting a poem. Yet in answering Socrates' subsequent questions, the student contradicts himself. The point Socrates makes with his line of questioning is not that the poet's words are untrue, but that memorizing what other people have said does not necessarily mean one has understood it or has arrived at true knowledge.

The method employed by Socrates has been called the "maeutic" form because, in *Theaetetus*, Socrates describes his work as a teacher to be like that of a midwife. The purpose of a mid-wife is not to give birth to her own children, but to assist others in the birthing of theirs. Likewise, Socrates does not present his own complete and conclusive ideas to the learner, but serves to draw ideas out of the learner herself, so that the learner gives birth, as it were, to her own intellectual offspring. In *Theaetetus* Socrates describes his maieutic technique:

> **Socrates:** Have you then not heard, you absurd boy, that I am the son of a noble and burly midwife, Phaenarete?
>
> **Theaetetus:** Yes, I have heard that.
>
> **Socrates:** And have you also heard that I practice the same art?
>
> **Theaetetus:** No, never.
>
> **Socrates:** But I assure you it is true; only do not tell on me to the others; for it is not known that I possess this art. But other people, since they do not know it, do not say this of me, but say that I am a most eccentric person and drive men to distraction.... Just take into consideration the whole business of midwives, and you will understand more easily what I mean.[128]

The mauetic form prevents the teacher from becoming too important or essential for the process of entering into relation with the truth. The teacher assists the seeker's quest for understanding of the truth, but because the truth is subjective and not simply an objective proposition to be dictated or handed off,

---

[127] Burrell, 48.

[128] Plato, "Theaeteus," in The Loeb Classical Library, ed. G. P. Goold, *Plato* VII, trans. Harold North Fowler (Cambridge MA: Harvard University Press, 1996) 31.

the teacher can only help the seeker understand that the seeker must herself be transformed by this truth—on some level this is, in fact, the truth. The teacher is only relevant so as to ask questions that illicit the knowledge already within the individual, after which time the teacher should fade out of sight and is unnecessary. Unlike the thought of Plato and Socrates, however, Climacus does ultimately emphasize that the Teacher is of utmost importance in the pursuit of religious truth. For the highest form of religion, which for Kierkegaard is Christianity, the Teacher (Jesus Christ) is always central and is the giver of knowledge, not the one who elicits inherent knowledge through recollection. However, teachers of the truth of Christianity are only to point to the Teacher, and are not essential to this truth, which is the comparison Climacus draws between Socrates as a midwife of sorts and a teacher's need to watch herself in order not to become important to others, "which, far from being inwardness is external, noisy conduct."[129]

It should not be surprising that this concept of inherent knowledge brought forth through the Socratic method is rejected by Climacus as it, for one, suggests a non-temporal form of existence as basic to humanity, which is actually contrary to existence. Climacus strongly opposes this idea of an inherent knowledge of God, even as it is developed in Christian forms as a natural immanence. According to Climacus, Plato emphasizes that knowledge is inherent in the individual in a way that is not fully developed in Socrates. While the idea that knowledge is a recollection is present in both philosophers, Climacus states that Socrates does not speculate upon it, whereas the elaboration of this concept is truly Platonic. He acknowledges the thesis that "all knowing is a recollecting" is a Socratic one, and that it is "an intimation of the beginning of speculative thought."[130] He argues, however, that Socrates did not develop it precisely because to do so would be speculation, and "Socrates essentially emphasizes existing," and his "infinite merit is precisely that of being an *existing* thinker."[131] Plato, however, charges Climacus, "forgets what it

---

[129] *Postscript,* 278.

[130] Ibid., 203.

[131] Ibid., 206. Climacus emphasizes the figure of Socrates as an "existing thinker": "The thesis certainly belongs to both of them, but Socrates continually parts with it because he wants to exist. By holding Socrates to the thesis that all knowing is recollecting, one turns him into a speculative philosopher instead of what he was, an existing thinker who understood existing as the essential. The thesis that all knowing is recollecting belongs to speculative thought, and recollecting is immanence, and from the point of view of speculation and the eternal there is no paradox. The difficulty, however,

means to exist" and "loses himself in speculative thought."[132] Climacus also opposes the speculative tendencies he witnesses in the philosophy of his day, particularly in Hegelian Idealism, as he believes speculative thought negates existence. In contrast to Hegel, who wrote seventeen volumes of direct communication, "so that if he has not found anyone who has understood him, it is all the worse for Hegel," Socrates, "artistically arranged his entire mode of communication so as to be misunderstood."[133]

The maieutic form is a philosophical method admired by Climacus, however, also because it serves to take away assumed knowledge. In Copenhagen during Kierkegaard's day, he found that the state church and Christendom created within people the assumption of a certain amount of knowledge of God and of Christianity. Thus, Kierkegaard felt that in his context it was necessary to first take away knowledge, as what was assumed were doctrinal propositional statements and not a knowledge of Christian existence—not a lived knowledge, which is the only authentic Christian knowledge. This taking away of knowledge is similar to what one finds in Socratic questioning. Socrates is considered wise because he realized that he knew nothing. Those with whom he dialogued presumed they had some knowledge of the virtues but, through his simple line of questioning, such as "What is virtue?" or "What is courage?" those questioned realized they did not have the knowledge they presumed. Likewise, Kierkegaard through indirect communication endeavors to take away the false assumption of objective and certain knowledge of God, which he saw prevailing in Christendom and under the influence of Hegelian Idealism. Climacus also applies this concept of "Socratic ignorance" to the lack of true knowledge of God one can gain through observation of nature or history. One can observe nature looking for evidence of God and see signs of

---

is that no human being is speculation, but the speculating person is an existing human being, subject to the claims of existence. To forget this is no merit, but to hold this fast is indeed a merit, and that is precisely what Socrates did. To emphasize existence, which contains within it the qualification of inwardness, is the Socratic, whereas the Platonic is to pursue recollection and immanence" (206). This stress at the heart of Kierkegaard's thought—that one's beliefs be enacted in one's life—will be highlighted again in chapter 5, when we consider Bakhtin's very similar conception. This writer of "Toward a Philosophy of Act" speaks of the incarnation of one's ideas, the embodiment of one's thought. See also Alexandar Mihailovic, *Corporeal Words: Mikhail Bakhtin's Theology of Discourse* (Evanston IL: Northwestern University Press, 1997).

[132] *Postscript,* 206.

[133] Ibid., 70.

"omnipotence and wisdom," but one also sees "much that troubles and disturbs." [134] The sum total of such observation is simply objective uncertainty. One cannot gain objective knowledge of God through the observation of nature or of history, something Climacus claims Socrates recognized as well: "When Socrates believed that God is, he no doubt perceived that where the road swings off there is a road of objective approximation, for example, the observation of nature, world history, etc. His merit was precisely to shun this road where the quantifying siren song spellbinds and tricks the existing person."[135]

In the Socratic-maeutic method Climacus sees a form of discourse that functions much the way Kierkegaard's pseudonymous works aspire to function. In the maeutic form of questions and answers, Socrates is able to evoke thought from the seeker of truth. It illustrates not only that the seeker must be involved in the pursuit with her own being, and not simply looking for answers to be given, but the form itself requires involvement from the seeker herself; it requires introspection and examination of the seeker's own life. Ultimately it evokes the question from the seeker as to whether or not her life reflects the truth discovered—i.e., whether or not her life is in truth. Theological writing, as it is writing on Christianity, should draw the reader to a personal response, which is essential to being a Christian. This is one intention behind Kierkegaard's use of the pseudonym in describing stages of life and decisions made as to what sort of person one is becoming. For Kierkegaard the questions evoked are: "Who am I in the process of becoming? Am I directed passionately toward the truth?"

Another method employed by Socrates upon which Climacus draws is that of irony, as Socrates uses irony to communicate philosophical ideas indirectly, particularly the concept of the infinite. "When Socrates specifically wants to emphasize the infinite, one of the forms his irony takes is that he initially speaks like a madman."[136] This ironic form also allows Socrates to retain his inwardness, an important aspect of communicating subjective truth. Socrates, in speaking the part of a madman, may be staying true to his idea of ignorance. "Perhaps some of those present actually considered him lunatic...perhaps someone else thought that it was a droll way of talking, perhaps. At the same time, however, Socrates perhaps kept a little tryst with his idea, with ignorance.

---

[134] Ibid., 204.

[135] Ibid., 210.

[136] Ibid., 83.

If he did grasp the infinite in the form of ignorance, he had to have this with him everywhere."[137]

Climacus suggests "manifold" forms of expression to convey what Christianity is. The forms may be confusing, as is sometimes the case with Socrates and some of Kierkegaard's pseudonymous works. The forms may be illusive. They may be creative, artistic, and poetic. They will certainly not be direct but will leave room for the reader to question, to struggle to understand, and finally to consider her own way of existence. The form should not present results, direct answers, or closed systems of thought, but should be open to the existence of the learner and the very paradox that emerges with that individual in relation to the eternal in time, the incarnate Christ.

The pseudonymous author Johannes Climacus gives an interpretation of Kierkegaard's pseudonymous authorship as another example of indirect communication, and at this point, one can hear Kierkegaard's own voice explaining his works and the intention behind them, at least the intention in retrospect. Climacus commends the ethical texts in *Either/Or* for not being didactic yet successfully communicating this important content: "to think is one thing and to exist in what has been thought is something else."[138] Climacus is pleased the pseudonymous authors have not produced a sort of official interpretation of the works, which one sometimes finds in a preface, and he suggests they perhaps avoid this because they are "aware of the relation of indirect communication to truth as inwardness."[139] He writes of the pseudonymous form that it

> won my complete approval, and I believed I had also found that in it the pseudonymous authors continually aimed at *existing* and in this way sustained an indirect polemic against speculative thought. If a person knows everything but knows it by rote, the form of the imaginary construction is a good exploratory means; in this form, one even tells him what he knows, but he does not recognize it.[140]

Climacus discusses his *Philosophical Fragments*, to which *Concluding Unscientific Postscript* serves as a "post-script," in the context of his discussion of the pseudonymous works, but he chooses not to provide a direct explanation of it. He does state, however, that the book was not written with the intention of

---

[137] Ibid., 84. Again note the abundance of "perhaps."

[138] Ibid., 254.

[139] Ibid., 252.

[140] Ibid., 264.

giving "nonknowers" "something to know," but that the audience for *Fragments* are people of the times, who are then always knowledgeable, which is precisely their problem—"that they know too much." He also states his intention in the work to be that of "placing Christianity indirectly into relation to what it means to exist, in bringing it through an indirect form into relation to a knowing reader whose trouble perhaps is precisely that he is one who knows.... It could not be done by direct communication, since this always pertains to a recipient only in terms of knowledge, not essentially to an existing person."[141]

The Hidden God

We now move to a closer consideration of the theme of hiddenness in Christian theology, looking specifically at the work of Luther, who struggled with this Hidden God and allowed his theology to be impacted by it, suggesting that his theology develops at the point where revelation confronts human existence, that his theology takes the God-relation as the point of reflection. In the work of Luther we discover the subjective nature of the theological task given significant attention and the development of the concept of the Hiddenness of God, both of which support the Kierkegaardian argument for indirect forms of communication to express the nature of Christianity. The concept of *deus absconditus*, in fact, not only supports Kierkegaard's concern that Christians not assume a form of knowledge we are not given and cannot possess of God, it also stems, at least in part, from the theologian's own struggle in the tension between revelation and human existence.

Luther not only serves as an exemplar theologian here because he takes the hiddenness of God seriously, but because he allows his experience of the world in faith to impact his theological writings to such an extent that they may be said to shape each other. Scripture and God revealed in Christ, particularly in Christ on the cross, provide the norm for his theology, but there is no separating this conceptualizing of God from his encounter with God in his own existence. Most Luther scholars agree that experience is one of the key principles at work in the development of Luther's theology; after all, Luther himself said: "Experience alone makes a theologian."[142] It is said that Luther transforms "the abstract question of a just god into an *existential quest* that concerned the *whole* human being, encompassing thought and action, soul and body, love and

---

[141] Ibid., 274.

[142] Martin Luther, *Table Talk,* in *Luther's Works*, vol. 54, ed. and trans. Theodore G. Tappet, gen. ed. Helmut T. Lehmann (Philadelphia: Fortress Press, 1967) 7.

suffering."[143] Mary Solberg makes this assessment: "There was an intimate relationship between what Luther lived as a historical subject, on the one hand, and what Luther said and wrote on the other. …he made it clear that for him theology had most emphatically to do with his own and other people's *lives* before God and with one another. Theologizing is existential."[144]

Luther's own existential struggles and spiritual trials play a significant role in his theology, and according to him such experiences should in fact impact one's theological development. It seems to be a very particular experience that Luther finds especially formative for the theologian—the *Anfechtung*— a difficult term for translators to give expression. It includes a sense of struggle and anguish, and is something that Luther considers central to the development of his theology and of himself as a theologian. He writes: "I did not learn my theology at one time, but I had to meditate deeper and deeper. Then my *Anfechtungen* carried me thither. For this cannot be acquired without experience."[145] Bornkamm calls it a "distress of the heart" and he poses a question that expresses the thrust of the term: "Is the God who demands our trust and pledges His help, which we often fail to see amidst our sorrow and tribulation, not just a dream, a great self-delusion of man?"[146] Solberg says that the meaning of the cross comes clear only "in the midst of the questioning and temptation, the doubt and near-despair that daily experience brings with it."[147] Faith, when confronted by life, is repeatedly challenged, and this conflict is an aspect of the *Anfechtung* that Luther considers essential for his work as a theologian. And it is also this wrestling, as we will see, that is most associated with the human experience of the hidden God.

Solberg sums up what *Anfechtung* and existence itself meant to Luther's theology: "There is nothing detached, abstracted, 'above-it-all' about true theology or about the truly Christian life. It unfolds in the thick of human experience, in all its contradictions, difficulties, and negations."[148] The person is very much involved, or at least should be, if it is to be true to the nature of the

---

[143] Heiko A. Oberman, *Luther: Man between God and the Devil,* trans. Eileen Walliser-Schwarzbart (New Haven: Yale University Press, 1989) 151.

[144] Mary M. Solberg, *Compelling Knowledge: A Feminist Proposal for an Epistemology of the Cross* (New York: State University of New York Press, 1997) 57.

[145] Martin Luther, LW 54:50.

[146] Heinrich Bornkamm, *Luther's World of Thought*, trans. Martin H. Bertram (St. Louis: Concordia Publishing House, 1958) 73.

[147] Solberg, 83.

[148] Ibid., 83–84.

subject discussed—the God-relation. After all, revelation is always revelation to someone; the subject, the individual, is always involved. Solberg notes that Luther concerns himself more with describing a *theologian* of the cross than simply the *theology* of the cross. In his Heidelberg Disputation (1518), for example, what he describes is the theologian him- or herself.[149]

> A true theologian is made by life, with its tribulations and struggles, not by philosophizing and speculating. But despite this frequently expressed warning, the popular image of Luther ignores these experiences, struggles, successes, hopes, and fears, and reduces his development to two stages: first the desperate monk and then the self-confident Reformer from the moment he—suddenly—grasped the true meaning of verse seventeen of the first chapter of St. Paul's Epistle to the Romans.[150]

It should not be a surprise, then, that someone who endured *Anfechtung* and held it in continual relation with his theology would develop a concept of the hiddenness of God in ways that other theologians who attempt to think and write in ways removed from their subjectivity have not.

> Small wonder that Luther declared that this God, who dwells in everything that lives and whom he beheld there as clearly as ever poet and philosopher did, is a hidden God, a God to whom no path of our philosophical contemplation leads us. If we assume that we can comprehend Him in a discordant and contradictory life, in which He is indeed hidden, then our reflections must carry us into insoluble contradictions. Luther knew that to faith there is no alternative but imprecision and blasphemy. He was well aware that the human mind can snap because of this question and be driven to insanity. All profound thinkers who skirted the rim of this precipice have either known or experienced this (Goethe, Holderlin, Neitzsche).[151]

Lutheran and Reformed theologians are well aware of Luther's concept of the Hiddenness of God, though significant differences abound both in

---

[149] Theses 19 and 20 of the Heidelberg Disputation serve as an example of this emphasis on the theologian him/herself rather than solely on theology itself. Theses 19: "That a person does not deserve to be called a theologian who looks upon the invisible things of God as though they were clearly perceptible in those things which have actually happened" (Rom. 1:20). And again in Theses 20: "He deserves to be called a theologian, however, who comprehends the visible and manifest things of God seen through suffering and the cross." Quoted in Solberg, 56.

[150] Doberman, 157–58.

[151] Bornkamm, 64.

interpretations of this in Luther, as well as stances on how valid his position is in light of revelation. The generally accepted understanding of Luther's use of the concept identifies two forms of hiddenness.[152] The first type of hiddenness conceives of God's hiddenness in revelation, which is the generally accepted position on God's hiddenness, and we will refer to it as Hiddenness I, following Brian Gerrish's study on the topic. It is not a concept derived from humanity's inability to comprehend, from limits of language or the mind's categories, but instead insists that without revelation we would remain ignorant even of the Hidden God. The second type of hiddenness, Hiddenness II, relates to a hiddenness not identical with revelation, a hiddenness that is sometimes described as behind revelation or in some sense distinct and separate from revelation.[153] It is this second form of hiddenness that comes under the most fire, especially from Reformed theologians. The concern, of course, is that this

---

[152] Brian Gerrish identifies two types of hiddenness attributed to God in the work of Luther. He recognizes that there are derivations within the groups, other ways to break down Luther's discussion of hiddenness that would result in more specific forms of hiddenness, for example, Luther's discussion of the Naked God. However, his two types simplify the discussion, and thus I will be following his breakdown here. See Brian Gerrish, "'To the Unknown God': Luther and Calvin on the Hiddenness of God," *Journal of Religion* 53 (1973): 263–92.

[153] Gerrish gives the example of Luther's concept of the "Naked God" as one category of hiddenness outside revelation: "To mention only the most important variation, he sometimes speaks...of the 'Naked God.' His language clearly indicates that, at this point, the image of God fades into sheer negativity: the *dues nudus* is God in himself, a strange, terrifying, unapproachable abstraction. This being so, it appears that one must take into account, not only a dual relationship of God to the world, but also a conception of God as *deus absolutus*, out of relation to the world. This God, too, stands in antithetical relation to the Revealed God, for the *deus revelatus* is the *deus indutus*—the God who is not naked, but clothed with his Word" (Gerrish, 267). He quotes Walther Koehler, saying: "The 'Hidden God' is the Unknown God of the ancient world, God beyond the reach of human intelligence.... It is the ancient myth of the hidden savior which reappears in Luther's notion of revelation, complete with the picture-language about the deceiving of the devil. And yet the other line of thought remains 'on the margin': it stands for the transcendence of the Naked God, who cannot be seen even with the eye of faith, but remains the Unknown" (Gerrish, 268). Walther Koehler, *Der verborgene Gott,* Sitzungsberichte der Heidelberger Akademie der Wissenschaftan, philosophisch-historische Klasse, vol. 33, no. 4 (1942/1943) (Heidelberg: Carl Winter, Universitätsverlag, 1946).

second type suggests that God is different from what God has revealed Godself to be.

Hiddenness I proceeds on the principle that God is revealed in Jesus Christ, but that God in the form of flesh is not recognizable to humanity by its own powers of perception, as God in a humble form runs counter to all human expectations. God is revealed in the flesh, but is also simultaneously hidden in that flesh. God is therefore most hidden in Christ on the cross, as reason itself cannot recognize God revealed in such a form, in suffering and rejection. However, God is also revealed in Christ on the cross to those given sight through the Holy Spirit to recognize God there. Thus the incarnation and the cross are both a veiling and an unveiling. This form of Hiddenness in the work of Luther is most often associated with his *theologia cruces*. Brian Gerrish describes it thus: "In Christ, God works in a paradoxical mode *sub contraries*. His wisdom is hidden under folly, his strength under abject weakness. He gives life through death, righteousness to the unrighteous; he saves by judging and damning. The Hidden God is God incarnate, crucified, hidden in suffering."[154] This type, Hiddenness I, has been utilized productively by Protestant theologians and is much appreciated.[155]

Protestant theologians, however, have not received Luther's second form of hiddenness with the same enthusiasm. In Hiddenness II, they find a God hidden behind revelation, a God different from who God reveals Godself to be in Christ. While both Luther and Calvin found the concept of God's hiddenness to be fruitful for their theologies, the notion became distorted and eventually fell out of use in the centuries after the Reformation. John Dillenberger gives a rather harsh assessment as to why hiddenness became so unpopular among

---

[154] Gerrish, 268.

[155] Dillenberger describes how this concept is developed in the theology of Brunner, for whom this type of hiddenness is understood as "the apprehension of God in the *person* of Christ. It means that God does not reveal himself direct as in paganism," an important distinction we find in Kierkegaard as he described the difference between the religion of Socrates and the Christian religion, that which truly requires faith in the uncertain, and is communicated indirectly in paradoxical form: the god-man. Further, for Brunner, it means that "God has veiled himself so completely that only faith can recognize in the man Jesus the Son of God," which is certainly a form of hiddenness that corresponds with Climacus's paradoxical conception of Christianity and his emphasis that the incarnation can only be grasped in faith. John Dillenberger, *God Hidden and Revealed: The Interpretation of Luther's "Deus Absconditus" and Its Significance for Religious Thought* (Philadelphia: Muhlenberg Press, 1953) 108.

theologians of Protestant orthodoxy. He says of these theologians that they "usually knew too much about the intricacies of the working of God to permit genuine mystery or hiddenness as a part of their heritage. They set the world of God, about which they knew too much, against the world of man." He goes on to charge:

> Orthodox thinkers bordered on arbitrariness in their formulations. They had little sense for the genuine mystery and hiddenness before which one's thinking stops. They represented a self-constructed picture of the mind of God in rigid contrast to the mind of man.... The net result was that they made an impossible claim to knowledge of God and attempted to impose it upon a world by and large convinced of the impossibility of knowledge under any path remotely related to what was not self-evident.[156]

Hiddenness was a lost theme because the claims of understanding and knowledge were too great to retain a genuine sense of mystery.[157] However, hiddenness also became an unfavorable theological position because it became systematized, especially as God's hiddenness was thought to relate to the doctrines of salvation and predestination, such that theologians seemed to know exactly where God was hidden, making it another form of knowing rather than unknowing.

However, Brian Gerrish makes a strong argument for the theme of hiddenness to again receive a place in theology. It should not be systematized, but the topic has an important theological function nonetheless. Regardless of how "disruptive it may be of theological tidiness," he charges, the experience of God's hiddenness "must be taken with the utmost theological seriousness especially at the present day."[158] Describing how religious experience supports a conception of the hiddenness of God outside Christ, Gerrish suggests that this

---

[156] Dillenberger, xvii.

[157] Rudolph Otto also laments the loss among Lutheran theologians of the elements in Luther's theology that dealt with the hidden and mysterious aspects of God. Otto charges that in the period of Lutheran Orthodoxy the "conceptual and doctrinal" began to overpower elements in Lutheran teaching on "the inexpressible, whose only life is in the conscious mental attitude of the devout soul." He says that because of this shift, "[t]he Church became a school, and her communications, in truth, found a more and more contracted access to the mind." See Rudolph Otto, *The Idea of the Holy: An Inquiry into the Non-Rational Factor in the Idea of the Divine and Its Relation to the Rational*, trans. John W. Harvey (London: Oxford University Press, 1950) 108.

[158] Gerrish, 269.

category might actually be a useful resource for a consideration of human experience and the existential struggle over the tensions between predestination and human freedom, and the magnitude of suffering in the world.

Hiddenness II pertains particularly to the anxiety of human experience. It is an affirmation of God's hiddenness based upon the human experience of the hiddenness of God in nature, history, and the mystery of salvation, and it arises out of a very real human terror and anguish. This form of hiddenness is not completely out of relationship with revelation, however, as the tension between what has been revealed of God in Christ and what one persists to experience in life can actually heighten the anguish. Luther

> insisted at the outset that he proclaimed nothing but Christ crucified. But one of the doctrines that "Christ crucified brings with him" finally forces us to acknowledge an inscrutable will of God behind and beyond the figure of Christ. We began from God's revelation in Christ as the only secure basis for a knowledge of God's gracious will; we end by discovering that, after all, God wills many things which he does not show us in his Word. And the problem is not merely that there is a hidden will *alongside* of the revealed will of God, but that the two are found to be in apparent *contradiction.*[159]

Gerrish explains that a range of religious experience lies within the concept of Hiddenness II and shows how aspects of this experience actually give shape to the concept of faith so central to Reformation thought. The very experience of such a contradiction emphasizes faith and the nature of faith's "certainty," that is, its objective uncertainty, its utter trust in God in the face of uncertainty. Describing Luther's theology of the cross, Hall writes that

> true *faith* is the antithesis of a triumphant confidence. To be sure, there is a certitude of faith. But it is not at all what men usually mean by it. The certitude of faith is not a matter of demonstration or success, but a matter of trust: trust in the promise of a God who gives life to the dead and calls into existence the things that are not (Rom., ch. 4).... This certitude of faith is not available for possession. In fact, it is experienced only here and there, now and then; and it lives in constant tension with its antithesis.[160]

Luther himself draws a link between faith and God's hiddenness; he writes: "Faith has to do with things not seen (Heb. 11:1). Hence in order that

---

[159] Ibid., 273.

[160] John Hall, *Lighten Our Darkness: Toward an Indigenous Theology of the Cross* (Philadelphia: Westminster Press, 1976) 120.

there may be room for faith, it is necessary that everything which is believed should be hidden."[161]

Other Reformation scholars stand in agreement with Gerrish's exposition of the relationship between faith and hiddenness. Luther historian F. Kattenbusch says: "Only when, regardless of all revelation, God still is and remains the *absconditusi,* can it be said that faith is the one and only [cognitive relationship] between man and God."[162] And Egil Grislis explains, "Luther is suggesting that the way into faith leads through such an ultimate level of trust which no longer has any objective grounds for confidence."[163] Gerrish understands the development of the hiddenness of God in the theology of Luther, particularly Hiddenness II, to be in many ways the result of Luther's experience of the hiddenness of God in a state of faith,[164] noting Luther's famous statement: "it is by living—no, rather, by dying and being damned—that a theologian is made, not by understanding, reading, or speculating."[165]

---

[161] Martin Luther, The Library of Christian Classics, Vol. XVII, *Luther and Erasmus: Free Will and Salvation,* ed. E. Gordon Rupp et al. (Philadelphia: The Westminster Press, 1969) 68.

[162] Ferdinand Kattenbusch, "*Deus Absconditus* bei Luther," in *Festagabe für D. Dr. Julius Kaften zu seinem* 70. Geburtstag, Tübingen: J.C.B. Mohr, 1920, 170–214. Quoted by Egil Grislis, "Martin Luther's View of the Hidden God: The Problem of the *Deus Absconditus* in Luther's Treatise *De Servo Arbitrio,*" *McCormick Quarterly* 21, no. 1 (November 1967): 85.

[163] Grislis, 85.

[164] Gerrish is not alone in this assessment. Dillenberger summarizes Karl Heim's position, according to which Luther emphasized both types of hiddenness, without creating "an uneasy alliance, [for] the two were germane to Luther's new intuition of the problem on the basis of his experience of faith" (Dillenberger, 41). A dual emphasis on both developed in relationship as "Luther experienced in his own life and recast it in faith" (Dillenberger, 41). Rudolph Otto also notes the close relationship between Luther's religious life and his conception of the hiddenness of God. These doctrines "stand in most intimate connextion with his own innermost religious life, of which they are a genuine first-hand utterance, and should be examined as such. Luther himself guarantees expressly that he does not teach such things merely as subjects of dispute in the schools or as philosophical deductions and corollaries, but because they are a central part of the religious experience of the Christian, who must know them in order to have faith and to have life" (Otto, 98).

[165] This oft-quoted statement is found in *D. Martin Luthers Werke: Kritische Gesamtausgabe* (Weimar: Hermann Böhlaus Nachfolger, 1883) 5, 28, 163.

Gerrish recognizes the limitations of Hiddenness II, and sees the methodological importance of speaking of the hiddenness in terms of revelation, affirming that we would not even know God is hidden if first God did not reveal Godself. He and Dillenberger do not fully deny Barth's famous critique of Luther's notion of God's hiddenness, as for example, we do not put categories like incomprehensibility upon God from our side, but affirm God's incomprehensibility because in God's revelation we learn of God's hiddenness. However, both scholars charge that an emphasis on revelation that does not give full credence to the experience of God's hiddenness, even when we see Christ, falls short in speaking to the reality of the human experience of God. John Dillenberger argues that when theologians limit talk of God's hiddenness solely to revelation, making hiddenness and revelation identical, they fail to "adequately take into account the unfathomable and abysmal nature of the God who has made himself known."[166] Egil Grislis finds in Luther an affirmation that despite revelation, God is still hidden from the individual in many respects. Grislis speaks against a "too easy and shallow 'Christocentricity,'" charging that when "such a limited and necessarily shallow 'understanding' of Christ is used to plumb the depths of God, then, by necessity, God also will be

[166] Dillenberger, 170. Gerrish also notes this and details the personal account of a man condemned to death as one of the conspirators against Hitler, as an example of this "anguish of the conflict between faith and experience." The man condemned, named Goerdeler, wrote: "In sleepless nights I have asked myself whether a God exists who shares in the personal fate of men. It is becoming hard to believe it. For this God must for years now have allowed rivers of blood and suffering, mountains of horror and despair for mankind.... He must have let millions of decent men die and suffer without moving a finger. Is this supposed to be a judgment? ...Like the Psalmist, I have a controversy with God because I cannot understand him.... And yet through Christ I am still looking for a merciful God. I have not found him." Gerrish sees this not only as the experience of the hiddenness of God, but related to nineteenth-century liberal theology, which "closed the door on Luther's *deus absconditus* and the Christ who was forsaken on the cross" [Gerrish, 289, taking the story from Julius Richter, "Luther's 'Deus Absconditus'—Zuflucht order Ausflucht?" *Zeitschrift für Religions—und Geistesgeschichte* 7, no. 4 (1955): 289]. Theology as it developed at that time had no room for this experience; it could make no sense of it, leaving an objective account of Christianity and God's ways in the world that denied the anguish of faith as it is experienced in an authentic human life and the contradiction between revelation and life in the world. These theologies are therefore unable, even, to express Christ's authentic human existence and crucifixion.

misunderstood."[167] The concept pertains most significantly to the human experience of God's hiddenness *despite* what is revealed in Christ, or because of what is revealed and the anguish endured when experience runs counter to it, and thus a direct correlation between revelation and hiddenness is too narrow and too precise. The depth of truth of this hiddenness cannot be packed up and dealt with in neatly delineated doctrines.

Scholars have noted a variety of places where discussion of God's hiddenness arises in theology: in terms of the believer's faith or a person's lack of it, predestination, suffering and wrath, world religions, and nature and history.[168] Gerrish describes Luther's struggle in faith with the doctrine of predestination, as "*there* faith cannot find the way out, but can only wait for the light of glory. And if it lingers too long, tries to penetrate the mystery of the hidden will, it can only lose itself in the abyss of the Unknown God."[169] A problem arises here, however, as Luther and others place predestination as a factual, objective doctrine within the Hiddenness of God, making it more a form of knowing than unknowing. When one defines where or what hiddenness is too concretely, it ceases to be a category to help one dealing with the contradictions between one's experience of the world and who God is revealed to be for the world in Christ. It becomes another structured, objective category, affirming that we know exactly where God is hidden instead of an affirmation of an experienced tension. It takes a category related to subjective experience and makes it objective, expected to reflect the real nature of God, instead of reflecting the reality of human experience with God.[170]

---

[167] Grislis, 93–94.

[168] Dillenberger lists these and others in his book on p. 165ff.

[169] Gerrish, 278.

[170] As an example of the dangers of noting exactly where or how God is hidden, Dillenberger tells the story of Emanuel Hirsch, who "spoke of the hiddenness of God in the sufferings of the German nation during the First World War and since that war. By shifting the emphasis slightly he was able to insist upon a close connection between the German people and God's working in the world. The hidden connection manifested in the conjunction of Protestant and German history became the basis for supporting the German revival in the interest of the revival of theology.... Further, the concept of hiddenness is meaningful in the context of the problem of theodicy, but not in that of ethics" (Dillenberger, 48). In contrast to this conception of hiddenness, which defines what is hidden, Dillenberger gives the example of an address by Bishop Otto Dibelius in 1947, who spoke of the plight of the German people. Bishop Dibelius said: "In this situation there is only the God whose purposes we cannot know, but yet must trust. That

When one views the natural world, it often seems violent, wasteful of life, and unjust, and one could easily question how a good God's purposes were being accomplished within it. History is just as violent, vicious, and terrifying, and one would ask how a good God is at work within it. But in faith, one is supposed to see something different revealed in Christ. Gerrish explains Luther's perspective thus: "When Luther looked directly at nature, apart from the Word, he was aware of an awesome, creative power quite other than the God he encountered in Jesus Christ."[171] Luther saw the same difficulty in history. Gerrish states that "when Luther turned his thought from nature to history and contemplated it apart from the Word of God, he could not claim that the fatherly providence of God was evident. The good cause is not always vindicated; the bad as often triumphs."[172] The problem of evil and suffering continues to bump up against faith; the friction is real and painful for the believer and non-believer alike. The anguish and pathos Luther experienced over the predestining God are matched by many over the God who allows suffering, whether or not it is temporal or eternal. And a God who would allow this runs counter to human expectations and to the concept of a loving, merciful God, which we find in Christ.[173] John Hall recognizes the relationship between Luther's very theology of the cross and this experience of human existence in the world. He writes that the theology of the cross "takes its stand *within* the experience of negation. It neither minimizes nor seeks to absorb the evil and impossibility of human existence into a finally triumphant goodness. The negative is not annulled by an overwhelming positive."[174]

The notion of the Hidden God does not provide comfort, but according to Gerrish, the acknowledgment of its reality in our existence may offer some assurance that we are not alone. "There may be a comfort in company—that is, in the recognition that we are not the first to have met him. Rather, hiddenness belongs essentially to the conception of God which we inherit."[175] We are not

---

there must be some sense in the senseless is all that we can affirm" (Dillenberger, 48). Dillenberger concludes, "It is better to insist upon the mystery of God without establishing a separate niche for it within the Godhead" (Dillenberger, 169).

[171] Gerrish, 276–77.

[172] Gerrish, 277.

[173] I do not deny, however, that this conflicted nature is even found within the revelation of Christ, as one might expect everyone who encounters Christ to be fed and healed. He could have turned all stones into bread and fed the world, but he did not.

[174] Hall, 120.

[175] Gerrish, 290.

the first to encounter the tension between what God is revealed to be in Jesus Christ and what we often experience. As Gerrish puts it, the "negative side of our religious experience has already been thematized."[176] He argues persuasively that speaking of the Hidden God does not have to be the "manifest inconsistency" with which it is often dismissed. Gerrish insists that revelation not be used as "the final, a logical resolution to an intellectual puzzle," but that one's "appeal to the *deus revelatus* must be understood within the concrete movement of experience."[177] Revelation is not to be looked at as a set of facts from which one can derive a logical system, one justifiable to the "objective" sciences (if there is such a thing). Revelation as the source for theological reflection is revelation as it is applied to the person in existence, or as Gerrish puts it, "understood within the concrete movement of experience." "Concrete" speaks to the historical existence of both Christ and the person of faith and the "movement of experience" addresses the ongoing process of human life. Revelation is always revelation to a person in existence and is not a bare, abstract fact. Therefore revelation as a point of reflection is the God-relation, a relation that includes both the experience of *deus revelatus* and *deus absconditus*. Talk only of the revealed God, without real acknowledgment that what is revealed appears even antithetical to our experience, in effect presents a conception of Jesus Christ as abstract, attainable, and objective knowledge.

Truly Luther's conception of this second form of Hiddenness has come under fire because it is more the result of reflection on human existence than on the hiddenness of God as revealed in the incarnation. Gerrish does not deny this, but he does assert that the "strangeness" and "terror of being human" that arise within the believer no less than in the unbeliever from questions about God and existence "are the other side of God's hiddenness."[178] Faith may persist in the face of this despair at human existence, but it does not eradicate the despair, which leads Gerrish to identify this as "an unresolved dialectic in Reformation faith corresponding to a dialectic in the conception of God."[179] Acknowledging that calling the distinction between the Hidden and Revealed God a "dialectic" is not representative of Luther's thought when conceived of as an objective relationship, however, Gerrish sees a "subjective dialectic" as "inescapably present: that is, a perennial exchange between two images of God. The art of

---

[176] Ibid.
[177] Ibid.
[178] Ibid.
[179] Ibid.

faith is to move the mind in *one* direction; but it cannot *halt* the reverse movement, only *counter* it."[180] Although the sources of anxiety may be different in some cases from that experienced in the world of the Reformers, Gerrish asserts that it is exactly here that our faith most resembles the faith of Luther and Calvin. Faith here means that, in the Revealed God, one "finds the possibility of affirming the meaning of life in spite of this anxiety—this other dark possibility that [one] really is lost in the boundless and senseless universe."[181]

Even for those theologians who want to keep God's hiddenness and revelation in correlation, thus affirming that God is not different than the manifestation of Godself in revelation, this manifestation is

> mystery as well as meaning, and comes out of a God who remains unfathomable, but of whom it may be affirmed that he is trustworthy on the basis of faith. God's dealing with the world, even in faith, points to an abyss which man cannot comprehend. Here, with Luther, one can say that the essence of faith is to believe God just who appears so unjust. Such a situation must be affirmed rather than explained.[182]

John Dillenberger concludes that for the Christian, "the world as such is neither fully rational nor is it irrational. It stands under the mystery of God, who yet in the midst of it has declared his sovereignty over it to the eyes of faith, to those who trust in the ever revealed and ever hidden sovereignty and purpose of God."[183]

The hiddenness of God is not another category in the nature of God that we have figured out, but points to the mystery of God and points to the limits of our comprehension at the place where the God-human relation cannot be systematized: the tensions between revelation and experience; the very tensions in scripture; predestination and freedom; and a good, loving, and merciful God paired with such conflicting evidence in the world. These tensions should not, and cannot be, resolved in a system, but remain a rub, a struggle, or a darkness. It allows us to talk about the nature of God revealed without denying the

---

[180] Ibid.

[181] Ibid., 291.

[182] Dillenberger, 171. Despite his anguish over the hiddenness of God, Luther continued to have faith that "in the providence of God all life, at its best and at its worst, lies within the domain of the purpose of God, though the events as they are cannot be equated with the final purpose of God" (Dillenberger, 172).

[183] Ibid., 172.

contradiction of it experienced in the world, the anxiety of human existence even in faith. The hiddenness of God is not a defined category that we understand and apply to specific cases as a sort of knowledge, but is a place where our experience finds resonance, where our experience is disposed instead of denied.

Conclusion: The Call for Inconclusive Theologies

I argue that because Christianity is in essence related to existence, is about a God-relation or God in relation to creation and humanity in existence, reflection upon this relation will include the contradictions of life and salvation. It is a paradoxical religion, after all, and these tensions cannot be reconciled in the sort of synthesis Kierkegaard saw Hegelians asserting in his day, nor should they be. Direct forms of discourse are not sufficient to express the nature of Christian faith, that Christianity is "a way," a transforming relationship lived passionately within the unresolved dialectic, within the very real tensions felt deeply by the individual but endured in faith.

If Kierkegaard is right that religious truth is relational and cannot only be communicated directly, and if Gerrish is correct that God's hiddenness is an important concept to be revived in Christian theology, and I think they are, then theologians need to foster ways to communicate that are appropriate to these forms of knowledge, lack of knowledge, and aspects of the God-relation. Theology is not simply self-projection by any means, but neither is it solely composed of objective propositions.[184] Our discourse should deal honestly with the persisting contradictions, tensions, and difficulties. One way to communicate Christianity responsibly and honestly is through indirect forms, through manifold genres that work to evoke something within the reader: appropriation and decisive action. And here I argue that literary forms are better suited to deal with these tensions and struggle with the hidden God. They can express the struggle without establishing a "niche in the Godhead" for this

---

[184] We see even in Luther, for example, a depth of subjective involvement and experiential influence evidenced in his theological writings. "At its heart Luther's theology of the cross unapologetically describes a life (one might hazard to say, Luther's life) under the cross. A significant part of what preserves it from being simply his private theology and commends it to other believers is that Luther did not identify and claim his own (or any other individual's) experience as authoritative—he rarely wrote or spoke of it—nor did he hesitate at any moment to direct attention away from himself, toward the God whose self-revelation comprised the very possibility of justification and of theological talk about it" (Solberg, 88).

hiddenness;[185] they have the potential to honestly portray that place of tension and strife at the God-human relationship without making darkness, uncertainty, and unknowing a form of knowing by putting it into a system.

Salvation comes through a temporal existence, Jesus', and is then to be applied to another life in process and time, as this salvation wrought through Christ's historical existence is then actualized in the present in the ongoing life of another concrete person. Thus, both aspects of revelation occur in process and in time. The scope of salvation is universal, but its appropriation involves the contemporary person and world. Salvation is not abstract, nor is it something distanced from the present. Though Christ's life, ministry, death, and resurrection were historical events, Christianity is not a set of beliefs about the past, but about how the past connects to the present and directs the future. Because Christianity exists in this transition of the benefits of Christ's work to the individual, community, and world, because of this movement and its dynamic nature from within a temporal existence, there is no absolute perspective on it, no view of it as a completed, entire whole. The revelation of God in Christ is so rich and multiform as to resist any complete articulation of its truth.

Christianity is also manifold because of faith or its relation to each dynamic person, which adds to its complexity and diversity. As it is concerned with God's revelation in Christ to a particular someone, and with that person's recognition of Christ and lifelong appropriation of this knowledge, there is not a single picture, or one set of doctrines to encompass this reality. Christianity is related to beliefs about this historical person Jesus Christ, but, as it is here briefly illustrated, it is far more than that. It includes a participation; it includes one's decisive action to pursue a life that embodies these beliefs, that one's life actually reflect one's thought.[186] Christianity is the relation of one's life to this living Christ. It is something lived, something that shapes one's existence in history.

Theology cannot of itself communicate the actual relationship of which Christian knowledge consists, and when systematic theology attempts to be

---

[185] Dillenberger, 169.

[186] I am less concerned here with actually detailing the "required" Christian beliefs, but in emphasizing that one's way of life reflect them. For example, if one believes we are saved by grace and not by works, one may then expect one's life not to be governed by guilt and fear, but to continue Christ's ministry actively, empowered by the grace one has received.

absolute or complete, it creates a barrier to this subjective appropriation. Christianity invites those in the present to appropriate the teachings of the church, but primarily, to accept a relationship to the Teacher, and as stated, this is a present relation directed to the future. However, traditional dogmatics do not communicate this contemporaneity and this movement. It can be a tool for the opening of eyes and hearts, for giving categories for each person to think through their lives with a Christian understanding, but it cannot hand Christianity over complete and packaged to another person; the one who takes it and considers it done never becomes a Christian, but only a holder of doctrines. Theology should then be stated in a way that allows contact with the present, with the contemporaneous existing individual, who is invited to encounter the living Christ here and now. It should place the possibility of a Christian existence, of redemption in Christ, as close to the reader as possible.

Theology as it has traditionally been articulated abstracts universal principles from the life of Christ, often organizing them into a system. Because of the nature of the discourse, it is distanced from the present, and often even from the historical context of Jesus' actual life. The accepted forms of theological discourse have limited potential for contact with the existing person because its objective forms move away from the concrete and detemporalize the message, distancing it from the present through an abstracted past. Such removal of the discussion of the living Christ from the present, and from contact with the person existing now in time, prevents these forms from communicating the contemporaneity of the relationship essential to Christianity. Such forms of discourse, therefore, as they are projected into an abstract stance, supposing a universal perspective, distanced from the present and from the historical existing person, cannot adequately communicate the lived nature of Christianity. The concepts are held far off, and salvation is thought to be applied to the individual by the hand of God, possibly from all eternity, and so even the very application of Christ's life to the person is decontextualized, detemporalized, and held off in a transcendental realm to which we have no access.

The inclusion of the person in the communication of Christianity inherently resists systematizing to the extent that systems form closed totalities. In order to give a comprehensive explanation of the workings of Christianity, traditionally accepted forms of theological discourse cannot include the individual and the person's participation in Christianity, for such inclusion would require an acceptance of the inconclusive. In the transition of the benefits of Christ's life to the current individual living in time, there is a movement and a continuing process, which disallows a comprehensive image of a completed product. The processes of Christ's life attaining the sanctification of human nature, and that of the human to which it is applied, constitute two concrete and lifelong movements. How can two movements in relationship, and ongoing, be accounted for and communicated in direct, propositional form? Systems by their nature cannot accommodate the inconclusive. Modern philosophy limited itself to the propositional form, with few exceptions, and theology did likewise. The accepted modes of theological communication barred other genres. Yet other genres are better able to communicate subjectivity and thus communicate Christianity more appropriately.

Indirect forms of communication are necessary because Christianity is such that the person should be set free in the communication of it, and set free to consider her life, her development, the movement of her soul, or simply put: her God-relation. Kierkegaard stresses the importance to communicate the Christian message and to have it communicated to particular persons; his very concern with the form of communication suggests an awareness of the role that others play in the development of one's religious knowledge. The communication should engage the other in a way that is not forceful, authoritarian, or imposed, but invites, introduces, and leaves the other in freedom to consider, develop, and work the ideas through in her own manner and for her context. Kierkegaard experiments with styles that will show the person her very self, that will evoke consideration and self-examination, that will take away the assumed knowledge that we do not have of God, and yet will not produce adherents to a system, as adherents are those who did not make the truth their own.[187]

---

[187] Kierkegaard eventually turned away from indirect communication and to a direct form of "bearing witness." He wrote in his journals: "The communication of Christianity must ultimately end in bearing witness, the maieutic form can never be final. For truth, from the Christian point of view, does not lie in the subject (as Socrates understood it), but in a revelation that must be proclaimed. In Christendom the maieutic form can certainly be used, simply because the majority in fact live under the impression that they are Christians. But since Christianity is Christianity, the maieuticer must become the witness." However, even here Kierkegaard distinguishes "bearing witness" from a "direct witness." [*The Journals of Søren Kierkegaard,* selection ed. and trans. Alexander Dru (Oxford University Press: London, New York, 1938) 259–60, entry #809.] However, it does begin with the maieutic or indirect form; both are necessary for Christianity to be communicated. Direct form, however, continues to be the one and only form of discourse accepted in the theological discipline, and the only form studied or attempted. If Socrates, Plato, and Kierkegaard are correct, that the subjective must be

An indirect form reflects the nature of the knowledge communicated by being embedded in existence and thus in the concrete. It will not, like a direct form, remove the discussion from existence through objectivity, speculation, and/or abstraction. An indirect form will not impose a systematic structure because existence cannot be systematized for humanity as they are constantly in the process of becoming.

An indirect communication is inconclusive; it is open in dialogue. As such it corresponds to the intersubjective nature of religious knowledge as described above—in relation to God and to others. For Kierkegaard, and for Mikhail Bakhtin as we will see in chapter 4, the forming of the consciousness is always due to a dialogue with the thought of another and developed through interaction. A Christian consciousness, then, would be formed through dialogue with a history of voices in and outside the tradition, one's community, history, and context.

Theology will look quite different if, instead of starting with revelation as an object for distanced, factual, scientific study, we start with the relation of revelation to the person, community, or world, and the transition of Christ's benefits to lived existence and the movement that entails. It will *not* be systematic in terms of whole complete and closed systems; it will not be *certain* or conclusive, but it may express faith; it may communicate the "God-relation," not as objective content, but as that into which one enters. If religious truth is found in the God-relation, then the tensions of that difficulty become theological themes worthy of attention.

We now turn our focus to the need for alternative forms due to the nature of Christian knowledge. My interpretation of genre is made in light of the nature of Christian faith, which in time is incomplete and therefore does not fit a rigid systematic structure or "direct" discourse. In keeping with the focus of this study, we will consider the nature of the articulation of Christianity with the understanding that revelation relates to a person in historical existence, and the relationship between these two is the point of reflection. Thus far we have discussed elements of temporality and process within Christian existence and the implications such things have for the inconclusive nature of Christian theology. We now turn to a consideration of the need for humility in theological

---

implied in the discourse itself, then the discourse should represent the nature of the object under consideration, which when discussing Christianity is not only the objective revelation of God in Jesus Christ, but also the subjective appropriation of this or of the embodiment of the belief in decisive action.

claims to better represent the inconclusity of religious discourse because of its relation to existence. Because Christianity invites response, it should be communicated informs that respect freedom, allow room for difference in appropriation, and involve the reader/hearer her spatial and temporal locatedness. The letter is thus an appropriate form.[188]

[188] These doctrines with paradox or tensions in the tradition include: predestination and the goodness of God and the conflicting scriptures on salvation for all or for the elect and election and free will. We have tensions in salvation as: God's act and human participation in election and human response, in predestination and freedom. Here we note the tension between God revealed and God experienced—faith as Christ's faith or ours in him.

2

The Epistemic Humility of Faith in Sor Juana's Letters

As detailed in the previous chapter, direct forms of communication are not fully, or at least exclusively, appropriate for theological discourse. Despite revelation, God remains hidden to much human experience and comprehension, and even though revelation may be considered an objective manifestation of truth, one's subjective appropriation of the Christ-event is still always essential for Christian knowledge. For these reasons indirect forms of communication are needed in order to express Christianity more fully. In the writings of Sor Juana Inés de la Cruz, we find not only examples of indirect forms of communication in drama, poetry, and epistle, but also perspectives expressed in these genres that correspond to the theological concerns discussed thus far. As I explained in the introduction, Sor Juana brought totalities into question, without naming them such, because these totalities were structured in such a way as to relegate her to a powerless role as a woman and colonial subject, without an approved voice. Thus, she had to break open the discourse to include her voice, to participate in the debates of her day in an alternative form.

Sor Juana's work recognizes limits on human knowledge of the divine, the inadequacy of human language to fully express religious knowledge, and the need for a subjective appropriation of religious knowledge; she accomplishes this through an invitation to dialogue, attention to the need for personal appropriation for ideas to truly be internally persuasive, and an insistence on epistemic humility in theological discourse. Writing on the heels of late scholasticism and the authoritarian revival of the Catholic Reformation and ongoing Inquisition, Sor Juana proposes a type of theology that does not make bold claims for itself and its objective knowledge of the divine. Despite writing at a time when religion was often imposed upon individuals, communities, and even nations, Sor Juana promoted a different form of religious conversation, one that could be described as "polite,"[1] respectful, and tolerant.

The seventeenth century is described as an age of crisis, or one composed of "cultures of crisis," which were "forged in the crucible of the largest battle between traditionalism and the questionable, problematic values of change and

[1] My particular use of that term will be thoroughly developed in the chapter.

modernization."[2] This was an era of instability and uncertainty, composed of radical shifts throughout the cultures of Europe. Stephanie Merrim summarizes it as follows:

> Financial recessions and poverty and plague, shifting demographics, inflation, a newly disempowered and impoverished nobility, among many factors, transformed its economic and social landscape. The revolutions of the Reformation and the Counter-Reformation continued to restructure the religious and political systems of Europe; the slow move toward the organization of the modern centralized state involved the breakup of empires and the configuration of national identities. Wars religious and secular, civil and international, consistently wracked Europe. Where the Reformation and Counter-Reformation had placed religious belief systems into question, the onset in certain countries of the scientific revolution during the latter half of the century subjected to systematic doubt all knowledge that had preceded it.[3]

The shift from the Baroque to the Modern period evoked tension and conflict as the culture seeking to preserve tradition and the past struggled against the culture pushing for change. One such place of transition is from traditional knowledge, resting primarily on dogma and the principle of authority backing it, to a more properly modern conception of knowledge, which proceeds via the scientific method rather than the Scholastic method, and rests on a particular construal of reason and empirical observation.[4] Whereas the seventeenth century understood reason to include emotion and will, interpreting the capacity broadly to encompass intuition, insight, poetic perception, and those things modernity would label "irrational,"[5] the Modern period saw a narrowing and restricting of this function to suppose an isolatable capacity, separate from emotion and involvement with the subject and community. The Modern period also witnessed the emergence of a focus on the individual and existentialism.

Additionally, the seventeenth century experienced a backlash against the freedoms of women acquired in the sixteenth century; in an attempt to regain order during this era of crisis and uncertainty, traditional gender roles were reinforced and gender difference was emphasized. With push for change on

---

[2] Merrim, *Early Modern,* xxxvi.

[3] Ibid., xxvi.

[4] See Yolanda Martínez-San Miguel, 19–20, and Elías Trabulse, *Ciencia y Religion en el Siglo XVII* (Mexico: El Colegio de México, 1974) 9–10.

[5] Martínez-San Miguel, 71.

multiple fronts, the enforcement of gender roles and the enclosure of women became the "prime weapon of control" used to reinstate order during what has been called "the crisis of patriarchy."[6] The seventeenth century was authoritarian and exhibited an increase in the centralization of power, with a tightening "grip of traditional conservative attitudes."[7] And because of this, according to Wilson and Warnke, the era "was not hospitable to the artistic and intellectual endeavors of women."[8]

Stephanie Merrim suggests that Spain during the Catholic Reformation may serve as "the most pronounced example of the conservative backlash against the progressive forces of modernization making its presence felt in other seventeenth-century European domains as well. This recontainment of the energies of change manifested itself, among other ways, in a resurgence of traditional and medieval values."[9] And in New Spain, the seventeenth century was a time of polarizing oppositions and conflict characterized by numerous ambiguities and tensions that are not easily resolved.[10] Some scholars present this era in New Spain as one of "paralysis" and "stagnation" due to the crisis facing Scholasticism as the method for gaining knowledge, and as the very idea of what constitutes knowledge or truth was questioned.[11] The time in which Sor Juana lived and worked was one of transition and conflict between traditional epistemologies governed by the church and an emerging modern one. Pronounced conflicts gave shape to the culture of seventeenth-century New Spain: conflicts between the church and the university; between the colonial government and the mother country of Spain; between the Spanish-born in New Spain and the *criollo*, among others. Sor Juana's context was one in which authorities and distinct centers of power challenged each other, battling for control of the hegemonic space.[12] Sor Juana's work is a product of this context and is profoundly marked by an environment made unstable through the ongoing battles for control over the field of knowledge, fought between the

---

[6] Merrim, *Early Modern*, xxxi.

[7] Ibid., xxxii. Merrim is quoting Katharina M. Wilson and Frank J. Warnke in their introduction to *Women Writers of the Seventeenth Century* (Athens GA: University of Georgia Press, 1989) xvii.

[8] Ibid.

[9] Merrim, *Early Modern,* xxxi.

[10] Martínez-San Miguel, 21.

[11] Ibid.

[12] Ibid.

government, church, and university.[13] We see this tension and strife in Sor Juana's writing, for example, in the pairing of oppositions throughout her work, something considered throughout this book.

Sor Juana's creative expression took a variety of forms, but she was most prolific in her correspondence. Although almost all of her letters are lost, she is still most widely recognized for a letter she wrote to Manuel Fernández de Santa Cruz, Bishop of Puebla, the letter known as *La Respuesta*, or "The Answer"; it has been called both an intellectual autobiography and a proto-feminist defense of a woman's right to study. Sor Juana wrote this letter in response to the publication of another letter she wrote to Bishop Fernández at his request.

The parlor to Sor Juana's convent cell is often compared to a salon, where ideas were discussed and debated and where Sor Juana's erudition and eloquence were regularly displayed.[14] It was there that Bishop Fernández heard her response to the exaggerated claims of famous Jesuit preacher António Vieira, and asked if she would record her arguments for him. She did so in a letter, which he published without her consent, and although he gave it the lofty title *Carta Athenagórica* ("Letter Worthy of Athena"), he published a letter along with it, signed with the pseudonym of a nun, Sor Filotea de la Cruz, chastising Sor Juana for giving too much attention to secular studies.[15] The

---

[13] Ibid., 42.

[14] Octavio Paz, *Sor Juana, or The Traps of Faith,* trans. Margaret Sayers Peden (Cambridge: The Belknap Press of Harvard University Press, 1988) 131.

[15] A number of scholars have investigated the situation surrounding the writing of the *Carta Athenagórica,* Fernández's request of it from Juana, and his publication of it both with acclaim and critique under the pseudonym; a number of theories abound. Paz wonders if Fernández requests the letter and publishes it as an implicit critique of the Archbishop Aguiar Seijas, who like Vieira was a Jesuit. Myscofski has also suggested the critique of Vieira is an implicit critique of the archbishop. [Carole A. Myscofski, "Review Symposium on *Sor Juana Inés de la Cruz: Religion, Art, and Feminism* by Pamela Kirk (New York: Continuum, 1998)," *Horizons* 25, no. 2 (1998): 303–306.] Others have suggested that Sor Juana was placed in the middle of a disagreement between the archbishop and Fernández, bishop of Puebla; Marie-Cécile Bénassy discredits this position. "Hipótesis Sobre la 'Conversion' Final de Sor Juana Inés de la Cruz," *Revista de la Universidad de México* 30, no. 3 (Noviembre 1975): 21–24. See also Elías Trabulse, who argued that her *Carta Athenagórica* was written in response to something written on the *finezas* by Nuñez de Miranda, the strict confessor Sor Juana had dismissed as her advisor. [*El Enigma de Serafina de Cristo: Acerca de un*

publication of her letter and castigation evoked Sor Juana's famous "Answer," which was addressed to Bishop Fernández's pseudonym, Sor Filotea, though it is clear that Sor Juana knew who was behind the name, the publication, and the public critique.[16]

Carta Athenagórica was a rebuttal of the claims made by Vieira in a Maundy Thursday sermon he wrote forty years previously. In the sermon he confronted the teachings of Augustine, Thomas Aquinas, and John Chrysostom on the greatest signs of Christ's love, his *finezas*.[17] Vieira claimed his position on the *finezas* exceeded that of these three theologians. Sor Juana found his bold assertions of the ultimacy of his ideas to be arrogant and stated that his attitude should be humbled. She proceeded in her argument, using the ideas of the three aforementioned theologians to expose Vieira's hubris and the inaccuracy of his claims to superior thought.

One of the primary concerns Sor Juana communicated in these letters is humility in theological discourse corresponding to the limits of human knowledge and language. She not only insists on theological humility for herself through the use of conventional expressions of modesty, but she also challenged the confident assertions of Vieira, demonstrating her frustration with both bold claims of knowledge and the accompanying arrogance in the theological discipline.

Manuscrito Inédito de Sor Juana Inés de la Cruz (1691) (Toluca: Instituto Mexiquense de Cultura, 1995).] See also Luciani, who summarizes Trabulse's findings: "Sor Juana's troubled relationship with Núñez de Miranda became more evident in the 1990s with Trabulse's publication and analysis of the 'Carta de Serafina de Cristo,' a pseudonymous satire penned around the time of the *Respuesta a Sor Filotea*, which appears to identify Núñez de Miranda—not Antonio de Vieira—as the real target of the *Carta Athenagórica*, and confirms that the relationship between Sor Juana and her ex-confessor remained acrimonious a decade after their break" (153). See also Irving A. Leonard, *Baroque Times in Old Mexico: Seventeenth-Century Persons, Places, and Practices* (Ann Arbor: University of Michigan Press, 1959). Leonard gives attention to the chief characters involved and offers great insight into the archbishop and his reputation.

[16] See Paz, *Sor Juana*, 397. For an English translation of this letter by Fernández, see *Sor Juana Inés de la Cruz: Selected Writings*, trans. Pamela Kirk (New York: Paulist Press, 2005).

[17] *Finezas* here refers to the gifts of Christ given to humanity during his lifetime. The debate concerns what is his greatest gift to humankind or the greatest sign of his love for humanity.

I first examine the ideas Sor Juana communicates in these two letters regarding the nature of human knowledge and language, particularly when considering sacred matters, showing her position to be close to what Kierkegaard later called "Socratic ignorance" and what is now often discussed as "epistemic humility." In the midst of astute arguments for women's intelligence and right to study, Sor Juana repeatedly calls herself ignorant and claims a lack of knowledge. Scholars have taken different approaches to make sense of these remarks.[18] Studies expose the way in which these rhetorical devices are fairly typical of medieval letters by women and men in deference to authority and the hierarchical power structures of the day. Yet beyond this, most recognize this as a style of self-effacement, expected particularly of religious women as a safeguard against censure because of their subjugated position in patriarchal society and the ecclesial hierarchy.[19] Further, some scholars understand these statements in the writings of particular women to be an intentional mimicking of what the authors perceived the rhetoric of meek women to be like.[20] I will consider some of these arguments, but first I examine

---

[18] See Electa Arenal and Amanda Powell, "Introduction," in *The Answer/La Respuesta, Including a Selection of Poems*, trans. Electa Arenal and Amanda Powell (New York: The Feminist Press at the City University of New York, 1994); Alison Weber, *Teresa of Avila and the Rhetoric of Femininity* (Princeton NJ: Princeton University Press, 1990); and Stephanie Merrim, "Toward a Feminist Reading of Sor Juana Inés de la Cruz: Past, Present, and Future Directions in Sor Juana Criticism," in *Feminist Perspectives on Sor Juana Inés de la Cruz,* ed. Stephanie Merrim (Detroit: Wayne State University Press, 1991).

[19] Women who wrote on sacred matters had to be particularly careful during this time as women were brought under the scrutiny of the Inquisition for teaching. Another strategy commonly used by women to write on theological matters in an acceptable manner was to write mystical or visionary literature. This allowed them to claim these ideas did not come from themselves and their own rationality, but came directly from the Holy Spirit, without their feminine interference. See Grace M. Jantzen, *Power, Gender, and Christian Mysticism* (Cambridge: Cambridge University Press, 1995).

[20] This interpretation was first proposed by Alison Weber in *Teresa of Avila and the Rhetoric of Femininity* (Princeton NJ: Princeton University Press, 1990). Stephanie Merrim follows Weber's conclusion saying Sor Juana "*contrives* to write like a self-effacing woman," and says further that Sor Juana is actually "parodying or mimicking" Theresa's style. Stephanie Merrim, *Early Modern Women's Writing and Sor Juana Inés de la Cruz* (Nashville: Vanderbilt University Press, 1999) 168. In her 2003 book, Michelle Gonzalez concludes that Sor Juana's self-deprecation is a form of self-defense, affirming Merrim's conclusion that Sor Juana writes as she believes women are

what Sor Juana may be expressing on the underside of these claims of ignorance, expanding the understanding of Sor Juana's employment of modesty with an analysis of her concerns with theological discourse. Through an analysis of Sor Juana's letters, I demonstrate that in addition to protecting herself, Sor Juana implements modesty clauses and claims of ignorance for theological purposes. She turns the expectations of women's writing on their head by exposing the overweening arrogance of the theological academy of her day, as it stands in contrast to her intelligent, learned arguments, hedged in such a way that leaves them open to dialogue.

She models epistemic humility in theological discourse as evidenced by tolerance, politeness, and non-combative forms of conversation. I conclude with a consideration of the form of the letter, arguing that it is a thoroughly appropriate form for the elaboration of these themes.

The Nature of Human Knowledge, or Socratic Ignorance

La Respuesta is best known as Sor Juana's strong defense of women's intelligence and right to study. She makes an extended argument not only for her own God-given love of learning,[21] but also for the importance of the education of women. To build her case, she uses: an exegesis of Pauline texts

---

expected to write. Michelle Gonzalez, *Sor Juana: Beauty and Justice in the Americas* (Maryknoll NY: Orbis Books, 2003) 105. Rosemary Radford Ruether analyzes similar phrases in the writing of medieval German mystic Hildegard of Bingen. Ruether finds multiple levels of meaning behind these statements by Hildegard. One aspect corresponds to those listed above: that this is the only way a religious woman could gain a public voice. However, Ruether finds three other levels of meaning within these phrases, and each of these is theological. For example, Ruether identifies Hildegard's theological anthropology in these statements and her view that this lowly state is true of the status of all sinful humanity in the light of God's majesty. Rosemary Radford Ruether, *Women and Redemption: A Theological History* (Minneapolis: Fortress Press, 1998) see esp. 84–86.

[21] "This shows only too clearly the strength of my inclination. Blessed be God for his will to direct it toward learning" ("*La Respuesta,*" in *Sor Juana Anthology,* trans. Alan S. Trueblood, with foreword by Octavio Paz [Cambridge MA: Harvard University Press, 1988] 218). The Spanish text can be found in *Obras Completas de Sor Juana Inés de la Cruz*, vol. 1–4, ed. Alfonso Méndez Plancarte and Alberto Salceda (México-Buenos Aires: Fondo de Cultura Económica, 1951–1957), hereafter, abbreviated as OC, followed by volume number, page number, and then the line number if applicable. OC 4:452.

traditionally used to silence women; her own life story of an innate desire to learn; philosophical arguments based on the inter-related nature of all knowledge culminating in theology; historical arguments cataloging a list of women leaders and scholars from a variety of sources, eras, and contexts; as well as an array of rhetorical arts like satire and irony. Numerous scholarly works are dedicated to examining these elements in *La Respuesta.*[22] For the purposes of this study, attention is focused on Sor Juana's epistemology and the way in which it relates to her ideas on theological discourse, as exhibited in the two letters: *Carta Athenagórica* and *La Respuesta.*

Throughout *La Respuesta,* Sor Juana makes repeated references to "not knowing."[23] She explains that she has studied a myriad of subjects, and she demonstrates her knowledge of scripture, the tradition, philosophy, history, mythology, and literature. However, despite this display of her informed ideas, she claims all the while to "not know." She begins the letter with such a disclaimer, recounting that Thomas Aquinas remained silent with his teacher Albertus Magnus out of humility, as he said he could not say anything worthy of Albertus. Sor Juana, not assuming the same position as Thomas, says that while Thomas declined to speak because of his humility, she actually does not know anything worthy of the recipient of her letter. Already in the opening sentences she provides the humility of Thomas, who kept silent, as an example, and claims to not know anything worth telling. She goes on for many pages, however, nonetheless telling what she cannot know fully and explaining why silence may be her ultimate response.

---

[22] See *Feminist Perspectives on Sor Juana Inés de la Cruz,* ed. Stephanie Merrim (Detroit: Wayne State University Press, 1991); Rosa Perelmuter Pérez, "La Estructurea Retórica de la *Respuesta a Sor Filotea,*" *Hispanic Review* 51, no. 2 (Spring 1983): 147–58; Nina M. Scott, "Sor Juana Inés de la Cruz: 'Let Your Women Keep Silence in the Churches,'" *Women's Studies International Forum* 8, no. 5 (1985): 511–19; Nina M. Scott "*La Gran Turba de las Que Nombres:* Sor Juana's Foremothers in *La Respuesta a Sor Filotea,*" in *Coded Encounters: Race, Gender, and Ethnicity in Colonial Latin America,* ed. Javier Cevallos-Candau (Amherst MA: University of Massachusetts Press, 1994) 206–23; and Jean Franco, "Sor Juana Explores Space," in *Plotting Women: Gender and Representation in Mexico* (New York: Columbia University Press, 1989).

[23] For an essay on the play between silence and "not knowing" in Sor Juana's work, see Josephina Ludmer, "Tricks of the Weak," in *Feminist Perspectives on Sor Juana Inés de la Cruz,* trans. and ed. Stephanie Merrim (Detroit: Wayne State University Press, 1991).

In another example, Sor Juana addresses the unexpected publication of her letter to Bishop Fernández (*Carta Athenagórica)* and says that, as a rational being, the thought of having her "poor scribblings" ("*borrones*") put in print would never have entered her mind.[24] She identifies herself as rational, while in the same breath effaces her ability to claim and give expression to knowledge. Her gratitude is so great, she says, that she is not sure what to say, or literally, that it "stretches the limited capacity of speech"[25] and that it is a favor so unmerited as to "leave the beneficiary speechless."[26] Thus at the offset she establishes the concept that language has limited capacity for expression. While she may be speaking hyperbolically and ironically about the supposed "favor" done her in the publication of the letter, she continues her argument made in the *Carta* that humans should not make bold claims of absolute or ultimate knowledge because our understanding of the divine is always imperfect and our ability to articulate the religious is restricted by language.

She gives examples from the Bible of those who, when blessed with recognition of the divine, are left with questions, doubts, or an inability to express the event. So it was with Elizabeth, the mother of John the Baptist, when she who was once barren became pregnant and realized that Mary, bearing the Word in her womb, was visiting her home. Sor Juana says Elizabeth's "mind went blank and words failed her," and so instead of giving

---

[24] OC 4:440. For a discussion of Sor Juana's use of *"borrones"* to describe her work—a word that refers to errors, smudges, corrections, mistakes, and edits—see Margo Glantz, *La Desnudez Como Naufragio: Borrones y Borradores* (Madrid: Iberoamericana, 2005), and *Borrones y Borradores. Reflexiones Sobre el Ejercicio de la Escritura (Ensayos de Literature Colonial, de Bernal Díaz del Castillo a SorJuana*) (Mexico: Coordinación de Difusión Cultural Dirección de Literatura, UNAM, Ediciones del Equilibrista, 1992). Glantz also considers Sor Juana's use of the word in other texts, particularly her *auto sacramental, El Divino Narciso.*

[25] "*La Respuesta*," in *Sor Juana Inés de la Cruz: Selected Writings*, trans. Pamela Kirk (New York: Paulist Press, 2005). Multiple translations of *La Respuesta* are available. I chose which translation to use based upon what I discern to be the most accurate and/or the most sensible reading. Trueblood's, though an older translation, is often the most readable. Powell and Arenal offer a parallel translation. Pamela Kirk gives the most recent translation, with some theological decisions made in translation. Hers is the only translation available of the *Carta Athenagórica* or the letter by Sor Filotea (Fernández) published with the *Carta Athenagórica*. OC 4:440.

[26] *Respuesta*, Trueblood, 205. OC 4:440.

thanks, she "burst out" with doubts and questions.[27] Sor Juana also gives the example of Saul, who, when selected and anointed as king, uttered questions. Finally she offers the example of Paul, who says he was taken to the third heaven and shown the secrets of God, yet "he does not tell what he saw; he says that he cannot tell it. Thus, of those things that cannot be spoken, it must at least be said that they cannot be, to make clear that keeping silent does not mean having nothing to say, but rather that words cannot encompass all there is to say."[28]

When the matter to be communicated is not simply the conveyance of fact from one person to another, limits of language resist the direct telling of it. However, if one wants to express it, one must determine how best to convey its meaning in an indirect form. Sor Juana explains that silence is one such option. Silence alone, however, is not enough. One must give some content to the silence. In fact, she says that she has almost determined to let silence be her response, but, she explains, that silence in and of itself is only something negative. "Although it explains a great deal by its insistence on not explaining, some brief label is needed to enable one to understand what it is intended to mean. Otherwise, silence will say nothing, since its function is precisely that: to say nothing."[29]

Using the example of the closing statements of the Gospel of John, Sor Juana remarks that with a few words a person can give expression to that which cannot be fully told. The gospel writer says that if he were to write down all of Christ's miracles, there would not be enough rooms in the world to hold all the pages. Sor Juana is referring to a remark by Vieira, who said that, in this statement, the Evangelist was expressing more than he ever had in anything else he had written. Sor Juana concurs, "Because with these words Saint John says all that he had left unsaid, and expresses whatever he had left unexpressed."[30] She thus concludes the introduction to her *Respuesta* by stating that she will give brief indication of that which she leaves to silence.

This conception of silence as a form of theological expression bookends her *Respuesta* as Sor Juana picks up this theme in the concluding paragraphs as well. In conclusion she gives an even stronger indication that she expects (or desires) to let silence be the culmination of her work, her last form of

---

[27] Ibid., 206. OC 4:440.

[28] Ibid., 207. OC 4:442.

[29] Ibid. OC 4:442.

[30] Ibid. OC 4:442.

expression. She has done much to preface it, to give her silence content, so that rather than saying nothing, the silence conveys intended substance. She reiterates that she is resolved to be silent, but that she would do the opposite of this, yielding her "decision" if the recipient determines speech rather than silence to be the better course: "If it be your pleasure, my Lady, I would do the opposite of what I have just proposed to your judgment and opinion. At the least indication of your desire I would cede, as is my right, my decision, which was, as I have told you, to remain silent."[31]

Progressing in her defense of her study and writings, Sor Juana faces the charge, printed along with her *Carta Athenagórica,* that she has not given enough attention to sacred matters. First, it is obvious in her *Carta* that she is well educated on the teachings of the church and its theologians, as well as scripture. This becomes even clearer in her "Answer" as she references an array of biblical texts, displays insightful exegetical skills, and exhibits her knowledge of the history of exegesis.[32] So, although Bishop Fernández instructs her to pay more attention to reading the "book of Jesus" rather than the secular subjects to which she devotes so much time, it is clear to the reader of Sor Juana's publications that she has not neglected the study of sacred subjects; in fact, she justifies her energies in subjects deemed "secular" by elucidating their connection to theology as preparatory for that advanced study.

Sor Juana appeals to the interconnectedness of all things to defend her secular studies, claiming that knowledge of one subject illuminates others, ultimately culminating in the study of theology. She writes:

> I, for my part, can assure you that whatever I do not understand from one author on one subject I am able to understand from another author on another subject that seems far removed. And these authors, as they explain themselves, employ metaphors from other disciplines. Mathematicians, for example, explain that the means in an equation functions as a measuring rod to the extremes. Similarly, we say that the arguments of the logician go in a straight line and those of the orator move like an arc along the longest path, but both are heading for the same point. The same is true when they say that the exegetes are like an open hand and the Scholastics like a closed fist. So there is nothing wrong, nor am I claiming that

[31] *Respuesta*, Kirk, 287. OC 4:472.

[32] She utilizes allegorical exegesis in a number of places, including an interpretation of crowns, and she notes the historical limitations placed on even men's study of Genesis and Song of Songs.

> there is, in having studied such a variety of things, because the disciplines complement one another.[33]

She attributes this interconnectedness to the creative intention of God: "It was to form this universal chain that the wisdom of their Author so put them in place that they appear correlated and bound together with marvelous concert and bonding."[34] She further defends her broad range of study by stressing the importance of understanding a variety of subjects so that one is better able to comprehend scripture and theology.

> In this way I went on, continually directing the course of my study, as I have said, toward the eminence of sacred theology. To reach this goal, I considered it necessary to ascend the steps of human arts and sciences, for how can one who has not mastered the style of the ancillary branches of learning hope to understand that of the queen of them all? How, lacking logic, was I to understand the general and specific methodologies of which Holy Scripture is composed?[35]

She also argues on a similar basis for the study of rhetoric, physics, music, arithmetic, geometry, architecture, history, law, and erudition. She concludes, however, that she has studied many things and yet knows nothing, an intriguing assessment given the display of knowledge she had just exhibited.[36]

She continues, further demonstrating her innate hunger for learning and intellectual prowess, saying she cannot stop herself from performing empirical experiments, whether they involve children's play tops on flour-dusted floors or observing the reaction of eggs in a variety of liquids. She taught herself Latin and seemingly reads everything available to her, and yet again she claims to "know nothing."[37] When one considers that this statement is the conclusion to her explanation of her studies, with the stated purpose to culminate in theological study, it seems this is not simply a claim of absolute ignorance in all of these subjects, but is instead an affirmation that studies cannot ultimately reach their goal, which is knowledge of God and God's ways in the world. Sor Juana explains that she has written less on sacred subjects, not because she has not applied herself to the study of them and not because she lacks the inclination, but because of "an excess of the awe and reverence due those

[33] *Respuesta*, Kirk, 264. OC 4:450.
[34] *Respuesta*, Trueblood, 216. OC 4:450.
[35] Ibid., 213. OC 4:447.
[36] OC 4:449.
[37] OC 4:451.

Sacred Letters."[38] She maintains that she is "ill-equipped" for the understanding of these matters, and considers herself "unworthy" of handling them. She hesitates to take on sacred subjects because of warnings from scripture, like: "Why do you speak my commandments and put my covenant in your mouth?"[39] Additionally she notes that even learned men were forbidden from reading the Song of Songs until they were thirty, and that the book of Genesis was also withheld from them until they were mature enough to deal with its obscure passages. She writes, "Then how should I dare to take this into my unworthy hands, when my sex, age, and especially my way of life all oppose it? And so I confess that many times this fear has taken the pen from my hand and caused the subject to sink back into the very mind from which it sought to emerge."[40]

Nonetheless she strove to direct her study as much to God's service as she could, because the goal to which she aspired was the study of theology. She writes that it seemed "no small incompetence, being Catholic, not to know everything about the sacred mysteries that can be attained by the use of natural reason."[41] Here we find Sor Juana yet again insisting on the importance of study. Throughout *La Respuesta* she argues for the right of women to study, for the importance that women be learned, and that those gifted with a capable mind, who avoid arrogance, should pursue knowledge. She details her intellectual development, the persistence of her mind, and her God-given desire for learning, and yet just as often as she makes arguments for her pursuit of knowledge, she insists that she has not attained it. "I envy those who say that the urge to study has cost them nothing. Blessed are they! For me, it has not been knowledge (which I still do not have), but rather the desire to know that has cost me dearly."[42] A similar attitude is conveyed in her poem *Primero sueño*, where the searching intellect is tormented by the intense longing and struggle to gain understanding, accompanied by the disappointment experienced when one realizes that arriving at certain, comprehensive knowledge is impossible.

---

[38] *Respuesta,* Trueblood, 208. OC 4:442.

[39] *Respuesta,* Kirk, from the Latin Vulgate, Ps. 49:16, 256. OC 4:442.

[40] *Respuesta,* Trueblood, 209. She also asserts that her writing on secular subjects at worst could only bring critics of the arts against it, whereas her writing on the sacred comes under the eye of the Holy Office. OC 4:443.

[41] *Respuesta,* Kirk, 261. OC 4:447.

[42] Ibid., 265. OC 4:451.

Although she says her ultimate goal is the study of theology and, therefore, knowledge of God, she repeatedly affirms that all she can really hope to gain at the end is to be less ignorant. She does not expect, despite all the study, the interconnectedness of subjects, and the way in which the natural order may demonstrate aspects of God, that she would ever attain a full or certain knowledge of the divine. Implicit within her humble claims are a serious proposal on the nature of theological discourse and a call for epistemic and discursive humility.[43] This becomes more evident when one examines the impetus behind her critique of Vieira's sermon.

Toward Theological Humility

Sor Juana states very clearly why she writes her rebuttal of Vieira's sermon in *Carta Athenagórica.* She claims to respect Vieira and his "creative genius," and she certainly may; she states his position on other matters and references him as an authority in her *Respuesta.*[44] She does not, however, find the arrogant claims surrounding his argument in this particular Maundy Thursday sermon to be appropriate to the task. She does not appear particularly concerned that she is actually able to truly define the absolute greatest sign of Christ's love. She begins her letter by stating that she formed these arguments to show that Vieira's claims of an ultimate position on Christ's *finezas* were not valid. And she concludes her letter similarly, by stating that her intention was to demonstrate that Vieira's declarations about the superiority of his thought, interpretation, and position on the topic were inappropriate, unwarranted, and even deserving divine punishment. One can read passion and frustration in her words that a preacher and theologian would make such bold statements about his knowledge into the divine mysteries and his ability to articulate them.

Sor Juana defends herself upfront from the likely charge that her refutation of Vieira's arguments is impudent by reminding the reader that Vieira himself opened up the way for such a response by "being the first to tread paths untouched," which, "in light of his great daring," makes such "less bold" ventures easier to undertake.[45] She asks: If in one of his sermons, Vieira "felt

[43] An interesting contrast is evident here between the tone in this carefully crafted letter to the bold and almost forceful tone in a recently discovered letter by Sor Juana, where she dismisses her powerful and oppressive confessor from his obligation to guide her. See *Carta de Monterrey.*

[44] *Carta,* Kirk, 220. OC 4:413.

[45] Ibid. OC 4:413.

strength enough in his pen to improve on three writers, imminently learned and canonized in one of his sermons," how much more so then will others, based on his example, "attempt to surpass his pen," which although learned, is not canonized?[46] Sor Juana repeatedly references Vieira's audacity and says she will "defend [her] position with the arguments of the three holy fathers," those three whom Vieira was so bold as to claim his arguments surpassed. She charges, quoting Vieira:

> He proposes to treat the position of the three holy fathers [Augustine, Thomas Aquinas, and John Chrysostom] with the following boundless audacity: "...that there is [sic] none of the benefits of the love of Christ that these same saints hold to which I will not add one that is better. Furthermore, I maintain that to the demonstrations of the love of Christ that I hold the greatest, there is not another one to be found to equal it."[47]

Sor Juana understands that if her response to Vieira is successfully persuasive, then it is attributable to God's desire to punish the pride of Vieira's assertion "*that there is no one who could maintain a demonstration of love equal* to his own."[48] She sees his declaration as evidence that "there was no one who could equal him" in "genius."[49] She also takes his arrogance to suggest that, whereas God did not create in Augustine, Chrysostom, or Thomas one whose arguments could not be surpassed or responded to, God did create such a person with Vieira. She says, with perhaps a bit of sarcasm, that if a woman could come up with this rebuttal off the cuff, without even taking the care she would if she knew it were to be published, perhaps his claims were excessive and grandiose. Utilizing a female metaphor to describe her work, she calls it "an embryo" and likens her production of it to "she-bear," who "gives birth to her unformed cubs."[50] Such a hastily written, embryonic rebuttal of his claims from a woman should be enough to prove Vieira's work wanting. She writes,

> Had I achieved no more than daring to answer him, this would have been sufficient mortification for such a man as he, illustrious in so many ways. It is no light punishment for a man who believes no man would dare to respond to him to behold an ignorant woman, for whom this type of study is so alien and remote

[46] Ibid., 220–21. OC 4:413.
[47] Ibid., 221. OC 4:414. For Vieira's sermon and this reference, see OC 4:674.
[48] Ibid., 243. OC 4:435.
[49] Ibid., 243–44. OC 4:435.
[50] Ibid., 243. OC 4:434.

from her sex, doing so. But then, so was Judith and she took up arms, and Deborah, who became a judge.[51]

Sor Juana, continuing in her David and Goliath metaphors, uses the illustration of "the pygmies" for whom "it was a sufficient demonstration of bravery merely to dare to challenge Hercules," stating that the genius of Vieira is so great that "even giants must appear as dwarfs" when confronting it.[52] And she asks, rather ironically: "What then is a poor woman to do?"[53] She follows with a reminder that a woman "took the club from the hands of Alcides, a deed considered one of the three impossibilities venerated in antiquity."[54] Moving into what she calls "a more Christian framework," she harkens on the words of Paul in 1 Corinthians 1:27–29: "The foolish things of the world God has chosen to confuse the wise, and the weak things God has chosen to confound the strong. What is ignoble and contemptible God has chosen, and what is not, so that he might destroy what is, so that all flesh will not glory in his sight."[55] Her brief catalogue of the achievements of those deemed weak and women also defends her right to take on the eminent Vieira, a defense she elaborates in her *Respuesta.*

Clearly then, Sor Juana's expressed intent is to temper Vieira's bold claims about his theological knowledge and insight, recognizing that, in his context, to have one's claims be at all wisely confronted by a woman would itself be a humbling event. She does not even seem to find it necessary to convince the reader fully that her arguments are stronger, and although she uses combat imagery, her goal is not one of "winning" the battle or being declared the victor by popular opinion. Rather, she is primarily making the point that Vieira should not claim his opinion is ultimate or announce that his view surpasses that of others, but that he should acknowledge in his work that this is his opinion, just as her learned response is a valid perspective as well.[56] Despite her warrior

---

[51] Ibid., 244. OC 4:435.

[52] Ibid., 243. OC 4:434.

[53] Ibid. OC 4:434.

[54] Ibid. OC 4:434.

[55] Ibid. OC 4:434.

[56] I do not argue that Sor Juana is making the case here for some extreme relativism, often attributed to postmodernism. She is not suggesting that every opinion, unlearned, uniformed, and irrelevant it may be, are all equal to those that have survived a long history in the Church. Rather, Sor Juana is confronting epistemic arrogance, one which makes superior claims for itself, and as an alternative she proposes a posture of

illustrations, Sor Juana is, in fact, directly rejecting combative tendencies in theology that would seek victory over alternative views and would seek domination of voice and opinion.[57] She expresses a sense of uneasiness concerning the possibility that her letter may appear as a refutation, and she explicitly welcomes differing views in response to her own work. The debate she proposes is closer to the fostering of dialogue for the sake of mutual learning than intellectual pugilism, with each in her/his corner attempting to beat the other rhetorically regardless of the uncertainty of the claims held. Her critique at its core is not directed at Vieira's specific arguments but rather at *the way* he argues.

In *La Respuesta* Sor Juana again picks up this theme of epistemic humility in theology. Despite the public chastisement she received, she does not back down from the primary case she made in her initial letter, but sustains the concern while simultaneously taking on the texts in Paul that would traditionally be interpreted to keep her from doing precisely what she did in her *Carta.* She considers 1 Corinthians 14:34, which says: "Let women keep silence in the churches, for it is not permitted them to speak," and responds with the apostle's statement in Titus: "The aged women, in like manner, in holy attire...teaching well."[58] She explains that according to these texts Paul's message is that, while it may not be appropriate for women to preach in the pulpit, "studying, writing, and teaching privately are not only allowable but most edifying and useful."[59] She continues, "Of course this does not apply to all women—only to those whom God has endowed with particular virtue and discernment and who have become highly accomplished and erudite, and possess the talents and other qualities needed for such holy pursuits."[60]

She makes an even bolder move, however, as she transitions from a defense of women's right to study and teach other women, to extend the biblical limitations on study and teaching to men as well. Sor Juana proclaims that men

---

epistemic humility. For evidence that she is not suggesting anything and everything goes and that all ideas are equally valid in reference to the Christian God, see *Respuesta,* OC 4:462–63.

[57] This becomes even more obvious in *Respuesta* when she talks about welcoming opposition because it keeps one humble, which is an essential feature of true wisdom. We also see this well demonstrated in her *loas.*

[58] Titus 2:3. *Respuesta*, Trueblood, 229. Translated from the Latin. OC 4:462.

[59] Ibid. OC 462.

[60] Ibid., 229–30. OC 4:462. Despite all her claims to ignorance and all her self-effacement, she seems to include herself in this group.

without the abilities and learning should no more be allowed to participate in these functions than those women of like limited abilities. For a woman of such strong intellectual skill, discipline, and learning to be prohibited from utilizing these abilities, while witnessing men with much less erudition and talent perform functions, exegete texts, and participate in the scholarly life as she would never be allowed, must have been a frustrating experience. She writes, "So true is this that the interpretation of Holy Scripture should be forbidden not only to women, considered so very inept, but to men, who merely by virtue of being men consider themselves sages, unless they are very learned and virtuous, with receptive and properly trained minds."[61] She asserts that the church's failure to place this limitation on men has, "in [her] view," "given rise precisely to all those sectarians and been the root cause of all the heresies."[62] She sees this as a particular flaw among those who are of an "arrogant, restless, and overbearing turn of mind," who seek out only new interpretations and will not rest until they have said something no one else has.[63] This shift from a defense of women's rights, to the broader issue of the care that should be taken by all who endeavor to study the powerful instrument of theology, is evidence that Sor Juana is not only addressing women's concerns but also making an argument about the theological task as a whole.

She again picks up the battle metaphor in reference to theological discourse, only to point out the negative and even dangerous aspects of such a posture and to highlight the violent nature of it. She says that theological study for those who are arrogant "is like putting a sword in the hands of a raging maniac. What is of itself a noble instrument meant for defense in his hands can cause his own death and the deaths of many others."[64] She again turns to Paul, quoting Romans 12:3: "Do not strive to know more than is necessary, but to know what is fitting for you each according to the faith that God has measured out to you."[65] She reminds the reader that when Paul says this, he is not addressing it to women but to men.

---

[61] Ibid., 230. OC 4:462.

[62] Ibid. I quote her phrase "in my view" specifically because this corresponds with her argument that theological discourse is sdhaped by a person's opinion, and as will be discussed later in this chapter, hedges of these sorts are strategies used by a speaker or writer to restrain her/his discourse from impinging on the freedom of the other, to retain an openness for discussion, and to show respect for the other. OC 4:462.

[63] Ibid. OC 4:462–63.

[64] *Respuesta,* Kirk, 277. OC 4:463.

[65] Ibid., 278. Translated from the Latin. OC 4:463.

> And so the *taceant* [being silent] is not only meant for women, but also for all those who are not adept at learning. Should I want to know as much or more than Aristotle or St. Augustine, if I do not have the aptitude of St. Augustine or Aristotle, were I to study more than both of them, not only would I not achieve this goal, but I would weaken and obstruct the operation of my weak mind through the disproportionate greatness of the object of study.[66]

Here she is not stating directly that she is without this aptitude, but posits this hypothetically for anyone without the abilities of Aristotle or Augustine competitively attempting to know more than these.

Sor Juana laments that people do not proceed in theological inquiry with more caution. Yet even worse than ignorant people with little talent for learning, but who undertake theological study anyway, are those who "write with a greedy ambition of equaling or surpassing others."[67] She recognizes a competitive aspect to much theological construction, and sees it not only as out of place in that context, but also as dangerous and deserving divine judgment, as expressed in her suggestion that God may use her as an instrument to humble the arrogant Vieira. If people only took heed to these warnings, she says, "how little courage would remain and how many errors we would have avoided, and how many twisted theories would not be circulating!"[68] The theological discipline, according to Sor Juana, is not a battle of intellects and opinions, verbally violent in attempts to outdo another, but a fruitful discourse where people learn from one another in respect and openness.

Responding to her critics, Sor Juana admits that the original letter (*Carta Athenagórica*) was unpolished because she did not expect it to be published, but asks if the critic finds something heretical in it, why does "he" not denounce it? Let people laugh at the roughness of style in the letter, she says; it does not bother her. She is not asking for anyone's applause or approval, for anyone is free to disagree with her, just as she was free to disagree with Vieira. She would not want to assume a posture that would exclude difference, nor one that would suppose the arrogant positioning like that taken by Vieira, asserting his ideas to be the last word on the subject.[69] She does, however, liken her sufferings from

---

[66] Ibid. OC 4:463.

[67] Ibid. OC 4:463–64.

[68] Ibid. OC 4:464.

[69] OC 4:469. Obviously the structure of power was a complex one in Sor Juana's ecclesial, colonial context. I do not intend to deny or obscure this fact, but wish to emphasize that Sor Juana is making *theological claims* here that scholars and

critics to the sufferings of Christ. He was hated and condemned not for faults but because of his good deeds, his signs, and miracles. Those who hated Christ because of these good things had "skewed reasoning," says Sor Juana, yet this is not surprising because, "when learned men become passionately involved, such inconsistencies in their reasoning are bound to occur."[70] This in turn serves as another example of the possibility to err among learned men. Reasoning can be "skewed" and inconsistencies in thought can emerge. She again insists that a person's opinion on such matters is not infallible.

Sor Juana tells of the custom in the Roman Empire to parade their victorious armies through the city, celebrating the glory of the empire and the generals who led the battle. Yet, while the conquering general heard the praise and adoration of the populace in the streets, soldiers, by order of the Senate, reminded him of his mortality and his flaws. Caesar, for example, marched through the city in victory, while the lowliest soldier proclaimed: "Beware, Romans, we bring you one who is bald, and adulterous."[71] Sor Juana illustrates that the very sort of intellectual victory that prominence in the theological field may provide is precisely the sort of prestige that ultimately endangers a person's judgment. She explains, "This was done so that in the midst of so much honor the victor would not become conceited because the ballast of these insults would be a counterweight to the sails of so much adulation and the ship of judgment would not be endangered by the winds of acclaim."[72] She then asks, "If this is what some of the pagans do, I say, with only the light of natural law to guide them, how much more ought we Catholics, with the commandment to love our enemies, tolerate those who insult us?"[73] She calls for "tolerance" for those who would oppose us, stating that fame and admiration for one's abilities should be countered with some opposition so as to keep one from taking glory for oneself when it is not due. "I hold the risk of fame a great one for human weakness, which is apt to appropriate that which is not its own."[74] Praise for and the unmitigated acceptance of one's ideas and work may actually impair one's reasonable judgment; some dissent is to be desired not only because it tempers

---

theologians should not ignore, and which continue to be relevant even in contemporary constructive theology.

[70] *Respuesta,* Kirk, 268. OC 4:454.

[71] Ibid., 288. Translated from the Latin. OC 4:472.

[72] Ibid. OC 4:472–73.

[73] Ibid. OC 4:473.

[74] Ibid. OC 4:473.

fame, but also because the very presence of differing views reflects the non-absolute form of anyone's theological claims.[75] She writes, "I therefore fear praise more than censure, my Lady, for the latter, by only the simplest act of patience, may be turned to advantage, while the former, if it is not to do one harm, requires many reciprocal acts of humility and self-knowledge. So in my case I recognize and realize that it is by God's special grace that I have understood this."[76]

In true Baroque fashion, with yet another metaphor, Sor Juana identifies tolerance and humility as the evidence of intelligence. Much like how statues on top of temples are covered with barbs to protect them from the birds, so those in a high position will be unable to avoid the barbs, or criticism and opposition by others. "Any eminence, be it in dignity, nobility, wealth, beauty, learning, is subject to this penalty, but most implacably subject to it is eminence of mind. First of all, because it is the most defenseless, since wealth and power punish anyone daring to challenge them; but not mind, for the greater it is, the more modest and long-suffering, and the less prone to defend itself."[77] True powers of the intellect are here recognizable in restraint from defensive counter-attack and self-justification and evidenced in "modesty" and "long-suffering." Genuine wisdom is not displayed in arrogance, but humility, as exemplified in Christ, whose sacred head and "divine brain were a storehouse of wisdom," but were crowned with thorns instead of silver or gold.[78]

Sor Juana explicitly states that she fears her confrontation of Vieira's attitude would be considered a refutation. She is nervous about the work being perceived as such, perhaps because of the Inquisition, but also, it seems, because this is contrary to her intention. In her *Carta* she tells the reader that she hesitated to write the letter because, among other things, she does not have a

[75] This is well demonstrated in her *loas* and *villancicos* and will be further considered in chapter 4.

[76] *Respuesta,* Trueblood, 242. OC 4:473. Some may argue that Sor Juana did seek fame for herself as she befriended the viceroyalty, those who could get her works published and keep her at least temporarily and partially out of danger of censure. She was close to those in power, and she enjoyed the benefits of it: in freedom, in money for books and scientific equipment, and in the prestige gained. In her *Respuesta,* she does not deny that she has received some amount of recognition, yet she admits that she hopes to receive criticism with grace because she knows it tempers that fame.

[77] *Respuesta,* Trueblood, 221. OC 4:455.

[78] Ibid. OC 4:455.

spirit of contradiction, but writes at the request of the Bishop of Puebla.[79] And in *La Respuesta* she says again that she was reluctant to write the letter on Vieira's sermon: "Because it treated sacred matters for which (as I have said) I hold such reverent dread; and, too, because it would appear to be an attempt at refutation, to which I have a natural aversion."[80] And she hopes that the fact that she has put dissenting words in writing at another's request, and specifically for his eyes, will temper its confrontational nature:

> Now I have done it so that you may know that I obey you in the most difficult matters, not only with my mind concerning such an arduous task as that of taking issue with the propositions of such a great individual, but also in that part of my character that finds loathsome anything which might appear to impugn anyone. Although this latter objection is modified to some degree, because in any case you alone will be witness to it and because the authority of your command will render honest the mistakes resulting from my obedience, which to other eyes might appear disproportionate pride.[81]

Also, Sor Juana expresses a concern that one not impose upon the rational freedom of another.[82] Here in her *Carta,* she describes human reason as a "free power" that assents or dissents based upon its own powers of deduction, what "it judges to be or not be the truth."[83] And in her *Respuesta,* she asks why she has been so chastised for exercising her rational freedom in forming an opinion contrary to Vieira's: "If my crime lies in the 'Letter Worthy of Athena,' was that anything more than a simple report of my opinion, with all the indulgences granted me by our Holy Mother Church? ...Is it bold of me to oppose Vieira, yet not so for that Reverend Father to oppose the three holy Fathers of the church? Is my mind, such as it is, less free than his, though it derives from the same source?"[84] In addition to noting that her mind is as free as a man's, coming from the same source in God, she makes an important distinction between theological opinion and revealed truth. She asks: "Is [Vieira's] opinion

---

[79] *Carta Athenagórica*, Kirk, 220. OC 4:413.

[80] *Respuesta*, in *The Answer/La Respuesta*, trans. Electa Arenal and Amanda Powell, 97. OC 4:471.

[81] *Carta Athenagórica*, Kirk, 219–20. OC 4:412.

[82] This is a position consistant with that at work in the dramas we will discuss in chapter 4, where she dramatizes approaches to coercion in contrast to internal conversion in the Conquest.

[83] Ibid., 220. OC 4:413.

[84] *Respuesta*, Arenal and Powell, 91. OC 4:468.

one of the revealed precepts of Holy Faith, that we should have to believe it blindly?"[85] The theological discipline should not be confused with revealed truth, but is instead composed of opinions formed through one's God-given intellectual freedom, which in turn is influenced by a variety of factors and thus always situated and interpretive, and therefore should be presented tentatively with an openness that does not suppose one's view to be the final or even the best word on the matter. She takes a daring stand on the inherent individual freedom of thought and equality of the rationality of female and male and colonized and colonizer. She applies this belief to a range of topics from doctrine to the sciences, all terrain over which the church claimed dominion.

In both letters reviewed here, we find a central concern that theology be approached in epistemic humility and not in a spirit of competition or in a combative manner. Alternatively, Sor Juana promotes an openness and a free sharing of opinions. While she does rebuke the "heretics," specifically naming Luther and Pelagius, she meanwhile calls for "tolerance" and love of enemies or of those with differing opinions. And although she writes what she nervously admits may be considered a "refutation," she all the while does so to make the case that such close-minded, self-promoting theology is false. She writes, "I say that I am not here engaging in a rebuttal but simply relating my opinion. In so doing, I am far from believing of myself what said preacher thinks of himself when he claims that no one can improve on his arguments,... Of course I think and believe that anyone could improve on my arguments to an infinite degree."[86]

Sor Juana's Socratic Ignorance

Sor Juana repeatedly references her ignorance and denigrates the quality of her argumentation and writing. Certainly she offers these statements denying her abilities and aptitude to protect herself. However, these claims in the context of her critique of Vieira also bear implications about knowledge of God and the limits of language to adequately give expression to claims about the divine. Some scholars assert that the epistemic humility demonstrated by Sor Juana in documents like *La Respuesta* is essentially a "false humility," a posture that Sor Juana artificially assumes in order to make her overall arguments more

[85] *Respuesta*, Trueblood, 237. OC 4:468.
[86] *Carta Athenagórica*, Kirk, 220. OC 4:413.

palatable to male readership and authorities.[87] I agree that this must be a part of her design, given her context as a woman in seventeenth-century New Spain and the common use of such phrases throughout religious orders of her time. Calling oneself "the worst of all" or "the worst sinner of all" was common practice, and Sor Juana is known to have written lines like this in the margin of a book and in the written final statements she made before she ceased writing.[88] In *La Respuesta*, however, Sor Juana directly references this "affected modesty" or "false humility," and denies that her position is anything of the sort. She knows full well that she has a keen intellect and that she is learned; she makes many statements that support this assessment, and her intellectual autobiography illustrates it. However, she likewise held a belief in the limits of reason, as evidenced in *La Respuesta* and in her poem *Primero sueño*, or "First Dream."[89]

In her *Carta,* she calls her comments there "unpolished, terse, and unlearned," but written in obedience.[90] She writes that she has never presumed herself to be a genius or even so learned as to be under an obligation to write, which, she explains, is what she tells people when they urge her to write. She appears even less comfortable writing when the subject at hand is theological. She says: "What understanding do I have, what course of studies, what material, or knowledge of it, except four superficial certificates?"[91] She refuses to claim a high level of understanding, particularly when the subject is God, because such knowledge is largely opinion, even if it is an educated opinion.[92] Granted, this is not without reference to the Inquisition; she continues: "I do not want any trouble with the Holy Office. I am ignorant and tremble at the thought of making a statement that sounds heretical or twisting the genuine meaning of any text. I do not study in order to write, and even less to teach (which would be for me disproportionate pride), but only in order to see if by studying I become less

[87] See Electa Arenal and Amanda Powell, "Introduction," in *The Answer/La Respuesta, Including a Selection of Poems*, trans. Electa Arenal and Amanda Powell (New York: The Feminist Press at the City University of New York, 1994).

[88] See Paz, 450–70. Evidence suggests she had begun writing again before her death.

[89] OC 4:468.

[90] OC 4:434.

[91] *La Respuesta*, Kirk, 258. OC 4:444.

[92] My overall point is not that theology is all opinion, but that as much as it is reflection on the God-relation, it is subjective (in the Kierkegaardian sense) and as thus related to the subject, then also contextual.

ignorant."[93] Imbedded in this statement shielding herself from the Inquisition, she claims she does not study in order to make declarative statements about the nature of things either in print or through teaching, but again, she studies that she become less lacking. Although she does not suppose she will come to a full, comprehensive knowledge of the world or the workings of God within it, she does find study valuable at the very least to make a person less unaware and less uninformed. Or, one might say: so as to be aware of the limits of one's knowledge, to be wise like Socrates in recognizing the little one knows. Sor Juana again demonstrates a form of Socratic ignorance, and although one can read within her words a concern or even fear of punishment from the Inquisition, in the same letter, she calls out those who slander her to go ahead and report her to the Holy Office, so fear does not seem to be the sole impetus in her statements.[94]

Sor Juana is not the only female writer who used these rhetorical devices with an additional purpose. A text that presents a well-received perspective on the self-deprecating language one finds in the texts of women like Sor Juana is Alison Weber's book *Teresa of Avila and the Rhetoric of Femininity*. Here Weber argues that Spanish mystic Teresa of Avila used, among other rhetorical tools, self-deprecation, and "feigned ignorance and incompetence" in order to give herself a voice to be heard in the church.[95] She introduces her study:

> As I read more and understood more clearly the conditions under which Teresa wrote, I was convinced that Teresa's self-depreciation was rhetorical but that it had a very non-traditional function. It seemed possible that Teresa's "rhetoric for women" was a "rhetoric of femininity," that is, a strategy which exploited certain stereotypes about women's character and language. Rather than "writing like a

[93] Ibid. OC 4:444.

[94] It seems likely that Sor Juana did endure some investigation from the Holy Office. The publication of her *Carta Athenagórica* brought with it a flurry of items written both to condemn her and also to support her. Some prominent theologians of Spain supported her and their words were printed in the front of an edition of her works published in Spain. The investigation and possible censure will be considered in chapter 5. See Elías Trabulse, *Años Finales de Sor Juana: Una Interpretación (1688–1695)* (Mexico City: Centro de Estudios de Historia de México Condumex, 1995).

[95] Weber, *Teresa of Avila and the Rhetoric of Femininity*, 159. Weber concludes, however, that in so doing Teresa also silenced other women.

woman," perhaps Teresa wrote as she believed women were *perceived* to speak.[96]

Using the work of Ernst Robert Curtius, who discusses the ancient history of modesty formulas and "affected modesty" as *captatio benevolentiae*, Weber gives attention to the likelihood that some of the phrases used by Teresa and others may be standard expressions used to "dispose the reader favorably toward the writer."[97] She explains that the "modesty formulas could also be used to offset the presumption implied when the writer expressed the expertise that conferred on him the privilege to take up the pen."[98] She provides a sampling of humility formulas in medieval and early Renaissance Spanish texts:

> The author is a sinner and inadequate to his literary task; it is only through divine intervention that he will be able to succeed; he writes under difficult conditions and therefore cannot produce a polished work; he writes only at the command of a superior or at the behest of friends; he bemoans his rustic speech; his work will doubtless require emendation by superior scholars.[99]

Although recognizing that one could then certainly expect Teresa's self-effacing language to serve these common functions, she does not attribute Teresa's modest rhetoric to this alone, but describes Teresa's linguistic strategy as "mixed."

A cursory survey of the two letters under examination in this chapter reveals Sor Juana's implementation of each of the six conventions listed by Weber: (1) She is unworthy or inadequate to her literary task: Sor Juana writes that she knows herself to be "incapable of understanding" and "unworthy of handling" sacred texts;[100] she asks how should she "dare" take sacred subjects into her "unworthy hands" when her sex, age, and, above all, custom oppose it?;[101] and she asks, as she is "distant" from "virtue and learning," how she could "find the courage to write?"[102] (2) She will succeed in her argument only because of divine intervention: Sor Juana says that if her letter "has achieved

---

[96] Ibid., 11.

[97] Ibid., 49. Weber is referencing Ernst Robert Curtius, *Literature and the Latin Middle Ages*, trans. Willard R. Trask, 1953 (reprint ed., New York: Harper and Row 1963) 84–85.

[98] Weber, 49.

[99] Ibid.

[100] *Respuesta,* Arenal and Powell, 45. OC 4:443.

[101] OC 4:443.

[102] OC 4:449.

some success, it is not the work of [her] understanding, but rather only that God desired to punish, through such a weak instrument, the pride of the author's assertion."[103] (3) Difficult conditions prevent the writer from producing a more polished piece of work: She says if she thought her "letter would be published, [she] would have polished its rough style,"[104] and that she had to write the letter with speed, which did not leave her time to polish her discourse.[105] (4) She writes only at the command of a superior or at the request of others: Sor Juana states that "although [her] arguments are unpolished, terse, and unlearned," she has "obeyed Your Grace's order";[106] she explains that she was never considered herself "to be learned or to have that kind of genius that carries with it the obligation to write";[107] and she claims that she has "never written anything of [her] own volition, but always at the request, and to the specifications, of others," stating that the only thing she remembers writing for her own pleasure "is a trifle called *The Dream*."[108] (5) She regrets that her writing is so unsophisticated: Sor Juana states that if her critic thinks her *Carta Athenagórica* "sounds uncouth," then "he is right" and his laughter is warranted.[109] And lastly, (6) Her work requires correction by superior minds: Sor Juana not only invites correction from Sor Filoeta/Fernández, but she claims to "think and believe that anyone could improve on [her] arguments to an infinite degree."[110]

Sor Juana may very well use such accepted rhetorical formulas to make her writing palatable to a society that is skeptical even of women's right to study, not to mention to critique the sermon of a respected priest. On one level, many of Sor Juana's statements fit the type, and one can, of course, hear the irony in these statements as she proves throughout her entire letter how learned she actually is and how confident she is that her love of learning is from God. However, when one examines the actual content of these two letters by Sor Juana, one discovers that she is not simply kowtowing to authorities and customs, but she is arguing for epistemic humility to be practiced by all those who would presume to take up the study of the sacred. We know Sor Juana was

[103] *Carta Athenagórica,* Kirk, 243. OC 4:434–35.

[104] *Respuesta,* Trueblood, 237. OC 4:468–69.

[105] *Carta Athenagórica,* Kirk, 243. OC 4:434.

[106] Ibid. OC 4:434.

[107] *Respuesta,* Kirk, 257. OC 4:447.

[108] Ibid., Trueblood, 239. OC 4:471.

[109] Ibid., 237. OC 4:469.

[110] *Carta Athenagórica,* Kirk, 220. OC 4:413.

not bashful or timid in her positions, as is well expressed in the recently uncovered *Carta de Monterrey* where she boldly confronts her confessor and Inquisitor Núñez de Miranda. Though one can hear some fear behind her rhetoric in her *Respuesta,* based upon her tenuous position as a woman in her context, it is clear that she is taking a strong and bold stance against the arrogance and theologically unsound nature of authoritarian control over sacred studies.[111]

According to Weber, Teresa of Avila uses phrases that suggest imprecision in her argumentation throughout her corpus.[112] Weber gives the example of Teresa's use of the verb "*parecer*" ("to seem") throughout the *Interior Castle*, and other expressions that suggest uncertainty in one's assertions. Teresa remarks on her own use of the phrase as a means of expressing that even though she believes this to be truth, there is still room for mistake: "In difficult matters even though it seems to me that I understand and that I speak the truth, I always

---

[111] In this *Carta de Monterrey,* for example, she makes arguments closely related to the heart of this study and our reading of her writings. For example, on the need for persuasion rather than authoritarian command or coercion, she writes: "Am I perchance a heretic? And if I were, could I become saintly solely through coercion? Would it were so, I should surely be saintly; but I judge that one is persuaded, not commanded, and if by command, I have had Prelates to so command; but precepts and external coercion that make one circumspect and modest when they are moderate and prudent cause despair when they are too strong; only God's grace and assistance can make a saint" (Paz, 500). When she discusses her decision to dismiss her confessor if he cannot find favor for her within himself, she writes about the varieties of human natures, and ways of relating to and thinking of God. She says salvation rests on God's grace rather than on "accurate" and certain knowledge or on "official" theological positions. If salvation is based on something within the individual, it is desire and not actual knowledge itself. She writes: "God, Who created and redeemed me and Who has bestowed so many mercies upon me, will supply a remedy in order that my soul, awaiting his kindness, shall not be lost even though it lack the direction of Y.R., for He has made many keys to Heaven and has not confined Himself to a single criterion; rather, there are many mansions for people of as many different natures, and in the world there are many theologians, but were they lacking, salvation lies more in the desiring than in the knowing, and that will be more in me than in my confessor" (Paz, 502).

[112] Or again, I suggest this may also serve as a rhetorical recognition of the tentative nature of objective truth claims.

use the expression 'it seems to me.'"[113] Teresa leaves an openness here for her arguments to be improved upon. She writes, "For if I am mistaken, I'm very much prepared to believe what those who have a great deal of learning say."[114] Teresa also claims ignorance and "repeatedly denies possessing literary skill, much less theological certainty or authority," much like Sor Juana does one century later in New Spain.[115] Teresa's use of expressions of feigned ignorance, humility, and uncertainty may be her attempt to write in a way she believed women were perceived to speak, as Weber argues. In the context of Sor Juana's work, however, and quite possibly here for Teresa as well, the expressions also serve to make a point about the tentative nature of theological claims and the way such claims should be communicated. These expressions suggest an openness to the ideas of others, room for the arguments to be improved upon, a tolerance of other opinions, and "politeness" in discourse.

"Politeness" Strategies and Epistemic Humility

Weber utilizes the work of sociolinguists Penelope Brown and Stephen Levinson to develop her case for Teresa's "mixed" linguistic strategy. I likewise find that the studies of Brown and Levinson and other socio- and feminist linguists offer insight into Sor Juana's epistolary communication, particularly her use of verbal hedges throughout to temper her statements and claims. These sorts of rhetorical techniques, found in texts by Teresa and Sor Juana, are not unique to their time, language, or gender. Brown and Levinson, through an examination of a number of unrelated languages and cultures, consider this a "universal in language usage."[116] They find these formulas and postures across cultures to actually signify "politeness," and they developed a model from their findings showing "politeness" to be a rational and strategic behavior, which utilizes differing strategies based on particular circumstances.

Brown and Levinson find that speakers use strategies of politeness in communication when they are attempting to preserve the hearer's "face," and to

[113] Weber, 107. Quote from *The Book of Her Life,* in *The Collected Works of St. Teresa of Avila*, trans. Kieran Kavanaugh and Otilio Rodríguez (Washington D.C.: Institute of Carmelite Studies, 1976) 74–75.

[114] Ibid.

[115] Ibid.

[116] Penelope Brown and Stephen Levinson, "Universals in Language Usage: Politeness Phenomena," in *Questions and Politeness*, ed. Esther N. Goody (Cambridge: Cambridge University Press, 1978). Weber applies some aspects of the Brown-Levinson study to Teresa's rhetoric as well.

prevent the speaker from "losing" his or her own. "Face" is a term derived from public usage in expressions like "losing face" and "saving face," and it refers to a person's public self-image and need to be respected. When a verbal interaction takes place, a person using a strategy of politeness will speak in a way as to not impose upon the other person or threaten the hearer's "face." Forms of politeness give "face" to the addressee or express those attempts by the speaker to actually "counteract the potential face damage" of the speech, "by doing it in such a way, or with such modifications or additions, that indicate clearly that no such face threat is intended or desired," and that the speaker recognizes, and actually wants to see, the "face wants" of the hearer to be achieved.[117]

Brown and Levinson identify two forms of politeness, which in turn serve to categorize a variety of hedges and verbal formulas. Positive politeness is a strategy by which the speaker demonstrates that she considers the hearer to be "the same," with "in-group rights and duties and expectations of reciprocity."[118] Negative politeness is aimed toward a preservation of the hearer's basic desire for self-determination and to guard against the address taking a coercive, forceful tone. Among the characteristics of negative politeness are hedges and "other softening mechanisms that give the addressee an 'out,' a face-saving line of escape, permitting him to feel that his response is not coerced."[119]

Politeness strategies are contrasted with Grice's Maxims, which are basic intuitive guidelines "for achieving maximally efficient communication."[120] The maxims are divided into those of Quality, Quantity, Relevance, and Manner, and the general principles are that one's communication be truthful, concise yet sufficient, relevant, orderly, and avoiding ambiguity and obscurity of expression. However, Levinson and Brown point out that most conversations do not proceed in such a "brusque" manner, and these sociolinguists set out to demonstrate "that one powerful and pervasive motive for *not* talking Maxim-wise is the desire to give some attention to face."[121] They explain that the primary reason for not using politeness strategies is that the speaker is more concerned with "maximum efficiency" than s/he is concerned "to any degree"

---

117 Brown and Levinson, 75.

118 Ibid.

119 Ibid.

120 Ibid., 100.

121 Ibid.

with the hearer's "face."[122] Levinson and Brown give two classes of reasons for this sort of communication: either emergency or those cases where the speaker ignores "face" or considers it irrelevant.[123]

A speaker may use verbal hedges, such as "I think," "I believe," and "I presume," in order to avoid the presumption that the hearer's assessment of the situation or contribution to the dialogue is the same as the speaker's, and to keep the communication from taking on a coercive force. Thus they prevent the statement from taking the form of a certain truth statement, which would seem to require the hearer's assent, and instead, the hedges give the hearer room to agree or disagree by creating a sort of distance for difference.[124] The study also concludes that strategies of politeness are used to convey a level of mutual respect between the conversing parties.[125]

The more controversial elements of the study reside in the discovery that, across cultures, women use politeness strategies more often than men, suggesting to Levinson and Brown that women are generally more sensitive to the "face-needs" of others. They also propose that one possible factor contributing to this phenomenon is the vulnerability of women in most cultures, such that more acts in which women engage are defined as "face-threatening." One example they give is that for a woman to speak to a man to whom she is not related is itself "face-threatening" in some cultures. So based on power dynamics in society, women proceed more often with such "politeness."[126]

Feminist sociolinguist Robin Lakoff published her assessment of similar patterns in her 1975 work, *Language and Woman's Place*. She goes beyond the observation of potential tendencies across genders to attribute value to one style of communication over and against the other, and concluded that the "negative" forms of politeness illustrated above actually constitute a weaker use of language. Lakoff assumes that many of the tendencies in women's speech are signs of weakness or subjection, of male dominance and female acquiescence. She interprets women's use of politeness hedges, for example, negatively such that the woman using them in speech is accepting the weak role assigned by

[122] Ibid.

[123] Ibid.

[124] Ibid., 169, 177.

[125] Ibid., 183.

[126] Ibid., 257. Sociolinguist Jennifer Coates asks if this tendency is due also in part to the nature of the conversations in which the two genders tend to engage.

society.[127] Lakoff's ideas were influential in sparking a growing debate in the field of gender difference in sociolinguistics, and though her conclusions are not particularly well received by the scholarly community, she did spur many rigorous research projects on the topic.[128] More recent research, like that of Jennifer Coates and Levinson and Brown, suggests that not only are there many factors involved, these tendencies in women's speech may actually be more appropriate for society at large. Lakoff is accused of judging women's speech by masculine standards in her assumption that the aggressive assertiveness of male speech patterns are stronger and more desirable, leading her to conclude

---

[127] Allyson Jule provides this summary of Lakoff's book and the debate it ignited: "In it, she argued that women have a different way of speaking from men—a way of speaking that reflects and produces a subordinate position in society. According to Lakoff, women's language is full of linguistic and paralinguistic devices that render women's speech tentative, powerless, and trivial. As such, Lakoff believed that women's use of language disqualified them from positions of power and authority. Their use of particular linguistic strategies, such as using rising intonation, hedges (such as 'kind of' or 'sort of'), intensifiers ('very,' 'so') or their use of more tag questions are examples of gendered linguistic tendencies. In this way, language serves as a tool of oppression, an oppression that women collude in by way of their using such strategies. Such patterns are learned as part of learning to be a woman, imposed on women by societal expectations, and used by women to rehearse themselves into supportive and submissive roles.... Her view that women and men talk differently propelled a central debate in the field of feminist linguistics, what became known as the Deficit/Dominance/Difference Debate that raged for 20 years or so. Those 1970s scholars who explained the difference as a woman's deficit (like Lakoff did) influenced others in the 1980s (like Dale Spender) to assert that women spoke in such submissive ways because they had been dominated and required by men to do so. Others in the 1990s (like Deborah Tannen) suggested that the differences are simply there and benign." Allyson Jule, "Silence as Femininity? A Look at Performances of Gender in Theology College Classrooms," in *Being Feminist, Being Christian: Essays from Academia*, ed. Allyson Jule and Bettina Tate Pedersen (New York: Palgrave Macmillan, 2006) 38.

[128] My assessment of Lakoff's work is informed by Jennifer Coates, Dale Spender, Levinson and Brown, and Allyson Jule. Spender says Lakoff looks at "lack" and deficiency in women's speech by comparing it to masculine speech—"she states that women *lack* authority and seriousness, they *lack* conviction and confidence. In her view, in comparison with the (ostensibly) forceful and effective language of men, women are tentative, hesitant, even trivial, and are therefore 'deficient'" (Dale Spender, *Man Made Language*, 2nd ed. (London: Routledge Kegan Paul, 1980) 8.

that this style should be assumed by women if the sex is to advance in society. Instead, Coates argues, and the research she cites suggests, that in many instances the goal might rather be to change the acceptable speech patterns themselves such that the conversational speech style more often employed by women becomes the desirable standard in many contexts.[129]

Coates explains how change in the status of women is closely related to this re-evaluation of accepted modes of speech in various situations. Using the work of social psychologist Henri Tajfel, who studied inter-group dynamics and social change, Coates outlines a variety of approaches taken by those assigned to an "inferior group," such as women historically have been.[130] One option, according to Tajfel's theory, is to reject the "inferior status." One way to accomplish this is to "assimilate with the superior group and demand equality."[131] In this stage women "redefine themselves in terms of *male*

---

[129] These studies may idealize women and women's ways. I do not intend to weigh in significantly on that debate, but to present their research to highlight the radical proposal Sor Juana makes subtly in these letters.

[130] Tajfel finds that those of a social group of "inferior status" would either accept the conditions of the "superior" group and attempt to assimilate according to the standards of the "superior" group or would accept the "inferior status" by comparing themselves to others in the "inferior" position, and strive to become the best within that group, according to the standards assigned to that group by the "superior" group. Coates sees this at work among women who compare themselves to other women in regard to their physical appearance, cooking, housekeeping, and the like, as these are values assigned to women by patriarchal society. The other approach in this category, when applied to women, suggests that some women instead model their behavior after perceived male behavior. Coates writes of those who utilize this strategy that the woman "operates successfully in the men's world and becomes, to all intents and purposes, a man," but she notes this does nothing for the group as a whole as it doesn't challenge the standards and only affords success for the one individual woman (J. Coates, 9). I remind the reader of Cixous's similar observation about women writers, quoted earlier in the introduction: "It is well known that the number of women writers…has always been ridiculously small. This is a useless and deceptive fact unless from their species of female writers we do not first deduct the immense majority whose workmanship is in no way different from male writing and which either obscures women or reproduces the classic representations of women" (Cixous, 1092). Both note that this last approach can actually hinder progress for other women. Weber draws a similar conclusion concerning Teresa's "rhetoric of femininity," which reinforced assumptions of "women's writing" and thus silenced other women.

[131] J. Coates, 9.

values."[132] Coates notes ways that women do this in speech, assuming the male standard: (1) "they use deeper voices (lower in pitch)"; (2) "they swear and use taboo language"; (3) "they adopt a more assertive style in group interaction"; (4) "they adopt prosodic features more typical of men (e.g., falls rather than rising intonation patterns)"; and (5) "they address themselves in public to traditionally male topics."[133] This approach shares some commonalities with Second Wave and Liberal Feminism where equality is emphasized to the point that some believe difference is denied. The skills and capacities highlighted tend to be those already valued by (male-dominant) society. The benefit of this approach is that it has paved the way for women to excel in fields once barred them, but one limit is the insistence on sameness does not challenge the predetermined values of patriarchal society.

Another strategy to reject the "inferior status" involves a re-evaluation of those characteristics that were once relegated as the weaker traits of the inferior group, such that the group rejecting their inferior status insist that certain characteristics typical of their group actually carry high social value at large. Tajfel finds this strategy to be the most effective for social change, and he notes that it most commonly follows chronologically the previous one described. Applying Tajfel's findings to her work in gender and sociolinguistics, Coates notes that some women "have begun to stress the value to society of stereotyped female qualities such as gentleness, caring for others, sensitivity. This has led in turn to a re-evaluation of stereotyped male qualities such as aggression and competitiveness, and an awareness that such qualities are not always socially functional."[134] What she describes sounds much like the feminist position stemming from the "cult of womanhood," often labeled "romantic feminism" or "essentialist feminism," usually pejoratively.[135] Such a move to highlight "women's ways" as nurturing, for example, while it can challenge public values typically labeled "masculine," nonetheless lifts traits that a patriarchal society has deemed "feminine," and so neither does it function outside a patriarchal framework. This approach also tends to universalize women's experience, denying significant differences among women of differing contexts—social class, race, sexual orientation, nation, and the like.

---

[132] Ibid., 10.

[133] Ibid.

[134] Ibid.

[135] What we have, then, are two strategies observed by Tajfel and Coates that loosely describe two types of feminism that have been at odds for decades.

As a sociolinguist, Coates examines how this approach is evidenced in language use; she writes:

> The most significant move seems to be a reappraisal by women of the relative merits of cooperative as opposed to competitive strategies in conversation. Research carried out in this field suggests that men typically adopt a competitive style in conversation, treating their turn as a chance to overturn earlier speakers' contributions and to make their own point as forcibly as possible. Women on the other hand, in conversation with other women, typically adopt a cooperative mode: they add to rather than demolish other speakers' contributions, they are supportive of others, they tend not to interrupt each other ...Researchers discussing this difference comment that women are beginning to value their style and to resent being forced to adopt the male mode in mixed interaction.... It seems that women's less assertive, more cooperative style in group interaction is being revalued positively by women speakers, and conversely, men's style is being criticized.[136]

Her work is seconded by the findings of Susan Gal, who, while not suggesting that less conflict occurs in female groups, likewise notes studies that find males more prone to interact competitively in conversation and to organize themselves hierarchically, whereas the females in the studies more often practice a collaborative approach, supporting each other's ideas and building upon the statements of others.[137] There is some evidence to support these

---

[136] Ibid., 10–11.

[137] Susan Gal in her sociolinguistic study, "Between Speech and Silence," notes studies on gender differences in conversation. She says: "boys and men organize into relatively large hierarchical groups, using direct commands and vying with one another for leadership positions by holding forth in competitive verbal display. Side comments and challenges are the proper responses by those who do not have the floor. Girls, by contrast, play in smaller groups, forming exclusive coalitions. There is plenty of conflict in all-girl groups, but their verbal interactions implicitly deny conflict and hierarchy, phrasing commands as proposals for future activity (Goodwin 1980). Girls and women carefully link their utterances to the previous speaker's contribution and develop one another's topics, asking questions for conversational maintenance rather than for information or challenge." She continues, "One way of interpreting the female strategies is as a set of practices that, whatever the actual power relations within the girls' or women's group, nevertheless enact values of support and solidarity that directly oppose and implicitly criticize the boys' and men's practices of heroic individuality, competition, and the celebration of hierarchy." (Susan Gal, "Between Speech and Silence: The Problematics of Research on Language and Gender," in *Gender at the*

findings in feminist theology, where many collaborative projects are published, for example, and "round tables" are a regular part of the publication of *The Journal of Feminist Studies in Religion* and are also a feature typical of feminist pedagogy.

The application of this research to Sor Juana's argument and interpretation of her letters is fruitful. Most of the studies relate to oral exchanges and conversation, but the dialogical style of the letter makes it an appropriate comparison, as Weber also found in her study of Teresa's linguistic strategies.

Some interpretations of Sor Juana's work emphasize her insistence on the equality of women's intellect to men's, which she does forcefully in *Respuesta*. Unfortunately the focus on her claims of equality resulted in the misunderstanding of her use of "modesty clauses" and hedges as inauthentic "false modesty," and thus her strategic use of them are overlooked. Her hedges, like those utilized by Teresa ("it seems to me," "I think," "I believe"), and her openness to have her arguments "improved upon" serve a purpose, as she insists that these ways of communicating are actually more desirable in theology. She clearly criticizes the combative and competitive style of religious discourse that sociolinguistic studies claim often typifies male manners of communication, and she models and proposes a dialogical style that sociolinguists find to be more typical of women.[138]

Therefore Sor Juana may, in fact, be making an even bolder claim than simply one of equality. She appears to be taking the step Tajfel describes as initiating actual social change, by stressing the value of a type of communication now understood to be more typical of women, critiquing the dominant approach to theological discourse, and encouraging all those who enter the debate to proceed in that style of communication she models in openness and epistemic humility.

My concern here is not to determine the cause of these observations in sociolinguistics or even the validity of the gendered claims: Do women work more collaboratively and less competitively in groups as Gal's research

---

Crossroads of Knowledge: Feminist Anthropology in the Postmodern Era, ed. M. di Leonardo (Berkeley: University of California Press, 1991)184. See also M. Goodwin, "Directive-Response Speech Sequences in Girls' and Boys' Task Activities," in *Women and Language in Literature and Society*, ed. S. McConnell-Ginet, R. Borker, and N. Furman (New York: Praeger, 1980).

[138] I do not deny that there are a variety of reasons persons utilize one style of communication rather than another.

suggests? Do women use hedges more frequently because they are less frequently in positions of power? Do women actually care more about the "face" of the other in communication? These and many more are all interesting questions. For the sake of this analysis of Sor Juana's message on theological communication, however, my conclusion does not require these answers. I am not even particularly concerned if it is true that women speak this way more than men and men more often proceed "Maxim-wise." What does interest me, however, is that Sor Juana, in her own way, long preceding these studies, takes a stand regarding the way in which religious discourse should proceed, and that is in a way that shows concern for "face." She uses these strategies not only because she is a woman religious, required to submit to the ecclesial patriarchy and hierarchy, but because she thinks arrogance and claims of certain knowledge in religious discourse are inadequate.

I understand that I must proceed with caution on a number of fronts. (1) Sor Juana was not a feminist in any proper sense of the term as a seventeenth-century figure. I also take to heart warnings like that issued by Carole A. Myscofski, when she writes of her worry "that our expectations of [Sor Juana]—to be the new feminist voice, the first feminist voice in the Americas, the inspiration for feminist writers or theologians—will result in a new and unrecognizable image."[139] I do not intent to suggest Sor Juana utilized these strategies with a feminist self-awareness. However, I also have a constructive proposal at work that utilizes Sor Juana's insight to challenge contemporary religious discourse and theology, much like a theologian may use the work of Calvin or Augustine or Julian of Norwich to further contemporary constructive theology. I simply want to highlight what views on theological discourse are operative here. (2) This very notion that there are "women's ways" and "men's ways" is highly contentious and problematic. Some women communicate one way and some another, as with men; truly today even those categories of male and female are themselves contested.[140]

I use these studies to point out not that women do this and so does Sor Juana, but (1) that Sor Juana identifies the way that most theological discourse proceeds and explicitly labels it arrogant, competitive, and even dangerous; and 2) that Sor Juana models a form of religious discourse that shows concern for "face." This modeling is, in part, related to her use of these hedges; thus, I

---

[139] Myscofski, 306.

[140] See, for example the influential works of Judith Butler, including her essay: "The End of Sexual Difference?" in *Undoing Gender* (New York: Routledge, 2004).

argue, they should not be discounted as false modesty or simply the expectation of women writers.

Positive politeness strategies communicate to the hearer that s/he is welcomed, is considered part of "the group" (or is not an outsider), and has the same rights to be heard and understood. It also suggests that there is expectation of reciprocity, a back and forth between the two persons. Politeness strategies also simultaneously convey a sense that the speaker does not think the hearer must agree, but presents an openness to difference of opinion. People use these strategies, according to Brown and Stevenson, specifically to create an environment of exchange in which the hearer does not feel pressured or coerced by what is communicated, but instead feels respected and free to self-determine. These strategies express that the speaker does not intend to offend or disregard the freedom of the other, but truly desires that the "face needs" of the other are met. Alternatively, one who is more concerned with efficiency than the "face" of the other will proceed "Maxim-wise," such that the speech is more likely to be coercive, forceful, and/or aggressive; the self-determination of the other is not a consideration.

Throughout her work and letters, Sor Juana says conversion and change of heart and mind cannot come through coercion, but must be reached freely. According to Brown and Stevenson, the best way to communicate so as to respect the freedom of the other is through these "politeness" strategies. Finally, not only does Sor Juana model this in her use of hedges, like "it seems" and "I believe," she calls theologians, preachers, and all involved in religious discourse to proceed in similar fashion—respecting the freedom of the other, recognizing that what they share is their opinion, and remaining open to the views of the other.

And she is not alone. I remind the reader of Kierkegaard's frequent use of "suppose" and "perhaps" in his *Concluding Unscientific Postscript.* As discussed in chapter 1, Kierkegaard's pseudonym, Johannes Climacus, encourages the use of "perhaps" following the example of Lessing. By using these hedges, the speaker keeps the conversation open to differing opinions and allows the hearer to respond without coercion, to appropriate the ideas for her/himself rather than sense the requirement that it be received word for word as in a direct form of communication. He writes:

> Suppose that someone wished to communicate the following conviction: Truth is inwardness: there is no objective truth, but truth consists in personal appropriation.* — *I say only "suppose": and in this form I have the right to posit both what is most certain and what is most absurd. For even the certain is

> not posited as certain, but only as a supposition, to throw light on the relationship involved (to the individual being addressed) and even the absurd is not posited essentially, but only hypothetically in order to illustrate the consequence of the relationship.[141]

Kierkegaard not only prefaces statements with politeness hedges under his pseudonym Johannes Climacus, he also argues that this softening of the absolute nature of the claims of systematic theology would make the project more honest, as well as more fitting to the task of introducing the reader to a moment of decision within her/himself for appropriation of Christian truth and the transformation of the person's life.

There are very few theological statements that one can absolutely affirm, and even those are still dependent on faith because the subjective appropriation of Christianity is at the heart of Christian knowledge. Even the most basic theological assertions assume at minimum a faith in the existence of God. It seems, therefore, that many theological works should simply begin with a "Perhaps" and then continue on with the argument, much like we find in the sort of theological discourse advocated in *Concluding Unscientific Postscript* and Kierkegaard's work as a whole. Kierkegaard stated in his journal that if Hegel had prefaced his *Logic* with the statement that what follows is a "thought-experiment," then Hegel would "have been the greatest thinker to have ever lived." Without such a preface, however, Hegel's system presumes a complete and absolute truth, which Kierkegaard says makes Hegel comical.[142]

The whole conception of indirect communication is such that the speaker does not impose something upon the hearer, but in the very moment of communicating must also attempt to remove her/himself from it, so the communication is not about the speaker, but about the idea. It is true that Kierkegaard eventually affirms a form of direct communication, but this is primarily a "bearing witness." It is a step away from statements such as "This is who God is" or a "defining" of God. It is more modest. It includes the politeness hedge "I believe," the very sort of distancing technique highlighted by Levinson and Brown, which in its personal form does not bear the coercive

---

[141] Søren Kierkegaard, *Concluding Unscientific Postscript*, trans. and ed. Howard V. Hong and Edna H. Hong (Princeton: Princeton University Press, 1992) 71.

[142] Søren Kierkegaard, *Søren Kierkegaard's Journals and Papers,* vol. 2, F–K, ed. and trans. Howard V. Hong and Edna H. Hong (Bloomington and London: Indiana University Press, 1970) 217, entry no. 1605.

weight of direct statements without such hedges, which they call "bald, on-record." The hedge is also used to indicate the non-spurious nature of the communication, its sincerity.

These modesty formulas and politeness hedges are not simply a gender issue. Certainly there are power dynamics at work, both in terms of social hierarchies and gender, that should not be ignored in the historical context of the works of Teresa and Sor Juana, but as Weber has pointed out in Teresa-studies, these women are not simply pawns of their context. They employ rhetorical strategies with intention and skill. In Sor Juana's case, we know she is highly educated, intellectually astute, and not without power and influence. Even as she humbles herself before the authority of the Bishop of Puebla and the Holy Office, she asserts her rights, her position, and her abilities. She brilliantly uses conventional modesty formulas and "polite" forms of dialogue to make a significant point about the posture all humans should take when communicating theological thought.

Both Kierkegaard and Sor Juana utilize a form of discourse that encourages the reader to develop her own response to the ideas presented. [143] Although in these letters Sor Juana does not use the hedge "perhaps" like Kierkegaard, nor does she use "*parecer*" as frequently or to the same purpose as Teresa, she does, however, uses modesty and politeness hedges throughout her letters. She uses "*parecer*" (to seem) as well as "*creer*" (to believe), and repeatedly highlights that what she is stating is her opinion or her view. Some examples, among many, of her use of these words and phrases are as follows: "I believe it is true that"[144]; "it seems" [145]; "I think and believe"[146]; "it appears to me"[147]; "I think I have"[148]; "in my opinion"[149]; "I say that I am not here

[143] I recognize that Sor Juana's situation was not simple but complex and tense due to her position, time, and social location. The differences between what may have led these two thinkers to develop similar expressions in their writing are significant. My analysis of Sor Juana's work asserts that she urges for limits on the arrogance of theological claims not only for herself because that is expected and even required of her in her day and context, but for everyone presuming to take up sacred matters.

[144] OC 4:434–35.

[145] OC 4:434–35.

[146] *Carta Athenagórica,* Kirk, 220.

[147] Ibid., 229.

[148] Ibid.

[149] Ibid., 244, and again on 245.

engaging in a rebuttal but simply relating my opinion";[150] "[W]as there anything more to that than simply setting forth my views without exceeding the limits of our Holy Mother Church allows?";[151] "I am not asking him to applaud me, since, just as I was free to dissent from Vieira, so anyone else is to dissent from my opinions";[152] "Failure to do so, in my view, has given rise precisely to all those sectarians and been the root cause of all the heresies."[153]

It seems unlikely, when read in the context of her concerns as here expounded, that Sor Juana is solely softening her claims with these hedges to make them more palatable because she is a woman, nor are her claims of ignorance solely feminine self-deprecation in order to not appear outside her rights as a woman. She has made clear that she believes what she is doing is very much within her rights and the rights of anyone else with strong intellectual abilities. "So what is there so criminal, considering that I refrain even from what is legitimate for women, which is to teach through writing."[154] She is acting according to her own view of the appropriate posture in theological discourse: non-coercive and tentative, open to the opinions of others, tolerant, and non-combative.

Sor Juana makes strong statements based on close study and vast knowledge, and meanwhile claims she does not know. Her move is not so different from that of Socrates, who proves himself to be the most wise by being the one who can recognize that he does not know. Sor Juana is not doing "women's theology," but I argue she claims that all engaged in the discipline should hamper their arrogant claims of ultimacy or assurance of accuracy through a stance more open to true dialogue and interplay of ideas, through a "perhaps" or the recognition that this is a thought-experiment or opinion, and through holding their positions in a way that is open for improvement. Religious discourse should take a turn to humility.

The open dialogical discourse modeled for us by Sor Juana and Kierkegaard is of a sort that takes into consideration the "face" of the other, that respects the reader's desire for, and right of, self-determination. It allows for a sort of internal persuasion without coercion. This is perhaps a strategy hardly avoidable for Sor Juana as she was a woman writing in a patriarchal church

---

[150] Ibid., 220. OC 4:413.

[151] *Respuesta,* Trueblood, 237. OC 4:468.

[152] Ibid. OC 4:469.

[153] Ibid., 230. OC 4:462.

[154] Ibid., 236. OC 4:468.

context.[155] Nonetheless she models a form of discourse quite different from what surrounded her. While the Inquisition kept a tight rein and a watchful eye, not only on what people wrote but also on what they read, she directly invited others to disagree with her and voice their opinions in opposition.[156]

Sor Juana welcomes views different from her own through her epistemic humility, "politeness" of discourse, and openness to the freedom of opinion. Recognizing the limits of human knowledge of the divine and the limits of language, Sor Juana does not dare to assume any ultimate perspective on divine truth, yet this does not keep her from seeking to understand and continuing to invite dialogue with others. One way in which she holds this stance successfully is through the use of the letter rather than the form of a theological treatise. Her *Carta Athenagórica* is the closest thing to a theological treatise we have by Sor Juana, but even this, with its pointed views on the appropriate form of theological claims and her perceptive arguments on the love of Christ, is written as a letter. Thus it is written to a particular person with: greetings and salutations, the personal elements that recognize both the other and the freedom of the other's rationality, and the inherent invitation to dialogue, which are so characteristic of the letter.

The Form of the Letter

The importance of correspondence in philosophical thought development is not a new concept. Leibniz and Clarke carried on a productive exchange of letters, as did Leo Strauss and Eric Voegelin. Franz Rosenzweig is also known to have formulated much of his philosophy and theology through correspondence. To develop one's theology in correspondence, and thus through dialogue, is to remain true to the nature of religious knowledge, which is not set, complete, or absolute, but relational. To develop one's theology through interaction with another person seeking truth reflects the open, progressive, and non-static form of religious knowledge that is found only through transformation, ongoing process, and relationship. To develop one's theology in respectful dialogue resists the entrenchment so common to much theological thought. Instead of coming at the other with one's position utterly determined, each brings ideas with the chance of learning from another, of change, and of discovery. This is reflected in theological method; it insists upon the dialectic, not a Hegelian

[155] See Leonard.

[156] See Leonard, especially "On the Book Trade, 1683," 157–71.

dialectic that ends in resolution and closure, but of the sort Kierkegaard proposes, one that remains open.

Janet Gurkin Altman provides a critical study of the epistolary form. Her analysis of the unique form of the letter in communication applies to many shared characteristics of the epistle, whether it is a fictive construction of the author or the real record of a correspondence. I will use her analysis of these characteristics to highlight exemplary features in the form of epistolary discourse for the communication of theological concepts in accordance with the concerns raised by Sor Juana in her own letters. If theological writing should be humble, "polite," and open to the opinions and views of others in a tolerant, non-combative posture because of the nature of Christian knowledge, then the letter in its very structure helps shape the discourse in a manner corresponding with this.

Altman identifies three features that distinguish epistolary discourse from other literary forms like memoir, rhetoric, or theater. First is the distinct "I-you" voice and context of the letter. The other two features deal with the particular temporal nature of the epistolary form. First, the present tense plays a pivotal function around which the past and the future orient. Second is the "temporal polyvalence" of the epistle.

Unlike other forms of discourse where there is no addressee, such as the memoir or diary, or those for which the addressee is anonymous or anyone, as in rhetorical works like a theological treatise, the letter always has a specific "you" who "stands in a unique relationship to the *I*."[157] The letter is open in its very consideration of the addressee, as Altman explains: "In no other genre do readers figure so prominently within the world of the narrative and in the generation of the text."[158] Note that the other, or the addressee, of the letter is integral to the formulation of thought and presentation. The letter, in its recognition of and personal address to the recipient, indicates a valuing of the other. Altman describes the intended recipient as one who "plays an instrumental generative role" from the letter's "very inception."[159] She contrasts it with straight autobiography, which is generally written "without regard for the eventual reader."[160] I include a contrast with a variety of forms of direct

---

[157] Janet Gurkin Altman, *Epistolarity: Approaches to a Form* (Columbus: Ohio State University Press, 1982) 117.

[158] Ibid., 88.

[159] Ibid.

[160] Ibid.

communication that express objective facts that stand outside a relation to the reader, thus making the reader insignificant to the construction. Alternatively, "the letter is by definition never the product of such an 'immaculate conception,' but is rather the result of a union of writer and reader."[161] Letters are not a product of the writer within her/himself but of a writer in relationship to another; ideas are not abstracted away from the person, the relationship, or time, but are at essence situated in a moment and relationship.

The "epistolary experience" is described as a "reciprocal one."[162] The recipient of the letter is considered both "influencing and influenceable," as the writer "simultaneously seeks to affect his reader and is affected by him."[163] The letter is distinguished from the diary, including those written with the purpose of publication in mind, as the letter exhibits "the desire for *exchange*."[164] Altman explains, "To write a letter is not only to define oneself in relationship to a particular *you*; it is also an attempt to draw that *you* into becoming the *I* of a new statement," and she calls those statements the "hallmark of epistolary language" that intentionally "elicit a response from a specific addressee." [165] In this form of communication, the specific reader/addressee is empowered to respond as an agent and writer in turn and thus to contribute to the thought-product.[166]

Discourse is personal and "characterized by the use of *I-you*," while history is nonpersonal, "characterized by the use of *il* (he or it)."[167] The application of this observation is obvious: if theological discourse is to be true to its title, it must preserve the personal, subjective, and dialogical elements of the discipline. The letter does not accommodate the abstracted, impersonal tone of the traditional rhetoric of theological writing. The subjective nature of the topic is inherent in the format of the letter, both in the personal narrative of the writer, who identifies herself, her status, and typically her location in the first lines of the letter and also again in the conclusion of the traditional letter. It is also found in the specificity of the recipient who is addressed directly in the

---

[161] Ibid.

[162] Ibid.

[163] Ibid.

[164] Ibid., 111.

[165] Ibid., 122.

[166] Ibid., 89.

[167] Ibid., 141. Altman here follows Emile Benvesiste's distinction between two fundamental linguistic subsystems (*Problémes de linguistique générale* [I]).

very first greeting and generally again referenced personally in the concluding lines.

The open dialogical form of communication through letter is also rooted in the multitude of perspectives confronted in the structure itself. The monovocal format of much authoritarian writing is bypassed in the multiplicity of voices inherent in the letter. As Altman explains, "epistolary writing, as distinguished from simple first-person writing, refracts events through not one but two prisms—that of reader as well as that of writer. We as external readers must always interpret a given letter in the light of its intended recipient."[168] When one reads a letter, one is already confronting at least three views: that of the writer, the addressee, and oneself reading the correspondence. In *Carta Athenagórica* the reader has four perspectives, when one considers it consists as a response to the words of Vieira.[169]

The other distinguishing characteristics of the letter, according to Altman, pertain to the role of time in the discourse. The traditional structure of the letter points to the very temporality of the discourse and of knowledge itself. The letter begins or ends with the date, stamping the temporal embeddedness of the discourse from the outset. A variety of temporal elements are found in the letter: time past as it narrates past events, as well as time past in the very delay of delivery itself. The present for the writer becomes the past for the reader, and despite all of this, Altman finds that letters are often future-directed. However, it is the present tense that anchors the narration of the letter; the future and past tenses pivot around the author's present. Whereas the preterit tense is dominant in certain forms of narration, like the memoir, the present tense is central to the letter. Yet the present possesses a future-orientation. According to Altman, "interrogatives, imperatives, and future tenses—rarer in other types of narrative are vehicles for expression" characteristic of the letter.[170] She says the letter is "preoccupied" with the future as "each letter arrests the writer in a present whose future is unknown."[171] Tense and time play such unique roles in the letter that it resists those universal abstractions that remove the idea from the temporality of existence and from the concrete. By keeping the ideas situated in

[168] Ibid., 92.

[169] And this presentation of a variety of views, often conflicting ones, is characteristic of Sor Juana's use of dialogue, as we will see in the following chapters, and also found in her *villancicos*.

[170] Altman, 124.

[171] Ibid., 127.

time, the letter provides a medium to call the reader to response, to transformation within temporal life. And with its unique future-directed tone, it is an ideal form for the discussion of ideas that pertain so significantly to the process of becoming, which itself contributes to the unknown nature of the future and resists certain, static knowledge. The letter is an excellent vehicle, then, for communicating the complicated temporal elements in the Christian message: the relation of past events (or most specifically, the Christ-event) to the present and the impact this relationship has upon the future.

This display of "temporal valence" is certainly true of Sor Juana's letters. In the *Carta Athenagórica*, Sor Juana records her past oral response to a sermon Vieira wrote forty years earlier. Her *Respuesta* is written after the considerable delay of the publication of the original letter with the inclusion of a response by the Bishop of Puebla under the guise of Sor Filotea. *La Respuesta* narrates Sor Juana's history from childhood to her present, provides an account of the past events that brought about the writing of the *Carta Athenagórica* and other works, gives argument for current views on women's right to study, and suggests her future intensions to "remain silent."[172]

It is impossible to write a letter that is true to form and yet be atemporal. This is a valuable feature for a theologian who, like Kierkegaard, seeks to avoid the pitfalls of a systematic philosophy that attempts a timeless perspective. His critique of Hegelian philosophy is shared by Rosenzweig, who, as mentioned previously, developed and communicated his philosophy primarily through correspondence. Michael D. Oppenheim highlights this similar concern with temporality in Kierkegaard and Rosenzweig. He states,

> They saw that the timelessness of Systematic Philosophy was not merely an oversight. They held, in fact, that the lack of attention to the individual's personal experience of time was a necessary result of philosophy's endeavour to be systematic and all-inclusive. In viewing the individual through the eyes of a system, the life of change and development was either ignored or redefined in terms of necessity.[173]

---

[172] "Si vos, Señora, gustáredes de que yo haga lo contrario de lo que tenía propuesto a vuestro juicio y sentir, al menor movimiento de vuestro gusto cederá, como es razón, mi dictamen que, como os he dicho, era de callar,..."(OC 4:472).

[173] Michael D. Oppenheim, "Taking Time Seriously: An Inquiry into the Methods of Communication of Søren Kierkegaard and Franz Rosenzweig," *Sciences Religieuses/Studies in Religion* 7, no. 1 (Winter 1978): 53–60.

According to Oppenheim, for Rosenzweig and Kierkegaard, "the element of time determines their selection of a method of communication."[174] Kierkegaard used pseudonyms as a form of indirect communication, and Rosenzweig used the epistolary form. Oppenheim writes:

> In rejecting previous philosophy's understanding of man, Kierkegaard and Rosenzweig saw that a radical departure from the traditional methods of communicating philosophical knowledge had become necessary. Kierkegaard and Rosenzweig found that their methods of communication had to correspond to their understanding of man's living in time. The content of philosophy could not be divorced from its form and except to be relevant to the individual in existence. Only new forms of communication could securely tie the new philosophy to the real life of man.[175]

As discussed in the previous chapter, the individual's existence in time means that one is always in the process of becoming, and thus, the truth of religion is dynamic, and this should be reflected in the communication of it. In the voice of Johannes Climacus, Kierkegaard calls for the form of the theologian's communication to be "in essential conformity with his mode of existence," which is necessarily temporal.[176] Oppenheim also describes the importance of the temporal for theological discourse in Kierkegaard's work in his contrast between direct and indirect communication. He explains that direct communication "treats knowledge as a fixed matter," and thus, "truth and falsehood can be determined by 'objective' criteria, without regard to the individual who is the recipient of this knowledge."[177] This form "presupposes that the individual stands in a timeless position where all is eternally clear and certain."[178] Direct communication, therefore, resists the personal and temporal dimensions intrinsic to the form of the letter. However, in philosophy and theology the person is central to the knowledge itself, and therefore her/his life in time has consequences for its communication and reception. When the ethical or religious are being communicated, objective certainty of truth cannot be claimed, because "the person who is aware of living in time recognizes that certainty is beyond his grasp. At any particular point in time he is still

[174] Ibid., 56.
[175] Ibid., 60.
[176] Søren Kierkegaard, *Concluding Unscientific Postscript*, 74.
[177] Oppenheim, 56.
[178] Ibid., 57.

developing, and he can have only a partial view of the truth."[179] Oppenheim explains that "since the hearer or reader is always undergoing development, only by relating the truth to his growing religious and ethical awareness does he stand in real relationship to that which is being communicated. …Thus the idea or insight must be formulated in such a manner that it is capable of being inwardly appropriated by the individual."[180]

This is something Jewish theologian and philosopher Franz Rosenzweig took to heart. He distinguished between what he considered "old thinking," that is, a way of doing philosophy as a monologue of the philosopher without regard to temporality, and "new thinking," which recognizes that it is time-bound, does not try to evade temporality, and considers the "you" essential to one's philosophy. "New thinking" sees the human thought process as something similar to human speech, which includes the other in both its address to another and in the expectation of reciprocity of communication. Writing to his fiancé in 1920 about the discovery of acting mutually rather that one-sidedly, Rosenzweig exclaims that he can "no longer write a 'book,' everything now turns to a letter," as he needs to "see the 'other.'"[181] And in a letter known as "Urzelle," in which he lays the intellectual groundwork for *The Star of Redemption*, Rosenzweig writes to Rudolf Ehrenberg in conclusion: "The remainder is philo-logy, i.e. silence. But seriously, what do you say to it? …And I mean you, too: it is certainly only formulated for you; even if I wished to formulate it for Rosenstock, I would have to write it quite differently…. I have written it 'looking at you.'"[182]

Oppenheim illuminates the significance of the epistolary form for the communication of Rosenzweig's philosophy, and his description highlights the appropriateness of this form for the communication of Sor Juana's thought and for the expression of all religious knowledge that takes its subjective nature seriously:

---

[179] Ibid., 56–57.

[180] Ibid., 57.

[181] Rosenzweig in a letter to his fiancée and future wife Edith Hahn, quoted in *Franz Rosenzweig: His Life and Thought*, presented by Nahum N. Glatzer (New York: Schocken Books, 1961) 90.

[182] Franz Rosenzweig, *Philosophical and Theological Writings*, trans. and ed. Paul W. Franks and Michael L. Morgan (Indianapolis: Hackett Publishing Company, Inc., 2000) 70. Rosenzweig writes: "looking at you" in Greek; I have included the editor's translation of the phrase in the text.

> The letter rather than the book or article is true to human time and to speech. A letter is written at a specific time and it reflects the mutual concerns of that time. Like speech, its being bound to the moment is recognized by the fact that it often loses meaning outside the context of a particular time. The letter is an event, a meeting between persons. Like all real meetings it has a special sequence, like the sequence in a conversation—of greeting, questions, answers to past questions, etc. The aspects of time and mutuality in this are easily contrasted with the static form of the book—title, table of contents, preface, etc. An exchange of letters provides the occasion for an open dialogue that may even bring about changes of mood and ideas by the correspondents over time. Of course, the letter needs the other, because it both answers and addresses questions to some other particular person or persons. It is not written "at all times and for everyone."[183]

Conclusion: Theology as Dialogical Correspondence

The need for personal appropriation of religious knowledge defies the direct forms of speech so common to concluded theological systems. How ought the theologian to get at these dynamic aspects of Christianity? One form available to the theologian is the letter, as Sor Juana's work demonstrates. A letter does not make universal claims in the way one finds in a treatise. The letter grounds the discussion in the concrete, keeps it personal, and thus prevents it from becoming grand, universalizing, abstract theory. Its very form suggests opinion, and a sharing of one's ideas with another, and as stated, the letter always has a specific "you" who "stands in a unique relationship to the *I*." It is a form that allows for the inconclusive, temporal, and ongoing nature of Christian knowledge, and takes a non-systematic mode to communicate Christianity's relation to existence. The letter invites dialogue. It is a form that can be true to human existence and the limits of Christian knowing based upon its essential relation to the existing person in time.

When theology takes the form of closed dialectics, or when it creates closed systems that assume completeness, at which point one system is pitted against another in a metaphysical battle, it becomes only another form of competition and warfare. These closed systems are the kinds over which wars are raged and conquests ignited; they are what postmodern thinkers call "totality systems," and it is as such that they have been used to batter and squelch others rather than welcome open dialogue. Sor Juana maintains that ideas of God should be communicated with openness and not in a combative posture or with

[183] Oppenheim, 59–60.

violence.[184] Theological discussion should proceed with patience and tolerance; tolerance does not assume one will surrender one's position, nor that all ideas are equally logical or worthy of support, but it does assume openness and willingness to understand the other. Sor Juana argues that religious discourse should proceed in epistemic humility, a stance that does not simply stem from her womanhood, for which modesty and gentleness have traditionally been considered "feminine" traits, but because of the nature of religious truth, because of the limits on our knowledge of the divine, and so as not to impinge on another's freedom, as coercive or direct communication would hamper true Christian knowledge, which is arrived at through personal appropriation.

Certainly the debate has not been settled in sociolinguistics and gender studies as to whether politeness hedges are simply more naturally common among women or if they are simply characteristic of the speech of those without power. My proposal here is that if theology is not to be a power play, if it is not to be an authoritative form of speech imposed upon the reader or hearer, then the discipline needs to accommodate itself to the speech forms used by those who are not enforcing power, or who are not seeking dominance of thought or language. If Christian knowledge requires subjective appropriation and is thus not absolute or entirely objective, theological discourse ought to take these limitations seriously and honestly reflect them. If theology is to invite the reader to participate in the dialogue so that the discourse may become internally persuasive, then the form it takes should not coerce the hearer, but should respect her selfhood and intentionally avoid language of dominance. Theology that desires to be internally persuasive or transformative should be "polite," should be dialogical, open, and not of a sort that causes the other to "lose face." One way to accomplish this is to situate it in time and context, to recognize the other and her freedom in the discourse, and to invite response as does the epistolary form. Theology needs to seek out alternative forms of discourse such as the letter, or poetry, to which we now turn.

---

[184] This theme will be developed even more thoroughly in chapter 4 when we consider her use of the narrative form.

3

Sor Juana's *Dream* and the Hiddenness of God

Chapter 1 examined the tension between the revelation of God in Christ and the encounter with this event in one's present existence. Even the event of revelation itself is rooted in an unveiling and a veiling. Here, as we turn to one important poem by Sor Juana, we consider poetry as a form to express this very real aspect of Christianity. I do not examine all the potential benefits and reasons for poetic expression in theological discourse, but focus primarily on this one: poetry's unique ability to communicate the truth that exists at those points of tension, or its proficiency for the expression of darkness, the struggle of faith, and the continued striving in existence that results in incomplete knowledge in this life.[1] I utilize Heidegger's theory on poetry to demonstrate how poetry can accomplish this.

I limit myself to one particular type of poem, the "night poem," and steer clear of any grand theory of poetic language and structures, though some consideration will be given to the form of poetry itself. I examine only one poem by Sor Juana, her long poem *Primero sueño,* or *First Dream*, a piece that Sor Juana describes in her *Respuesta* as the only thing she's written for her own pleasure. The poem, set between sunset and sunrise, deals with one's inability to find full answers that satisfy the rational mind outside of faith, the failure of totality systems to adequately explain the nature of the world or convey

---

[1] Octavio Paz speaks of poetry as the form for protest and resistance, particularly against the values of rationalism and the bourgeoisie: "Bourgeois rationalism is, in a manner of speaking, constitutionally averse to poetry. Hence poetry, from the beginnings of the modern era—that is, since the last years of the eighteenth century—has been a form of rebellion. Poetry is not a genre in harmony with the modern world; its innermost nature is hostile or indifferent to the dogmas of modern times, progress and the cult of the future. Of course some poets have sincerely and passionately believed in progressive ideals, but their works say something quite different. Poetry, whatever the manifest content of the poem, is always a violation of the rationalism and morality of bourgeois society." Octavio Paz, *Sor Juana or, Traps of Faith*, trans. Margaret Sayers Paden (Cambridge MA: Harvard University Press, 1988) 5. This description of poetry corresponds with my interpretation of poetry as resistant to the demands and claims of modernity and responsive to the concerns of postmodern concerns.

knowledge of God, and the impossibility of gaining a detached view of the nature of things beyond one's embodiment and history. The poem gives expression to the struggle of faith, the tensions of Christian existence and the failure to find conclusivity and rest in the quest for understanding. Yet the poem concludes that one ought to keep pressing for understanding, even though one will ultimately fail and will be left with silence.

These aspects of existence communicated in Sor Juana's poem share similarities with those described by Kierkegaard: the sense of immortality within the soul while facing mortality, one's temporal existence in relation to the eternal, as well as the tension of salvation and hope in the face of suffering, world history, and a violent natural world.

Poetry in form illustrates the limits of knowing and the fragmenting of language, and can well express the frustration of seeking both to know and to communicate. Poetry can communicate in form the theological task of interpreting revelation, while representing the uncertainty and instability of this knowledge. The space of poetry as explained by Heiddeger and illustrated by Sor Juana is one of conflict, struggle, and striving. It is a space of concealing and revealing. It provides room to claim a knowledge while simultaneously affirming those experiences that deny that knowledge. It accounts for the struggle for knowledge and certainty, as well as the recognition that one's human existence impacts and limits one's perspective and understanding.

However, Sor Juana does not simply present oppositions or construct binaries. Here she gives voice to challenging oppositions and tensions while offering a third way or alternative; she does this both regarding theories of acquiring knowledge and also with ways of communicating knowledge. Ultimately she proposes a form of knowledge that is aware of its contextuality in contrast to Aristotelian and Platonic thought, and she suggests neither a systematic nor a direct expression of the fallibilistic knowledge she proposes, but a poetic one.

Primero Sueño

Primero sueño is Sor Juana's longest and most philosophical poem. It is a complicated composition of mythology, cosmology, medieval science, philosophy, and theology that serves as an extended metaphor describing Sor Juana's ambitious and frustrated quest for knowledge. The poem, composed of 975 lines, is a *silva*, a poem constituted of seven- and eleven-syllable lines and no fixed rhyme pattern. The adjective "*primero*," "first," was added to the title when it was printed in the second edition of Sor Juana's works in Seville in

1692, and therefore some debate surrounds whether it should be titled *Primero sueño* or *El Sueño*. Sor Juana's editors may have added the "*primero*," but she was certainly aware of it, and so I follow Paz and others in referring to the poem as *Primero sueño*, "First Dream."

"*Sueño*" can mean both "dream" and "sleep" in Spanish, and as Octavio Paz points out, the word is used to describe a variety of experiences: "the act of sleeping, the fantastic and irrational images we 'see' while we sleep, the psychic or physiologic faculty that produces those images, desires, ambitions, and dreams, and finally, the strange experience to which Sor Juana refers."[2] The different connotations to the word add strength to the various interpretations of the poem. Paz explains: "The word *sueño,* in the text, has four principle connotations: *sueño* as sleep; *sueño* as dream that is vision, not deception; *sueño* as the name of that vision; and *sueño* as ambition, desire, or an unrealized dream."[3] Georgina Sabat-Rivers also catalogues different interpretations of *sueño* in literature and of Sor Juana's use of it here in the poem. One interpretation of "dream" particularly interesting for this study is Sabat-Rivers's pairing of dream as both death and life. Here is one of the many oppositional pairings throughout the poem. Sabat-Rivers explains that all are equal in death as in sleep, and considers the suspension of the senses during *el sueño* to be, in Sor Juana's words, "*muerte temporal.*"[4] This dream, however, is more than an image of death. It is also the dream of a dream, as José Gaos puts it;[5] it is the dream of the realization of one's dream, of one's most intimate desire. Therefore, the dream also images life; and this particular dream prepares one to accept the reality that one is not able to achieve the maximum level of understanding one so desires, and it shows that the valor found in life is in the attempt to reach the goal, not actually in the attainment itself.[6]

Some debate persists as how best to classify this poem. Some critics consider it representative of the Baroque poetry of disillusionment, highlighting the similarities between Sor Juana's poem and the *Solitudes* of Góngora, which

---

[2] Ibid., 359.

[3] Ibid., 368.

[4] Georgina Sabat-Rivers, *El "Sueño" de Sor Juana Inés de la Cruz: Tradiciones Literarias y Originalidad* (London: Tamesis Books Ltd, 1976) 53, vv. 192–203 in *Sueño*.

[5] José Gaos, "El Sueño de un Sueño," *Historia Mexicana* 10, no. 1 (1960): (54–71).

[6] Sabat-Rivers, *El "Sueño,"* 54.

is considered an exemplar poem of Spanish disillusion, and upon which Sor Juana's poem is said to be modeled "in imitation."[7] Sabat-Rivers notes the similarities between *Sueño* and those of the great poets of the Spanish Golden Age and details comparisons between *Sueño* and poems by Trillo y Figuero and Salazar y Torrez.[8] Other critics suggest that the poem prefigures Enlightenment philosophical poetry or agree with a general modern-looking assessment of the "dream."[9] Octavio Paz, although arguing that the poem can be classified neither as an emulation of the popular Baroque forms of Sor Juana's day, like the poem of disillusionment, nor as a purely philosophical poem without the evinced influence of the great poets of the Golden Era, still assesses that the poem is a prophecy "of the modern poetry that centers on the paradox at the heart of her poem: the revelation of nonrevelation."[10] This interpretation of the poem as an expression of the paradox of "the revelation of nonrevelation," is something we will return to after a prose summary of the subjects, movement, and themes of *Primero sueño*.

Paz notes that "most critics believe that the poem is about 'the dream of knowledge.' They immediately invest the word 'dream' of the title with the sense of illusion and vanity. The soul 'dreams' of knowing, fails, and now awakened, realizes that knowledge is a delusion."[11] And this is a reading not far from the one presented here. The "dream" is that one can gain such knowledge,

---

[7] The full title and description of the poem is published as: "First Dream, so entitled and so composed by Mother Juana Inés de la Cruz, in imitation of Góngora." Georgina Sabat-Rivers notes the similarities between *First Dream* and a poem by Francisco de Trillo y Figueroa, "Portrait of a Night from Dusk to Dawn," in Georgina Sabat-Rivers, *El "Sueño" de Sor Juana Inés de la Cruz* (London: Tamesis, 1977). Other works and comparisons are listed by Octavio Paz, *Sor Juana, or Traps of Faith*, trans. Margaret Sayers Paden (Cambridge: Harvard University Press, 1988) 61–63.

[8] Sabat-Rivers, "*El Sueño,*" 55–64.

[9] Paz attributes this view to Vossler, and Paz himself interprets Sor Juana's work as prefiguring modern poetry, as does Benassy-Berling, while Electa Arenal suggests her work foreshadows aspects of Enlightenment thought. Sabat-Rivers also sees the ideas in *Sueño* as a foreshadowing of the perspective of future generations, and Stephanie Merrim calls her a "bridge to the Enlightenment." ("Toward a Feminist Reading of Sor Juana Inés de la Cruz: Past, Present, and Future Directions in Sor Juana Criticism," in *Feminist Perspectives on Sor Juana Inés de la Cruz*, ed. Stephanie Merrim (Detroit: Wayne State University Press, 1991) 11.

[10] Paz, 381.

[11] Ibid., 379.

detached, objective, and comprehensive, unhindered or unlimited by one's embodiment in a particular history, location, and community; it is the dream that one's context and interpretive framework will not interfere with the garnering of sheer, pure truth and knowledge of reality. The poem shows this dream to be just that, a dream or fantasy, but it also shows the deep longing for knowledge, the dream itself, to be a worthy aspiration, and the "first" in the title suggests a second, a continuation of the struggle, of another and further attempt to understand.

The poem tells the story of the descent of night upon the world, beginning with the movement of darkness and shadow over the earth, while the stars glow and the moon rules over the silenced landscape. The domain of night is a "silent realm," and the only sounds are the "muted voices" of the night birds whose sounds are "so deep and dim as not to break the silence."[12] The poem goes on to detail mythic birds of the night whose sluggish flight and song lulls everything living to sleep.[13] "Shamefaced Nyctimene" is mentioned, recalling the story of the girl from Lesbos who is changed into an owl because she committed incest with her father and is too ashamed thereafter to go out in daylight.[14] Nyctimene is said to drink the oil from the "brightly shining holy lamps" in order to extinguish them. Also present are three bats, once three sisters, who "create an added fog, fearing even in darkness to be seen."[15] They were condemned to this form because they would not celebrate the rites of Bacchus, and instead of going to his festival, stayed inside spinning wool and telling stories at the suggestion of one of the sisters, who says they should not leave their work for a

---

[12] Sor Juana Inés de la Cruz, "First Dream," in *A Sor Juana Anthology,* trans. Alan S. Trueblood (Cambridge, MA: Harvard University Press, 1988) 171. For an alternative English translation see *Sor Juana's Dream,* trans. Luis Harss (New York: Lumen Books, 1986). OC 1.333:15–24.

[13] For a study of the many mystical female figures and female personifications used by Sor Juana in *First Dream*, see Electa Arenal, "Where Woman Is Creator of the Wor(l)d. Or, Sor Juana's Discourses on Method," in *Feminist Perspectives on Sor Juana Inés de la Cruz*, ed. Stephanie Merrim (Detroit: Wayne State University Press, 1991); Stephanie Merrim, *Early Modern Women's Writing*; and Sabat-Rivers, *El "Sueño."*

[14] *Sueño,* Trueblood, 172. OC 1.336:27. Stephanie Merrim in *Early Modern Women's Writing* explains all these mythological characters as women who transgressed the patriarchal order in the realm of knowledge and were severely punished. She interprets the sacred oil that Nyctimene steals or drinks to be hard-earned knowledge and draws parallels with Sor Juana herself (Merrim, *Early Modern*, 192).

[15] *Sueño*, Trueblood, 172.

false religion but stay true to Pallas, a truer goddess, keeping to the looms and telling tales to pass the time. According to Ovid, the creatures they were condemned to become hate the light, "fly at night, and derive their name, '*vespertiliones*,' from '*vesper,*' the evening."[16] These night fliers, all human females condemned to the form of night animals, are joined by the screech owl, which Sor Juana identifies as "Pluto's telltale one-time henchman," an ill omen "to superstitious persons."[17] She is referring to Ascalaphus, a nymph of Hades who is turned into a screech owl for tattle-telling. Together the bats and birds create a "dismal intermittent dirge."[18] Harpocrates, the god of silence, joins the mythic night birds in bringing all things to rest and to quiet. The dog sleeps. The winds cease. Nothing stirs lest a "sough or sigh should make a sacrilegious noise, however slight, to violate the reign of silence."[19] Even the fish, "mute always," are now "doubly silent" as they sleep.

The poem continues with further description of the stretching blackness and quiet of the night, as lions, birds, and the stag Actaeon fall into deep slumber. "All was now bound in sleep,/ all by silence occupied./ Even the thief was slumbering,/ even the lover had closed his eyes./ The hour of silence is drawing to a close,/ the dark time is half over."[20] The poem expresses the fatigue of limbs and of body, weary both with labor and with pleasure, with leisure and with toil, as they give up the bodily senses for sleep. "[H]ence Nature is always shifting weight/ from one side of the balance to the other."[21] And now with body and the senses at rest, silent, and asleep, the soul is released from the governance of the external things that keep it "materially employed" throughout the day. The body is described as "a corpse with soul," and is said to be "dead to living, living to dead,"[22] yet warmth, breath, and the regular pulsing of blood through the veins, like the rhythm of the clock, show evidence of continued life.[23] The poem details some ideas from medieval biology on the heating of the body through the stomach, the balancing of the humors (blood, phlegm, yellow and black biles), and their vapors. The brain is given fuel for

---

[16] Ovid, *Metapmorphoses,* Book IV, 389–415.

[17] *Sueño,* Trueblood, 173. OC 1.336.54–55.

[18] Ibid.

[19] Ibid. OC 1.33:80–85.

[20] Ibid., 175. OC 1.339:147–53.

[21] Ibid. OC 1.339:160–61.

[22] Ibid., 176. OC 1.340:202–203.

[23] Sabat-Rivers in *El "Sueño"* notes how the inclusion of the household clock here shows signs of modernity in the poem, 135.

memory and imagination, and fantasy displays images to the partially freed soul, which then contemplates the divine spark within, "that portion of highest being in whose likeness in herself she took delight."[24]

Once the body sleeps, the soul of the narrator begins an ascent to knowledge. The climb is not unlike scaling the pyramids, as the soul, whose gender is not revealed at this point in the poem,[25] attempts to move from the most basic forms of knowledge in order to progress to high knowledge, ultimately culminating in knowledge of the Supreme Being.[26] The soul feels herself to be "almost loosed from that bodily chain,/ that always blocks her path," that always interferes "with the flight of intellect."[27] And because of the loosening of the body's restraint on the soul, the soul proceeds on a spiritual-

---

[24] *Sueño,* Trueblood, 178. OC 1.342:292–96. Octavio Paz claims that this "divine spark" discussion in the poem does not have Christian origins; however, it is most definitely the way in which some strands of Christian throughout the tradition have considered the image and/or likeness of God within humanity. "Nor does she say that the soul was created by God; rather, it is a 'spark of divine fire'" (Paz, 373). He claims this is un-Christian and instead neoplatonism and/or hermetic. It seems she was influenced by Kircher and hermticism, but Kircher himself was a Jesuit and neoplatonism has a long history of impacting Christian theology, even influencing Augustine, so this influence does not necessarily indicate that Sor Juana's reference to the divine spark was an un-Christian statement.

[25] The soul is a feminine noun, but the gender of the author or sleeping person whose soul takes flight is not revealed until the concluding line. Much is published on the genderless soul in the work of Sor Juana as well as the identification of the gender of the person in the conclusion of the poem. For investigations on this aspect of the poem and the implications of an interpretation of the soul as genderless or of the significance of the feminine gender of the questing soul revealed in the last line, see Licia Fiol-Matta, "Visions of Gender: Sor Juana and the First Dream," in *Nepantla: Views from the South* 4.2 (2003): 345–374. And for other studies that consider gender in *Primero sueño,* see Arenal, "Where Woman Is Creator of the Wor(l)d. Or, Sor Juana's Discourses on Method;" Georgina Sabat-Rivers, "A Feminist Rereading of Sor Juana's *Dream,*" in *Feminist Perspectives on Sor Juana Inés de la Cruz*, ed. Stephanie Merrim (Detroit: Wayne State University Press, 1991); and Yolanda Martinez-San Miguel, *Saberes Americanos: Subalternidad y Epistemología en los Escritos de Sor Juana* (Pittsburgh: Instituto Internacional de Literatura Iberoamericana, University of Pittsburgh, 1999).

[26] This is similar to the description given in *Respuesta* written a number of years later, in which Sor Juana explains her pursuit of a variety of disciplines of study for the sake of gaining a better understanding of the Queen of the sciences, Theology.

[27] *Sueño,* Trueblood, 178–79. OC 1.342–3:296–98.

intellectual voyage. During such a journey, the soul may investigate "the vast immensity of the firmament" or consider the orbits of the celestial bodies as they run their various courses.[28] The soul imagines herself viewing her surroundings from a vantage point so high it dwarfs Atlas, that mountain that makes Olympus appear a foothill. The lower levels of the mountain the soul climbs are themselves beyond the reach of even the strongest bird, the eagle. And she compares this mountain to the two Memphis Pyramids in Egypt, the tips upon which one's gaze cannot focus, for as they reach higher "in smooth and level stages, their vast bulk,/ shrank so in girth and with such art/" that as the "observing eye approached the heavens,/ the more it lost its way amid the winds, unable to discern the minute tip," and so one's sight becomes "worn out by sheer astonishment" and its gaze plummets to the wide base of the pyramid, which is "no minor punishment for the wingèd boldness of the eyes."[29] Homer considered these pyramids to be visual representation of the inner movement of the spirit, whose ascent takes on a pyramidal shape "in ever aspiring to the one First Cause,/ the center toward which the straight line tends,/ if not indeed the circumference containing every essence ad infinitum."[30]

---

[28] Ibid., 179. OC 1.342–43:300–306.

[29] Ibid., 180. OC 1.344:354–61. Recent readings of the poem suggest the pyramids in this poem may refer to Mexican indigenous cultures. They may also show evidence of the influence hermeticism had upon Sor Juana through Kircher and the idealization of ancient Egypt.

[30] Ibid., 181. OC 1.345:408–11. This description, again, though not referencing the Christian God explicitly, could be influenced by Greek philosophy, which would seem fitting with a reference to the Greek Homer, but the First Cause argument was also utilized by Thomas Aquinas, of whose work Sor Juana was clearly aware. Also, the description of this First Cause as the center and circumference of everything is an image not foreign to Christian theology. See Maximus Confessor, for example, who speaks of God as one who "contains, gathers, and limits" all things, while maintaining as "cause, beginning, and end all beings," which God makes "converse in each other by the singular force of their relationship to him as origin" [Maximus the Confessor, "Church's Mystagogy," in *Selected Writings*, trans. George C. Berthold (Mahway NJ: Paulist Press, 1985) 186]. Here Maximus speaks of God as origin and that which gathers and limits all creation, very similar to the center and circumference argument given here by Sor Juana. Thus, I again disagree with Paz, who found this reference also evidence of influences on Sor Juana other than Christian ones. Paz pushes an interpretation of her work as extremely influenced by hermeticism. The translator of the poem, Alan Trueblood, does agree that this reference of Homer's interpretation of the pyramids "must allude to a

The mountain is also compared to the Tower of Babel,[31] which was built in an attempt to ascend high enough to reach God and considered so blasphemously arrogant that its builders were punished by the imposition of many different languages upon them. Humanity was condemned to "divers tongues which still obstruct the easy intercourse of humankind," for the assumption that they could reach a vantage point on God. Yet the Tower of Babel and the Pyramids of Memphis would be far below the "elevated pyramid of mind," which the soul was now summiting. The soul had seemingly limitless vision over all creation, yet the understanding was so overcome by the magnitude of the vision that it recoils. The attempt of the soul to see and to understand things in their entirety is described as an impudent ambition, prideful, and an arrogant presumption. Sor Juana references Icarus, who flies too close to the sun, melting the wax on his artificial wings, and plummets into the sea.[32] The poem describes at length the condition of the mind and its attempts to comprehend the created order: "it foundered, bearings lost,/ and, trying to look at everything, saw nothing."[33] In the face of the masses of species, the mind was unable to perceive even one. And like one who loses sight by the excessive brightness of light, the intellective faculty dimmed.

The shocked soul recovers itself in recoiling, like one whose eyes are accustomed to the dark when confronted by a blinding flash of light will cover her eyes with her hand and, by restoring darkness, recover sight, or like a doctor who is able to give doses of what might poison in such a way as to give remedy, or to use a poison in order to develop an antidote.[34] The soul is astonished and withdraws its attention from the chaotic, disordered mass she had formed in her mind as her reasoning powers were blocked by the shock. The soul is like an overconfident ship that presumes the sea is loyal, but is beaten by the winds and forced aground, off "the vast sea of knowing," with a broken rudder and yardarms, and is ultimately relieved to be on land, where she recovers. The soul

---

hermetic interpretation of [Homer's] text" (181). Elena Feder also critiques Paz's position and his insistence on the non-religious or non-Christian reading of the poem.

[31] The Tower of Babel was an important metaphor for Bakhtin in reference to heteroglossia. See chapter 4.

[32] Some of the words and phrases used to describe this attempt and presumption include: "*ambicioso anhelo*" (429); "*osado presupuesto*" (454); and "*ufana*" (lines 487 and 488). OC 1.346–47.

[33] *Sueño,* Trueblood, 183. OC 1.347:476–80.

[34] Here Sor Juana actually goes on to talk about how the physicians test their remedies on animals first and do empirical experiments.

was beaten about on the "sea of knowing"; it could not navigate something so vast, could not comprehend all things, and for recovery had to come away from "the knowing." The soul restores her intellectual capacities and "considers it more appropriate" to restrict thought to a single subject at a time, rather than attempting to gain a comprehensive understanding at once. So, the soul turns to "those artfully constructed categories, ten in number," and determines to consider things one by one.[35] Such an approach is described as a "metaphysical reduction" that teaches the art of forming universals "by encompassing generic entities in the purely mental constructs of abstract thought, eschewing embodiment in matter."[36] This systematic method is thought to compensate for the human intellectual deficiency in its inability to comprehensively understand the cosmos in one cognitive move. It allows one, rather, "to move up, step by step,/ as on a ladder, from one concept/ to the next, adopting of necessity/ the relative order of understanding/ required by the restricted power of Mind,/ which must entrust its progress/ to a graduated form of reasoning."[37]

The narrator says, "My mind desired to pursue the method: namely, from the basest level of being…to move on to the nobler hierarchy."[38] Moving through each kingdom, from the most simple to the most complex, the soul proposes to begin with the inanimate objects and then move through the vegetable kingdom, before moving on to the animal kingdom. Finally then the soul would consider humanity, which is the link between the animal and the angelic, as the human and the angel share the inner faculties of will, understanding, and memory.[39] Humanity is called "the goal of all his [the creator's] works, the circle/ clasping heaven and earth in one, utmost perfection

---

[35] *Sueño,* Trueblood, 185. OC 1.349:581–82. Sor Juana again turns to Aristotle, in keeping with the tradition of scholastic theology.

[36] Ibid. OC 1.350:583–88.

[37] Ibid., 186. OC 1.350:593–99.

[38] Ibid. OC 1.350–51:617–24.

[39] Augustine lists these three as vestiges within the self of the Trinity. See *De Trinitate* Book X. The poem's discussion continues like any neoplatonic idea of the chain of being—common to Pseudo-Dionysius, Augustine, and most of the tradition of Western mysticism. Humanity is a link between the fallen earthly realm, that with matter, and the spiritual realm. The human has the spirit within, the soul, but also body—capable of "the loftiest aspiration heavenward, yet only mortal" (from Trueblood's prose summary of "First Dream," 169). Sor Juana talks of humanity as represented by John's apocalyptic vision of a creature belonging to both heaven and earth and of the statue in Nebuchadnezzar's dream, which is gold with feet of clay.

of creation, utmost delight of its Eternal Author,/ with whom well pleased, well satisfied,/ His immense magnificence took His rest."[40] Like the creature in John's vision, humanity has arms stretched to heaven but has a mouth filled with dust; humanity is of both heaven and earth, is the "circle clasping" both in one, or, like the statue in Nebuchadnezzar's dream in Daniel, formed of the "most prized metal," but on "flimsy feet."[41] She asks why humanity would be so composed as to resemble "angel, plant, and beast alike," and conjectures that perhaps it is that humanity may be lifted even higher "by a grace of loving union."[42]

The poem's narrator says, "These then were the stages over which [she] sometimes wished to range"; yet at other times she considered it too bold, as she had failed to understand even the smallest, easiest parts of nature that were close at hand for observation, such as the causes of the course of a brook and its many meanderings, or the reason behind the blending of colors in a flower, "why its scent is of amber" and why it "unravels in the breeze." If she couldn't even fully comprehend the intricacies of these seemingly simple natural occurrences, how could she expect to scale any higher? "If reason, overwhelmed, recoils before so difficult a challenge,/ ...doubting in her cowardice/ that she can grasp even this single object,/ how can she hope to function in the face/ of so astounding and immense a system?/ Its burden, terrible, unendurable—were it not upheld at its very center—would make the shoulders even of Atlas sag." The "task of

---

[40] This is most definitely a depiction of the Christian understanding of creation. *Respuesta,* Trueblood, 188. OC 1.352:664–67.

[41] *Sueño,* Trueblood, 188. OC 1.352:670–76. Kierkegaard discusses a similar tension endured by humanity, as they have a sense of immortality within their souls, but face mortality.

[42] Ibid. OC 1.352:693–99. This is another example of the influence of the Christian tradition on this poem. Numerous theologians speak of contemplating the natural world as one step toward knowledge of the divine: Bonaventure, Augustine, and Thomas. See Bonaventure's *Soul's Journey into God.* Even Augustine's *Confessions* are often understood as depicting this structure, beginning with contemplation of the external, moving to contemplation of the interior, and finally moving on to contemplation of the superior, that is, of God. McKenna's reading of the poem corresponds with my understanding of it in this regard: "The soul's aspiration toward the light from above is to know God, not in the sense of a mystical union, but rather to contemplate the Supreme Being in the full comprehension of the universe" [Susan M. McKenna, "Rational Thought and Female Poetics in Sor Juana's 'Primero sueño': The Circumvention of Two Traditions," *Hispanic Review* 68, no. 1 (Winter 2000): 43].

investigating Nature" is deemed a heavier burden than upholding the "sphere of heaven."[43]

At other times, however, the narrator wonders if this is not merely cowardice, or "yielding the laurels" without attempting "to meet the challenge of the lists."[44] In these bolder moments, she would "seize upon the brave example set by" Phaethon.[45] When the narrator finds the boldness necessary to make the investigations, to do the intellectual lifting required in such feats, she considers Phaethon: "that famous youth, high-minded/ charioteer of the chariot of flame;/ then courage would be fired/ by his grand and bold, if hapless, impulse,/ in which the spirit finds/ not, like timidity, a chastening lesson/ but a pathway summoning it to dare;/ once treading this, no punishment can deter/ the spirit bent upon a fresh attempt/ (I mean a thrust of new ambition)."[46] Fear of neither failure nor punishment will deter "the soaring spirit once resolved,/ in lofty disregard of living, to pluck from ruin an everlasting fame."[47] And Phaethon, despite the warnings that it could not be done, that he could not control his father's chariot, the sun, tried nonetheless, and although he perished in the attempt, he is considered "the very type, the model" for the pursuit of one's ambition.[48] She writes: "Rather, that youth, is…a most pernicious instance/ (causing wings to sprout for further flights)/ of that ambitious mettle,/ which finding in terror itself a spur/ to prick up courage, pieces together the name of glory/ from letters spelling endless havoc."[49] Such attempts give the actor a heroic image even in failure or demise, such that the narrator suggests the act should never be made known to the public, as even the punishment brings glory: "Either the punishment should not be known so that the crime would never be contagious."[50] She suggests it would be better to let ignorance

---

[43] Ibid., 190. OC 1.354:770–80.

[44] Ibid., 191. OC 1.355:781–84.

[45] Ibid. OC 1.355:785–86.

[46] Ibid. OC 1.355:786–95.

[47] Ibid. OC 1.355:800–802. The phrases she uses to describe him include: "al ánimo arrogante," arrogant spirit (line 800); "ejemplar pernicioso," pernicious example (line 804); and "del ánimo ambicioso," ambitious spirit (line 806). Luis Harss's translation of this description of Phaethon speaks of his "unfettered pride" that did not heed the "thunderbolt sent against arrogance," and pronounces his "pernicious model" broadcast in its punishment as "flatter[ing] such a crime" (Harss, 64).

[48] Ibid. OC 1.355:803.

[49] Ibid. OC 1.355:803–10.

[50] Ibid. OC 1.355:811–12.

of his attempt prevail, "for broadcasting makes the wickedness of the greatest crime the greater/ till it threatens a widespread epidemic, while, left in unknown isolation, repetition is far less likely/ than if broadcast to all as a would-be lesson."[51]

The narrator shows a desire for knowledge, but an awareness of the impossibility of attaining the knowledge she seeks. She considers pursuing it despite the inevitable failure, but wonders if this is not reckless glory-seeking. The poem shows her oscillation, frustration, and even some confusion over what to do with such a strong desire for knowledge when it cannot be satisfied. Perhaps the mind should not take after the example of Phaethon after all, because it encourages reckless, bold behavior. Such feats of knowledge seek glory for oneself and represent that selfish ambition that Sor Juana finds ill-suited to theology. She is frustrated by the dilemma: she knows that when she attempts conclusive, comprehensive understanding, it is doomed to failure and a painful cognitive experience, but a strong desire to know persists, and before she is able to decide her route, the environment changes.[52] "But as judgment foundered in confusion/ amid the reefs and skirted whirlpools of no return, no matter which direction it sought to follow."[53] She is not as inexperienced now as when first her ship was thrown onto the beach; she has skirted whirlpools but she is still among them and among the reefs. She faces frustration in either direction, and she sees no way out of the conflict, confusion, and inability to make sense of it all. In that moment her body begins to awaken from hunger, and the poem returns to a consideration of the vapors and humors that induced the sleep as they relax their influence on the body. She stirs, limbs move, eyes

---

[51] Ibid. OC 1.356:821–26. As Sor Juana lived during the reign of the "Holy Office," that is, the Inquisition, her inclusion of the use of public punishment, particularly for "crimes" of ambitions of knowledge, different views, or "heresy," is particularly relevant. Giordano Bruno, the famous hermetic priest, for example, was burned at the stake in 1600. Could there be a subtle critique here of such practices? She could not openly question the fear tactics of her day and the use of violence to force assent to the Church's official teaching, as one notices in her *Response,* where she repeatedly noted that she does not want trouble with the Holy Office; however, she does offer a critique of the violence utilized by the Church in the Conquest in her *loas*, so it would not be out of line with concerns voiced in other texts.

[52] Sabat-Rivers argues that the poem leads one to believe she will absolutely try the feat again and again repeatedly, knowing she will fail, but she will pursue it again nonetheless.

[53] *Sueño,* Trueblood, 192. OC 1.356:827–32.

flutter, and light slowly illumines the room. The shadows flee and the morning star shines, birds herald the dawn, and the Night gathers "her swarthy squadrons in" and makes "an orderly retreat" as the sun returns for its rule of the day.[54] And when the sun is bright and fully risen, "flooding with light whatever had been opaque/ throughout the world," it wakes her, or in the concluding words of the poem: "y yo despierta."[55] At this point, the gender is finally given for the narrator whose soul the reader has observed and heard, and being feminine and descriptive of much we know about Sor Juana's pursuits and desires, this first-person poem, *Primero sueño,* is considered autobiographical.

Analysis

Trueblood uses the adjective "first" in the title of the poem to emphasize the narrator's prolonged debate over whether or not to dare a second flight, another attempt at full comprehension. Nearly half of the poem is given over to a consideration of the "pros and cons of undertaking a second flight."[56] And here his description of the narrator's internal struggle and conflict mirrors that of the entire shape of the poem and its pairings of oppositions: "We are there introduced into the speaker's most prized intimacy, the workshop of her mind, where thought swings in pendular fashion between the resolve to try again and the fear of a second failure."[57] Before the sleeper is able to determine in her dream which course she should take, she is awakened, reminded of her body, of her embeddedness in time and space, the human existence that keeps her from the unifying and universal vision sought in the *Dream.* And the reader is reminded that the title itself suggests that such comprehensive and certain knowledge is, after all, a dream, a fantasy.

The poem illustrates a tension between a desire to know and the ability to think critically, and the frustration of that desire as one can never gain a full, abstract, and perfectly coherent understanding. Such a vision is for God alone. And so, the human lives in this tension and struggle. As Sabat-Rivers explains:

> For as much that she desired to understand everything, the mind is not capable of an infinite or divine intuition. Her discursive intellect barely serves to comprehend the smallest aspects of reality. And nevertheless the exercise of reason is the unique glory of humanity. In this ambiguity, that of the greatness

[54] Ibid., 194. OC 1.358:937–38.

[55] Ibid., 195. OC 1.359:974–75.

[56] Ibid., 21.

[57] Ibid.

and the misery that is to be human, rests the essential valor and the romantic tragedy of Sor Juana's *Sueño.*[58]

The mental journey of Sor Juana narrated in the poem is represented by the figures of Icarus and Phaethon, who symbolize sheer audacity; they signify the risk, the danger, and the boldness of the cognitive task undertaken. Sabat-Rivers proposes that in her use of these two figures in *Sueño*, Icarus and Phaethon, Sor Juana personally summarizes not only the tension in the age of transition in which she lived, that is, between the optimism of the Renaissance and the disappointment of the Baroque, but also illustrates the perspective of the generations to come.[59] Icarus is a figure of failure and disappointment, and is commonly used as such throughout literature of the time, but Phaethon is reinvented by Sor Juana to figure not only the failure but also the exemplary boldness of his fearless attempt. Throughout Sor Juana's works, Icarus is a symbol of human disappointment, of what the human is unable to become or accomplish, of frustrated human desires and aspirations;[60] he is the figure of one discouraged and dejected. He is also an example of "necedad, locura y escarmiento," of foolishness, madness, and punishment—or of learning one's lesson.[61]

The interpretation of Phaethon in the history of literature is complex, and Sor Juana's use of the figure in this poem is no less so. Her purpose behind this imagery is debated. A number of scholars interpret Sor Juana's use of Phaethon in this text to serve as an example to follow, suggesting that one is encouraged in Sor Juana's treatment to be as daring and as bold as Phaethon, despite the consequences. He is then a figure of both virtuous rebellion and bravery. Sabat-Rivers sees Sor Juana's use of the figure to suggest the ongoing struggle for knowledge, and a repeated attempt at the feat, and says that Sor Juana uses the figure in ways uncommon in the history of literature. With Phaethon, Sor Juana is innovative. Paz makes a similar assessment: "for the majority of Spanish poets of her time, Phaethon is an example of imprudence and its punishment. For Sor Juana that punishment is consecration."[62] Sabat-Rivers sees this reading mirrored in the personified Night in *Sueño* as both "represent an urge to succeed

[58] Sabat-Rivers, *El "Sueño,"* 128, my trans.

[59] Ibid., 96.

[60] Ibid., 91.

[61] Ibid., 89.

[62] Paz, 123.

and to rebel, even though in vain."[63] I argue, however, that the poem's assessment of Phaethon's brazen action is not simply unfaltering approval.

Critics highlight the parallels between *El Sueño* and *La Respuesta*, as both describe Sor Juana's desire for knowledge and struggle to gain it either because of social or ecclesial limits placed on her as a woman or because of the limits placed on all human understanding because of the nature of existence. I note a further similarity between the warning and criticism of arrogant claims of knowledge in *La Respuesta* and the characterization of the arrogant boldness of Phaethon and Icarus and the builders of the Tower of Babel. In *La Respuesta* she chastises those who would claim dominance of opinion and ultimacy of thought in favor of a posture we could call epistemic humility. In this poem she is less concerned with the claims of knowledge people make, but instead stresses the limits of human knowing and again warns against the pursuit of fame and glory through heights of knowledge, much like she does in *Respuesta,* where she reminds her readers that Christ did not receive a crown of gold around his head of wisdom but one of thorns. One should not expect glory for knowledge, but suffering, which is true of Sor Juana and of Phaethon, who, though achieving fame, received it only through suffering failure.[64]

Whether one reads Sor Juana's Phaethon as a model of brave rebellion or of dangerous arrogance, it is clear that Phaethon is also a symbol of the virtue in the struggle to understand. The virtue is found in the striving itself, in the continued pursuit, and not in a successful grasp on an unattainable height of comprehension. It is more important to keep at the pursuit than to actually gain a certain and sure knowledge. As we saw in Kierkegaard, which he finds in Socrates and Lessing, the poem shares an emphasis on the life lived in pursuit and striving and not on the attainment of a concluded, stable state of knowledge. As Sabat-Rivers notes, the dream is not only a symbol of death, but also of life, a life lived in the struggle and tension described throughout the verse.[65] The following analysis of *Sueño* examines the tensions, conflict, and oppositions throughout the poem in both structure and content, considering how this creates

---

[63] Georgina Sabat-Rivers, "A Feminist Reading of Sor Juana's Dream," in *Feminist Perspectives on Sor Juana Inés de la Cruz*, ed. Stephanie Merrim (Detroit: Wayne State University, 1991) 157.

[64] When I refer to Sor Juana's "failure" here, I mean her repeated assertions of her failure to know, failure to gain full knowledge that I stress through my reading of her work.

[65] Sabat-Rivers, *El "Sueño,"* 53–54.

a space for unknowing and for the revealed and concealed to co-exist in the strife of truth, or as we will see in Heidegger, how the poem is situated as an "Open." I examine: (1) dueling epistemologies and Sor Juana's response; (2) the conflict between day and night and within the soul itself; and (3) the role of silence in this space.

Dueling Epistemologies. Most scholars affirm that the *Primero sueño* directs a challenge at traditional Western epistemology, both against claims of certain knowledge and the proposed ways of acquiring that knowledge. Elena Feder claims that the poem "dissects Western culture's ontological and epistemological foundations and formations."[66] The thinker, whose gender remains hidden throughout the intellectual exercises described, is finally revealed to be a female who dares to critique the dominant systems of thought of her day: the inductive reasoning of Plato and the deductive of Aristotle, both mystical attempts at gaining comprehensive vision and the systematizing of Late Scholasticism.[67]

As Sabat-Rivers positions the poem between Baroque disappointment and Renaissance optimism, while foreshadowing the perspective of "future generations," Feder locates the poem "historically and formally, in the space of rupture where two powerful epistemological currents of the time coexist and confront one another: scholastic tradition, bulwark of the Counter-Reformation, and Renaissance humanism, which reached Sor Juana through the filter of Florentine neo-Platonism."[68] The poem stands between these forces of thought, challenging both fronts and proposing another alternative, a view that recognizes the limits on human understanding, of fallibility, or one that encourages epistemic humility while never ceasing in the pursuit to understand. She says of the Platonic view that the soul "trying to look at everything, saw nothing,"[69] and describes the scholastic method as a "metaphysical reduction" that teaches the art of forming universals "by encompassing generic entities in the purely mental constructs of abstract thought, eschewing embodiment in matter."[70] Her pursuit and intellectual journey even begins by asserting that the body limits the mind's vision, as the soul felt herself to be "almost loosed from

[66] Feder, 475.

[67] See Martínez-San Miguel, 70.

[68] Feder, 475.

[69] *Sueño,* Trueblood, 183. OC 1.347:476–80.

[70] Ibid., 185. OC 1.350:583–88.

that bodily chain,/ that always blocks her path," that always interferes "with the flight of intellect."[71]

Primero sueño illustrates the incomplete nature of knowledge and the impossibility of attaining full knowledge or of gaining a universal perspective, detached from human limits of embodiment and context. The method Sor Juana employs is similar to what she later describes in *La Respuesta.* She sees the accumulation of knowledge like a ladder, or here like a pyramid, which one ascends rung by rung until one reaches the study of theology, the "Queen of the sciences." One does not assume a knowledge of God can be gained immediately, but she understands this to be gained throughout a life of study and pursuit. Similarly here, after failing to gain a comprehensive knowledge of the whole initially, she determines that perhaps one could proceed systematically and thereby gain understanding. However, even when following a scholastic method, even when proceeding systematically, the mind still cannot grasp the necessary steps ever to reach theological understanding, as one cannot even gain full knowledge of the first building blocks of the structure. The weight of what the mind is trying to understand is too much for the system; it is too much even for Atlas.

The detached perspective, high upon the pyramid, is itself a dream, an illusion, or a fallacy, as is the assumption that one can reach heights of full comprehension by systematic process. Humanity cannot gain such perspective or knowledge; the view of which humanity is capable is one embedded in existence, embodied, and one cannot gain a view of God or God's ways in the world that is removed from this. I posit further that knowledge of God, or Christian knowledge, occurs at the point of the God relation, at the place where Christ's life and work are transitioned and transitioning to our own lives; it is applied to our lives, and transforms them through time. Therefore these aspects of human existence (time, space, embodiment) impact Christian knowledge and understanding.

Feder calls the space in which the poem's narrative is located to be both "of rupture and encounter" and describes the "laws regulating this space" as "conceptualized dialectically."[72] And she finds among the oppositions a "polarization between center and margin" that "is exacerbated as the cycle of the poem draws to a close. Here, Sor Juana divides the planet into two opposing halves ('antípoda[s] opuest[as]' [l. 890] and has night and day reigning

[71] Ibid., 178–79. OC 1.342–43:296–98.

[72] Feder, 483.

separately, joined, however, by a dividing line that becomes progressively more unstable and conflicted, and where a series of images of struggle abound (ll. 888-894)."[73] The realm of knowledge is exposed as unstable, just as the hierarchies themselves and the state of things are shown to be uncertain. Martínez-San Miguel makes a similar assessment: "the space of knowing is posed as an unstable and conflictual zone. In order to reject the two accepted methods of knowing, the poem stops being a traditional didactic text in order to become what Octavio Castro López calls a '*historia de una tension intelectual*.'"[74] She continues, "The knowledge that is proposed in the text, is a knowledge of its own contingency, its particularity and its limits."[75] And this proposed knowledge—a knowledge of its own limits—is generated through the "constant battle of the subject in a specific social and institutional moment."[76]

Not only does the mind recoil at its exposure to the chaos, but before the subject can even decide whether or not to try the feat again, the body stirs, reminds the subject of its bodily existence through hunger pains, and then wakens to the material, corporeal, and sensual world in which it lives. The subject's existence in time and space, particularly located, concludes the illustration of a person's attempt to gain universal, abstract, and non-contextual knowledge; after the failure to gain that perspective and declarations of its impossibility, the point is made: the subject is embodied and knowledge is "situated," localized, and impacted by the knower's human existence and particular context.[77] Truly, the final statement of the poem reminds the reader that knowers are, in fact, gendered. Martínez-San Miguel argues that the struggle of the subject is not the intellectual struggle of one who has "essentially achieved separation from the external world, as the knowledge process itself demonstrates the inseparability of the cognitive experience from the body that lives in the world."[78] The poem may be read as an argument that detached, non-

---

[73] Ibid., 509.

[74] Yolanda Martínez-San Miguel, 83, quoting Octavio Castro López, *Sor Juana y el Primero Sueño* (Mexico: Centro de Investigaciones Lingüístico-Literarias. Instituto de Investigaciones Humanísticas, Universidad Veracruzana, 1982) 10, my trans.

[75] Martínez-San Miguel, 83, my trans.

[76] Martínez-San Miguel, 84, my trans.

[77] See Yolanda Martinez-San Miguel's analysis of Sor Juana in *Saberes Americanos*, where she uses Donna Haraway, "Situated Knowledge: The Science Question in Feminism as a Site of Discourse on the Privilege of Partial Perspective," *Feminist Studies* 14.3 (1988): 575–99.

[78] Martínez-San Miguel, 77, my trans.

contextualized knowledge is impossible, that one always knows in one's embodied and gendered form, in time and space. It may also assert that one's situation, community, and context impact one's ways of conceiving, interpreting, and processing ideas; one's "situatedness" influences the very formation of the categories one utilizes to sort information and experience. It is a poem of tensions and struggles both internal and external, and they will not be resolved: day/night, knowing/unknowing, revelation/hiddenness, body/soul.

Sor Juana's poem tells of one who dares to attempt the comprehensive, detached perspective, to ascend to that height and gain a universal, abstract picture of the world, universe, and the Supreme Being. Not only does the thinker fail to attain this knowledge but is faced with chaos at the attempt. And through the figures of Phaethon and Icarus, and the images of the Tower of Babel and the pyramids, the poem suggests that assuming such a vantage point is tantamount to placing oneself on level with God, or is an attempt to gain a vantage point on God. "*First Dream* is not a confession…but an accusation and a denunciation of those who, by confusing human with divine power, turn the latter into a travesty."[79] The supposition that one has gained such a vision and certain knowledge of God and God's ways in the world, after all, undermines faith as described in chapter 1. It supposes a level of certainty, objectivity, and detached, factual knowledge that is counter to faith—faith as certainty only of one's uncertainty, but yet trusting God. Yet, José Gaos may be right in suggesting that skepticism gets the last word in this poem; one is left with the failure to know and understand.[80]

Paz makes the assessment that in *Primero sueño* "the soul finds that what opens before it is a bottomless abyss," and says the poem is a denial of revelation, or rather that the revelation is that there is no revelation.[81] This conclusion is partly drawn from Paz's insistence that there is no God referenced in the poem and no Christian underpinning.[82] Though he admits that "the theme

---

[79] Feder, 499.

[80] Gaos, 68.

[81] Paz, 359.

[82] Paz again interprets ascent to knowledge as Sor Juana describes it as one unrelated to the Christian tradition, because in his perspective, it is not representative of the mystical tradition. He writes, "'The Categories' ends by evoking union with God as the goal of knowledge. Sor Juana knew perfectly well, however, that knowledge of the divine is essentially different from knowledge of worldly sciences. Unlike the philosophical schools of antiquity, whose ultimate goal was wisdom and an upright life, no manual of Christian mysticism prescribes the study of geology" (Paz, 377). As I

of the voyage of the soul is a religious theme and is inseparable from revelation," he nonetheless asserts that "in Sor Juana's poem not only is there no demiurge, there is no revelation."[83] Though I would argue that more Christian foundation is present in the poem than Paz recognizes, and that the themes of light and dark, disclosure and concealment, are more suggestive of the unveiling and veiling of revelation and hiddenness than Paz gives account for, I do agree that the poem is very much a poem at that tension, exposing human frustration and struggle:

> *First Dream* is the first example of an attitude—the solitary soul confronting the universe—that later, beginning with romanticism, would be the spiritual axis of Western poetry. The solitary confrontation is a religious theme, like that of the voyage of the soul, but religious in a negative way: it denies revelation. More precisely, it is the revelation of the fact that we are alone and that the world of the supernatural has dissipated. In one way or another, all modern poets have lived, relived, and re-created the double negation of *First Dream:* the silence of space, and the vision of nonvision.[84]

The poem illustrates the terror of the solitude of the individual in a massive, impersonal universe, and of the conflict and confusion between the promise of knowledge and the seemingly God-given hunger for such understanding, suggested by Sor Juana's reference to the "divine spark" within the soul, and yet the inevitable failure of attainment; it demonstrates the terrible limits on understanding. This may just as well be the poem of a believer and woman of faith, who still struggles with the hiddenness of God and the tension between what is said to be known (revelation) and what is actually experienced

---

argued earlier, there is a tradition within Christianity going back as least as far as Augustine, which considers the contemplation of the external world to be the beginning of one's growth in knowledge toward God. Also, the tradition of natural theology would serve as a Christian example of this pursuit. In the earliest questions of his *Summa*, Thomas Aquinas discusses the possibility of gaining some knowledge of God through the observation and contemplation of nature. See also Bonaventure *Soul's Journey into God,* where he lays out steps of an ascent to contemplation of God beginning with the contemplation of the nature. Book 1 of this work is titled, "On the Stages of the Ascent into God on Contemplating Him through His Vestiges in the Universe," and Book 2 is called, "On Contemplating God in His Vestiges in the Sense World."

[83] Paz, 367.

[84] Ibid.

(lack of knowledge). I argue that this is a poem on that rift, and a poem of the tension in Christianity as it exists as a God-relation.

Feder agrees that this poem represents the struggle of a woman of faith more than Paz accounts for: "Octavio Paz has correctly rejected the interpretation that inserts the poem within the mystical tradition. According to him the theme of the *Sueño* is the 'inverse of revelation.'"[85] However, she continues, "Paz implies that the refusal of mystical experience is equivalent to a denial of the existence of God."[86] She finds Paz's reading of the poem an anachronistic imposition of romanticism and existentialism upon the thought of Sor Juana.[87] "Sor Juana does not belong to the episteme that shares the post-Nietzschean vision of the death of God, the absence of a center. Her Christian universe is real and God is synonymous with meaning and truth."[88] I appreciate Feder's insistence that Sor Juana's search belongs to a religious worldview, and that these questions are posed in the midst of her struggles within that worldview. Though the center (God) is not absent for Sor Juana, as Paz claims, the poet acknowledges that she does not understand this center fully and addresses this complication to life, knowledge, and the quest for understanding the world and God's ways within it. Feder does not deny that the poem could illustrate "the inverse of revelation," but clarifies that this is only possible "in the religious sense of this experience."[89] She continues:

> In the context of Renaissance rationalism, however, the revelation that follows the encounter of the soul with the First Cause is of another kind. Sor Juana toys with the possibility of reaching a balance between religion, whose immutable truths were unquestionable at the time, and scientific reason, whose methods promised a more correct *approximation* to the truth. As we have seen, Sor Juana believed that the human spirit has the ability to come close to the First Cause because it is everyone's origin and *telos,* regardless of earth-bound differences. But to come close is not the same as to transcend. To transcend implies a denial of the distance separating words from things, signs from referent, representation from the real—a distance language is forever condemned to try to bridge.[90]

---

[85] Feder, 496.
[86] Ibid., 497.
[87] Ibid.
[88] Ibid., 516.
[89] Ibid., 497.
[90] Ibid.

Night and Day. Primero sueño stands between realms of thought, confronting both, as the soul also remains locked in a struggle between revelation and hiddenness or knowledge and failure to understand. The oppositions not only constitute the themes of the poem but also the poem's very structure. Franco points out that the author "fabricates an intricate labyrinth" in the complex poem that both "conceals and reveals," just as the God of Sor Juana's universe is understood to work, constructing a mysterious reality that both reveals and conceals. [91] *Primero sueño* is framed within a battle of domains: night and day, one ruled by the moon and the other by the sun. Trueblood agrees: "It is to the celebration of the surge of mind, despite a clear-eyed acknowledgment of inevitable ultimate frustration, that *First Dream* is ultimately addressed. The poem is seeded with imagery of conflict, especially of light against dark, lucidity against obscurity and even obscurantism."[92] The contrast between light and dark in the poem is personified in a conflict between Night, with its "mist, shadows, darkness, and confusion," which McKenna interprets as metaphors for "intellectual darkness," and the light of Day, which reveals, illumines, and chases the shadows.[93] It is between the luminous and the shadowy, that which illuminates and that which conceals. Paz also sees the oppositions as conflicting: "Throughout the poem—tacitly, not explicitly—two series of oppositions are in conflict; day and night, body and soul."[94] The dialectical structure of the poem is noted also by Franco, who contrasts: "Light and dark, revelation and secrecy, enlightenment and confusion, melancholy and joy" in the poem.[95] *Primero sueño* is a poem of revealing and concealing, of dueling oppositions, something one also finds in Sor Juana's *villancicos* and *loas*.[96] Though the poem begins and ends with light, which not only is what gives human eyes the ability to see but also represents understanding as

[91] Jean Franco, *Plotting Women: Gender and Representation in Mexico* (New York: Columbia University Press, 1989) 33.

[92] Trueblood, "Introduction," in *A Sor Juana Anthology*, 22.

[93] Susan M. McKenna, "Rational Thought and Female Poetics in Sor Juana's 'Primero sueño': The Circumvention of Two Traditions," in *Hispanic Review* 68, no. 1 (Winter 2000): 42.

[94] Paz, 368.

[95] Franco, 33.

[96] See Mabel Moraña, "Poder, Raza, y Lengua: La Construcción Étnica del Otro en los Villancicos de Sor Juana," *Colonial Latin American Review* 4, no. 2 (1995): 139–54.

illumination and enlightenment, most of the poem belongs to the reign of darkness.[97]

A number of Sor Juana scholars conceive of the night in *Sueño* as a "space" that functions in a variety of ways. Arenal suggests that the night serves as a space where a woman can embark on a quest for knowledge and understanding that brings into question accepted ways of knowing and traditional knowledge without risking censure from the Inquisition.[98] Martínez-San Miguel argues that the night is associated with a space where one is able to propose alternative ways of acquiring "official knowledge," a proposal that eventually leads to the questioning of rationally accepted methods of gaining knowledge and the "official knowledge" itself.[99] Martínez-San Miguel concludes, "The night is, then, the alternative space for the search for knowledge that transgresses the institutional order, particularly because the subject that knows is a woman during the day and asexual (or simply abstract as the soul), during the night."[100]

The poem also passes through liminal spaces, and it is in these places that Feder identifies some of the most radical suggestions of the poem. The gloaming and loss of light before darkness sets in and the growing light before dawn are periods of liminality, as are the phases between waking and sleep. The majority of the poem does not proceed only in those specifically liminal states of fading and emerging light or the transition from sleep to waking, but such phases do bookend the poem, and the themes explored certainly make such a label appropriate. In liminal space, hierarchies are (temporarily) dissolved and status fades, and here in the space described in Sor Juana's poem, a woman's intellect is able to explore realms barred to her because of her status as a woman under the authority of the church (the ecclesiastical hierarchy) and the Spanish

---

[97] See Rosa Perelmuter Pérez, *Noche Intellectual: La Oscuridad Idiomática en el Primero Sueño* (Mexico: UNAM, Instituto de Investigaciones Filológicas, Centro de Estudios Literarios, 1982). Close to half of the poem, lines 445–870 of the 975-line poem, is devoted to a description of the soul's failure to gain the knowledge desired and a vacillation between whether or not it should even dare attempt the feat again: 425 lines are given to the soul's failure to know. 191 introductory lines are given to a description of the reign of the night, darkness, and silence, which is the time in which the following 700 lines proceed, until finally the sun makes its appearance in line 943, leaving only 30 lines to the reign of the sun.

[98] Arenal, "Where Woman," 132.

[99] Martínez-San Miguel, 70.

[100] Ibid. My trans.

Empire to which she was a colonial subject. Here she is not confined to the role assigned and regulated by society and church, but is free to pursue intellectual, philosophical, theological, and scientific concepts, which she would be unable to do freely outside this space. Feder goes so far as to say that in *Sueño*, "Sor Juana inverts the values of the hierarchy and suggests that a system that privileges one extreme, calling it 'noble' (l. 624), to the detriment of the lower levels, which serve it as base and support, is not only unjust; it is also unstable."[101]

Liminal space provides room for ambiguity and is characterized by openness, and may also include chaos. Not only is the sex of the dreamer ambiguous until the final line of the poem, but the soul is free to explore in an open, unrestricted manner, and in this journey (or pilgrimage) the soul encounters chaos as the instability of the realm of knowledge is exposed.[102] Feder also asserts that "liminal spaces are revelatory," and in a way similar to the Open we will discuss in Heidegger, it is a space that reveals the struggle of disclosure and concealment. She writes, "The fall of night hides but at the same time exposes the unequal struggle between darkness and light."[103]

All of these levels of tension and conflict throughout the poem between light and dark, body and soul, day and night, highlight the soul's own struggle, the conflict experienced by the narrator in a longing for understanding and the quest for it, and the rebuff because it cannot be attained. Even the mythological characters upon which Sor Juana draws have some element of tragic fate in their stories, struggle and failure, or a striving/rebellion and a casting down into some inescapable limitation; this is true of all of the figures of night, the night birds, and of Icarus and Phaethon. For example, three sisters are turned into bats for rebelling against Bacchus in favor of the goddess Pallas, and so bound to the form, silence, and the night. Another woman is transformed into an owl and bound to the night and an endless cycle of drinking the sacred oil, or as Stephanie Merrim notes, to Sacrilege.[104] Sor Juana's use of the biblical images of the human with arms stretched to heaven but a mouth filled with dust, and the statue formed of the "most prized metal" but standing on feet of clay, also

---

[101] Feder, 503.

[102] Jean Franco, "Sor Juana Explores Space," in *Plotting Women: Gender and Representation in Mexico* (New York: Columbia University Press, 1989).

[103] Feder, 490.

[104] Merrim, *Early Modern,* 192.

points to this idea of heavenly aspirations, but earthboundedness, binding limits.[105]

The Role of Silence. As stated, *Sueño* transpires in the domains of night and silence, appropriate placement for a discussion of the inability to know, the limits of understanding, and the conflict between revelation and hiddenness, or light and dark.[106] It is also an appropriate context for a discussion of one's failure to gain comprehensive knowledge of God, or of the spark of the divine within the soul, or even the course of a brook under the ground.

The poem foretells of Sor Juana's declarations in *La Respuesta* that her intention was to remain silent and that silence only has meaning when it is first given content, which she sets out to do.[107] McKenna also sees this theme emerging in *Sueño* and the relationship of silence to what Sor Juana is trying to express: "The predominant images of silence in the first few stanzas suggest the likelihood of non-communication in the poem. Harpocrates, the Egyptian god of silence, stifles the muffled sounds of all of earth's creatures.... It becomes evident that Sor Juana does indeed desire to communicate. This communication, however, is realized through silence."[108]

McKenna also notes how naming, or direct saying, has long been associated with the masculine. She says that "women authors often refrain from naming the object or the idea to which their writing refers."[109] Since the time of Adam's naming of the animals, "the power to name has traditionally been a male-inscribed tradition," and therefore, McKenna asserts, women writers

---

[105] *Sueño,* Trueblood, 188. OC 1.352:670–76. Kierkegaard discusses a similar tension endured by humanity, as they have a sense of immortality within their souls, but face mortality.

[106] The reign of night is also the reign of silence in *First Dream.* The poem begins with a description of the muteness of all creatures with the expectation of those mythic birds. "Mute" is also a term highly relevant in current sociolinguistic studies, possibly beginning with the work of Edwin Ardener (1975), who noted the muted women in anthropological research and methodology. See Dale Spender, *Man Made Language*, 2nd ed. (London: Routledge Kegan Paul, 1980) 76ff.

[107] On Sor Juana's silence, see Josefina Ludmer, "Tricks of the Weak," in *Feminist Perspectives on Sor Juana Inés de la Cruz*, trans. and ed. Stephanie Merrim (Detroit: Wayne State University Press, 1991) 86–93; and Mabel Moraña, *Viaje al Silencio: Exploraciones del Discurso Barroco* (México: UNAM, 1998).

[108] McKenna, 48–49.

[109] Ibid., 49.

"learn to exploit their disadvantage by alluding to a particular subject without ever naming it."[110] She also asserts that

> the power of silence to communicate is a strategy employed by women writers throughout the ages.... Sor Juana encoded her writings with hidden currents and images rife with multiple meanings. Concealed within the exaggerated, ornamental verse of "Primero sueño," Sor Juana relates the circumstances of her "politico silencio," "fingida ignorancia," and "secreta pena." In the final verse Sor Juana breaks her self-imposed silence and reveals to the reader the gendered identity of the poet.[111]

Thus, she finds in Sor Juana's use of "baroque circumlocution" the "expressive circularity of feminine poetics," and the theme of silence as a way in which to "bypass the male discourse of naming."[112]

Josefina Ludmer also notes the importance of silence, both in Sor Juana's *Respuesta* and here in *Primero sueño*. She traces a relationship between saying and knowing, and the negation of them in the life and work of Sor Juana, particularly as they relate to superiors and power. She sees the use of silence as a "trick of the weak," of those assigned subservient roles in society. She says that in the relationship between knowledge and saying, or unknowing and silence, one can also

> see the relationship between the *Respuesta*...[and] *Primero sueño*. From one point of view the *Respuesta* can be read as a gloss of the *Sueño,* to the degree that the poem sets forth a theory of knowledge and of epistemological impulses, as well as positing the impossibility of attaining the Absolute. Both the *Respuesta* and the *Sueño* open with the theme of muteness and silence; silence

---

[110] Ibid.

[111] Ibid. Paz comments that "the parallel between *First Dream* and *The Response* is complete," but he considers this to be the case because he says that Sor Juana's conclusion to *The Response* indicates "that *she will continue to write:* there is not the slightest sign of any intention to stop writing, nor is there any notice of a renunciation or a surrender to silence" (Paz, 380). I find a very different intention in *The Response*, as do Arenal and Powell and Ludmer, all of whom note voiced intention toward silence, which I will argue more thoroughly in chapter 5. I argue with Paz that the parallel between *First Dream* and *The Response* is a strong one, but I see a core aspect of that similarity to be in the function of silence.

[112] McKenna, 49.

also constitutes the terminus of the poem: at the peak of understanding—perplexity, silence.[113]

Even when language is the theme (rather than silence), it is viewed as a problem, prone to confusion. The poem signals the problem of language through reference to Babel.[114] Jorge Checa suggests that the poem may express "a crisis of linguistic mediation in the production and transmission of knowledge." [115] Words cannot achieve precise and universal meaning because of the polysemy that results from the contamination and babelization of language. [116] Sabat-Rivers interprets Sor Juana's use of the Tower of Babel as similar to her use of Icarus and Phaethon. It serves as a symbol "of confusion, pride, and failure."[117] And she notes that none of Sor Juana's predecessors used the image in the way she does to emphasize the confusion of language.[118]

As Sabat-Rivers saw in *Sueño* a foreshadowing of the perspective of future generations, Feder sees an affinity between what Sor Juana expresses here and the concerns of some postmodern thinkers. She draws on Foucault, René Girard, and Derrida, saying:

> Over three hundred years before René Girard noticed the symbolic importance of contamination as well as the dangers it presents to the survival of culture, and equally as many before Derrida observed the same process in the mode of functioning of writing itself (Derrida, *Dissemination*), Sor Juana reached the same conclusions. When she analyzes the relation between dominant discourse and its margins, she uses an almost identical conceptual paradigm, describing it in astonishingly similar terms. The dissemination of alternative experiences, she writes, is the greatest threat to the hegemonic order.[119]

---

[113] Ludmer, 89.

[114] On the role of Babel in *Primero Sueño,* see Jorge Checa, "Los Caracteres del Estrago: Babel en *Primero Sueño*," in *Mujer y Cultura en la Colonia Hispanoamericana*, ed. Mabel Moraña (Pittsburgh: Biblioteca de América, 1996) 257–71.

[115] Martínez-San Miguel, 82, my trans. She describes Checa's contribution.

[116] Ibid.

[117] Sabat-Rivers, *Sueño,* 104, my trans.

[118] Ibid.

[119] Feder, 508–509. Feder also draws on Derrida for her interpretation of the Sun in *Sueño*, saying her reading "is based on an application of Jacques Derrida's insights in 'White Mythology'" (523).

Feder goes on to provide an interpretation of Sor Juana's lines on Phaethon to again suggest that the poem challenges not only the dominant tradition's ways of gaining knowledge and claims of that knowledge, but also the forms of discourse used for the communication of said knowledge. Feder writes,

> The dissemination of alternative experiences, she writes, is the greatest threat to the hegemonic order,
>
> "for broadcasting makes the wickedness
> of the greatest crime all the greater
> till it threatens a widespread epidemic,
> while, left in unknown isolation,
> repetition is far less likely
> than if broadcast to all as a would-be lesson." (Trueblood, 191)
>
> Sor Juana was not alone in recognizing the transgressive power of language, and especially of its dissemination's "contaminating" potential.[120]

Feder describes Sor Juana's project in terms very similar to the extended argument laid out throughout this work. She writes, "Her object is to transform a hostile reality, to imagine alternatives, and to find linguistic structures that will re-present them adequately." And she continues,

> Sor Juana's project is as much aesthetic as it is political; her search as much intellectual as ethical, her relationship to language as lucid as it is functional. Her purpose is not to paint reality with "falsely colored syllogisms" ("falsos silogismos de colores"), but rather to try to understand and re-produce it in all its complexity. This singular vision is Sor Juana's greatest contribution to the baroque (and probably to our understanding of postmodernism).[121]

Sandra Harding has highlighted, with thinkers like Foucault and Rorty, that certain epistemologies function to rationalize "the legitimacy of the beliefs of the powerful."[122] Sor Juana's questioning of the dominant epistemologies of her day and the proposition of an epistemology that emphasizes limits due to embodiment, among other things, is, therefore, also a questioning of the beliefs of the powerful these epistemologies serve to legitimate. And here in *Sueño*, she posits these questions and tensions with a series of multilayered oppositions in

---

[120] Ibid., 509.

[121] Ibid., 514.

[122] Sandra Harding, "Feminism, Science, and the Anti-Enlightenment," in *Feminism and Postmodernism*, ed. Linda J. Nicholson (New York: Routledge: 1990) 87.

the fragmented poetic form. Sor Juana critiques the dominant methods of acquiring knowledge, official claims of certain knowledge, and the official forms for communicating knowledge through her questioning of the communicative potential of language. And her moves are mirrored in contemporary philosophy currently. Her work illustrates what Heidegger develops in his later work on poetry, to which we now turn.

Heidegger, Poetry, and Truth at the Rift

In each chapter on a different genre, I use a theorist to assist in uncovering the theological function that genre may particularly accomplish. In my discussion of letters, I use the thought and example of Rosenzweig to underline the temporal and concrete nature of the form, as well as the work of a scholar of epistolary literature. In my chapter on drama, I chiefly utilize the thought of Bakhtin to highlight elements in Sor Juana's *loas* that not only bring out the temporal nature of existence, but specifically bring out her arguments for discourse that persuades internally as contrasted with unifying, authoritative discourse. In this chapter on poetry, I use the thought of Martin Heidegger, whose work is known for its starting point in temporality, to discuss how poetry can express the tensions between the revealed and the hidden. I am not using him as some philosophical hero, but find his concepts on art a useful and interesting metaphor for a discussion of knowledge in Christian existence.[123]

I have argued that the tension between revelation and human existence has been thematized in the tradition as the hiddenness of God; here I want to focus on the conflict itself in order to build a case for the particular function poetry can play in the expression of this aspect of Christianity. I have argued that the "hiddenness of God" does not belong in a theological system such that it there becomes another form of knowledge, suggesting we know exactly where and how God is hidden instead of serving to point to unknowing. Here, utilizing Heidegger's work on poetry and art, I highlight the role of poetry in expressing, while avoiding systematizing, this theme and the conflict itself.

---

[123] There are many limitations to using Heidegger in this project. Obviously there is his support of the Nazis in Germany, which makes his thought suspect and should possibly lead to a complete rejection of it. There is also the consideration of the extent to which his early philosophy may have been the construction of a unity and totality of its own. Then there is the very opacity of his writings themselves, particularly his later works, which we are concerning ourselves with here. See William Spanos on Heidegger and Nazism.

I recognize that my application of his thought here to express the tension in the God-human relationship from the perspective of human existence is stretching the intention of Heidegger's project as a whole, because he did not expand upon the relation in such specific terms; however, I think it will be clear that his insistence that art and poetry express the aspect of veiling and unveiling one encounters in *Dasein*, and of truth's location at the rift between the concealed and the disclosed, are useful arguments for the nature of poetry to deal with these aspects in Christianity. I believe it will also be evident that poetry serves well as a form that can communicate the rift: the unresolved tension experienced in a Christian existence as we have been describing it, that is, in motion, transition and transformation, lived in time but in relation to the eternal entered into historical time, bringing salvation through the historical process of Jesus' life, death, and resurrection, but applied now to our present and aimed at a continued social and personal transformation into the future. Poetry here functions theologically not simply in expressing the hiddenness itself, or solely communicating the Hiddenness of God, but in considering the rift, the veiling and unveiling, the concealedness and unconcealedness; it expresses the struggle between the known and unknown in Christianity as we saw illustrated by Sor Juana's *Primero sueño*. Heidegger's project also functions well here because his philosophy proceeds with an understanding of knowledge much like that with which we have been working, as something lived and not simply propositional or conceptual. He has, in fact, been compared to Kierkegaard on some of these issues and is known to be indebted to him.

I have not denied the facticity of the God-human, but our access to that fact or event when truth is understood as "correct" in a fact-based framework. Scripture gives a historical account, but even that as "history" is not "objective." The truth of the God-human may rest there at the relationship between Christ and humanity, that is, the incarnation. So, too, theology is a reflection upon that God-relation, which exists in the person of Christ and persists in the world through the continuing work of the Holy Spirit. Yet there is a rift, a rift not dissimilar from that experienced by Christ's very disciples; his existence as the God-human had to be revealed by the Spirit to the heart of the person. The God-relation is never simply objective fact, empirically observable. This double-revealing, both of the God-human relation that constitutes the person of Christ, and of the ongoing God-human relationship now experienced through Christ, has been called the objective and subjective side of revelation. Though Kierkegaard in *Postscript* spoke of Christian knowledge as relating only to subjective truth when talking about faith, it would be appropriate to see his work as moving away from the very dichotomy of subject and object, subjectivity and objectivity, and instead to speak of a different kind of understanding of knowledge altogether, one that does not fit into this schema. This other view on knowledge and truth is closer to that developed under the influence of Kierkegaard's work and Heidegger. That is: knowledge is not static but relational, and because it is relational, on some level "subjective" may be an appropriate label, but it is more than this term traditionally signifies and does not simply stand in opposition to an objective knowledge; instead it involves a more holistic view including the individual and the world in which the individual is situated, including context, community, and action, past experience, present embodiment, and future expectations and trajectory. For the purposes of theology, this perspective opens the possibility to pursue Christian reflection on the God-human relation, allowing the person and work of Christ to serve not simply as an objective text from which propositional statements can be derived, but as the key to understanding the very God relation itself, upon which Christianity in turn reflects: God in relation to creation, the world, and humanity. I am proposing that it is the very relation itself that is the point of theological reflection.[124]

I primarily draw from Heidegger's lectures "The Origins of the Work of Art," which are considered the most important essays for understanding the later Heidegger and his work on poetry. Heidegger describes the field of the arts in general, but he considers poetry to be the highest expression of the artistic impulse: "the poem in the narrower sense, has a privileged position in the

[124] Kierkegaard makes the argument in *Postscript* (216) as noted in chapter 1 that systematic theology treats Jesus as if he had been a professor and the disciples as if they were a society of scholars. In his journals he makes a similar argument for the activity of Christ's life, which reveals his nature and God-relation and contrasts the Christian religion to Islam, which is in fact based on direct teaching with an objective relation to the text. He writes: *"Christian dogmatics…must grow out of Christ's activity, and all the more so* because Christ did not establish any doctrine; he acted. He *did not teach* that there was redemption for men, be *he redeemed men.* A Mohammedan dogmatics…would grow out of Mohammed's teaching, but a Christian dogmatics grows out of Christ's activity. Through Christ's activity (which actually was the main thing) his nature also was given; Christ's relationship to God, man, nature, and the human situation *was conditioned by his activity.*" Søren Kierkegaard, *Søren Kierkegaard's Journals and Papers,* vol. 1, A–E, ed. and trans. Howard V. Hong and Edna H. Hong (Bloomington and London: Indiana University Press, 1967) 168, entry no. 412.

domain of the arts."[125] Art, but poetry in particular, is a happening of truth: "Truth, as the clearing and concealing of what is, happens in being composed, as a poet composes a poem. *All art,* as the letting happen of the advent of the truth of what is, is, as such, *essentially poetry.*"[126] Heidegger's account of poetry is particularly interesting and useful for our purposes here because he explains poetry (and art) as that which projects a strife, conflict, or rift between the unconcealed and the concealed—poetry is an "instigation of the strife of truth"—and he understands truth to be exactly this conflict, struggle, or tension between what is disclosed and what is hidden.[127] In poetry, says Heidegger, one may "come to learn what is unspoken," and he proposes a dialogue with poetry within philosophy, recognizing that "scholars of literary history inevitably consider that dialogue to be an unscientific violation of what such scholarship takes to be the facts. Philosophers consider the dialogue to be a helpless aberration into fantasy."[128]

If poetry is particularly well suited for expressing the happening of truth, as Heidegger suggests, then it seems that the form is especially appropriate for the expression of the tension within Christian existence, between the revealed and the hidden God, between what theology proclaims and what is encountered in life. The poem, as it locates truth in that rift itself, in the conflict which holds together the two, not in a resolved union, but in a continual movement of struggle together (yet not as posited as opposites), is especially well suited to communicate Christian knowledge, as both knowing and unknowing, while avoiding the systematizing of said "knowledge." It is also well illustrated in *Primero sueño* as we saw its composition of tension and opposition, of light and dark, of knowledge and lack of knowledge.

In the pages that follow, I will provide a reading of this difficult text of Heidegger, understanding his work in many ways to serve as a useful metaphor to get at a conception of religious truth as the relationship I have described and as such in tension. I will not try to exegete the entire thought of later Heidegger or even to exegete the full lectures, but will note the aspects important to my project. (1) I begin with a brief description of his understanding of truth,

---

[125] Martin Heidegger, "The Origin of the Work of Art," in *Poetry, Language, Thought*, trans. Albert Hofstadter (New York: Harper & Row, 1971) 73.

[126] Ibid., 72.

[127] Ibid., 76.

[128] Martin Heidegger, "What Are Poets For?" in *Poetry, Language, Thought*, trans. Albert Hofstadter (New York: Harper & Row, 1971) 96.

knowledge, and language in order to situate his thought in the suppositions of this work regarding the nature of truth, knowledge, existence, and communication, as well as to give a foundation for a better understanding of what he has to say about poetic discourse. (2) I then move on to his description of "world" and "earth" as the unconcealed and the concealed and the rift of opposition between them. (3) Lastly I consider his essay "What Are Poets For?" in which he talks about the world's night that he sees occurring, as this opens the way for us to consider poetry's unique relation to the night and darkness, or that struggle of faith with the hiddenness of God.

Truth and Knowledge. In "The Origin of the Work of Art," Heidegger builds upon his critique of Western philosophy and its "logical prejudice" and takes on the nature of propositional statements and what they are assumed to accomplish.[129] He sees a relationship between the structure of a propositional statement and the common conception of the structure of a thing: a combination of subject and predication, substance and accidents, or an object with attributes. Heidegger is helpful for us because he does not work from a conception of truth as static fact or of knowledge as correct information. He views truth as a happening, and knowledge consists of an active willing. His philosophy endeavors to reconceive the way one knows by overturning the subject-object dualism dependent upon a conception of an autonomous subject and of objects independent and outside that subject to be purely observed or perceived.[130] He identifies the whole of Western philosophy from Plato through Descartes and Kant to be guilty of this disconnect between being and world and blames this in part on the elevation of theory and propositional claims. He asks: "Is the structure of a simple propositional statement (the combination of subject and predicate) the mirror image of the structure of the thing (of the union of substance with accidents)? Or could it be that even the structure of the thing as

---

[129] See Daniel O. Dahlstrom, *Heidegger's Concept of Truth* (Cambridge: Cambridge University Press, 2001).

[130] In this sense Feder may not be off base in viewing *Sueño* as a precursor to post-modern concerns, as we saw Sor Juana emphasizes the knowing subject's embodiment and the limits to knowing based on the impact one's embeddedness in time and space has upon the perspective one can achieve, making knowledge contextual or "situated" and not objective or detached. For example, in her lines, "She thought herself almost loosed from that bodily chain that always blocks her path, obstructing crudely and grossly interfering with the flight of intellect through which she plumbs the vast immensity of the firmament" (Trueblood, 178–79), and the conclusion of the poem where her body stirs and her gender is known.

thus envisaged is a projection of the framework of the sentence?"[131] He accuses the commonly accepted Western way of understanding the relations between subject, object, and knowledge of only seeming to be critical while actually "being rash and ill-considered," and claims it is only "seemingly well founded."[132]

Because the propositional statement is composed of a subject with its predicate, he wonders if this is not why such a composition is considered the nature of a thing along Aristotelian lines—a substance and its accidents. And he wonders if this view of the nature of a thing is not simply accepted because this is the way of a proposition and not the other way around, that is, not because this is truly the nature of things and thus propositions follow suit. He asks which comes first,[133] and critiques Aristotelian categories and the way in which aspects of being in the world are divided up into different components, being separated conceptually, as we already saw Sor Juana critiquing in her poem.[134] He also questions the predominance of thought understood as theoretical reasoning. He says:

> Occasionally we still have the feeling that violence has long been done to the thingly element of things and that thought has played a part in this violence, for which reason people disavow thought instead of taking pains to make it more thoughtful. But in defining the nature of the thing, what is the use of a feeling, however certain, if thought alone has the right to speak here? Perhaps however what we call feeling or mood, here and in similar instances, is more reasonable—that is, more intelligently perceptive—because more open to Being than all that

---

[131] Heidegger, "Origins of the Work of Art," 24.

[132] Ibid.

[133] Heidegger writes: "Actually, the sentence structure does not provide the standard for the pattern of thing-structure, nor is the latter simply mirrored in the former. Both sentence and thing-structure derive, in their typical form and their possible mutual relationship, from a common and more original source. In any case this first interpretation of the thingness of the thing, the thing as bearer of its characteristic traits, despite its currency, is not as natural as it appears to be. What seems natural to us is probably just something familiar in a long tradition that has forgotten the unfamiliar source from which it arose. And yet this unfamiliar source once struck man as strange and caused him to think and to wonder" ("Origins of the Work of Art," 24).

[134] Interestingly we encounter Sor Juana in *First Dream* attempting to use the categories to gain knowledge, but she finds that system unable to accomplish what it proposes. She discovers the categories unable to offer a way to real knowledge despite its most systematic structure.

reason which having meanwhile become *ratio*, was misinterpreted as being rational.[135]

He sees these conceptions of the nature of the thing, propositions, and thought as driving the dominant understanding of truth, which Heidegger sets out to revolutionize. He describes the accepted view of truth as "the agreement or conformity of knowledge with fact."[136] According to the Western tradition, Heidegger says, "A proposition is true by conforming to the unconcealed, to what is true. Propositional truth is always, and always exclusively, this correctness. The critical concepts of truth which, since Descartes, start out from truth as certainty, are merely variations of the definition of truth as correctness."[137] This view of truth inadequately restricts it to what is unconcealed, not giving room for the hidden. Yet, a fact cannot show itself to be such unless it stands in the "unconcealed," and so Heidegger asserts that this very conception of truth as correctness "stands and falls with truth as the unconcealedness of beings."[138] Unconcealedness is the prevailing way in which Heidegger discusses truth, which he complicates in his later writings, a development to which we will shortly turn. Heidegger offers a more literal translation of the Greek word traditionally translated as "truth," *aletheia*, as "unconcealedness," and through this emphasis he develops a more active notion of truth, in which truth moves from concealed to disclosed, where truth is "setting itself into work," or to give his concrete example: where the truth which "occurs is the act that founds a political state."[139] Truth is a "happening."

He says that when we conceive of truth as unconcealedness, "we are reminding ourselves of what, unexperienced and unthought, underlies our familiar and therefore outworn nature of truth in the sense of correctness."[140] Heidegger recalls what we encountered in *Sueño;* he writes that: "there is much in being that man cannot master. There is but little that comes to be known. What is known remains inexact, what is mastered insecure."[141] He, like Socrates and Sor Juana, asserts that he, and humanity, know little. And his depiction of the little knowledge we do have shows it to be unstable. Knowledge in this

---

[135] "Origins of the Work of Art," 25.

[136] Ibid., 52.

[137] Ibid.

[138] Ibid.

[139] Ibid., 62.

[140] Ibid., 52.

[141] Ibid., 53.

description is not primarily a matter of information, nor is it based on traditional conceptions of certainty, but the active conception of it shows truth as a movement to unconcealedness and back into the concealed, giving unknowing a place within the very concept of truth. The term itself serves as a reminder of all that is unknown and the insecure nature of what is known.

In terms of art and poetry, Heidegger speaks of truth as fixed on some level, as it is set back in stone, wood, words, and the like. It is also "thrown," a typical Heideggerian term, again showing the active movement involved in being and truth.[142] Those to whom such truth in art is thrown are called its "preservers." Preservers are a historical group of people who read or hear a poem, or observe a piece of art, and perceive the truth. They are essential to art, just as are the author and the work of art itself. He describes the knowledge of such a preserver as an active willing: "This 'standing-within' of preservation, however, is a knowing. Yet knowing does not consist in mere information and notions about something. He who truly knows what is, knows what he wills to do in the midst of what is."[143] Despite the seemingly abstract nature of poetry, as it often has neither an addressee nor explicit historical location, Heidegger insists that art as truth thrown at preservers is done so to a specific, historical group, and that it is therefore "never an arbitrary demand."[144]

---

[142] Ibid., 67. It is described this way by the translator of *Poetry, Language, and Thought*, Albert Hofstadter: "Thrownness is understood in *Being and Time* as an existential characteristic of *Dasein,* human being, its thatness, its 'that it is,' and it refers to the facticity of human being's being handed over to itself, its being on its own responsibility; as long as human being is what it is, it is thrown, cast, 'im Wurf'" (*Poetry, Language, and Thought,* 72).

[143] Heidegger further elaborates, relating his later work here to what he had accomplished in *Being and Time:* "The willing here referred to, which neither merely applies knowledge nor decides beforehand, is thought of in terms of the basic experience of thinking in *Being and Time*. Knowing that remains a willing, and willing that remains a knowing, is the existing human being's entrance into and compliance with the unconcealedness of Being. The resoluteness intended in *Being and Time* is not the deliberate action of a subject, but the opening up of human being, out of its capacity in that which is, to the openness of Being. However, in existence, man does not proceed from some inside to some outside; rather, the nature of *Existenz* is out-standing standing-within the essential sunderance of the clearing of beings" ("Origins of the Work of Art," 67).

[144] The full quote from Heidegger here, reads: "The poetic projection of truth that sets itself into work as figure is also never carried out in the direction of an

The view of language related to the view of truth and knowledge Heidegger identified with Western philosophy conceives of language as a conveyer of information. Heidegger, however, develops a far more active view of language to compliment his likewise active conception of knowledge and truth. Language is the means of bringing what is into the Open, into the clearing where the conflict between the unconcealed and concealed occurs. Because language brings this about, poetry is a higher art than visual or musical arts. Because knowledge is no longer, then, retaining information, language is also viewed differently, much more akin to the Kierkegaardian view of communication discussed in chapter 1. Heidegger describes the "current view" of language, that which corresponds to the Western tradition's understanding of knowledge, truth, and the nature of the thing: "It serves for verbal exchange and agreement, and in general for communicating."[145] He continues, "But language is not only and not primarily an audible and written expression of what is to be communicated. It not only puts forth in words and statements what is overtly or covertly intended to be communicated."[146] Language is used to push the reader to reconceive of the relationship between self and world in the complex matrix of Being.[147]

---

indeterminate void. Rather, in the work, truth is thrown toward the coming preservers, that is, toward an historical group of men. What is thus cast forth is, however, never an arbitrary demand. Genuinely poetic projection is the opening up or disclosure of that into which human being as historical is already cast" ("Origins of the Work of Art," 76).

[145] "Origins of the Work of Art," 73.

[146] Ibid.

[147] "Projected" or "projecting" is another term used by Heidegger to assist in his reworking of traditional conceptions of existence and the divide between being and knowing. He writes: "Projecting is the release of a throw by which unconcealedness submits and infuses itself into what is as such. This projective announcement forthwith becomes a renunciation of all the dim confusion in which what is veils and withdraws itself. Projective saying is poetry: the saying of world and earth, the saying of the arena of their conflict and thus of the place of all nearness and remoteness of the gods.... Projective saying is saying which, in preparing the sayable, simultaneously brings the unsayable as such into the world"[147] ("Origins of the Work of Art," 73–74). Heidegger uses words like "throw" and "projected" in order to convey that what occurs in this use of language is not the sort of communication one is used to conceiving; it is not information transmission. It is not the speaking of a static fact to be held cognitively, but the words "thrown" and "project" have an array of meanings when used by him, including a movement toward one's possibilities, decision, and decision itself for

In his essay on Rilke's poetry, "What Are Poets For?", Heidegger makes a helpful distinction in the sorts of knowledge he is here discussing, and its purposes for our argument should be obvious. He distinguishes between the knowledge described by two modern thinkers: Descartes and Pascal. Heidegger is trying to get at what is "essentially inner," or the "sphere of the invisible interior," which he says modern metaphysics along the line of Descartes define as "the realm of the presence of calculated objects."[148] The inner, interior, or invisible realm according to this tradition is understood as the realm of cognitive reason. Yet, there is an alternative. Contemporary with Descartes, Pascal discovered "the logic of the heart as over against the logic of calculating reason."[149] In this understanding, "the inner and invisible domain of the heart is not only more inward than the interior that belongs to calculating representation," but it is only there that a person is inclined toward that which is for her to love.[150] Heidegger lists the things there to be loved as: "the forefathers, the dead, the children, those who are to come," but others could be added, and Pascal would certainly include "God" among those things to love.[151] Heidegger says this "interior of uncustomary consciousness" is the realm "in which everything is for us beyond the arithmetic of calculation, and free of such boundaries, can overflow into the unbounded whole of the Open."[152] And he asserts, "Only what we thus retain in our heart (*par coeur*), only that do we truly know by heart."[153] The implications for this project of such a conception of knowing as "inner," "of the "heart," or that which shows humanity what there is

---

Heidegger suggests the rift, because without that tension there would be no decision properly speaking. Heidegger's translator, Hofstadter, gives this explanation of "projection": "Projection, on the other hand, is a second existential character of human being, referring to its driving forward toward its own possibility of being. It takes the form of understanding, which the author speaks of as the mode of being in which human being *is* in its possibility *as* possibilities. It is not the mere having of a preconceived plan, but is the projecting of possibility in human being that occurs antecedently to all plans and makes planning possible. Human being is both thrown and projected; it is thrown project, factical directedness toward possibilities of being" (*Poetry, Language, and Thought,* 72).

[148] "What Are Poets For?" 127.

[149] Ibid.

[150] Ibid., 127–28.

[151] Ibid., 128.

[152] Ibid.

[153] Ibid., 130.

to love, are clear. This is the sort of inner persuasion we find Kierkegaard seeking to convey, and will find in chapter 4 with Bakhtin through his description of inner persuasion contrasting authoritarian coercion and Sor Juana's similar pitted contrast in her dramas. Knowing resides in the movement of the whole person, not in an isolated cognitive exercise.

The Rift Between the Earth and the World. Heidegger's conception of the work of art and the truth "thrown" to the preserver rests upon his conception of the "earth" and "world," terms very difficult to define and almost resisting definition in Heidegger's usage. They exist not in a static opposition to each other but in a dynamic unity with openness that does not "exclude motion from itself but includes it."[154] It is a happening; thus, its close relation to his conception of truth is not surprising. Earlier I described truth for Heidegger as *aletheia*, unconcealedness. However, in his important later essays in *Poetry, Language, Thought,* Heidegger modifies this somewhat, adding hiddenness or concealment to this understanding, so that truth is both disclosure and concealment.[155] This tension is also described in terms of earth and world. At times in his work, it appears as if the world itself is the Open, the clearing which allows for truth to happen, yet as the lectures progress, it seems evident that it is actually the strife, the tension there between the revealed and the hidden that creates the Open and the clearing where the disclosing and concealing occur.

World is associated with being unconcealed, or a "self-disclosing openness."[156] Earth is described as the "spontaneous forthcoming of that which is continually self-secluding and to that extent sheltering and concealing."[157] These two, earth and world, are in relationship to one another but in a conflictual manner: "The world, in resting upon the earth, strives to surmount it. As self-opening it cannot endure anything closed. The earth, however, as sheltering and concealing, tends always to draw the world into itself and keep it there."[158] Thus, although the two are "essentially different from one another," they "are never separated."[159] This dialectical relationship between earth and

---

[154] "Origins of the Work of Art," 48.

[155] For a work helpful in gaining an understanding of Heidegger's later work on poetry, see Gerald L. Bruns, *Heidegger's Estrangements: Language, Truth, and Poetry in the Later Writings* (New Haven: Yale University Press, 1989).

[156] "Origins of the Work of Art," 48.

[157] Ibid.

[158] Ibid., 49.

[159] Ibid., 48–49.

world, however, "does not wither away into the empty unity of opposites unconcerned with one another."[160]

The relationship between what is concealed and what is revealed can be one of "dissembling," as the revealing of one conceals another. He describes this interaction as one in which "one being places itself in front of another thing, the one helps to hide the other, the former obscures the latter, a few obstruct many, one denies all. Here concealment is not simple refusal. Rather, a being appears, but it presents itself as other than it is. This concealment is dissembling."[161] His description of a concealment that occurs through appearing as other than it is resonates with my description in chapter 1 of Hiddenness I. There I described God's hiddenness in Christ, where, for example, God is said to be most revealed and most concealed in Christ on the cross. There God is hidden in the form of a suffering, abandoned human being. The integral relationship between hiddenness and revelation in the incarnation is recognized in the theme here called Hiddenness I. However, the comparison between Heidegger's work and that of the Christian conception of the hiddenness of God is limited as Heidegger calls this "dissembling," described above as a form of deception because it presents itself as other than it is. Nonetheless, when he describes the Open as that place of revealing and concealment, it does resonate with the Christian experience of revelation in that God's revelation of Godself in Christ is not an obvious, open, stark uncovering of truth, but always requires the Spirit's work in faith, much like what Luther described as that assurance that comes now and then, here and there, but is not always and lasting. It is not a permanent vision before the empirical eyes. Heidegger writes:

> The open place in the midst of beings, the clearing, is never a rigid stage with a permanently raised curtain on which the play of beings run its course. Rather, the clearing happens only as this double concealment. The unconcealedness of beings—this is never a merely existent state, but a happening. Unconcealedness (truth) is neither an attribute of factual things in the sense of beings, nor one of propositions.[162]

The concealment is not wholly negative, however, as it is "not simply and only the limit of knowledge in any given circumstance, but the beginning of the clearing of what is lighted."[163] Again, here Heidegger notes the important

---

[160] Ibid., 49.

[161] Ibid., 54.

[162] Ibid.

[163] Ibid.

relationship between the concealment and the revelation. This concealing is not only what we think of as the limits of understanding, or for our purposes: the inability of humanity to comprehend God, but the concealing is actually related to the revealing. The concealment is not something to be lamented but is the "beginning of the clearing." Heidegger states that "the clearing is pervaded by a constant concealment in the double form of refusal and dissembling. At bottom, the ordinary is not ordinary; it is extra-ordinary, uncanny."[164] The clearing and dissembling are not simply a denial of knowledge, but are perhaps best understood as what occurs when the "ordinary is not ordinary," but "is extra-ordinary." Again the application of this concept to the discussion of the hiddenness of God may be apparent: God concealed in human flesh, or God's incarnation in a humble carpenter from Nazareth, would be an extra-ordinary occurrence, yet such a human existence itself appears ordinary.

Heidegger continues:

> The nature of truth, that is, of unconcealedness, is dominated throughout by a denial. Yet this denial is not a defect or a fault, as though truth were an unalloyed unconcealedness that has rid itself of everything concealed. If truth could accomplish this, it would no longer be itself. *This denial, in the form of a double concealment, belongs to the nature of truth as unconcealedness.* Truth, in its nature, is un-truth.[165]

He is not stating that truth is at its core only falsehood, but boldly expresses "that denial in the manner of concealment belongs to unconcealedness as clearing."[166] Nor does this statement "mean that truth is never itself but, viewed dialectically, is always also its opposite."[167] But again, it is not the simple negation of each other; it is a dynamic opposition. This conflict between the disclosing and concealing of world and earth creates the Open and the clearing.

> Truth is un-truth, insofar as there belongs to it the reservoir of the not-yet-uncovered, the un-uncovered, in the sense of concealment. In unconcealedness, as truth, there occurs as such in the opposition of clearing and double concealing. Truth is the primal conflict in which, always in some particular way, the Open is won within which everything stands and from which everything withholds itself that shows itself and withdraws itself as a being. Whenever and however this

[164] Ibid.

[165] Ibid.

[166] Ibid., 54–55.

[167] Ibid., 55.

> conflict breaks out and happens, the opponents, lighting or clearing and concealing, move apart because of it. Thus the Open of the place of conflict is won.[168]

He calls this struggle, and the clearing it constitutes, the "primal conflict." "The nature of truth is, in itself, the primal conflict in which that open center is won within which what is stands," and "truth happens as the primal conflict between clearing and concealing."[169] The picture Heidegger gives of truth and reality is one of conflict and opposition, and he asserts poetry as the best form to communicate this strife that creates the Open. Again Sor Juana's poem portrays a similar reality as it narrates the dream of objective knowledge in contrast to the reality of embodiment and limits on knowing through her series of oppositions.

The word Heidegger gives this site of conflict is *Riss*, "rift." This rift, however, is not to be understood "as a mere cleft is ripped open."[170] Instead, Heidegger describes it as "the intimacy with which opponents belong to each other."[171] He says, "This rift does not let the opponents break apart; it brings the opposition of measure and boundary into their common outline."[172] Heidegger says that "in the strife the unity of world and earth is won"; however, this intimacy of opposition is not resolved in such a way as to form a closed dialectic.[173] The opposition creates the Open, and so stands in an open dialectic like that proposed by Kierkegaard, who pushed for a dialectic without the synthesis of Hegel's closed dialectic. "Truth establishes itself in the work. Truth is present only as the conflict between lighting and concealing in the opposition of world and earth. Truth wills to be established in the work as this conflict of world and earth. The conflict is not to be resolved."[174] "Knowing" for Heidegger is actually standing in the conflict, the rift, a space in which Sor Juana positioned herself, at the struggle between knowing and unknowing.

The work of art is "fitted into the rift," fixes it in place, and makes the conflict "manifest." The poem, according to Heidegger, fixes the rift in place, so to speak; it holds the disclosing and concealing conflict of truth to be "thrown"

---

[168] Ibid., 61.

[169] Ibid., 55.

[170] Ibid., 63.

[171] Ibid.

[172] Ibid.

[173] Ibid.

[174] Ibid.

toward preservers. "There lies hidden in nature a rift-design, a measure and a boundary and, tied to it, a capacity for bringing forth—that is, art."[175] The poem somehow presents this Open, this conflict as truth, to the "preserver," to the one who hears, understands, and makes it her own.

To make the application of this idea to our arguments more explicit: Not only is truth not simple disclosure of fact or correctness as earlier described, but further, truth neither exists as direct disclosure. Truth is also the denial of such disclosure. Christian truth, then, is not only the *deus revelatus* but also *deus absconditus*. Christian knowledge, then, is not only knowing but also unknowing. This conception of truth stands within a framework that does not look at the life of Christ as a composition of factual propositions off which one can read direct doctrinal statements, but looks at the relation between the lived existence of Jesus Christ and that of the human being in time.

Heidegger also calls this opposition a "striving." This corresponds for us with the Kierkegaardian conception of authentic existence as a striving or quest never concluded in this life.[176] To view truth as this dynamic opposition in movement and counter-movement, as striving, also underscores the limits of propositional statements and conclusive systems because the movement or striving that continues through life is an aspect of the truth under consideration. The tension between God revealed and God hidden to humans in existence does not cease in the age of theology. The opposition between known and unknown continues in the striving and so the God-relation that is Christianity cannot be honestly portrayed by a conclusive system, which does not make sense of the religion or its truth.

This striving is not chaos, however, nor is it even simply disorderly. An alternative to closed dialectics and totalizing discourses is not disorderly or confused discourse. "The opposition of world and earth is a striving. But we would surely all too easily falsify its nature if we were to confound striving with discord and dispute, and thus see it only as disorder and destruction. In essential striving, rather, the opponents raise each other into the self-assertion of their natures."[177] He says the work of art, or poem, instigates the striving, but he clarifies that the work does not set up the opposition so as to "settle and put an end to the conflict in an insipid agreement, but so that the strife may remain a

---

[175] Ibid., 70.

[176] This is a theme expounded upon in Sor Juana's *First Dream*, especially through the figure of Phaethon.

[177] Ibid., 49.

strife."[178] This is certainly true of *Sueño,* which sets up the continued and unending striving as the virtue of life, even as the "dream" also recalls death and the recognition that one's goal of understanding will never be satisfied in life. Christian knowledge is not to be "in truth" in some static way as if one could simply assent to "revealed" dogmatic "truths," but it is to live in this tension of and between the concealed and the unconcealed, what is revealed in Jesus Christ and the mystery of salvation and the state of the world. It is the movement that persists between the history of the world and humanity and the hiddenness of God within it and what is revealed of God in Christ and the prophets, which as we learn from Luther, is not only an unveiling but also a veiling. That relation endures, and as time progresses, so does the relation exist in movement. The happening of truth, then, is at that rift, not simply some pure, abstract, divine revelation in propositional form, but truth is in the movement: Christian truth as God's relation to those in existence. It is dynamic on all sides. The goal is not then to attempt to put existence, history, suffering, darkness, or hiddenness aside, as if truth exists only on one side of the rift, only in the unconcealed or in the light. Instead, that struggle and striving between the two are actually the Open itself, where truth happens, where being is and becomes.

> Only this clearing grants and guarantees to us humans a passage to those beings that we ourselves are not, and access to the being that we ourselves are. Thanks to this clearing, beings are unconcealed in certain changing degrees. And yet a being can be *concealed,* too, only within the sphere of what is lighted. Each being we encounter and which encounters us keeps to this curious opposition of presence in that it always withholds itself at the same time in a concealedness. The clearing in which beings stand is in itself at the same time concealment.[179]

So the Christian should not run from the tensions, should not fear they jeopardize faith because they are what make faith, faith. Nor should theologians try to resolve them: "Truth happens only by establishing itself in the conflict and sphere opened up by truth itself. Because truth is the opposition of clearing and concealing, there belongs to it what is here to be called establishing. But truth does not exist in itself beforehand, somewhere among the stars, only later to descend elsewhere among beings."[180] Truth is that conflict and in that conflict (the relation-existence) and not out there somewhere as static fact.

[178] Ibid.
[179] Ibid., 53.
[180] Ibid., 61.

Poetry and the Night. Now we turn to Heidegger's discussion of the relationship between poetry and night in his essay "What Are Poets For?" In this, Heidegger writes: "Night is falling. Ever since the 'united three'—Herakles, Dionysos, and Christ—have left the world, the evening of the world's age has been declining toward its night. The world's night is spreading its darkness. The era is defined by the god's failure to arrive, by the 'default of God.'"[181] He does not consider such a statement to be a denial of the relationship of God to Christians and the church, but he believes the default of God "means that no god any longer gathers men and things unto himself, visibly and unequivocally, and by such gathering disposes the world's history and man's sojourn in it."[182] God's work in the world is not clear or obvious and not even necessarily discernible by people of faith. For example, is God unequivocally gathering humanity to Godself? It would be even more difficult to argue that God's presence is clearly discernible in history or in humanity's activity or in nature. Heidegger says, "Not only have the gods and the god fled, but the divine radiance has become extinguished in the world's history. ...It has already grown so destitute, it can no longer discern the default of God as a default."[183]

He describes the "world's night" as a time so destitute it is "no longer able even to experience its own destitution."[184] And he speculates: "Perhaps the world's night is now approaching its midnight. Perhaps the world's time in now becoming the completely destitute time. But also perhaps not, not yet, not even yet, despite the immeasurable need, despite all suffering, despite nameless sorrow, despite the growing and spreading peacelessness, despite the mounting confusion."[185] To be a poet, then, according to Heidegger, is to be such in a time of darkness, when God's ways in the world are not clear, when the time is one of "immeasurable need," "suffering," "growing and spreading peacelessness," and "mounting confusion." "To be a poet in a destitute time means: to attend, singing, to the trace of the fugitive gods."[186] He calls the time "destitute" because "the nature of pain, death, and love" remains concealed. Humanity

[181] "What Are Poets For?" 91.

[182] Ibid.

[183] Ibid.

[184] Ibid., 93.

[185] Ibid.

[186] Ibid., 94. "The time is destitute because it lacks the unconcealedness of the nature of pain, death, and love" ("What Are Poets For?" 97).

seems to have lost the "track" leading to the divine, according to Heidegger.[187] He says, "It remains undecided whether we still experience the holy as the track leading to the godhead of the divine, or whether we now encounter no more than a trace of the holy. It remains unclear what the track leading to the trace might be. It remains in question how such a track might show itself to us."[188] What is the track leading us to a trace of the divine? How is this disclosed to us? His voice sounds of frustration, asking for a clear meaning in the world, for sense to be made of it, when the answers given do not seem to correspond.[189]

According to Heidegger, this is the world's night. We are in the night, and the poet's calling, then, is to attend to the trace of God. Poet and literary theorist Edward Hirsch has also noted the unique relationship between poetry and night, or as he calls it: the "night mind." We now move into a brief consideration of "night poems" using the work of Hirsch in order to elucidate this reading of Sor Juana's *First Dream*, which is located primarily in the night and displays features of the night poem.

The Night Poem

Edward Hirsch provides an analysis of the differences in time of day depicted in poetry. First is the dawn song, which he associates primarily with the aubade, or poems of lovers who must part at the break of day. These poems recall the joy of love experienced and lament the impending separation. The morning parting scene between Romeo and Juliet stands as a classic example. However, some poets use this theme to express the loss of something besides the human lover at daybreak; Philip Larkin, for example, is reminded of the impending loss of life at the break of a new day in his poem *Aubade*. The second type of poem Hirsch considers is the morning poem, which celebrates life and nature; it is a song of praise. The afternoon poem is one of questioning and skepticism, irony and doubt. Hirsch includes poetry of witness or poetry of social and/or political challenge in this time of day. The poem of sundown marks the transition between "daylight mind" to the "night mind," from the light to the darkness, from the visible to the invisible, and "thereby takes us into the domain of

---

[187] Ibid., 97.

[188] Ibid.

[189] Again, my interpretation of Heidegger here is not intended to deny revelation but to highlight, as we found in Luther, that this revelation often runs counter to human experience, and in such moments cannot be comprehended comprehensively, and as noted in the last section, leaves one with uncertainty, but trusting God in faith.

psyche, of soul.... It defamiliarizes the objective world and estranges us from our ordinary selves."[190] Hirsch groups these poems of dusk and the poems of night together. Here he moves to a discussion of Spanish poet Frederico García Garcia Lorca and the *duende,* which he describes as a "form of dark inspiration, and it means something like artistic inspiration in the presence of death."[191] He writes, "The night poem puts us in the presence of nothingness.... The sundown poem turns into a nocturne of sleeplessness, the cry of the solitary and bereft ensouled in poetic form."[192] The poem of "a clear midnight" is quite different from the despair associated with the night poem.

> At this culminating hour in the nocturnal realm...everything must be let go that is associated with day, with daylight mind. Rather, the mind is now completely loosened for reverie and illumination, and poetry feels its metaphysical aspiration, its spirituality, its grandeur. This is the moment when lyric poetry, one of the soul's natural habitats, seeks to release something that dwells deeply within us. It seeks to contact the mysteries and shows its deep kinship with prayer.[193]

He says the midnight poem "seeks transcendence and dwells under the sign of the eternal."[194]

Sor Juana's poem encompasses the transition from daylight to darkness to daybreak. It shares characteristics of the sundown poem as it moves from the visible to the invisible realms. It also exhibits features of the night poem as it expresses the frustration of the solitary soul. And it certainly displays the characteristics of the midnight poem as the mind is loosed in "metaphysical aspiration," yet as it includes the breaking morning, it may convey some elements of the aubade. The loss experienced in the morning may be the loss of the soul's ascent, the failure of knowledge and the loss of the illusion that a universal perspective can be reached. It may speak of the loss of the "dream" of

---

[190] Edward Hirsch, "The Work of Lyric: Night and Day," *Georgia Review* 57, no. 2 (Summer 2003): 379. For Lorca's own work on *duende,* see Federico García Lorca, "Deep Song," in *Deep Song and Other Prose,* trans. and ed. Christopher Maurer (New York: Marion Boyars, 1991); and also Lorca, "Lecture: A Poet in New York," in *A Poet in New York,* trans. Greg Simon and Steven F. White, ed. Christopher Mauer (New York: Farrar, Straus and Giroux, 1988).

[191] Hirsch, "The Work of Lyric," 379.

[192] Ibid.

[193] Ibid., 380.

[194] Ibid.

attaining full knowledge, loss of the hope of ever gaining sure knowledge; it speaks of disillusionment. Yet here we will focus on the elements of the night mind as a general account spanning sunset to sunrise, including the shift from visible to invisible, from body to spirit and the deep concerns of the soul, including loss and frustration.

As mentioned, Hirsch associates night with the *duende*, particularly as it is described in the work of Andalusian poet Frederico García Lorca. Hirsch uses Garcia Lorca's *duende* as something of a starting point in his own investigations of artistic forms in his book *The Demon and the Angel: Searching for the Source of Artistic Expression*. In this work, he not only considers the source of artistic inspiration, but investigates those expressions which portray the anxiety of human existence, the confrontation with mortality and limitedness; he considers those works of art that express the depth of human existence, particularly the darkness confronted there in the "night." The *duende*, a word which in Andalusia is used to describe a particular form of life expression, is found especially in poetry, song, and dance. It is present in those works of art exhibiting "an element of mortal panic and fear."[195] In works with *duende,* "there's some sense of our humanness, some sense of our strangeness, and some sense of our mortality."[196] Hirsch says this spirit emerges in a work "only when something enormous is at risk, when the self is imperiled and pushed against its limits, when death is possible."[197]

Hirsch also highlights the role of dreams in this night mind. "Art is born from struggle.... Art is inexplicable and has a dream-power that radiates from the night mind. It unleashes something ancient, dark, and mysterious into the world," and paradoxically, in so doing, "it conducts a fresh light."[198] He goes on to say that this spirit of expression "favors dreams that spill over into waking spells. It favors nocturnes of sleeplessness— the cry of the solitary and the bereft ensouled in poetic form. It favors the urgent reveries and warnings of the night mind."[199] Sor Juana's "Dream" and its frustration, struggle, and flight to impending fall and failure exhibit some element of this spirit described by

---

[195] Edward Hirsch, *Demon and Angel: Searching for the Source of Artistic Inspiration* (New York: Harcourt, 2001) 11.

[196] "A Conversation with Edward Hirsch," interview by Donna Seaman, *Triquarterly* 117 (Fall 2003): 66.

[197] Hirsch, *Demon and Angel,* xiii.

[198] Ibid., ix.

[199] Ibid., 92.

Hirsch and Lorca. Such poems are also associated with silence.[200] "Poetry begins and ends in silence," and yet it is the expression of the "speechless," thought in lived language.[201] Hirsch does well to remind us of the words of John Keats, who wrote in a letter to Benjamin Bailey in 1817 that he is "more zealous" in his poetic task because he has "never yet been able to perceive how any thing can be known for truth by consecutive reasoning."[202] Hirsch also sees this affirmation in the apophatic tradition and in scripture itself: "'no one has ever seen or ever will see the being of God in all its hiddenness."[203] Or finally, in the words of Garcia Lorca himself: "Our people cross their arms in prayer, look at the stars, and wait in vain for a sign of salvation. The gesture is pathetic but true. And the poem either poses a deep emotional question with no answer, or solves it with death, which is the question of questions."[204] It is in the desperate search for clear sight of something that does not come: assurance of God, of salvation, of life beyond, or of certain knowledge. Poetry poses these questions of existence and its relation to God.

Hirsch admits that he finds this spirit more often in Hispanic cultures. He notes that "Spain is a country where death is a particular kind of cultural construction," and that it is perhaps only rivaled by Mexico's "culture of death," citing Octavio Paz's *The Labyrinth of Solitude* as an example of this.[205] He says that other Western cultures tend to relegate such "dark nostalgia" to the

---

[200] Thus, this night mind is related to silence, the awareness of suffering around you, and of solitude (Hirsch, *Demon and Angel*, 40). Hirsch describes the spirit expressed in these night poems beautifully: "It is still dark, but outside, to my great relief, I can see the shadowy figure of trees slowly emerging from the night, I can hear the early-morning birds stirring—blue jays calling up the brightness of day, crows singing out the blackness. It has been a long insomniac night, and I cannot shake the feeling—the felt thought—that the task of poetry begins and ends in silence" (Hirsch, "The Work of Lyric," 369–70). He describes these as "nights of mute terror," referring to the work of psychoanalyst George Groddeck, who gives the term "inner muteness" to humanity's "most personal thought," which he says "is speechless, subterranean, unconscious" ("The Work of Lyric," 370).

[201] Hirsch, *Demon and Angel*, 113.

[202] Ibid., 6.

[203] Ibid., 113. Hirsch is quoting Pseudo-Dionysius.

[204] Federico García Lorca, "Deep Song," in *In Search of the Duende*, ed. and prose trans. Christopher Maurer; poem trans. Norman di Giovanni, Edwin Honig, Langston Hughes, et al. (New York: New Directions, 1998) 11–12.

[205] Hirsch, *Demon and Angel*, 35.

"category of sentimentality, thereby trivializing and dismissing it," whereas "the Hispanic sensibility has wisely saved it as a poignant and durable feeling relating to the transitoriness of life."[206] He and Garcia Lorca see this spirit at the heart of Spanish Catholicism—in the "apses, crypts, and chapels, in the extravagant cathedrals of Mallorca and Toledo, in religious chants and festival dances, in the innumerable blood-soaked rites of Good Friday."[207] Hirsch says that the image of the "flesh-and-blood figure dying moment by moment" in the lyric poetry of Lorca, for example, "becomes the heroic emblem of [his] own anxieties and fears, inscribed and transformed" in verse.[208] The relationship of Sor Juana's dream to death has been noted previously and is explored in the work of Sabat-Rivers.

Works of this sort seem to express an "aspect of the night mind," and Hirsch likens this to the story of Jacob, who wrestles with an angel (God?) in the night. Jacob's night-long wrestling with an unknown figure, and finally his wounding by this one he could never quite see in the darkness, are much like the struggle of the artist.[209] Hirsch says that the "story probably has such great resonance for poets and prose writers because writing itself is an encounter with the unknown, a hard struggle with the unsaid. To write is to stand on the edge of a dark gorge guarded by a mysterious stranger.... Jacob may embrace the angel, but that embrace must also be agonistic, since it is an uncanny confrontation with the unknown."[210] Hirsch finds the night to be the indispensable setting for Jacob's struggle, as this particular form of expression somehow expresses the dark and struggling nature of human existence.

To expand the metaphor, the story is then much like the struggle of the individual with the hidden God, or with that figure one cannot quite make out, whose purposes seem hidden in the world despite the light of revelation. The story is an image of that conflict between who we believe God to be in Christ, and the dark suffering of the world and the mystery of salvation. It involves a "dark gorge" and a "hard struggle with the unsaid," and even a "confrontation with the unknown." This is not to deny trust and faith, but is all the more to insist upon them.

---

[206] Ibid., 11.

[207] Ibid., 16.

[208] Ibid., 21.

[209] Hirsch, "Conversation," 67.

[210] Hirsch, *Demon and Angel*, 124.

Conclusion: Theology as Discourse at the Rift

Sor Juana held a marginalized position in church and society, kept outside the official realm of theology, but the poetic form she employed enable her to propose alternatives to the theological system of her day. The form in its Baroque layering of metaphor not only disguises some of its boldest positions, resulting in a sort of dissembling (Heidegger) or a subtraction (Kierkegaard), but suggests that the subject with its "rational capacity, its body, and its language" is unable to produce a "stable, coherent, and universal knowledge."[211] The fragmented style of poetry along with the "baroque circumlocution" illustrates the confusion and tension of Sor Juana's time, "the crisis of the scholastic paradigm." She gives, then, what might be the "'first' baroque hint of the problem of knowledge."[212] Sor Juana leaves her reader finally with the unmistakable "notion of knowledge as exceedingly contextual, such that one is not able to postulate it as independent of the historical, cultural environment."[213] The best of poetry is a form of expression that conveys the transvergence of many layers and aspects of reality, the emotional and spiritual encounter of the person and the world, of a community with diverse forces, of the soul and a God it cannot fully know or comprehend.

Poetry is a form that is fragmentary. Its very structure gestures to the idea of something, or to an experience, and it endeavors to bring the reader into a memory of such a moment or thought, or to evoke that experience or thought within her; its purpose is generally to stir the reader, to move her. And its fragmented form does not give completed accounts or explicit instruction. Its fragmented lines and dependence upon metaphor and imagery make it a form well suited for the sort of indirect communication I propose. It is a form uniquely appropriate for conveying the inconclusive nature of knowledge, as it is not a form that can suppose itself to be the last word on a matter. It is not a form that communicates information. Its purpose is not to record fact, though it may express reality and true events. Or, as Heidegger argued, it may convey truth, that is, the truth that resides there at the rift, here interpreted as the tension between lived existence in a troubled world and God as revealed in Jesus Christ and interpreted by the church. Or it may be expressed in the terms of Luther, the

211 Martínez-San Miguel, 82, my trans.

212 Ibid., my trans.

213 Ibid., my trans.

Anfechtung, an existential state of faith and despair, together in "a highly intensified tension."[214]

The poem belongs with those theological works that express the hiddenness of God, those works of apophatic theology like "The Cloud of Unknowing" that encourage the Christian to silent prayer, where a contemplation of God is a peering into the darkness or the cloud through which one's sight cannot penetrate, where words cannot describe God. It stands in the tradition of works of those, like Pseudo-Dionysius, whose ideas on the incomprehensibility of God form the foundation of Western Christian mysticism. Though they give words to their quest for God, all these works indicate a search in the blinding darkness; they are works that give content to the silence that they otherwise promote and encourage.

This form does not solidify a darkness in Christian teaching. It does not categorize the frustration of Christian knowledge, but in its fragmented (and fragmenting) form, it gives expression to these very tensions deep within Christianity as it is a religion pertaining to God's activity in the world and the God-human, God-world relation. It does not take a form that suggests this hiddenness can be explained, but it leaves room for it within Christian existence, within theology nonetheless, and gives it voice. Poetry expresses the dynamic movement as the progression of a poem is a matter of movement: ongoing pursuit and striving, lacking in completeness or conclusion, that is the Christian existence described by Kierkegaard and poetized here by Sor Juana. *Primero sueño* alludes to more dreams to come in the very title and the ongoing internal battle illustrated in the soul's own struggle to know while cognizant that she will never attain full knowledge. The pursuit will never reach conclusion in this life. It is as ongoing as the God-relation itself and the transformative process of Christian existence. There is no rest. As we found in Heidegger's description of poetry and in Kierkegaard's conception of the inconclusive search of Christian knowledge, so does Sor Juana's poem depict the experience of the soul in this life: embodied, in time, and in the progression of days.

A night poem, says Hirsch, "is language in action against time, against death"[215] Such an active view of the function of language as one seeks to communicate Christianity to another in existence is the view of language I want

---

[214] Margaret R. Miles, "'The Rope Breaks When It Is Tightest': Luther on the Body, Consciousness, and the Word," *Harvard Theological Review* 77, no. 3–4 (1984): 243.

[215] Hirsch, "The Work of Lyric," 369–70.

to emphasize, recalling *Postscript* and why indirect communication is necessary in the expression of Christian knowledge. When expressing the nature of faith in the face of doubt and uncertainty, or when faith is defined as certainty only of objective uncertainty, the purpose is not to express that God is in fact hidden and hidden particularly behind history or devastating natural events or in a predestining decision, but to show that faith includes faith at the rift, faith under the cover of darkness, faith despite the tension between revelation and existence itself. Or even more, the theological forms for which I argue function to communicate that faith is exactly faith at those points and not despite them. They serve to express faith as a lived activity throughout the process of existence and not a cognitive explanation for exactly how God is or is not in the world.

Another theorist who highlights the struggle for knowledge, particularly the struggle for authentic knowledge in the face of authoritative coercion and official forms of discourse backed by power, is Mikhail Bakhtin. He, too, values dialogue, temporality, and non-coercive forms of discourse so as to persuade the person internally as she makes the ideas her own. We turn to his ideas on genre in the next chapter in order to offer a reading of Sor Juana's use of drama to communicate theology in what we are calling an "indirect" form.

4

Internal Persuasion in Sor Juana's Dramas

Introduction

Sor Juana lived in an age of transition, when forces to conserve and forces for change struggled across European culture. Not only did the Baroque period experience a conflict over methods of gaining knowledge and the nature of certain knowledge itself, but the changes described also impacted the form of discourse themselves. Sor Juana lived in and at the cusp of the era that birthed the modern novel, and within her work, one can see the emergence of tendencies that became characteristic of the novel as described by literary theorist Mikhail Bakhtin. Most scholars date the novel's appearance to the seventeenth or eighteenth centuries; Cervantes's *Don Quixote,* for example, is often considered one of the first representatives of the genre, and the first part of it was published in 1605, almost fifty years before Sor Juana's birth.

Literary theorist and philosopher Georg Lukács argues that the novel developed because of the breakdown of totality, or the dissolving of the hold the church had over truth and knowledge and certainty of that belief; he asserts that the novel can only emerge with the shifts in culture, knowledge, truth, and the sense of destiny that occur with the Modern era. He goes so far as to say that the novel could only arrive in modernity with the death of God, as previously with the epic, the hero of literature knew that whatever challenges or adventures "he" encountered were "his" destiny and determined by the gods. The novel, however, does not trace the hero's search for his or her destiny in accordance with the plan of the gods, but the search for him- or herself in the god-abandoned universe. The epic and the novel are often contrasted in literary theory, and here in Sor Juana's work one can see the literary transition taking place along with the cultural shifts that birth it;[1] one can see traces of both the epic and features Bakhtin says are characteristic of the novel.

---

[1] See Wlad Godzich and Nicholas Spadaccini, "Popular Culture and Spanish Literary History," in *Literature Among Discourses: The Spanish Golden Age*, ed. Wlad Godzich and Nicholas Spadaccini (Minneapolis: University of Minnesota Press, 1986).

Describing the medieval worldview, Lukács writes: "In Giotto and Dante, Wolfram von Eschenbach and Pisano, St. Thomas and St. Francis, the world became round once more, a totality capable of being taken in at a glance; the chasm lost the threat inherent in its actual depth; its whole darkness, without forfeiting any of its somberly gleaming power, became pure surface and could thus be fitted easily into a closed unity of colours."[2] This perspective, however, changed in the transition to modernity. And so "the novel is the epic of a world that has been abandoned by God. The objectivity of the novel is the mature man's knowledge that meaning can never quite penetrate reality."[3]

The literature of Sor Juana's day likewise reflects this shift; as Lukács and Bakhtin indicate in different, though complimentary ways, the novel emerges because of a different worldview than that which went before. The epic made sense in a world that believed in destiny and God's perceptible ways in the world, at a time when society invested authority in the church, when society believed the church's ways of accumulating knowledge of God, the world, humanity, and God's ways in the world, and the conclusions based on this knowledge—that is dogma or Truth. But as this authority was brought into question, and as the answers these authorities give were likewise brought into doubt with the Reformation, the church lost its grasp over the totality it once had. The epic and official discourses rely on this totality to give it meaning, and the novel emerges with the crumbling of this totality. If society no longer believes in this form of destiny, of God's interaction in the world as historically affirmed, then the epic does not communicate meaningfully to society any longer. The shift pushed for multiple voices and opinions, according to Bakhtin, and perspectives were invested with authority because they resonated and spoke meaningfully to the person, not simply because official power backed them.

Mikhail Bakhtin details the slow development of the novel, tracing its origins back to Socrates and certain aspects even in Homeric literature. His treatment of the novel positions it in contrast to the conservative, preserving elements in literature that rely on power and official backing to gain authoritative force. He points to elements emerging throughout literature that push against this conservative force and that finally develop into the modern novel. His juxtapositions mirror those highlighted in the culture in which the

---

[2] Georg Lukács, *The Theory of the Novel: A Historico-Philosophical Essay on the Forms of Great Epic Literature*. Trans. by Anna Bostock (Cambridge MA: The MIT Press, 1977) 88.

[3] Ibid.

novel emerges: he sets up a series of oppositions between the traditional, conserving, and official literature, with those forces moving for change and the inclusion of alternative voices. He traces the development throughout the history of literature of certain characteristics that stand in opposition to those of the genres that have gone before and serve a preserving function. Bakhtin shows how conserving or centripetal forces struggled against this push to diversity, dialogue, and open-endedness, and these forces to conserve resonate with those preserving forces described of the Baroque context, as the church and political authorities struggled to retain prominence and power. If Bakhtin is correct, it is not surprising to see these characteristics emerging in Sor Juana's work, even if they do not reach their most complete form in her work as she still writes within the genres deemed acceptable by the authorities. Sor Juana did not entirely restrict herself to genres deemed acceptable for nuns, however, as she did write many secular pieces, and poetry that has even been described as "raunchy burlesque."[4] In the following pages, I analyze Sor Juana's work as reflective of the tension and transitions of her time. Her work is positioned at a time of a shift from the medieval worldview to the modern one, or the early modern period that witnessed the changes in culture because of the Reformation and its sweeping impact for the following centuries.[5]

We embark on a discussion of Sor Juana's dramas, specifically the *loas* to her *auto sacramentales*. The form of the drama itself is already a dialogue, a form of communication noted by Kierkegaard as appropriate for indirect communication. I use the thought of Mikhail Bakhtin to bring out the elements in the *loas* that relate to the heart of this study: temporality, openness to alternative views, and dialogue. Bakhtin offers an argument for the function of certain forms of discourse that include a plurality of voices, and do not impose upon the reader externally as the centralizing and unifying forms of authoritative discourse do. Instead this discourse persuades internally through dialogue, heterogeneity, and room for appropriation. Bakhtin's definition of the novel is distinct from the traditional conception of the genre. While most literary theorists consider the novel a literary genre that emerged in the

[4] Harss, 6.

[5] For an argument that identifies the sixteenth and seventeenth centuries as "early modern," see Stephanie Merrim, *Early Modern Women's Writing*; and Leah S. Marcus, *Redrawing the Boundaries: The Transformation of English and American Literary Studies*, ed. Stephen Greenblatt and Giles Gun (New York: Modern Language Association of America, 1992).

seventeenth or eighteenth centuries, Bakhtin traces its development much further back, focusing on elements that are not restricted to the particular structure one now expects to be the defining feature of the "novel," but locates it in the anti-canonical spirit, the diverse speech of characters, and elements of common life and contemporaneity, among other things.[6] And whereas literary theorists generally focus on plot or structure in their designation of the novel, he uncovers a series of novelistic characteristics that begin to emerge in Socratic dialogue and Greek tragedies, and which show up in a variety of forms, although they reach their most comprehensive development in the novel proper. Bakhtin's English translator, Michael Holquist, clarifies that literary scholars would:

> within their own terms, be correct in asserting that there were no novels in Plato's Athens or during the Middle Ages, or at least no novel as we have come to know it. But Bakhtin is clearly not referring to that concept of a novel that begins with Cervantes or Richardson. These books, and especially the nineteenth-century psychological novel that evolved from them, have become the canon of the genre-novel. The majority of literary scholars are most at home when dealing with canons, which is why Bakhtin said that literary theory is helpless to deal with the novel. What is more conventionally thought of as the novel is simply the most complex and distilled expression of this impulse.[7]

Bakhtin notes the "anti-canonical" spirit of the novel, which explains why his work on the novel contrasts those theorists who look at the novel within a canon. Instead, Bakhtin's work on the genre highlights the use of voices from different social contexts, calling it "heteroglossia," and he considers the inclusion of local dialects and of characters from different social locations, classes, and ethnicities to be representative of these aspects of "novelization."[8] This is also an element that contributes to the centrifugal force of such discourse, that which pushes away from centers of power. Discourse which has

---

[6] Michael Holquist, "Introduction," in *Dialogic Imagination: Four Essays by M.M. Bakhtin,* trans. Caryl Emerson and Michael Holquist, ed. Michael Holquist (Austin TX: University of Texas Press, 1981) xxxi.

[7] M. M. Bakhtin, "Epic and Novel," in *Dialogic Imagination,* trans. Caryl Emerson and Michael Holquist, ed. Michael Holquist (Austin TX: University of Texas Press, 1981) 12.

[8] Of course, just because multiple voices are included does not mean that others are not still excluded, intentionally or unintentionally. There is still a power dimension at work.

only one dialect, one class, and one social context seeks a unified discourse, and is described by Bakhtin as monovocal. This type of discourse with one accepted linguistic meaning is that which is spoken by the ruling class, those in power, and those with authority. This is the way of authoritative discourse and "high" genres. They possess a centripetal force that seeks to draw everything under its dominion. The novel, a "low" genre, and those pieces of literature that share these characteristics, work in opposition to these forces through polyvocality and an anti-canonical movement, serving as a centrifugal force pushing away from those centers of power.[9]

Bakhtin identifies features that correspond to the themes we find in Sor Juana's work and that are consistent with Kierkegaard's argument for indirect communication. The *loa* exists as a literary, dramatic invitation to consider and appropriate Christian teaching displayed in allegorical and dramatic form. The *loas* also provide a perspective on effective modes of theological discussion in both form and content. Regarding the former, the genre itself makes the case for a demonstration of Christian teaching rather than direct theological instruction, and in content, as the *loas* specifically address the issue of theological debate both across religions and within Christianity. The dramas engage not only the intellect, but also the individual's imagination and emotions. Thus these pieces are of particular interest to this study in the use of genre to communicate indirectly, to persuade the reader to appropriate religious knowledge, and the subjective nature of religious truth. Rather than a direct explication of a creed or doctrine, Sor Juana tells stories, sometimes even secular stories, to convey Christian knowledge.

In the *auto*, and its accompanying *loa*, an array of arts are used to communicate the Christian message to the audience. Elements of the form of the *loa* are invaluable to the theological discipline, particularly if one of the goals of theology is to present Christianity to the individual in such a way that he or she is invited to appropriate it and be transformed by it.[10] Although, the

---

[9] An aspect of Bakhtin's thought that will not be thoroughly developed here, but which is also related to the thrust of this project, is what he calls the chronotope. It includes both spatial and temporal aspects of human existence. See "Forms of Time and of the Chronotope in the Novel," in *Dialogic Imagination*, trans. Caryl Emerson and Michael Holquist, ed. Michael Holquist (Austin TX: University of Texas Press, 1981).

[10] I acknowledge that the *loa* and the *auto* belong together, as argued by Yolanda Martínez-San Miguel, but it is also argued that the two are in many ways unrelated. [See Francisco Javier Ceballos, "La Alegoría del Deseo. La 'Loa para el auto *El Mártir del Sacramento, San Hermenegildo*,' de Sor Juana Inés del la Cruz," *Teatro y America* No.2

auto sacramental would most likely fall into the category of "high" genre, as it has a fairly standard form, is authorized by the Roman Catholic Church, and is thus placed not only in the hierarchy of literary forms, but also aligned with the powerful ecclesiastical hierarchy, such high genres have been influenced by the movement or "novelizing" spirit Bakhtin traces to centuries before Sor Juana. Bakhtin identifies this spirit in forms that would be considered "high genres," such as: drama (the work of Ibsen, for example), epic poetry (especially Byron's *Don Juan*), and lyric poetry.[11] Sor Juana utilized a traditional genre, one that has historically been used by the church to disseminate its doctrine, and one that is used to bring about conversion. In fact the genre we will be examining has been described by Anthony Pasquariello as "propaganda."[12] However, a shift does occur in her use of the genre from its traditional purpose. Certainly it remains educational, as it teaches the potential audience about the Eucharist and the salvation history it represents, but in so doing she incorporates more radical

(1992): 44; and Yolanda Martinez-San Miguel, *Saberes Americanos: Subalternidad y Epistemología en los Escritos de Sor Juana* (Pittsburgh: Instituto Internacional de Literatura Iberoamericana, University of Pittsburgh, 1999) 172–73.] Melveena McKendrick says they are usually on the same themes and use similar symbolism but they aren't even necessarily written by the same author. [See Melveena McKendrick, *Theater in Spain 1490–1700* (Cambridge: Cambridge University Press, 1989) 248.] The themes are carried through into the *auto* as argued by Martinez, but here I look primarily at the *loa* because it uniquely exemplifies so many novelistic tendencies, which aren't necessarily present in the subsequent *auto*, particularly in terms of heteroglossia and contemporaneity.

[11] Bakhtin, "Epic and Novel," 6.

[12] For a discussion of the development of the *loa* in New Spain, see Anthony M. Pasquariello, "The Evolution of the *Loa* in Spanish America," *Latin American Theater Review* 3, no. 2 (Spring 1970): 5–19. Pasquariello's discussion considers both the secular and the sacred *loas* and gives some attention to the work of Sor Juana (6–9); his description of the form is mostly negative, as he considers the secular form to be primarily for the flattering of the political authorities, and he calls Sor Juana's sacred *loas* "largely propaganda pieces" (6). Of Sor Juana's *loa* to *El Divino Narciso*, he says it "suffers from didactic dullness." And "As for the Indian characters, they are strange, shadowy figures, mere toys of the imagination, too intellectual to be natives. We look in vain for indigenous traits. The best that can be said for the *loas* of Sor Juana is that they are less strained than most" (9). Granted, his assessment of the genre as a whole is rather bleak: "one cannot help but feel that many a spectator was bored by their stilted language and mechanical, monotonous form" (5). See also Lee Daniel, "The *Loas* of Sor Juana Inés de la Cruz," *Letras Femeninas* 11, no. 1 (1985): 42–48.

elements that show signs of the shift in culture or of her own personal desire to see loosened, the tight hold the church and the colonizing country have over the standards of rationality and knowledge. Sor Juana revolutionizes the *loa* to make it less a document of praise for the political powers that be (though this is not entirely absent), into a subversive argument for *criolla* subjectivity, agency, and participation in the debates that were controlled and dominated from the European continent.[13]

What is important for our purposes is to identify what elements in Sor Juana's *loas* show evidence of this push for decentralization and heteroglossia. I will argue that in her *loas* one finds characteristics that Bakhtin links with this movement toward the genre of the novel, such as: (1) importance of the present, (2) heteroglossia, and (3) story told through dialogue; and that she utilizes these features to develop themes of the novelistic spirit, such as: (1) concern with epistemology and limits of knowing; and (2) the inconclusiveness of human assertions of religious truth. I conclude that these function in Sor Juana's dramas to produce an internally persuasive discourse, not void of tradition, but open in ways authoritative discourse lacking these elements cannot be and does not desire to be. I begin with a description of the *loa* and *auto sacramental*, then move into a consideration of three specific *loas* to Sor Juana's *auto sacramentales*: *El Divino Narciso* (The Divine Narcissus), *El Cetro de José* (The Scepter of Joseph), and *El Mártir del Sacramento, San Hermenegildo* (The Martyr of the Sacrament, St. Hermenegildo).[14] Lastly I analyze these pieces as

[13] See Martínez-San Miguel for an extended argument on Sor Juana's epistemological project in terms of her colonial and gendered identity.

[14] When I move to a discussion of Sor Juana's plays themselves, we will be dealing with only words and texts, but the *auto sacramental* and its *loa* in their true form, according to McKendrick, may not even exist outside of its performance. However, it is unlikely that any of the *auto sacramentales* or the *loas* preceding them were ever performed. (See A. A. Parker, Lee Alton Daniel, and N. D. Shergold on the evidence that these plays were never produced and performed.) McKendrick states that "the *autos* arguably can have no true *theatrical* existence other than in a performance which has some capacity at least to inspire awe and wonder, to move the faithful to devotion" (McKendrick, 249). An example of the union of text and performance can be found in the work of Calderón, who gave very explicit instructions for production, including stage direction. Due to the allegorical nature of these plays, they possess a "fusion of themes, symbolism and staging," with "everything on stage—scenery, effects, action, patterns of movement, characters and their costumes and the identifying objects they often carried—becoming an integral part of the imagery and symbolism"

theological literature in the spirit of the shift in literature described by Bakhtin and the emergence of the novel in modernity. In conclusion I highlight how theological works that proceed in this spirit function to persuade respectfully, recognizing the limits on theological knowledge and difference in knowledge because of context and the relation of Christianity to human inter-subjectivity.

The *Loa* and the *Auto Sacramental*

The *auto*, popular from the late fifteenth to early eighteenth centuries, is a dramatic production for the festival of Corpus Christi, a feast known for the elaborate festivities that were a highlight in Baroque Spanish culture. The *auto*s were not always particularly religious in nature, and it has been suggested that the *auto sacramental* may have been intentionally introduced to infuse the festivities with more overtly Christian content.[15] Not only were the dramas lavish with complex staging, scenery, and luxurious costumes, but the celebration included many other festival elements: "secular plays and comic interludes, dances, singing and even conjuring tricks, and since the pageantry included the traditional tableaux, the *tarasca* (a dragon with the mechanical figure of a woman on top) which knocked off onlookers' hats, and from 1580 on giant figures to frighten small children."[16] The substantial costs of the festivities were typically subsidized by the authorities.[17]

The *auto sacramental* is a one act play for the purpose of instruction on the Eucharist, performed in the open air on elevated carts, or *carros*, which were moved through the streets. These sets could be quite elaborate, and sometimes were composed of two-stories with room for the actors to change. Pedro Calderón de la Barca (1600–1681), the master of the form, is said to use as many as eight carts and a center stage.[18] With candles burning behind stage even though the plays were performed in broad daylight, they were a form of ritual, part of the liturgical year, and called "devotional" by Calderón. They are allegorical in nature and typically Baroque in the variety of arts used, as the

---

(McKendrick, 250). Sor Juana gives some explicit costume instructions, particularly when she is describing what the characters playing/representing the Aztecs would wear in *Divino Narciso*.

[15] McKendrick, 241.

[16] Ibid.

[17] Ibid.

[18] Ibid., 248–49.

form is an amassing of artistic representations: choral singing, instrumental music, poetry, dance, and moving sets.

The *auto* is introduced by means of another short play, called a *loa*. The *loa* preceding an *auto* typically poses a situation that sets up the need for the explication of the Eucharist, leading one of the characters to suggest that they watch the subsequent play as it will explain it, thus resulting with a play within a play as its standard form.[19] Though the Eucharist is the general focus, the plays are often more sweeping, covering a range of Christian doctrines, as the whole story of fall and redemption is directly linked to the institution of the sacrament. Sor Juana's *Cetro de José,* in particular, gives an impressive account of the entire Christian story, surpassing the *auto* by Calderon that she most likely used as a model. The plays use a variety of material for this exposition: the lives of saints, stories from the Bible, and classical mythology, all of which are found in Sor Juana's corpus.[20]

Calderón was the chief playwright for the Corpus Christi festivities at the height of the *auto sacramental*, which ran from 1648–1681.[21] He also developed the clearest sense of a theory of the genre and articulated a distinct purpose in the production of these theological dramas; Sor Juana's works were clearly influenced by him. A. A. Parker says Calderón's *auto*s function as: "poetry of the invisible beauty which can be vaguely yearned for on earth but never found, and which is not accessible to the senses apart from symbols."[22] He also explains the intention behind these allegorical dramas as related to the nature of religious knowledge. He writes: "The divine and eternal can only be known, though imperfectly, through analogy with the human and the temporal. Since drama can present such an analogy with particular vividness, it can legitimately be placed at the service of theology."[23] Parker also calls the *auto* in the hands of Calderón "the perfect method of conveying the mysterious and incomprehensible through the senses," as he explains, "eternal truths should not

[19] *Loas* do not only serve as introductory plays. They can also be independent. Lee Daniel notes that although most *loas* do serve to introduce a longer piece, "thirteen of the eighteen *loas* by Sor Juana are independent" [Lee Daniel, "The *Loas* of Sor Juana Inés de la Cruz," *Letras Femeninas*, 11, no. 1 (1985): 43].

[20] McKendrick also notes the use of medieval ballads, legend, everyday life, and contemporary history (McKendrick, 256).

[21] These dates are given by McKendrick.

[22] A. A. Parker, *The Allegorical Drama of Calderón: An Introduction to the "Auto Sacramentales"* (Oxford: The Dolphin Book Co. Ltd., 1968) 28.

[23] Ibid., 67.

be presented in the cold fomulae of metaphysical abstractions: they should be fused with the poetic form in such a way that the allegory comes to life, and allegorical characters do not only mean something but become real living beings."[24]

Allegorical dramas may seem abstract and remote, particularly for contemporary readers, as the characters are often concepts, virtues, and vices. In two of Sor Juana's *loas,* we encounter characters such as Faith, Religion, Idolatry, and Natural Law, but she sets these allegorical characters in the context of New Spain and its very real clash of cultures and religions. Sor Juana may have written these *loas* in reaction to one of the largest revolts of Amerindians against colonial New Spain and the action of missionaries that provoked the revolt. [25] In this way she is able, like Calderón, to keep "close and

---

[24] Ibid., 28.

[25] These two *loas* to *Cetro de José* and *Divino Narciso* may be written in reaction to Indian revolts. McGaha explains: "We do not know when exactly Sor Juana wrote the *auto sacramental* entitled *Joseph's Scepter (El Cetro de José).* Ezequiel Chávez has argued that the preoccupation with human sacrifice and polygamy in the *auto*'s prologue suggests a date in the 1680s, when one of the most massive Indian rebellions of the colonial period took place, threatening to restore those practices. [Ezequiel Chávez, *Ensayo de Psicología de Sor Juana de la Cruz* (Barcelona: Araluce, 1931) 194.] The rebellion was provoked by the excesses of some Spanish missionaries who sought to convert the Indians to Christianity by force. The Jesuit father Alegre described their conduct as follows: 'One of them wanted to become the apostle of the Tubaris. He entered their lands by surprise with five or six armed Spaniards. He and his companions lived off the Indians for some days. Willy-nilly, he baptized the infants he found at their mothers' breasts. His zeal to make the adults submit was so extreme that, when some refused baptism, he tied them up and loaded them down with chains until they begged to be baptized. ... His imprudence lighted a fire that would not be extinguished for many years, and placed all those new Christian communities in danger of perishing' [Father Alegre, *Historia de la Compania de Jesus en Nueva Espana, 3:52; cited in Luis Gonzales Obregon, Rebeliones indigenas y precursors de la indepnedencia Mexicana en los siglos XVI, XVII, y XVIII* (Mexico City: Ediciones Fuente Cultural, 1952)]. Beginning in 1684 in the northwestern coastal region of Sinaloa and in the western Sierra Madre, the revolt quickly spread as far east as Casas Grandes. Many different tribes united under the leadership of the Tarahumara chief Corosia, and began to attack Spanish missions and villages at the onset of winter 1684. Fighting would continue sporadically until 1690, resulting in many casualties on both sides and great destruction of property." [Michael McGaha, "Sor Juana Inés de la Cruz: *Joseph's Scepter,* 186–

constant contact" between the "externally supernatural world" of the ideas they communicate and "the here and now of human life."[26] These allusions to contemporary and common life are a tool to catch the attention of the audience by bringing the topics close to their lives in recognizable features. Maria E. Pérez writes:

> The *loas*, *sainetes*, *entremeses* and *fin de fiesta* that Sor Juana Inés de la Cruz wrote are another good example of how these inserted pieces have a popular character and relate the customs and reality of the environment. [...] It is here where one senses the beat of the pulse of the *criollo*, of the American, for the social classes are reflected in verse, the language used is generally the colloquial speech of the new village, the customs and the ambiance are none other than those of the American continent.[27]

The third *loa* of Sor Juana we will consider here is set primarily in a contemporary setting with a scholastic student debate. In these ways she uses every day life and contemporary history within her *loas*, characteristic resources for the form, and thus her *loas* connect specifically to the present and not simply to an abstract past, even though the figures are themselves often allegorical.

These dramas are not only liturgical and devotional, they are also sermonic, offering doctrinal instruction in a form that may be a more effective venue of communication than a traditional sermon, as Parker explains: "a sermon acted possesses greater didactic value than a sermon preached. It is better to demonstrate to an audience the meaning of Redemption than to tell it to them."[28] He explains that according to Calderón one could produce a play which demonstrates the story of Christ's life, but this itself would not be instruction in redemption. In order for this to be explained, one of the characters would have to comment "on the significance of the events presented on the stage," resulting basically with a character giving a sermon, which is hardly any different than a sermon itself. Calderón therefore strives to avoid this "because [the character's] 'sermon' would then be separated from the dramatic action. A sermon preached is only heard, a sermon acted is seen as well as heard."[29] This

225," in *The Story of Joseph in Spanish Golden Age Drama*, trans. Michael McGaha (Lewisburg: Bucknell University Press, 1998) 188.]

[26] Parker, 29.

[27] María E. Pérez, *Lo Americano en el Teatro de Sor Juana Inés de la Cruz* (New York: Eliseo Torres, 1975) 59. Quoted in Martínez-San Miguel, 172–73, my trans.

[28] Parker, 66.

[29] Ibid., 65–66.

form is considered more effective because the drama is "illustrative in a concrete way," which other forms of Christian instruction are not.[30] The *auto sacramental* transforms "a set of theological abstractions into drama which not only explained their relevance to man but projected that relevance with a force and an immediacy which commands the imagination and the emotions as well as the intellect."[31]

McKendrick explains the role the *auto* played during Sor Juana's day:

> The seventeenth century's pursuit of the marvelous and the sublime finds its ultimate expression in this art form at the very heart of which lie belief in the miraculous, faith in the unknowable, and awe before the power and mystery of God. The admiration and suspended disbelief experienced by the audience as the carts performed their magic to the accompaniment of impressive music was a paradigm of the religious wonder and faith which the *auto*'s text set out to provoke. Calderón himself stressed the importance of the technical effects and the music to the *auto*'s message in the preface he wrote to the twelve *autos* he published in 1677. The magic does not have to be the magic of the Baroque carts, but magic of some sort there has to be. The finest *autos* are stunning theater, the consummate example of...art in the service of religion. Even the most abstract of them work on their audience emotionally rather than intellectually in spite of their theological rigour, and that emotion, for all the artistry of Calderón's text, depends on a performance which does theatrical justice to those two linchpins of drama which Calderón exploits so effectively in his exploration of the Fall and Redemption of Man—conflict and metamorphosis. The *carro* system with its possibilities for variable pairings of carts was perfectly suited to the dualities and contrasts that Calderón saw at the heart of man's nature and predicament, and the productions could be so powerfully visual as to render words scarcely necessary to an understanding of the play for a contemporary audience.[32]

Note that McKendrick highlights "faith in the unknowable" as one of the responses the *auto* endeavors to evoke and makes clear that the intention is to engage the audience not only intellectually but also emotionally. The very "magic" of the production is in some sense an analogy to the splendor of the divine plan for human redemption. The many artistic dimensions shape a form of communication to invite personal response from the audience. It does not require literacy or education for the audience to be moved to a consideration of

---

[30] Ibid., 67.

[31] McKendrick, 255.

[32] Ibid., 250.

the topics displayed, and neither does it require money to procure the opportunity to witness such a lavish production. It is not religious discourse for the elite, but performed in the streets for all to witness, inviting all to appropriate the truths demonstrated.

A. A. Parker's conception of the perfect *auto* requires "that the theology, by the demonstration of its relevance to experience, should be rendered so effective as drama that even an unbeliever should be convinced that the dogmas expressed are viable."[33] McKendrick, however, does not require the same "exacting criterion" for a successful *auto*.[34] She sees the suspended disbelief, awe, and internal movement experienced during the performance to be enough to make the *auto* a success within its genre. Regardless, it is this "demonstration" of theology's "relevance to experience" that I find particularly significant, as this is exactly the purpose of indirect communication—that the reader will realize that Christianity involves her and her very existence. Such theology is not composed of abstract ideas that remain outside the person, but touch the very core of living, of one's being in time, even at the very moment. All of the splendor of the genre, however, along with "the mixing of the sacred and the profane," brought the *auto* under fire during the Reformation and it eventually fell out of use. "The very act indeed of using earthly symbolism for sacred truths...was deemed to be an offence against reverence and good taste; the place for religion was tucked away in church."[35]

El Divino Narciso. Sor Juana's *loas* function as a form of indirect communication and contrast the direct address of dogma through the novelistic features of her *loas*. Her *loas* are not only open-ended in form through connection to the present but also in the message of their content. Her *loas* to the *Divino Narciso* and *El Cetro de José* incorporate heteroglossia as cultures converse, and those without power play a leading role.[36] An argument for

---

[33] Ibid., 258–59. This is McKendrick's assessment of Parker.

[34] Ibid.

[35] Ibid., 260.

[36] Sor Juana's use of indigenous characters is mixed. On one hand her work affirms the equal rationality of the colonized and of the indigenous. She puts the history and the culture of the Americas on equal footing with Europe, writing in a native language (Nahuatl) and creating indigenous and black characters in her poetry and plays; however, despite the positive portrayal she gives of these peoples, cultures, languages, customs, and religious traditions, it is also from a position of some power over them that she writes this. She is the one giving and authorizing the voice. Ludmer says Sor Juana "grants the word to the Indians" and that "both the granting the word and identifying

openness to other views can also be found in the content of her *loa* to *San Hermenegildo*. The *loas*, as drama, additionally are most obviously composed of dialogue, an essential feature of this shift in literature as Bakhtin describes it and for any discourse which strives not to be a monologue or suggestive that it communicates an absolute, whole truth.

The *loa* sets the stage for the demonstration of the Christian story, which proceeds in the *auto*, and grounds the play. The *auto* itself, though the longer of the two, becomes the play within the play. The characters of the *loa* in essence watch the *auto* along with the audience and for the same purpose, to gain an understanding of Christianity, to be moved by the scene and therefore to be persuaded of its truth. The *loa* thus establishes the contemporaneity of the message. Despite the allegorical characters in two of Sor Juana's *loas* set at the time of the conquest, they are nonetheless symbolic of the contemporary racial clashes of which her audiences would have been aware had the play been performed in New Spain.

El Divino Narciso is considered the masterpiece of Sor Juana's three *auto-sacramentales*. Octavio Paz calls it "more complex and of greater intellectual and lyrical richness than the work" of Calderón using the same Greek myth, *Eco y Narciso*.[37] In the *loa* to *Divino Narciso*, Sor Juana presents the characters of Occident: a gallant "*Indio*," wearing a crown; and America: an "*India*" "of poised self-possession."[38] They are described in her text as wearing elaborate cloaks and tunics. The scene is set as they sit down on two chairs, and *indios*

---

oneself with the other involve the same imperative: the weak must accept the superior's project" ("Tricks of the Weak," 90). For a more extended look at the context in which Sor Juana is writing and the levels of power involved, see Yolanda Martinez-San Miguel, *Saberes Americanos: Subalternidad y Epistemología en los Escritos de Sor Juana* (Pittsburgh: Instituto Internacional de Literatura Iberoamericana, University of Pittsburgh, 1999). The power relations at work in a situation like Sor Juana's are of course famously explored in Gayatri Chakravorty Spivak's "Can the Subaltern Speak?"

[37] Paz, 351.

[38] *The Divine Narcissus/El Divino Narciso*, trans. Patricia A. Peters and Renée Domeier, O.S.B. (Albuquerque NM: University of New Mexico Press, 1998) 7. OC 3:5. Pamela Kirk translates the descriptions of the *indios* as a handsome Indian man and an Indian woman "gorgeously attired" (Kirk, 69). For a study of the significance of Sor Juana's inclusion of subaltern characters in such a production, see Yolanda Martinez-San Miguel, *Saberes Americanos: Subalternidad y Epistemología en los Escritos de Sor Juana* (Pittsburgh: Instituto Internacional de Literatura Iberoamericana, University of Pittsburgh, 1999) 169–204.

and *indias* "dance with feathers and rattles in their hands, as is customary for those doing this dance."[39] The other primary characters are also a man and a woman: Zeal is a Captain General in armor with Spanish soldiers, and Christian Religion, a Spanish lady.

The *loa* opens with a song honoring the residents of New Spain, *Mejicanos*, whose ancient ancestry is compared to the "brilliance of the Sun," and who have an abundance of fertile land.[40] It shows the Amerindians in full festivities celebrating the "God of Seeds" who makes their crops fertile. Sor Juana describes the rites of blood sacrifice practiced in this celebration and the use of human victims through the voices of Occident and America. A mixture of blood and seeds constitute a cake shaped in the form of a large man that is eaten by the people in the ritual. The God of Seeds is, therefore, said to feed them "with his very flesh, (first purified of every stain)."[41] The two Amerindians say, "We eat his body, drink his blood, and by this sacred meal are freed and cleansed from all that is profane, and thus, he purifies our soul."[42] The context is thus quickly set for an explanation of the Christian feast, which celebrates God giving God's own blood for the purification of humanity's sin, rather than requiring human sacrifice in order to procure cleansing. Christian Religion and Zeal enter, and although initially upon seeing the pagan ritual, Religion asks Zeal how he can contain his righteous wrath, Religion proceeds by peacefully approaching Occident and America in order to persuade them to Christian truth with rational arguments before Zeal can revert to violence. She says: "And I, in peace, will also go (before your fury lays them low) for justice must with mercy kiss; I shall invite them to arise from superstitious depths to faith."[43] When Religion first speaks to Occident and America, she begins by honoring them: "Great Occident, most powerful; America, so beautiful and rich."[44] Yet she continues, "you live in poverty amid the treasures of your land. Abandon this irreverent cult with which the demon has waylaid you."[45] And she identifies love as that which compels her approach for persuasion.

---

[39] Peters and Domeier, OC 3:3.

[40] Ibid.

[41] Ibid. OC 3:5.

[42] Ibid. OC 3:5.

[43] Ibid., 9. OC 3:6.

[44] Ibid. OC 3:7.

[45] Ibid., 9–10. OC 3:7.

Zeal quickly rises up with violent threats, and America and Occident exchange passionate words with him, both sides firmly holding to their belief in their god, and offended at the words and actions of the other. America eventually calls Zeal blind, crazy, and barbarous, saying that he comes with "mystifying messages" trying to disturb the "calm and peace," and "destroying the tranquility" that their people enjoy.[46] She instructs her husband Occident: "close off your hearing and your sight to all their words; refuse to heed their fantasies of zealous might; proceed to carry out your rite. Do not concede to insolence from foreigners intent to dull our ritual's magnificence."[47] Zeal responds with a call to take up arms, yelling "To war! To war!"[48] Occident and America appear shocked and confused, not sure why this terrible violence has befallen them, and therefore evoke sympathy from the reader. Occident, though instructing his soldiers to aim their arrows at the enemy, asks: "What miscarriages of justice has heaven sent against me? What are these weapons, blazing fire, before my unbelieving eyes?" And America: "What lightning bolts does heaven send to lay me low? What molten balls of burning lead so fiercely rain? What centaurs crush with monstrous force and cause my people such great pain?" Meanwhile, the call from the lines of Christians comes: "Long life to Spain! Long live her king!"[49] Religion shouts to Occident to surrender. And Occident responds profoundly: "I must bow to your aggression, but not before your arguments."[50]

Religion seems to recognize the truth of Occident's statement, and she commands Zeal to refrain from killing America. Conversion can only come through internal persuasion and not via external force and domination. America insists that the mind is free and cannot be forced to yield. She says: "If your petition for my life and show of Christian charity are motivated by the hope that you, at last, will conquer me, defeating my integrity with verbal steel where bullets failed, then you are sadly self-deceived. A weeping captive, I may mourn for liberty, yet my will grows beyond these bonds; my heart is free."[51] And Occident concurs: "Forced to surrender to your power, I have admitted my defeat, but still it must be clearly said that violence cannot devour my will, nor

---

[46] Ibid., 15. OC 3:9.

[47] Ibid. OC 3:9–10.

[48] Ibid. OC 3:10.

[49] Ibid., 17. OC 3:10.

[50] Ibid. "Ya es preciso que me rinda tu valor, no tu razón." OC 3:11.

[51] Ibid., 19. OC 3:12.

force constrain its right. Although in grief, I now lament, a prisoner, your cruel might has limits. You cannot prevent my saying here within my heart I worship the great God of Seeds!"[52] Physical violence cannot evoke real change, nor can rational rhetorical violence or intellectual weapons.[53] One cannot be forced to belief, be it through the arm or the voice of power and authority. Here we encounter the repeated theme of Sor Juana's letters. In a variety of genres, Sor Juana insists on the freedom of will and reason. This is also an example of Sor Juana's drama in correspondence with the themes of novelization. She clearly demonstrates her own understanding of the difference between discourse that persuades one internally and that which relies on the force of power and authority.

Religion responds by backing down in her verbal aggression. Where a few lines before she stated that she would "gently make [America] yield,"[54] she now explains: "What you perceive as force is not coercion, but affection."[55] Religion seems convinced by the statements made by America and Occident regarding the nature of internal persuasion—that which is held "within [one's] heart."[56] Religion proceeds to ask the Aztecs about their god, this one to whom their hearts cling with such devotion. After Occident describes a god who gives them fertile crops, who cleanses them from sin, and invites them to share a meal with him that he prepares, Religion speaks in an aside, as she considers the rite a dark shadowing of Christian truth. America notes Religion's expression and asks why she seems perplexed, thus opening the way for Religion to instruct them on the Christian God.

Beginning as Paul did with the Athenians, she claims she is not introducing a new God, but that when they adore the one who brings rain and causes their crops to flourish, this is actually the Christian God.[57] America concedes that this could be the case, but asks if this God is as kind as the god they worship, who allows human hands to touch him through the sacred rite of the image made with seed and blood. Religion responds: "Although the Essence of Divinity is boundless and invisible, because already It has been eternally

---

[52] Ibid., 21. OC 3:12.

[53] "Intellectivas armas." OC 3:12.

[54] *Divino Narciso*, 18–19. OC 3:19.

[55] Ibid., 21. "No es fuerza, sino caricia." OC 3:12.

[56] Ibid. OC 3:12.

[57] Ibid., 25. OC 3:13–14.

united with our nature, He resembles us so much in our humanity that He permits unworthy priests to take Him in their humble hands."[58]

Religion goes on to explain that although God is incorporeal, the human nature "he" assumed becomes present in the Mass. Bread made of the seeds of wheat is transformed into his body, and the sacred cup contains his holy blood, transformed the elements thus to offer himself for humanity.[59] But before such a meal a person must "bathe," and so Religion tells America and Occident of the sacrament of baptism or penance. America says that because Religion has inundated her "poor mind with concepts of theology" she is just beginning to understand but she wants to see more and her "desire to know is now by holy inspiration led."[60] And Occident agrees that he wants to know more about "the life and death of the God you say is in the bread."[61]

"[Religion] comes to realize that America will not find faith through scholastic syllogistic reasoning, but through 'objects of sight instead of words,' the 'sensate experimentalism' practiced by Sor Juana herself in her search for truth. Yet what Religion gives to America *is* words in a play, the symbols that mediate between language and experience."[62] Religion offers an explanation of the theological form of the drama they will witness, saying: "I shall make for you a metaphor, a concept clothed in rhetoric so colorful that what I show to you, your eyes will clearly see; for now I know that you require objects of sight instead of words, by which faith whispers in your ears too deaf to hear; I understand, for you necessity demands that through the eyes, faith find her way to her reception in your hearts."[63] Here Sor Juana displays her methodological justification for drama to be close to that discussed previously for the genre. Direct verbal instruction is not the only way to demonstrate Christian thought in a way that moves the individual to faith, and in fact, story, characters, visual images, and allegory may be a better way to invite subjective appropriation of Christian truth.

---

[58] Ibid. OC 3:15.

[59] Ibid., 27. OC 3:16.

[60] Ibid., 29–30. OC 3:17.

[61] Ibid., 31. OC 3:17.

[62] Peters and Domeier, Introduction to *The Divine Narcissus/El Divino Narciso,* xxi, quoting line 407 of the *loa*, p. 31 in the translation.

[63] Ibid., 31. OC 3:17–18.

The two natives agree to watch the play, and Zeal asks Religion what metaphor she will use to represent the holy mysteries.[64] She explains that she will use an *auto* to make the mysteries visible through allegorical images "of what America must learn and Occident implores to know about the questions that now burn within him so."[65] Religion describes the setup of the play, that it will be titled *Divino Narciso*, explaining that if this native woman's religion hid the mystery of the Eucharist, then she suspects this will also be found within the ancient myths.[66]

Sor Juana presents the Amerindians as noble, articulate, and intelligent, holding passionately to their beliefs and not easily pushed around as a weaker race. They represent the voice of reason, particularly the *India,* while the masculine Christian figure knows only force, violence, and coercion. This is a radical suggestion on Sor Juana's part, and the scene she sets leads the audience to believe that it is perfectly reasonable that the *indio/as* would not trust these "foreigners" who come "intent to dull" the magnificence of their beliefs and practices, and the natives seem justified in their distrust when Zeal comes breathing threats of violence and war.[67] Sor Juana's work does ultimately assert that the Christian God is the one true God, but she suggests in her syncretism that these faithful pagans are not far from the Christian religion. They have been led away by pagan practices of human sacrifice, but she suggests that underlying their polytheist beliefs is a surprising Christian foundation.

El Cetro de José. These themes are also present in the short *loa* to the *auto sacramental, El Cetro de José* ("Joseph's Scepter"). Here the characters Faith, Nature, The Law of Grace, and The Natural Law converse with one another on

---

[64] Ibid. OC 3:18.

[65] Ibid., 33. OC 3:18.

[66] Religion explains that it will be performed in Madrid, which Zeal suspects may be presumptuous. He asks: "that you should write in Mexico for royal patrons don't you see it to be an impropriety?" (*Divino Narciso*, 33. OC 3:19). She responds: "Is it beyond imagination that something made in one location can in another be of use? Furthermore, my writing it comes, not of whimsical caprice, but from my vowed obedience to do what seems beyond my reach. Well, then, this work, however rough and little polished it might be, results from my obedience, and not from my arrogance" (*Divino Narciso*, 35. OC 3:19). Here Religion's words echo *La Respuesta* and *Carta Athenagórica.*

[67] One wonders likewise of a marginalized and oppressed status in her society, if in showing these *indio/as* to be the reasonable characters, if she is not suggesting that other groups in her society, like women, are not equally rational even in contrast to those with power and force behind them and their opinions.

issues related to the conversion of natives in the Americas, setting the scene for the allegorical representation of the Eucharist through the Old Testament story of Joseph. The issues addressed in the *loa* may relate to a fear arising in the 1680s of a return to pagan practices after a significant and wide spread Indian revolt in New Spain.

After a song and general greetings among the characters, the plot proceeds with a speech by Faith who addresses the other characters one by one. She states that the "recent conversion of the conquered Indies" deserves a celebration.[68] These "vast provinces of fertile America" had been a place where all the individuals living there were deprived of herself, that is of Faith, and where The Law of Grace was once "trodden underfoot by blind Idolatry, whose sacrilegious altars [were] stained with human blood."[69] She continues to condemn this practice, while expanding her critique to all violence perpetrated by humans upon humans:

> Men are more barbaric than the cruelest animals (for among them there is none who turns his ferocious claws against his own kind; and among men not only is there hatred, but animosity has become an art, and rage is cultivated, for why else are swords sharpened, guns loaded with powder, lances armed with iron...? Oh, insane human ambition, heedless even of yourself, whom you destroy just when you think you are triumphing!).[70]

But after this aside where Sor Juana clearly critiques not only the practice of human sacrifice, but also the violent methods used in the conquest of the Americas, and what in today's context we might call "militarization," she returns to the topic of the celebration and suggests they do something to commemorate the happy reception the American people have given her. A discussion ensues in which proposals are given: the demolition of pagan altars for human sacrifices, abolition of polygamy, and the destruction of idols placed on pagan altars. Faith has an alternative proposal, however, for the commemoration of the conversions: "I think the best thing to do would be to place the consecrated Host on the altar, because it is the very substance rather

---

[68] Sor Juana gives no costume direction for these characters, and it is unclear what gendered pronoun would be used for them, and so I am using the feminine pronoun here because each of these characters is a feminine noun. *Joseph's Scepter*, in *The Story of Joseph in Spanish Golden Age Drama,* trans. Michael McGaha (Lewisburg: Bucknell University Press, 1998) 195. OC 3:186.

[69] *Joseph's Scepter,* 195. OC 3:186.

[70] Ibid., 195–96. OC 3:186.

than a mere image."[71] And Faith explains how all of the wishes of the others would be met through the successful completion of this final proposal.

The character of Idolatry enters dressed as an Amerindian woman, and she is outraged at Faith's plan. She says: "In spite of my resistance you've managed to strip me of the crown I held so peacefully for centuries, introducing your dictatorial rule in my empires and preaching the Christian Law, but you couldn't have done it if your weapons hadn't first violently cleared a path for you."[72] Here again Sor Juana contrasts, as she did in *El Divino Narciso*, the peaceful rule of the Aztecs with the violence of the Conquest and the cruel irony of violent means used under the pretext of introducing faith, linking the methods of evangelism directly with violence. Also, again the Amerindians are shown to not be passive and weakly acquiescent to the conquest.

Idolatry continues,

> And yes, it's true that almost all my people, worn down by your aggressive propaganda, have embraced your dogmas. You may be powerful, but I repeat that you will not succeed in obliterating my customs—they are too deeply rooted for that! So you may see me prostrate right now, but that doesn't mean I won't be able to keep you from demolishing the altars where human victims are sacrificed.[73]

Again force imposed by the dominant power is shown to be something which can force physical submission, while internal persuasion of belief cannot be so imposed, and again Sor Juana emphasizes the freedom of the will, as we saw she also did in her letters.

Idolatry explains that the sacrifices function to placate the Deity and lengthen the life of whoever eats of it. Faith asks who this is who would dare to interfere and Idolatry responds:

> Insult me all you like! You can't keep me from defending rights I have held for so long. I am an allegorical idea, an abstract consideration, and as such I embrace practically the entire kingdom. Therefore, speaking on everyone's behalf, as plenipotentiary of the Indians, I'm here to tell you that it's fine for you to brag about how many converts now follow your holy banners, but you'd better not try to force them to give up their ancient custom of offering sacrifices.[74]

[71] Ibid., 196. OC 3:189.

[72] Ibid., 198. OC 3:192.

[73] Ibid. OC 3:192–93.

[74] Ibid. OC 3:193.

Similar to the speeches made by the Amerindian in *Divino Narciso,* this *India* calls the church's missional practices "aggressive propaganda" and declares that their religious beliefs, idolatrous or not, are strongly and deeply held.[75] These Christian characters can brag about those who seem to follow their lead, but such dearly held ideas and customs are not so easily eradicated, despite appearances. Again we have a contrast between authoritative discourse enforced with power and violence and that which is truly held within the individual's sense of identity and consciousness.

She represents Amerindian culture, though negatively in the name Idolatry, and with an emphasis on human sacrifice in a way that would shock Europeans, but in speech, this character is noble and in many ways represents the perspective of faith proposed by Sor Juana, as Idolatry's description of herself sharply contrasts the negative depiction of dogma and its aggressive function. Sor Juana again shows an Amerindian woman as the voice of reason, to a similar result of what we saw in *Divino Narciso*. We hear her deliver the most elegant speech of the *loa*, critiquing a forceful dogmatic communication of the gospel and the use of violence and power in an attempt to change people's minds. This will not succeed, after all. They will bow physically, but those ideas held internally will survive. They may recite a creed, but it will not in this manner become deep and sustaining. Verbal assent is superficial: externally imposed, it is externally maintained. Dogma is contrasted with deeply rooted customs and religious practices, thus an external "conversion" in which an individual gives verbal assent to dogma does not necessarily signify internal conversion or persuasion. And here the use of power to bring about such conversion is viewed negatively as dictatorial, violent, and "aggressive propaganda."

Nature, Natural Law, Faith, and Law of Grace explain why human sacrifice is not the way to get what Idolatry seeks, and that there is another way to obtain the benefits "but in an infinitely higher degree."[76] She agrees to watch the allegorical sacramental play in order to be able to understand "how bread could turn into flesh and blood and produce the astonishing effects" of satisfying God and giving eternal life.[77] She is eager to have this explained,

---

[75] Ibid. OC 3:192.

[76] Ibid., 199. OC 3:196.

[77] Ibid., 200. OC 3:198. In the *auto* sacramental following this *loa*, *Cetro de José*, the character of Prophecy makes this statement, very much in line with the themes under discussion: Prophecy: "…I who formerly was Prophecy, speak now with the voice of

saying that if they can prove this to her then the matter is settled, and she will be satisfied.[78] Idolatry agrees to watch the play, and one can only assume the message is to convey that she is convinced by the brilliant allegory displayed; Sor Juana is writing this for a Christian festival after all. However, we do not see the Indian woman convert.

The *India* is reasonable and intelligent. She says if they can convince her rationally or with their allegorical play, she will concede; she, too, will believe in this Christian God. She is not inflexible or simply stubborn. She will listen to other views and if they are convincing, she will yield; her belief structure will shift in correspondence. She is also insistent, like the Amerindians of the *loa* to the *Divino Narciso* that externally imposed dogma is artificial; conversion comes only when a person grows truly convinced and makes something his or her own.

El Mártir del Sacramento, San Hermenegildo. Lastly we turn to the *loa* introducing the *auto sacramental El Mártir del Sacramento, San Hermenegildo.*[79] It begins with two students arguing off stage, using syllogistic reasoning. They enter arguing over the premises from which their conclusions are drawn, one citing Augustine as the authority supporting his ideas and the other claiming Thomas Aquinas. An older student "of serious aspect" enters. He asks that the other two relax their obstinance and the fire in their opinions and to stop trying to make their arguments more convincing through the volume of their voices. He explains: "This is not a question of voices but a battle of concepts and as reason is the judge, the winner, I think, will be the one with the subtler arguments and not the one who shouts the loudest. Nowhere more than

---

faith. This is no contradiction, for it is an act of faith to believe in what is yet to be without having seen it. Believing in God means believing what He said, believing against time, or in this case, against the evidence of the senses" (*Scepter of Joseph*, McGaha, 224).

[78] "La cuestión está acabada y yo quedo satisfecha" (OC 3:199). McGaha translates this phrase: "then the argument is over, and you win!" (200). However, I don't find the sort of competitive language in Idolatry's response here. It is not that religion "wins," but that this character's reason is satisfied. She simply says: "Let's go see this play that explains how it is that God is placated in a human sacrifice which I can also eat to receive eternal life, as you say; the matter is settled and I am satisfied!"

[79] No English translation of this text is available. All translations here are my own, and so I include the Spanish texts in reference. The citations follow Vol.Page:Line.

in the Schools, I believe, does the one with the weaker case rely on voice."[80] The first student responds with a Thomistic argument about the relationship between the body and the soul. He states that as the soul has no way to express itself other than through the body, and specifically through the voice, tongue, and chest, these instruments must be used to more adequately communicate the meaning which the soul is attempting to convey. Thus, "if the soul is intense, then the body expresses this with vigor; if the soul is reluctant, then with fear. So that for me, as a student, I do not agree that one must argue without shouting because if one doesn't, then I think, one does not demonstrate the soul outwardly, but instead forces reason inward," and therefore it is unexpressed.[81]

The third student does not appear impressed by this argument, stating that he could answer with a similar line of reasoning, but this is not his purpose for coming there, which is rather to mediate their rage. He does not fear the duel of a question but is aware that arguments such as the one in which the two students are engaged, become combat of another sort, "the kind young boys like you are accustomed to, that is to want to turn to the use of hands to demonstrate your talent as if it were the same to have a vigorous arm as to have strong arguments."[82] The two students had left a lecture in this state of impassioned debate, and the third student followed behind them, hoping that his age, friendship, and position as an instructor, would be enough to compose the two of them. They agree that their voices did not convey the respect they should have. "The voice is excessive where one's facial expression is enough," responds Student 2.[83]

The third student states that although he heard the arguments raised by the two of them inside the lecture hall, he would like them to repeat them now, so that he can discern whose arguments are most reasonable, explaining that if they simply let the argument go because they were flattered by his attention to them

---

[80] "Ésta no es cuestión de voces/ sino lid de los conceptos; y siendo juez la razón,/ que será vencedor, pienso,/ el que más sutil arguya,/ no el que gritare más recio./ En ninguna parte tanto,/ como en las Escuelas, creo/ que es el que lo mete a voces/ el que tiene más mal pleito" (OC 3.99:23–32).

[81] "Si es intenso, con vigor;/ y si es remiso, con miedo./ De modo que, para mí, por Estudiante no tengo al que arguye sin gritar,/ porque no le hace, pienso,/ al que no la muestra fuera,/ fuerza la razón adentro" (OC 3.99:45–52).

[82] "Que suele, y más en los mozos/ como sois, el del ingenio/ querer pasar a las manos,/ como si fuera lo mesmo/ tener el brazo vigor,/ que fuerza el entendimiento" (OC 3.100:59–64).

[83] "Es muy sobrada la voz/ donde basta vuestro aspecto" (OC 3.100:81–82).

and not because of reason, they will ultimately be unsatisfied, as they would have submitted only to authority and not to reason, which is the right thing to which to yield. Already here we have the third student making the point that authority itself is not something to which the intellect should simply surrender, but that one should yield to sound reasoning first and foremost, a theme held in common with all three *loas*.

The two students proceed to give their arguments for the greatest *fineza*, a concept and debate that are not new to us, as Sor Juana's critique of Vieira's sermon was on the same topic.[84] The first student argues that the greatest *fineza* after the incarnation itself is Jesus' death. The second states that although this is a great sign of love, he asserts that it is still more for Christ to be present in the Eucharist. The two proceed to make their scholastic arguments. The third student, however, rather than simply pronouncing whose argument is the strongest, demonstrates his response through a short drama, which becomes a play within a play, within a play. The third student explains that the understanding makes its objects visible with allegorical figures when empirical demonstration is not possible, another example of Sor Juana's *loas* justifying the use of theological drama. The drama which follows serves to demonstrate for the two students, the view of the third. The two students press him to pronounce a judgment as to which opinion most pleases him, but he responds: "What I have to answer you with is that which you will see; I do not have any further response that you will hear from me."[85]

The first scene of this small drama within the *loa* begins with soldiers celebrating Hercules. They discuss setting up columns as a sign marking the end of the world and that there is no more of the world beyond that which has been discovered by Hercules. A choir sings about the Pillars of Hercules, which serve as an eternal record of his name and as a sign to future generations that there is no more world beyond that which they have seen. "No man will pass by here arrogantly, being the *non plus ultra*."[86] And all the players in this mini-drama

[84] "Let us investigate more closely what a *fineza* is. Does it designate, perhaps, to have love? No, certainly not. Rather, it refers to the proofs of love. Those are called *finezas*. Those external demonstrative signs and actions that the lover practices, which have as their cause the motive of love, these are called *finezas*" (*Carta Athenagórica,* Kirk 232; OC 3.423–24).

[85] "Con lo que he de responderos,/ es con lo que habéis de ver;/ que más respuesta no tengo/ que me oigáis" (OC 3.104:92–95).

[86] "¡De aquí hombre ninguno/ pasará soberbio,/ siendo el *Non plus ultra* " (OC 3.105:211–13).

repeat the refrain: "*Non plus ultra! Non plus ultra!*" or "Nothing further beyond" and "Here the universe ends!"[87] The third student has painted the scene of the ancients, proudly asserting that they have reached the end, the ultimate point, and that no one can surpass what they have discovered. The second student does not understand how this scene relates to their debate. He is unsure why such a well-known story about the error of the ancients in believing that the end of the world was reached at the Strait of Gibraltar illuminates their discussion. The third student instructs them to watch yet another scene, one of Columbus and his men hitting ground in the Americas. Columbus makes a grand speech about fertile Spain and her strength at sea. He congratulates Europe, saying:

> There are more worlds, more empires for your weapons to subjugate and your breath to restrain. Abandon that past error your Ancients held that the end of the earth did not exceed the Strait! Oh Hercules! From your columns erase the arrogant heading of *Non plus ultra*, as my rudder broke the seal that existed for such a long time on the narrow of Abila and Calpe. And you all, my happy, brave companions, the first discoverers of such an expanded world, announce with bugles and drums in sweet echoes that there are more worlds, that there is *Plus Ultra*, and that you already see it![88]

And now the chant is "*Plus Ultra*" rather than "*Non Plus Ultra.*" There is more. That which was once considered the end and the ultimate has now been surpassed. One can hardly help but hear Sor Juana's critique of Vieira in these scenes. He claimed his argument was insurmountable, and she argued that his opinion could be improved upon, just as could her own.

The second student questions why the third used the secular examples of Hercules and Columbus to make his point, as he certainly could have found ample examples in scripture. But the third student says he does not have to

---

[87] "¡Aquí acaba el Universo!" (OC 3.105:216).

[88] "¡Más Mundos hay, más Imperios,/ que tus armas avasallen/ y sujeten tus alientos!/¡ Sál de aquel pasado error,/ que tus Antiguos tuvieron,/ de que el término del Mundo,/ no pasaba del Estrecho!/ ¡Oh Hércules! De tus Columnas/ borra el rótulo soberbio/ del *Non plus ultra*, pues ya/ rompió mi timón el sello/ que Ábila y Calpe cerrado/ tuvieron tan largos tiempos!/ Y vosotros, mis felices/ animosos comañeros,/ de tan dilatados Mundos/ descubridores primeros,/ con los clarines y cajas/ publicad, en dulces ecos,/ ¡que hay más Mundos, que hay *Plus ultra*,/ y que ya venís de verlo!" (OC 3.106–107:254–74).

respond to this, that the "sweet choirs of music" will do it for him. And the choirs proceed to argue with one another in song:

> Music:
> The Supreme Power could not enact another greater *fineza* of his immense love to than come to suffer.[89]
>
> Chorus 1:
> Yes he could![90]
>
> Chorus 2:
> No he could not![91]
>
> Chorus 1:
> To die, in my understanding, exhausts what can be considered of Love.[92]
>
> Chorus 2:
> Submerge oneself in the waters of his love and you will see that there is more to do.[93]

The first student sees the point that even suffering for love can be surpassed, but still does not understand why Hercules and Columbus were used to make this point.

The third student responds: "Consider if they are superfluous. Hercules in his coat of arms believed there was not more world, but Columbus set ship in the water and he saw that there was more world. Thus when it was understood that getting to suffer for the Supreme Power was the greatest task that he endured, he lay down in the water, and he knew that there was more left to do."[94] As the discussion continues between the three students, the music and the

[89] "No pudo el Sumo Poder/ otra fineza mayor/ obrar con Su inmenso Amor,/ que llegar a padecer" (OC 3.110:349–52).

[90] "¡Sí pudo hacer!" (OC 3.110).

[91] "¡No pudo hacer!" (OC 3.110).

[92] "El morir, en mi entender,/ agota de Amor la fragua" (OC 3.110).

[93] "Échese Su Amor al agua, y verá que hay más que hacer" (OC 3.110).

[94] "Pues mirad si son superfluos./ No haber más Mundo creía/ Hércules en su blazón,/ mas se echo al agua Colón/ y vio que más mundo había. Así cuando se entendía que el llegar a padecer/ era del Sumo Poder/ la empresa mayor que vieron,/ Se echó al agua, y conocieron/ que quedaba más que hacer" (OC 3.110–11:363–76).

choir continue contradicting each other, much like the theological debate between the two students at the opening: Music: "It cannot be!" Choir 2: "Yes it can be!"

The stage is set for the Eucharist to be considered the greatest *fineza*, as the drama suggests there is something more than to suffer, but the pronouncement is never explicitly made. Rather, the discussion moves in the direction of a third *fineza* for consideration, the foot-washing. Rather than a clear pronouncement of the greatest, the play simply transitions into an acknowledgment and honoring of those who may witness the production of this play if it is ever staged in Spain. The students honor the royal family, the court, tribunals, city council, dedicating the proceeding play to the nobility and also to the common people. Thus, the final message rings out as the surpassable nature of theological opinions rather than a coherent argument for the greatest *fineza*, which one might expect.

The representative of authority in the *loa*, the third student, does not pronounce a judgment on whose opinion is best but gives a picture. The third student shows two short dramas that are to "press their opinions." They want him to judge who has the sounder argument, and he responds with images depicting moments when a powerful figure declares he has reached the ultimate, the end, but is then surpassed. The greater meaning of the dramas explain that there is always more, more to be discovered, and that those like Hercules who claim to reach the end are foolish and arrogant, because it will be surpassed.

In her *Carta Athenagórica*, Sor Juana presents arguments for the greatest *fineza* similar to the views of the three students. There she supports the views of three church fathers against António Vieira's claims that his surpasses their views. Simply stated, Augustine argues for the death of Christ as the greatest example of Christ's love. Thomas argues that it is in instituting the Eucharist that Christ most demonstrates his love. And John Chrysostom argues that it is the foot-washing that is the greatest *fineza*. The first two students easily correspond to the views of Augustine and Thomas. The third student hints toward Chrysostom's position with his emphasis on the water, and a suggestion of cleansing, be it baptism, penance, or the washing of feet. The conclusion of the third student, however, is to gesture toward that argument in order to call for more, for further inquiry, and even indicating that greater demonstrations of love may still be to come.

In the *Carta Athenagórica* Sor Juana presents yet another view, one she does not compare to that of the three fathers', however, because her proposal is not a *fineza* of Christ's love, but of God's. She says it is of a different category because it belongs to the workings of God in eternity rather than specifically of Christ in Christ's lifetime. Octavio Paz, however, sees this difference between her view here and what she presents in that discussion of the *finezas* to be an inconsistency. I disagree with Paz, however, when he writes that Sor Juana's offering of differing arguments "indicates either that she was uncertain when confronted with several possible answers or, more probably, that she slanted her judgment to the circumstances of the moment. It is not easy to take her theological opinions seriously."[95] First, in the *Carta* her argument is clearly of a different sort, pertaining to God's *fineza* and not Christ's. Second, her ultimate argument in this *loa* mirrors that of the *Carta*, as both emphasize the multiple reasonable arguments to be made on the matter, all in accordance with church authorities, but yet also all surpassable. Just as Hercules's discovery was surpassed by Columbus's, so Augustine's argument was possibly surpassed by Thomas centuries later, and so forth.[96] Her texts address the theological arrogance of claims of superiority, display a variety of reasonable views on a topic, and demonstrate dramatically that there is always more to be said and improved upon, while never reaching the ultimate articulation or knowledge. She is absolutely consistent; on one level, her disregard for her "theological inconsistency" here only supports this position.

She does, however, value the discussion itself, as evidenced in the affirmation Student 3 gives to the conversation. The searching, the inquiry, and the discussion matter; the quest for understanding is the point, and not the final conclusion to be judged as best and highest. The refrain of the chorus rings out across this piece and her work as a whole "*Plus Ultra*," there is more. This phrase and her images here depicted, applied to theological debate and inquiry is a move to break open the canon: the authorities are not the end though they may help point to the continuing line of discovery. The canon suggests something closed, completed, and determined, but her work, in drama and other forms, and her use of Hercules and Columbus when one would expect her to use any of the number of sacred illustrations at her fingertips, point to the opening of the canon, to the world beyond the Pillars of Hercules, to the possibilities not yet seen.

---

[95] Paz, 343.

[96] See Georgina Sabat-Rivers, "*Loa* del *Auto* a San Hermenegildo: Sor Juana Frente a la *Auto*ridad de la Sabiduría Antigua," in *En busca de Sor Juana* (Alicante: Biblioteca Virtual Miguel de Cervantes, 2005) esp. 326–29.

The point where the mountains Abila and Calpe meet were considered the Pillars of Hercules and created a narrow passage into the sea thought to contain no more land, and thus served to mark the end or border, and legend says the coat of arms of Hercules stood there, engraved with the phrase: *Non Plus Ultra*. Yet through that narrow, Columbus found that the world opens and eventually set foot on land never before considered by the Christian European continent. The Pillars, instead of marking the end of the world, become the gate to more, and now the monument should read "*Plus Ultra*."[97] At the edge of the Christian empire, and what it represented and believed of itself and its knowledge, Sor Juana recalls the phrase emblazed on the coat of arms: There is More: more world, more culture, more knowledge, more beyond our comprehension and our language. We do not have it understood, wrapped up or concluded; we have not reached the end. Those like Hercules who claim to reach the end are foolish and arrogant because it will be surpassed. And if a monument were to be erected to mark the borders of Christian dogma and theological articulation it would also read: *Plus Ultra*.

In this *Estudiante* 3 we seem to encounter Sor Juana if she were able to be such a student and to teach. Through this character Sor Juana criticizes the use of loud voice and hostile argumentation, as if strength of arm could force the understanding. She critiques the forceful, masculine, combative, and competitive posturing in theology, that is, in her words, much like boys fighting in the school yard, who are taking it to fists, verbally. She could out argue them, but that is not her intention. She asks them to restate their view as she will use them as material for her drama, including Hercules and Columbus, and all pointing to the open-endedness of theological assertions and "discoveries." The two students gather from the dramas that the third student is mocking their debate, and although it is clear that the third student does value theological discussion, the *loa* certainly suggests that the nature (or fervency) of such discussions are verging on the humorous, in that they do not warrant the fire given them. Each side vehemently argues its position, but Sor Juana asserts that someone will eventually come and improve upon them nonetheless. There may

[97] "*Plus Ultra*" was the motto of Charles V and ultimately referred to how expansive the Spanish empire was—"further beyond, more beyond." Sor Juana's use of it here positions this *loa* also within colonial Spain, gesturing toward New Spain, as did her other *loas*. Here she uses the motto of Spain, typically used to glory in Spanish conquest of the Americas and its supremacy, as a warning against arrogance and claims of ultimacy!

be some mockery of the minutia fought over in scholastic debate when whole knowledge on such matters cannot be attained. Sor Juana is certainly not opposed to rigorous study; she devoted her life to it, but bold claims of ultimate argumentation is something to which she is certainly opposed to, as is also documented in her letters.

Also in this *loa* we encounter a juxtaposing of positions similar to that of another genre employed by Sor Juana, the *villancico*. These carols also take on dialogic form with different characters addressing one another. Most *villancicos* pose "a series of simultaneous explanations in diverse verbal and intellectual registers, in order to communicate the same" theological concept. [98] The *villancicos* begin with the "centralizing voice" of the metropolitan Catholic church and move to a multiplication of voices, "culminating in a mixture of diverse popular voices."[99] Sor Juana uses "this verbal and literary strategy to...produce a diversified epistemology," while still shielded by the catholic faith "in order to propose a new way to approach the problem of knowledge."[100] For example, Martínez-San Miguel writes of the *villancico* of San José: "The text initially presents four voices that propose different offices for San José: pastor, laborer, and carpenter. Each participant is supported and negated by the other two contradictory voices:[101] '!No fué tal!/4-Si Fué tal!'"[102] The final voice that closes the first part of the poem asserts the office as: father, protector, and intercessor.[103] Similarly we see the juxtaposing of differing viewpoints in the *loa* not only in the students opposing opinions, but especially in the chorus: "Yes he would!" responded to with: "No he would not!" Also: "It cannot be!" and "Yes it can be!" And perhaps the point is made most poignantly with: "Plus Ultra" and "Non Plus Ultra," because not only do the voices stand together in disagreement but their very message is that there are more views, more to be discovered, possibly even suggesting that there are other truths.[104]

---

[98] Martínez-San Miguel, 152. See also Mabel Moraña, "Poder, Raza, y Lengua: La Construcción Étnica del Otro en los Viallancicos de sor Juana," in *Viaje al Silencio: Exploraciones del Discurso Barroco* (Mexico: UNAM, 1998).

[99] See above.

[100] Martínez-San Miguel, 153.

[101] Ibid., 162.

[102] "Villancico de San José," OC 2.142.

[103] "La voz final que cierra esta primera parte del juguete lo presenta como 'Patrón/ Protector y Abogado'..." (Martínez-San Miguel, 162).

[104] Sor Juana's *villancicos* to St. Catherine of Alexandria bear similar themes to those we have considered throughout this study. Carol VI (poem 317), for example,

M. M. Bakhtin's Oppositions and the Emergence of the Novel

As indicated earlier, not only does Sor Juana utilize oppositions and expose tensions between the epistemological debates and cultural shifts of her day, but her work also reflects the tension between historical genres and the newly emerging novel. Bakhtin's theory of the novel helps highlight these features, and points to the elements at work in Sor Juana's *loas* that push theological discourse in the direction of the proposal here developed: forming indirect communication that expresses the relational aspect of Christianity, allowing for contact with the human in existence in the present, with room for subjective appropriation of the ideas expressed.

Bakhtin understands "the novel" to be "whatever force is at work within a given literary system to reveal the limits, the artificial constraints of that system."[105] Not permitting "generic monologue," the novel insists "on the dialogue between what a given system will admit as literature and those texts that are otherwise excluded from such a definition of literature."[106] Thus, they may function to open the way for a diversity of marginalized voices. "Novelization," according to Bakhtin, "sparks the renovation of all other genres, it infects them with its spirit of process and inconclusiveness."[107] Notice that "novelization" does not mean a piece of literature representative of another genre is actually a novel, but that this same spirit throughout the history of literature that pushed for openness, for contact with the present, and away from centers of power, that Bakhtin sees reaching its culmination in the novel, can be seen in other genres, such that the pieces of literature that share some of these features, is "novelized." When other genres become novelized, according to Bakhtin, "they become more free and flexible,... they become dialogized...— the novel inserts into these other genres an indeterminacy, a certain semantic open-endedness, a living contact with unfinished, still-evolving contemporary reality (the open-ended present)."[108]

The similarities here between the function of novelization and Kierkegaard's indirect communication are easily apparent. Both serve to reveal the limits of a "given system," insist on "living contact with unfinished, still-

bears a refrain praising Catherine for her intellectual victory over the "profane arrogance" of the learned men of her day.

[105] Holquist, Introduction to *Dialogic Imagination*, xxxi.

[106] Ibid.

[107] Bakhtin, "Epic and Novel," 7.

[108] Ibid.

evolving contemporary reality," and emphasize dialogue. When Bakhtin describes the novel in contrast to the epic, the similarities between the generic system of the epic and dogma in Kierkegaard's description are even greater. Dogma and the epic both tend to deal with the abstract rather than the concrete, hold a view of the past that can be called timeless or valorized, and both serve the hierarchy of knowledge, and the status quo. Both the novel and forms of indirect communication, according to these two thinkers, stand in direct contrast to systems that claim access to the one Truth and proceed to communicate it directly, a contrast we also saw in Sor Juana's *loas*. Thus this look at novelization shows how these literary characteristics of the novel function to communicate in ways very different from and even in opposition to certain forms of discourse, like dogma, and therefore, uncover how these same features in Sor Juana's *loas* function as a form of indirect communication in contrast to closed dogmatic systems.

The Epic vs. the Novel. Bakhtin looks at the epic as the representative form of the high genres and those that dominated the literary scene before the full development of the modern novel; he sets up a contrast between its features and those of the novel. He uses "absolute" to describe the epic, as it is "absolutely completed and finished" in its form, deals with the "absolute past" and is a genre distinguished by its "absolute fusion of subject matter and spatial-temporal aspects with valorized (hierarchical) ones."[109] Because of its perspective on an absolute past, "contemporary reality as such does not figure in as an available object of representation."[110] Time in the epic, then, is viewed as a whole; "it is not localized in an actual historical sequence; it is not relative to the present or to the future; it contains within itself, as it were, the entire fullness of time."[111] The epic is thus situated in a completed time, distanced from a present reality that is open-ended. This distancing is used to preserve it, to keep it from contact with actual existing persons who, in their contemporaneity, are in flux, are incomplete, and thus put the absolute, conclusive perspective of the epic at risk.

Because of this distancing and absolute past, "memory" serves as the "source and power of the creative impulse" in the epic, whereas the novel, with its connectedness to the present, "is determined by experience, knowledge and

[109] Ibid., 15, 17.

[110] Ibid., 18.

[111] Ibid., 19.

practice (the future)."[112] Additionally Bakhtin explains that "in distanced images we have the whole event, and plot interest (that is, the condition of not knowing) is impossible," but in those genres connected to the present and thus the open-ended future, unknowing is a reality. Because of its perspective on the "absolute past," the world of the epic is "inaccessible to personal experience and does not permit an individual, personal point of view or evaluation. One cannot glimpse it, grope for it, touch it; one cannot look at it from just any point of view; it is impossible to experience it, analyze it, take it apart, penetrate into its core."[113]

The *loa,* however, as we saw earlier, does not distance the material from the contemporary audience, but instead utilizes elements of daily common life specifically in order to connect to the audience.

Because unknowing becomes a possibility and theme, a concern with epistemology emerges in the novel as well.[114] The epic represents a dominant force and its view of truth is considered conclusive. Such high genres, with their formal restrictions on what is an acceptable expression of truth, create a hierarchy of form and language. Genres considered acceptable by those in power perform according to strict rules, and those that fall outside, which use common language or form are considered "low" and not valid communicators of truth. Such a stance, assuming an absolute perspective on the past, on language and meaning, according to Bakhtin restricts the subject, or results in its "unfreedom," which is only overcome through "active polyglossia and interillumination of languages."[115]

Directly related is the epic's utter reliance on tradition. Epic narrative is "given solely as tradition, sacred and sacrosanct, evaluated in the same way by all and demanding a pious attitude toward itself."[116] Because of its formal structure and these inherent characteristics, the epic cannot be open to alternative viewpoints. Its generic structure is complete and closed, its perspective is absolute, and its content is offered only for acceptance and pious

[112] Ibid., 15.

[113] Ibid., 16.

[114] Ibid., 32.

[115] Ibid., 15. Regardless of whether Bakhtin speaks of subject matter (which in theology is God or the God-relation) or the subject as the reader, the freedom of both is of crucial importance for theology. The form should communicate the freedom of both God and the individual, as it is to convey the invitation for the reader to take Christian knowledge to heart for transformation, to appropriate the truth.

[116] Ibid., 16–17.

reverence.[117] The similarities in this description of epic and Kierkegaard's conception of dogma are easily apparent. Both forms are closed systems which remain distant from the relative nature of present existence. Both convey an objective conception of truth, which is communicated directly in a set form without room for the consideration and appropriation of the existing individual.

In contrast to the complete, conclusive, and absolute stance of the epic, the novel is precisely inconclusive and open. The epic is associated with official language and powerful traditions, distanced from the present, contemporary persons, and popular language in an absolute past, and makes memory the foundational element and impulse. The novel, however, "is associated with the eternally living element of unofficial language and unofficial thought."[118] Rather than memory, epistemology is the driving force, along with experience, and practice conceived as a future orientation.[119] And the category of unknowing not only becomes possible, but the admission of it, a virtue.[120] These themes and concerns are certainly recognizable in all the literature of Sor Juana's we have examined thus far.

As stated earlier the novelistic spirit exists in part when contemporary reality serves as the subject, "inconclusive and fluid."[121] Bakhtin sees evidence of this influence in the instances within literature where "the subject of serious literary representation…is portrayed without any distance, on the level of contemporary reality, in a zone of direct and even crude contact. Even where

---

[117] Bakhtin explains that the epic's content and meaning must be accepted as is, in total: "One can only accept the epic world with reverence; it is impossible to really touch it, for it is beyond the realm of human activity, the realm in which everything humans touch is altered and re-thought" ("Epic and Novel," 17). It cannot be brought so close to the contemporary person that it can be touched, reconceived, or altered in the least. The epic relies "on impersonal and sacrosanct tradition, on a commonly held evaluation and point of view—which excludes any possibility of another approach—and which therefore displays a profound piety toward the subject described and toward the language used to describe it, the language of tradition" ("Epic and Novel," 16–17).

[118] Bakhtin, "Epic and Novel," 20.

[119] The future orientation of the novel, resting in its inherent presentness, is a characteristic shared with the epistle. Thus it is not surprising that epistolary literature is one of the places in which Bakhtin recognizes the process of novelization.

[120] Bakhtin says explicitly: "When the novel becomes the dominant genre, epistemology becomes the dominant discipline" ("Epic and Novel," 15).

[121] Ibid., 39.

the past or myth serves as the subject of representation in these genres there is no epic distance, and contemporary reality provides the point of view."[122]

Contemporaneity does not mean absence of tradition or exclusion of the depiction of the heroic past. Bakhtin gives the example of Xenophon's *Cyropaedia*, which is set in the past with a heroic protagonist, but, according to Bakhtin, "the starting point of representation is Xenophon's own contemporary reality; it is that which provides the point of view and value orientation."[123] We also find this in Sor Juana's *loas,* in *El Cetro de José*, for example. Though the story is set at the conquest a century earlier, it still addresses contemporary concerns and reality if it is written in response to re-emerging pagan practices among the Amerindians in the region as some scholars believe. Bakhtin further explains: "The world has already opened up; one's own monolithic and closed world (the world of the epic) has been replaced by the great world of one's own plus 'the others.'"[124] This is certainly evident in Sor Juana's *loas* not only depicting this world opened up and including "others" in their dramatic representation and dialogue, but demonstrating exactly that break from a closed world of *Non Plus Ultra* to the shocking reality that there is more world. It is opened, and there are others. Despite her use of Greek myth and other classic or historical tales in her *auto sacramentales,* Sor Juana is introducing them in a world no longer closed but opened to whole new cultures, religion, lands, languages, and peoples in the Americas.

Sounding not unlike Kierkegaard in *Concluding Unscientific Postscript*, Bakhtin describes the present as necessarily inconclusive, as "by its very nature it demands continuation, it moves into the future, and the more actively and consciously it moves into the future the more tangible and indispensable its inconclusiveness becomes."[125] Bakhtin calls the novel "the genre of becoming," a fitting form, then, it would seem to communicate that Christianity involves a process of becoming, a development we found described by Kierkegaard. According to Bakhtin, in the novel, through contact with the present,

> an object is attracted to the incomplete process of a world-in-the-making, and is stamped with the seal of inconclusiveness. No matter how distant this object is from us in time, it is connected to our incompleted, present-day, continuing temporal transitions, it develops a relationship with our unpreparedness, with our

---

[122] Ibid., 23.
[123] Ibid., 29.
[124] Ibid.
[125] Ibid., 30.

present. But meanwhile our present has been moving into an inconclusive future. And in this inconclusive context all the semantic stability of the object is lost; its sense and significance are renewed and grow as the context continues to unfold.[126]

Monoglossia vs. Polyglossia and Heteroglossia. In addition to the contrast between epic and novel, Bakhtin erects other binaries: monoglossia and polyglossia/heteroglossia;[127] centripetal and centrifugal forces; and authoritative and internally persuasive discourse. Some of these oppositions are more polemical than others, but they are very much set in opposition. Polyglossia, heteroglossia, centrifugal linguistic forces, and the potential to function as a form of internally persuasive discourse all relate to his conception of the novelizing spirit and to "the posited/open/concrete modes of being," while monoglossia, centripetal force, and authoritative discourse are characteristic of traditional high genres or voices of power and to "the given/closed/abstract."[128]

Heteroglossia and polyglossia are essential features of Bakhtin's conception of the novel, illuminated through contrast with monoglossia, which Bakhtin sees as the language of high genres. These high genres operate with the unitary and uniting language of the ruling class. Bakhtin describes this common unitary language as "a system of linguistic norms," not simply as a set of imposed rules, but as "forces that struggle to overcome the heteroglossia of language, forces that unite and centralize verbal-ideological thought, creating within a heteroglot national language the firm, stable linguistic nucleus of an officially recognized literary language, or else defending an already formed

---

[126] Ibid.

[127] Bakhtin scholar Ruth Coates explains the difference between polyglossia and heteroglossia in Bakhtin: "Polyglossia is introduced as the coexistence of a variety of national languages in one cultural space (such as the Romans' familiarity with Greek as well as Latin),… heteroglossia denotes the variety of 'social' languages at work within the boundaries of any national language" [Ruth Coates, *Christianity in Bakhtin* (Cambridge: Cambridge University Press, 1998) 105].

[128] Ruth Coates notes the relationship between this series of oppositions: "As a preliminary hypothesis, I should like to suggest that all these oppositions closely resemble the opposition of the given/closed/abstract and the posited/open/concrete modes of being of 'Philosophy of the Act,' and…the opposition of monologism and polyphony of *Dostoevsky's Creative Work*" (R. Coates, 104).

language from the pressure of growing heteroglossia."[129] Discourse that is monoglot (not only in the sense of being of one language, but especially of being of one meaning, one social context, one class, and one culture) is, then, the language of those in power and reinforces that particular world view. Monoglossia is generally considered the "official" language, and it traffics in "official meanings." It is infused with ideology, and therefore, while monoglossia strives for linguistic dominance, it is at same time fighting for ideological dominance.[130] He explains further:

> What we have in mind here is not an abstract linguistic minimum of a common language, in the sense of a system of elementary forms (linguistic symbols) guaranteeing a *minimum* level of comprehension in practical communication. We are taking language not as a system of abstract grammatical categories, but rather language conceived as ideologically saturated, language as a world view, even as a concrete opinion, insuring a *maximum* of mutual understanding in all spheres of ideological life. Thus a unitary language gives expression to forces working toward a concrete verbal and ideological unification and centralization, which develop in vital connection with the processes of sociopolitical and cultural centralization.[131]

Monoglossia is not innocent. Ruth Coates describes Bakhtin's view: "The dominant, official language is presented as a destructive force, opposed to linguistic and ideological diversity in principle. Bakhtin makes his position on this struggle very plain: a language's claim to be the only language, and its truth to be the only truth, is a 'myth,' and its imposition an unpardonable violence."[132] One finds a similar position in Sor Juana's work. Not only does she denounce rhetorical violence and the supposition of one truth discernible and claimed, in her *loas* she also posits reason and the alternative views of the Amerindians against the use of force and violence of those claiming possession of Amerindian land and of the One Truth.

Bakhtin writes: "the dominant 'unitary language' still aspires to the destruction of all other languages, all other 'truths,' and it does this subscribing to the view that there is a 'sacrosanct and unitary linguistic medium for

---

[129] M. M. Bakhtin, "Discourse in the Novel," in *Dialogic Imagination,* trans. Caryl Emerson and Michael Holquist, ed. Michael Holquist (Austin TX: University of Texas Press, 1981) 270.

[130] R. Coates, 106.

[131] Bakhtin, "Discourse in the Novel," 270.

[132] R. Coates, 106.

containing ideological thought.'"[133] According to this approach, there is a right way to communicate truth, and it is the way that abides by established rules and norms. [134] The only discourse accepted as a conveyor of truth is that which abides by its particular standards set by the ruling, powerful, and elite. Discourse that moves outside these boundaries is rejected as unable to communicate truth, as lowly rather than lofty, and therefore inappropriate for the subject matter. By pushing beyond boundaries of high genres, or of discourse labeled appropriate in form by authorities, discourse sharing these characteristics with the novel is anti-canonical. Here Bakhtin's description of these different forms of discourse resonates with one of the concerns of this project. His work highlights the enforced boundaries around what is deemed theological discourse as they are imposed by those in privileged positions, which also bars "low" discourses and those expressions of religious meaning that push against these centers of power.

The unitary languages Bakhtin describes are driven by centripetal forces, and are called Ptolemaic; they are ruling, dominant, and undergird the ideology of those in power. This unitary impulse of Ptolemaic language contrasts the Galilean perception of language found in the novel, which:

> denies the absolutism of a single and unitary language—that is, that refuses to acknowledge its own language as the sole verbal and semantic center of the ideological world. It is a perception that has been made conscious of the vast plentitude of national, and, more to the point, social languages—all of which are equally capable of being "languages of truth," but, since such is the case, all of which are equally relative, reified and limited, as they are merely the languages of social groups, professions and other cross-sections of everyday life. The novel begins by presuming a verbal and semantic decentering of the ideological world, a certain linguistic homelessness of literary consciousness, which no longer

---

[133] Bakhtin, "Discourse in the Novel," 367.

[134] Kierkegaard also brings into question the rigid creation of boundaries defining truth, particularly that of revelation: "Whether it is a word, a sentence, a book, a man, a society, whatever it is, as soon as it is supposed to be a boundary, so that the boundary itself is not dialectical, it is superstition and narrow-mindedness. In a human being there is always a desire, at once comfortable and concerned, to have something really firm and fixed that can exclude the dialectical, but this is cowardliness and fraudulence toward the divine. Even the most certain of all, a revelation, *eo ipso* [precisely thereby] becomes dialectical when I am to appropriate it;... As soon as I take away the dialectical, I am superstitious and defraud God of the moment's strenuous acquisition of what was once acquired" (*Postscript,* 35).

possesses a sacrosanct and unitary linguistic medium for containing ideological thought.[135]

The novel is then the genre of unofficial discourses, of "dialogised heteroglossia," of the "low," the concrete, and the personal, and it has been "historically shaped by the current of decentralizing, centrifugal forces."[136] The heteroglossia of genres in this spirit incorporate languages of diverse social classes and cultures.[137] Dialogues develop with characters other than those simply of the ruling classes and authorities in their official language. But this heteroglossia does not exist simply in contrast to the "the accepted literary language (in all its various generic expressions)," which serves as "the linguistic center of the verbal-ideological life of the nation and the epoch," but rather it is "aimed sharply and polemically against the official languages of its given time."[138]

Coates explains that this genre "stands for the freedom of languages to express themselves, the freedom of multiple truths to exist."[139] Bakhtin alludes to the Tower of Babel and Coates notes its significance: "In order to prevent humankind from gaining inordinate power, God proceeds to 'confuse their language' and scatter them over the earth; linguistic unity in the account is equated with arrogance and the will to power; linguistic diversity, on the other hand, is equated with cultural diversity, and diversity as such with the containment of power."[140]

Literature infused with this novelistic spirit therefore serves to oppose the dominant ideology of the powerful through an insistence on multiple meanings as illustrated in heteroglossia. The diversity of cultures, languages, and meanings, by their very presence in the work, serve to oppose the centralizing

---

[135] Bakhtin, "Discourse in the Novel," 366–67.

[136] Ibid., 273.

[137] Fundamental to the novel's decentralizing force is its acknowledgement of differing social groups interacting in the narrative: "The decentralizing of the verbal-ideological world that finds its expression in the novel begins by presuming fundamentally differentiated social groups, which exist in an intense and vital interaction with other social groups" ("Discourse in the Novel," 368).

[138] Ibid., 273.

[139] Coates continues, "Here we can see the extension of the polyphonic principle, the same debunking of the single authorial truth, now expressed in linguistic terms" (R. Coates, 107).

[140] Ibid., 108.

of power. The Tower of Babel illustrates God's desire to encourage diversity and polyglossia in order that ideological power be diffused and spread among all peoples and cultures and not controlled by one group, who claims the one meaning, language, and truth, and thus multiplies its power. We saw this image used for similar purposes in *Primero sueño.* Heteroglossia is important in theology in order to resist those characteristics of monoglossia to which theology tends. Without heteroglossia, God-talk is restricted to the interpretation of one social class, culture, and gender, such that theology is determined by the minority in power and imposed upon others.

In the end Sor Juana fails to fully develop a heteroglossia. In the *loa* to *Divino Narciso,* for example, as the Christian God of Spain usurps the pagan religion and rituals, claiming them for Christianity, and the Amerindians speak in the tone of *criollo* New Spain. Yolanda Martínez-San Miguel also finds this true of Sor Juana's *autos*, noting that they illustrate the point made by De Certeau about the complication in attempts to represent the "other": "But the written discourse which cites the speech of the other is not, cannot be, the discourse of the other. On the contrary, this discourse, in writing the Fable that authorizes it, alters it."[141] However, Sor Juana's work does move toward heteroglossia. She presents a diversity of voices in *Divino Narciso*, and she does leave some surprising openness to other cultures for her time and position in that the last song is to the God of the Seeds sung by all of the characters of the *loa*, including the Christian ones. We are to assume, of course, that they now take this to be the Christian God found in the Eucharistic bread, yet the song does not make this claim but simply rings out to the God of the Seeds. Considering the nature of the topic is truth in other religions, her stance is not among the rigid and dogmatic sort. Boundaries are still to be expected in a piece of Christian theology, and this was a didactic piece after all. In the realm of Christianity, boundaries remain, but here we see them with fluidity and the communication of them suggests an inclusiveness and not an absolute claim of closed, complete truth. It shares similarities with discourse of the novel, as Bakhtin describes the process of developing individual consciousness and internal persuasion as partly a matter of "getting familiar with the boundaries" and "exposing the weak sides."

---

[141] Michel de Certeau, "Montaigne's 'Of Cannibals': The Savage 'I,'" *Heterologies: Discourse on the Other* (Minneapolis: University of Minnesota Press) 19. Quoted in Martínez-San Miguel, 199.

Direct vs. Indirect Discourse. Bakhtin not only finds the unifying force and tendency within official discourse to be false, but asserts that "all direct meanings and direct expressions" are false, especially when the meanings and expressions relate to the emotions.[142] The novel, in contrast, utilizes "indirect, 'qualified' speaking."[143] In some forms of the novel, Bakhtin recognizes the beginnings of "a radical skepticism toward any unmediated discourse," bordering on a "rejection of the very possibility of having a straightforward discourse at all that would not be false."[144] Direct discourse in matters related to the individual's subjective state of being, then, is shown to be misleading and even a lie. Thus, the buffoon and the clown in a novel exist not simply for comedic affect, but they signify the falsehood of direct discourse of which other characters assume they have clear understanding. For Bakhtin, stupidity in the novel is incomprehension, where it is "always polemical."[145] Stupidity in the novel is the inability to comprehend the discourse of another who has attempted through the direct word to "appropriate the world" and to "conceptualize it." It is the failure to understand these "generally accepted, canonized, inveterately false languages with their lofty labels for things and events: poetic language, scholarly and pedantic language, religious, political, judicial language and so forth."[146] Therefore, for Bakhtin, stupidity is "justified, as it is the failure to

---

[142] Bakhtin, "Discourse in the Novel," 401. Bakhtin, like Kierkegaard, notes the distinction between what form of discourse is appropriate for mathematics and the natural sciences and what is more appropriate to the humanities, specifically "in the humanities there arises the specific task of establishing, transmitting, and interpreting the words of others" ("Discourse in the Novel," 351). Whereas in mathematics and the natural sciences the entire methodological apparatus "is directed toward mastery over *mute objects*, *brute things*, that do not reveal themselves in words, that do not *comment on themselves*. Acquiring knowledge here is not connected with receiving and interpreting words or signs from the object itself under consideration" ("Discourse in the Novel," 351).

[143] Ibid., 413. The similarities here between Kierkegaard's notion of indirect communication and his critique of direct communication is obvious, but also worthy of note is a comparison between such "'qualified' speaking" and the verbal hedges discussed in chapter 2, which serve to temper the boldness of certain statements and claims.

[144] Ibid., 401.

[145] Ibid., 403.

[146] Ibid.

understand a lie."[147] In novelized narrative, to not understand is to expose the lie that the world or the whole can be understood. It is to be honest, and like Socratic ignorance, it is also to be wise. Bakhtin explains that stupidity "interacts dialogically with an intelligence (a lofty pseudo intelligence) with which it polemicizes and whose mask it tears away."[148] The comic novel in particular, according to Bakhtin, unmasks the falsity, hypocrisy, and greed of certain ideological belief systems, which are revealed to be "limited, narrowly rationalistic, [and] inadequate to reality."[149] The languages of these systems, "already fully formed, officially recognized, reigning languages that are authoritative and reactionary," are the material of the comic novel's parody.[150]

As Socrates served as a hero for Kierkegaard and indirect communication, so he does for Bakhtin and the novel. Bakhtin "comes very close to naming Socrates as the first novelist,"[151] saying the Socratic dialogues can be considered "the novels of their time."[152] He elevates numerous elements in the Socratic dialogues which he understands to be characteristic of the novel. He explains that the Socratic dialogue characteristically

> arises as *apomnemoneumata*, that is, as a genre of the memoir type, as transcripts based on personal memories of real conversations among contemporaries; characteristic, also, is the fact that a speaking and conversing man is the central image of the genre. Characteristic, too, is the combination of the image of Socrates, the central hero of the genre, wearing the popular mask of a bewildered fool...with the image of a wise man of the most elevated sort (in the spirit of legends about seven wise men); this combination produces the ambivalent image of wise ignorance. Characteristic also is the ambivalent self-praise in the Socratic dialogue: I am wiser than everyone, because I know that I know nothing.[153]

---

[147] Ibid., 404. Bakhtin finds "novelization" even in epistolary literature. Also helpful is his identification of the spirit that refuses to accept a lie as knowledge as "ignorance." For Bakhtin knowledge is truly not certain or attainable, and so this "ignorance" is honest and true. This serves to shed light on Sor Juana's repeated claims to "lack of knowledge" throughout her works, which we considered specifically in her letters and in her "failure" to gain comprehensive knowledge in her poem *Primero sueño*.

[148] Ibid., 403.

[149] Ibid., 312.

[150] Ibid.

[151] Holquist, xxxii.

[152] Bakhtin, "Epic and Novel," 22.

[153] Ibid., 24.

The wise man conceived as wise because he recognizes that he knows nothing is a feature of the novel discussed by Bakhtin through an analysis of the comic novel and the buffoon. For our purposes, the important point to note is that the novelization of genres includes an emphasis on epistemological concerns, particularly a stress on lack of knowledge, or inconclusive knowledge, something we see not only in these *loas* by Sor Juana, but across the genres she utilizes. The highlighted virtues of Socrates shared between Bakhtin and Kierkegaard is easily recognized. Both applaud his "wise ignorance" as well as his chosen form of communication: the dialogue.[154] Also found in Socratic dialogue and characteristic of the novel "is the spoken dialogue framed by a dialogized story."[155] Not only are characters speaking with each other, but the work or story itself shows differing views and alternative and opposing ideas. This is characteristic of the *loas* we have examined, as well as Sor Juana's *villancicos.*

Internally Persuasive vs. Authoritative Discourse. The last contrast proposed by Bakhtin we will examine is between authoritative discourse and internally persuasive discourse. Internally persuasive discourse is related to "the tendency to assimilate other's discourse" in such a way that it impacts "an individual's ideological becoming."[156] When this occurs the other's discourse serves not only to provide "information, directions, rule, models, and so forth," but it influences "the very basis of our ideological interrelations with the world, the very basis of our behavior."[157] Such a description of discourse that persuades one internally corresponds with a conception of Christianity as something which transforms the life of the individual to whom it is related. Internally persuasive discourse, according to Bakhtin's description is of "decisive significance in the evolution of an individual consciousness."[158]

These two types of discourse, authoritative and internally persuasive, are most often encountered as sharply distinct forms in one's ideological becoming,

---

[154] The wise ignorance as exemplified by Sor Juana was discussed previously, and here we highlight her use of the dialogue to communicate religious thought through the form of drama.

[155] Bakhtin, "Epic and Novel," 26. Bakhtin notes other novelistic characteristics found in the Socratic dialogues, such as irony and popular language.

[156] Bakhtin, "Discourse in the Novel," 342.

[157] Ibid.

[158] Ibid., 346.

though not necessarily so.[159] On one side is the authoritative word, which Bakhtin identifies as "religious, political, moral; the word of a father, of adults and of teachers, etc.," a word that is not typically internally persuasive but is imposed from without. On the other side is the "internally persuasive word that is denied all privilege, backed up by no authority at all, and is frequently not even acknowledged in society (not by public opinion, nor by scholarly norms, nor by criticism), not even in the legal code."[160]

Bakhtin recognizes that there are different degrees of authoritativeness which as a topic lies beyond the scope of his essay, as it does not offer an in depth look at the varieties of authoritative discourse, though he does list these additional examples: "the authority of religious dogma, or of acknowledged scientific truth or of a currently fashionable book."[161] He also offers a general description of the nature of authoritative discourse:

> The authoritative word demands that we acknowledge it, that we make it our own; it binds us, quite independent of any power it might have to persuade us internally; we encounter it with its authority already fused to it. The authoritative word is located in a distanced zone, organically connected with a past that is felt to be hierarchically higher. It is, so to speak, the word of the fathers. Its authority was already *acknowledged* in the past. It is a *prior* discourse. It is therefore not a question of choosing it from among other possible discourses that are its equal. It is given (it sounds) in lofty spheres, not those of familiar contact. Its language is a special (as it were, hieratic) language. It can be profaned. It is akin to taboo, i.e., a name that must not be taken in vain.[162]

He explains that authoritative discourse may gather around itself "great masses" of other discourses which serve to "interpret it, praise it, [and] apply it in various ways," but the authoritative discourse itself is separate from these supplementary discourses; it is set apart. The *loa* and *auto sacramental* as genres were originally intended to serve this function. They explicate official church teaching and praise the authorities in power. Sor Juana, however, is among the writers of the *loa* that were transforming the genre. The *loa* evolved

[159] A discourse can, though rarely, function as both authoritative discourse and internally persuasive discourse. The two can be joined in a single expression, or as Bakhtin says, "in a single word," even though these two types of discourse possess "profound differences" ("Discourse in the Novel," 342).

[160] Ibid.

[161] Ibid.

[162] Ibid.

during the seventeenth century "from the laudatory genre closely linked to the metropolitan and viceregal centers of power" such that it became "a critical space and on occasion became a satire of the colonial order." This evolution of the *loa* is evident in the work of Sor Juana, as some critics have noted in her work "a stylistic culmination of this process of distancing from the official discourse praising those in power."[163] Martínez-San Miguel notes that not only does Sor Juana subvert and invert the genre itself as her *loas* question the limits of knowledge and epistemological method, but also by questioning the boundaries of the dialogical space themselves, that were set by the power relations of the colonial context: colonial government and viceroy, mother country, and ecclesiastical hierarchy.[164] The genre is transformed from a colonizing discourse where the victor assimilates the speech of the defeated into a space where a colonial subject asserts equality, through fictitious characters and illusory tactics.[165] As a defender of the equal rationality of the colonial subject to colonizer and by illustrating a reciprocal exchange of knowledge between the colonial subject and colonizer, Sor Juana's *autos* and *loas* are subversive. This is true also because the *loas'* original function as a tool for assimilating the colonial subject into the conquering culture and religion is replaced with an affirmation of the colonial subject as "rational subject-agent" participating in "a process of transculturation" instead of assimilation.[166]

---

[163] "La loa también evolucionó durante el siglo XVII de un género laudatorio muy vinculado a los centros de poder metropolitano y vierreinal a ser un espacio crítico y, en ocasiones, hasta satírico del orden colonial" (Maldonado, 84–88). "Esta evolución de la loa es significativa en la obra de Sor Juana, en la cual algunos críticos han señalado una culminación estilística de este proceso de distanciamiento del discurso official que alababa al poder" (Martínez-San Miguel, 173, my trans.).

[164] Martínez-San Miguel, 196.

[165] Ibid., 174.

[166] "Para insertarlo en un espacio más amplio de del conocimiento teológico y a su consiguiente rol de difusor y confirmador de ideologías entre dos polos de poder desiguales—i.e. el auto como discurso colonizador y asimilador dirigido a los vencidos por los vencedores. Esto lo convierte en us espacio donde el sujeto colonial puede, ficticia e ilusoriamente, intercambiar recíprocamente conocimientos con el colonizador y defender su igualdad racional. De este modo el auto sacramental como género es subvertido, pues su rol asimilador se sustituye por un gesto equiparador, en el cual el sujeto colonial puede acceder al saber en su calidad de sujeto racional, y se convierte así en sujeto-agente en el proceso transculturador" (Martínez-San Miguel, 174).

Unlike an unofficial discourse which persuades one internally through a process of questioning, acceptance, and rejection, strictly authoritative discourse does not seek "a free appropriation and assimilation of the word," but instead "it demands our unconditional allegiance."[167] It therefore "permits no play with the context framing it, no play with its borders, no gradual and flexible transitions, no spontaneously creative stylizing variants on it."[168] Bakhtin sees authoritative discourse as an "indivisible mass," such that "one must either totally affirm it, or totally reject it. It is indissolubly fused with its authority—with political power, an institution, a person—and it stands and falls together with that authority. One cannot divide it up—agree with one part, accept but not completely another part, reject utterly a third part."[169] Authoritative discourse, as such, resists representation and can only be "transmitted."[170] He explains, "Its inertia, its semantic finiteness and calcification, the degree to which it is hard-edged, a thing in its own right, the impermissibility of any free stylistic development in relation to it—all this renders the artistic representation of authoritative discourse impossible."[171]

Internally persuasive discourse, in contrast, is another's discourse that becomes authoritative to you. As you wrestle with another's, or an "alien discourse," it becomes internally persuasive to you based on the way you appropriate it, incorporate it into one's own world view, and make it one's own. "In the everyday rounds of our consciousness, the internally persuasive word is half-ours and half-someone else's. Its creativity and productiveness consist precisely in the fact that such a word awakens new and independent words, that it organizes masses of our words from within, and does not remain in an isolated and static condition."[172]

Bakhtin cannot overestimate the importance of struggling with another's discourse in the process of coming to one's own ideological consciousness. Initially we distinguish "between internally persuasive discourse and authoritarian enforced discourse," and reject "those congeries of discourses that do not matter to us, that do not touch us."[173] He explains that internally persuasive

[167] Bakhtin, "Discourse in the Novel," 343.

[168] Ibid.

[169] Ibid.

[170] Ibid., 344.

[171] Ibid.

[172] Ibid., 346.

[173] Ibid., 345.

discourse is recognizable when consciousness is awakened "to independent ideological life precisely in a world of alien discourses surrounding it, and from which it cannot initially separate itself." However, although people's voices may have been "born of another or dynamically stimulated by another," their own voices and discourses will begin to emerge independent as they "liberate themselves from the authority of the other's discourse."[174] This internal conversation with the persuasive word which may begin as resistance, eventually takes shape as a questioning; one puts the discourse to the test "in order to expose its weak sides, to get a feel for its boundaries, to experience it physically as an object."[175] This contrasts authoritative discourse which, as mentioned previously, "permits no play with its borders."

Authoritative and internally persuasive discourses are distinguishable finally "when thought begins to work in an independent, experimenting and discriminating way."[176] Whereas authoritative discourse does not allow for the individual consciousness to alter its language or meaning, as it comes to the individual from the outside, imposed as a complete whole to be accepted as is, "the semantic structure of an internally persuasive discourse is *not finite*, it is *open*; in each of the new contexts that dialogize it, this discourse is able to reveal ever newer *ways to mean*."[177]

The relationship between the form religious discourse typically takes and epic and authoritative discourse is clear in "Notes Made in 1970–1971," where Bakhtin describes the proclamatory genres of "priests, prophets, preachers, judges, leaders, patriarchal fathers, and so forth," as "the word that retards and freezes thought."[178] He explains that their word functions this way "because of its sacrosanct, impenetrable boundaries," which make it "inert," leaving it with very few "possibilities of contacts and combinations."[179] This word is one "that demands reverent repetition and not further development, corrections, and additions."[180] It is "removed from dialogue: it can only be cited amid rejoinders;

[174] Ibid., 348. Bakhtin clarifies: "the process of distinguishing between one's own and another's discourse, between one's own and another's thought, is activated rather late in development" ("Discourse in the Novel," 345).

[175] Ibid., 348.

[176] Ibid., 345.

[177] Ibid., 346.

[178] Bakhtin, "Notes Made in 1970–1971," 132–33.

[179] Ibid., 133.

[180] Ibid.

it cannot itself become a rejoinder among equally privileged rejoinders."[181] He says "this word had spread everywhere, limiting, directing, and retarding both thought and live experience of life," but the modern person could no longer tolerate it. He describes the development of modern languages as "a lengthy and complex process of expunging the other's sacred word, and expunging the sacred and authoritarian word in general, with its indisputability, unconditionality, and unequivocality."[182] The rigid stability and certainty with which things were stated in the past is no longer acceptable. Bakhtin describes the shift as one from "proclamatory genres" to one of simple speaking, that is to speak with reservations.

Bakhtin is certainly not arguing that all kinds of religious discourse are authoritative in the most rigid manner described—that is, utterly imposed externally and inflexible to the interpretation of the individual, and distanced from contact with the present; neither am I. Rather, I am highlighting differences in types of discourse, affirming that religious discourse can be internally persuasive, and encouraging such open forms of discourse which incorporate the stretched boundaries of discourse that allows for both the centripetal forces of a language which offer a level of understanding and recognized intention, but also the centrifugal forces that push toward non-dominant meanings and languages. Centripetal forces ensure some boundaries, keep language from utter linguistic chaos, and prevent the loss of some shared understanding, while centrifugal forces ensure that the meaning assigned by one group does not assert ultimacy or claim an absolute position on truth. Centripetal and centrifugal forces work together to allow for diversity and openness while protecting meaning from the edge of chaos.

The novel is a form that recognizes the multitude of voices, views, and languages for the description of beliefs and world views. Bakhtin is particularly concerned not with destroying all tradition and attention to the past, but with bringing such history into real contact with the person and contemporary reality. He wants the story to be available to be touched by the individual, not distanced and walled off from her. He is encouraging a form of discourse that brings the meaning of another's discourse into contact with the meaning of one's own, and that brings the meaning of traditional language into relationship with the meaning of contemporary language and with the language of the "common" people. The discourse here proposed involves listening to the meaning in the

[181] Ibid.
[182] Ibid.

language of those from other classes and cultures. Official discourses and high genres, which serve as the language of the elite, are described as "semi-moribund" and will not survive because they will not retain a living witness if they do not allow the influence of novelizing, that is if they do not bring their discourse into contact with the present, if they do not accept an inconclusive openness, and some fluidity. This does involve risk, however, as one exposes tradition to the touch of the contemporary person. Coates notes that Bakhtin is opposed to a "finalization," which is similar to this project's critique of conclusiveness, but similarly Bakhtin also leaves room for the finalization within God, whose authority is acceptable. And, I would add, the only one in the relationship with a perspective on the conclusive or final. Remember that Kierkegaard/Climacus, while not denying a "system" from God's perspective, did deny its possibility for those remaining in existence. Coates writes, "as far as human or authorial finalization is concerned, Bakhtin is its resolved opponent.... However, he clearly reserves a space, his 'loophole,' as it were, for surrender to the loving authority of an absolute Other, a peculiarly spiritual, and radical, solution, to an otherwise apparently hopeless existential situation."[183] If the goal of Christian communication is to evoke personal and social change, and if forms of novelistic discourse can function to invite such active engagement, theology should utilize these forms, creating flexible boundaries, acknowledging its "weak sides," and incorporating novelizing features, such as we find in Sor Juana's *loas*.

The novelistic features in the *loas* include connectedness to the present, dialogue, and the speech of characters from multiple cultures, including those out of social power. The *loas* thus push toward heteroglossia, and the centrifugal forces are evident in the nobility and speeches made by the Amerindians that persuade Spanish Religion of the truth existent in their religion and in their conception of the freedom of mind and will. Sor Juana's work is subversive in that "she claims an equal intellect and culture with the Spanish conquistador, at the same time that she denounces the violence and illegitimacy of the conquering act."[184] And the *loa* to *San Hermenegildo* also opens up the dialogical space through the debating voices and the theme of *Plus Ultra*. They therefore also demonstrate a recognition of the contrast between

---

[183] R. Coates, 123.

[184] "Se reclama una igualidad intelectual y cultural con el conquistador español, a la vez que se denuncia la violencia e ilegitimidad del acto de conquista" (Martínez-San Miguel, 175, my trans.).

internally persuasive and authoritative discourse, or subjective appropriation and dogmatism. The form itself as "spoken dialogue framed by a dialogized story" stands in contrast to dogmatics and closed systems of thought. The *loa* in its dialogue, story, characters, and presentness, promote an openness in theological discourse and a tolerance in religious debate. It pushes away from the centers of power of traditional theological discourse and its implicit assertion of ultimacy of form and meaning. It presents a self-critical view of Christianity in the context of other languages, cultures, and meanings, even hinting at other truths. The *loa* as Sor Juana utilizes it, then, becomes critical of dogmatism within the very form once used to instruct in dogma. Her critique is shielded by the authoritative form of the genre itself, but the themes and way in which she uses it, shows evidence of the impact of the cultural shifts and questioning that produced the novel as defined by Bakhtin. Her *loas* demonstrate an invitation for consideration and the possibility of appropriation of the ideas illustrated dramatically, but in this self-critical form, they do not suggest an absolute perspective inflexible to the sort of process of development and appropriation Bakhtin describes as possible with discourse that becomes internally persuasive. This medium of Christian instruction is not of an authoritative sort in Sor Juana's hand, in that it does not present Christianity as closed, absolute, and sacrosanct, to be taken as a whole on the word of those in power, but instead it openly invites interaction and dialogue.

Bakhtin and Sor Juana both expose and critique the potential for discourse to be violent and coercive. This is one reason for Bakhtin's concern with dialogue, which he preferred over the dialectic. For Bakhtin the "dialogic sphere" is "where the word lives," but "this sphere is very fragile;" the slightest violence to another in dialogue destroys it, and this "violence" could simply be "references to authority."[185] One can only invite dialogue, therefore; one cannot demand it. For Bakhtin one way to avoid coercive or violent discourse is to avoid "finalization"; he says that the activity of an author without the use of conclusivity has more chance to function as "persuasion through love."[186] Bakhtin, like Kierkegaard, rejects Hegelianism and Idealism partly because of its conclusiveness in synthesis.[187] He reads Dostoevsky's novels as exemplary

[185] Bakhtin, "From Notes Made in 1970–1971," 150.

[186] Bakhtin, "Towards a Reworking of the Book on Dostoevsky," 292.

[187] See *Dostoevsky's Creative Work*. Bakhtin's thought shares many similarities with Kierkegaard: both have clear theological concerns, particularly regarding religious discourse, both reject Hegel's dialectic and Idealism, and both resist the "direct" word

presentations of opposites that are not "cancelled out dialogically," the contradictions are not smoothed out or resolved in a synthesis.[188]

As Bakhtin sets up oppositions between forms of discourse that mirror the change in culture at the time of the novel's birth, so Sor Juana's work sets up a series of oppositions. We have already seen how dueling oppositions pervade the atmosphere of *Primero sueño*; scholars have also noted this in her *Carta Monterrey* and in numerous *villancicos*.[189] In the *loas* to her *auto sacramentals,* one also finds oppositions and dueling voices of agreement and disagreement. Her *loas* and *villancicos* proceed especially with a particular opposition between force or strength (*fuerza*) and reason. Reason is related particularly to freedom, and so is likewise linked with the struggle for freedom, agency, and "epistemological subjectivities," in a colonial context.[190] It has also been noted that the side of reason, and therefore the specific struggle for freedom and agency, is represented in Sor Juana's works by women, and force, by male characters. This is especially evident in *Divino Narciso* where the process of reasoning and persuasion is dramatized primarily by the female characters America and Christian Religion, while Zeal and Occident, move to war and physical aggression.[191] This whole structure of a multiplicity of oppositions and difference reflects the time in which Sor Juana lived. In her form and in the voices she inserts into the debates, Sor Juana creates space and opens the

---

and encourage the "indirect," and consider the ways the indirect word functions in genres. Bakhtin says that modernity no longer has room for the direct word, while Kierkegaard thought it was far too comfortable with the direct, but both admire those thinkers and writers who resist the use of direct discourse.

[188] Bakhtin, *Dostoevsky's Creative Work*, 25–26.

[189] For studies on this in the *Carta de Monterrey,* see Antonio Alatorre, "La Carta de Sor Juana al P. Núñez (1682)," in *Nueva Revista de Filología Hispánica* 35, no. 2 (1987): 591–673; and Nina Scott, "If you are not pleased to favor me, put me out of your mind…': Gender and Authority in Sor Juana Inés de la Cruz: And the Translation of Her Letter to the Reverend Father Maestro Antonio Núñez of the Society of Jesus," *Women's Studies International Forum* 11/5 (1988): 429–38.

[190] Martínez-San Miguel, 145.

[191] Margo Glantz has noted this same opposition that appears in the *loa* to the *Divine Narcissus*, where "the strength/force is on the side of the males, the capacity of reason on the side of the women." *Borrones y Borradores. Reflexiones Sobre el Ejercicio de la Escritura (Ensayos de Literature Colonial, de Bernal Díaz del Castillo a Sor Juana)* (Mexico: Coordinación de Difusión Cultural Dirección de Literatura, UNAM, Ediciones del Equilibrista, 1992) 183, my trans.

discussion. She does not propose one ultimate position but through these oppositions creates a space, or an Open, between and beyond them for alternative voices and views, a space where true dialogue can occur from a variety of perspectives—including those of women, colonial subjects, and those who speak in non-European languages. She opens space for this difference, asserting that subjectivity impacts the field of knowledge, the methods of gaining knowledge, and the forms for the dissemination of this knowledge.

Conclusion: Theology as Dramatic Invitation

For centuries, enlightenment ideals of objective, detached, abstract, and universal knowledge claimed dominance over all fields of knowledge, and the principles of modern philosophy possessed control over the argumentation and debates in theology; today decentralizing forces again erupt and push for change and openness, creating an environment of opposition and struggle reminiscent of the transition occurring in Sor Juana's day.[192] Martínez San-Miguel comments on Sor Juana's proposal that when knowledge and experience are held together, they "point to the impossibility of postulating a single mode of knowledge."[193] Likewise because of the dissonance between the said knowledge of Christian revelation and life, and because of its the connection to the human in the God-human relation, Christian knowledge will take a variety of shapes in accordance with the diversity of subjectivities relating to it.[194]

The form of Christian discourse here proposed pushes away from one, unified meaning held as utterly authoritative truth and toward an openness to other views and meanings, such as Sor Juana encourages. We saw this in her letters, poems, and now in these *loas* through heteroglossia, the incon-

[192] This counter-Enlightenment current emerged with the Enlightenment itself, and has become more pronounced with broad postmodern response to modernity. See Adorno and Horkheimer, *The Dialectic of the Enlightenment*; and Jonathan Israel, *The Radical Enlightenment: Philosophy and the Making of Modernity 1650–1750.*

[193] Martinez-San Miguel, 163.

[194] "Saber y experiencia se vuelven a vincular para apuntar hacia la imposibilidad de postular un solo modo de conocer que pueda contener la diversidad de subjetividades que intentan entablar un diálogo en los textos comentados. Las voces que intervienen en los villancicos estudiados coexisten sin asimilarse completamente, trazan puntos de contacto al mismo tiempo que evidencian los límites del proceso didáctico, de identificación comunitaria de una fe, y del proceso representativo mismo que se extraña y exterioriza en la construcción de ciertas voces que le resultan un tanto incomprensibles" (Martínez-San Miguel, 167–68).

clusiveness of *Plus Ultra*, and presentness. As the characters are invited to watch, listen, and consider, so is the audience—they in essence join the characters of the *loa* in attending to the proceeding drama. The connection to the present moment could hardly be more explicit. They press outward away from official discourse, away from centers of power and authority, in heteroglossia. Bakhtin noted that even reference to authority is a violence that could destroy the fragile dialogic sphere.[195] The proposed discourse critiques rhetoric that relies on authority for persuasive force,[196] through the anti-canonical use of omitted texts, stories, cultures, and languages.

Not only is literature influenced by the novelizing spirit a more appropriate form for communicating the elusive nature of Christian knowledge, but it is also an effective means to resist unitary, systematic tendencies in traditional Christian discourse. Such authoritarian discourse supports and is supported by those of power, or is Ptolemaic in nature according to Bakhtin, but the Galilean nature of Christian discourse was not originally a discourse of the powerful, but of the lowly, of those outside centers of power.[197] Its centrifugal force pushed against the centripetal forces of the temple system of the first century, with its strict codes criticized by Jesus in many instances as he advocated the spirit over the letter of the law.[198] Much of Jesus' ministry pushed these boundaries against

---

[195] He writes: In rhetoric "there is complete victory and destruction of the opponent. In dialogue the destruction of the opponent also destroys that very dialogic sphere where the word lives.... This sphere is very fragile and easily destroyed (the slightest violence is sufficient, references to authority, and so forth)" ("From Notes Made in 1970–1971," 150).

[196] This is found in all three *loas*.

[197] For discussion of the differences between Ptolemaic and Galilean discourses, see Bakhtin, "Discourse in the Novel," 366–67; and "From the Prehistory of Novelistic Discourse," 65. In "Prehistory of Novelistic Discourse," Bakhtin writes: "Where languages and cultures interanimated each other, language became something entirely different, its very nature changed: in place of a single, unitary sealed-off Ptolemaic world of language, there appeared the open Galilean world of many languages, mutually animating each other" [M. M. Bakhtin, "From the Prehistory of Novelistic Discourse," in *Dialogic Imagination,* trans. Caryl Emerson and Michael Holquist, ed. Michael Holquist (Austin TX: University of Texas Press, 1981) 65].

[198] For a discussion of the development of increasingly strict purity laws and behavior codes in Second Temple Judaism, see Martha Himmelfarb, *A Kingdom of Priests: Ancestry and Merit in Ancient Judaism* (Philadelphia: University of Pennsylvania Press, 2006).

the institutional authorities: healing on the Sabbath, touching the unclean, allowing his disciples to pick grain on the Sabbath.[199] It is no accident that Jesus spoke in parables, and that they included characters representing those without power in that system—the Samaritan and the widow, for example. The boundaries set for acceptable Christian discourse were established centuries ago, going back as far as Nicaea and the church's alignment with Constantine's empire. The official discourse of the church has since been determined by those in power within the institution, which is controlled by men of specific cultures and education. During modernity, Enlightenment standards of knowledge and propositional form, reflecting the Western philosophy of its day, dominated forms of theological discourse. Dogma in the language of the elite, enforcing strict standards on language, form, and meaning, excludes the "lower," and claims ownership of the tradition, keeping it sealed, preserved, and distanced, while the "lower" genres put tradition in contact with the present, with the individual, and therefore put its "purity" at risk. Christian dogma proceeds according to an established set of rules, setting up its own generic hierarchy and canon. Those discourses which abide by this system of rules are considered acceptable transmitters of truth. However, "not knowing" is impossible for a genre that claims an objective perspective on the truth, with a bird's eye view on an absolute, completed past. And this is the direction of traditional Christian theology which looks at revelation in Christ as a completed event to which we have access through the Bible. Thus, like other high genres, the tradition is distanced from the contemporary existing person, and the category of not knowing cannot survive.

This, however, excludes the inter-subjective aspects of Christian knowledge, that the Christ-event means salvation only as it is applied to the lives of those in existence, who in their spacio-temporal locatedness are in process, involved in an ongoing and unconcluded relationship with God and others, and actively pursuing the Kingdom of God which is ever emerging, but not yet fully actualized. As much as faith rests in the completed work of God it may be considered objective and conclusive, but faith relates to the person and community in the present; it is in process and not yet concluded, but growing, changing, and emerging. Thus so should theological discourse include this spirit of inconclusiveness, which gives expression to the inter-subjective aspect of faith and Christian knowledge. Because religious knowledge is only such in

---

[199] See Richard A. Horsley, *Jesus and Empire: The Kingdom of God and the New World Disorder* (Minneapolis: Fortress Press, 2003).

relationship, involving the Other and others, one cannot claim an objective certainty. An acceptance of one's lack of such complete knowledge is, then, a part of honest theology. A Christian perspective is not of an absolute, completed past, but a past event as it relates to the present existing people who continue in a process of an incomplete future.

The meaning of Christian discourse exists partly as it is appropriated in the life of the individual and community, and is directly related to an ongoing process of transformation which by its very nature is incomplete. This makes one meaning and full complete knowledge of it impossible. Unknowing is the admission of this vulnerable state of knowledge and meaning; it is the acceptance of a life of process and development and the relative uncertainty that such a state necessitates. Christian knowledge is not abstract, but exists as Christ's work is applied to the living person by the Holy Spirit and in persons and communities struggling for justice in the world. As much as its meaning is found in this relation to the complexities of human life, personal and social, it is open-ended and incomplete, and therefore, should be communicated in forms of discourse that allow for this, that seek contact, appropriation, and internal persuasion. Thus, they cannot be absolute, distanced, or monoglot, and so I propose theology should function like the *loas* by Sor Juana here discussed.

As mentioned earlier novelization includes a "spirit of process and inconclusiveness." Bakhtin sees this novelizing force as that which infuses discourse with inconclusiveness, with movement as it relates to the present and the person in the present with all of its uncertainty pointed to an open future. In terms of theological discourse, novelizing would communicate this continuing process and relation to the present. It breaks open the closed discourse and concluded dialectic of totality systems. It is vulnerable to contact with the present, to speak to society as it exists, such that those appropriating this word can actively engage society through it. It is non-canonical. Thus, for a theological discourse to be novelized, it will not speak only in the language of those in power. It will not attempt to persuade based solely on an authoritative voice or position, but will invite the readers to consider and appropriate it to their own lives and communities, making such discourse a sort of hybrid, part of the discourse of others, but also one's own. It is not to be taken verbatim as an authoritative discourse most often is,[200] but to be sifted through one's life,

---

[200] Recall Kierkegaard's critique that systematic theology and direct discourse teach Christian knowledge as something memorized by rote, and his argument that this is the opposite of Christian knowledge (see ch. 1).

experience, and context. It does not lose its connection to the original word, but yet becomes something new in contact with the present and a living person in existence. As stated, the semantic structure of internally persuasive discourse is open "in each of the new contexts that dialogize it, [and] this discourse is able to reveal ever newer ways to mean."[201]

[201] Bakhtin, "Discourse in the Novel," 345–46.

5

Beyond the Limits of Theological Language

Sor Juana's Silent Action

In November 1690, Sor Juana's *Carta Athenagórica* was first published in New Spain. In March 1691, she wrote her *Respuesta* in response to the publication of the letter and the attached prologue of criticism and praise, written by Bishop Fernández de Santa Cruz under the pseudonym Sor Filotea.[1] During the summer of 1691, a crisis began to erupt in her region, as the Valley of Mexico endured incessant rains that destroyed most crops and flooded the capital. Adobe homes collapsed; there was a shortage of fuel, fruit, vegetables, and poultry, bread, and maize were scarce. A plague of weevils ate what crops were left, and the people blamed all the events on a solar eclipse that took place on 23 August of that year. Suppliers and residents of other areas of the country began to hoard their supplies, unwilling to share, and hiding them in fear. As would be expected "those most affected by the shortages were the poor," but, Paz notes, "the most vocal complainers were groups of *criollos* and clergymen..., the same social classes that a century later would fight for independence."[2] In June 1692, the situation had not improved and a panic spread through the region as people caught rumor that the food supplies had run out. After two Indian women were beaten by officers, and these women were paraded through the city for all to see and to stir resistance, a riot broke out. The way in which the riot was handled weakened the viceroyalty, while magnifying the power of the church; the people grew superstitious and turned to the church for a theistic resolution to the crisis. Death was everywhere.[3] Fear was not have been limited to the people in the streets. Between 24 April 1691, one month after penning *Respueta,* and 5

---

[1] *La Respuesta* was not published until after her death in *Fama y Obras Póstumas* (1700), although Paz suspects it was circulated among friends and admirers before that time.

[2] Octavio Paz, *Sor Juana or, Traps of Faith*, trans. Margaret Sayers Peden (Cambridge MA: Harvard University Press, 1988) 439.

[3] Dorothy Schons, "Some Obscure Points in the Life of Sor Juana Inés de la Cruz," in *Feminist Perspectives on Sor Juana Inés de la Cruz*, ed. Stephanie Merrim (Detroit: Wayne State University Press, 1991) 55.

August 19692, two of Sor Juana's lifelong friends died and ten nuns died in her convent between 24 April 1691 and 5 August 1692.[4]

On 25 November 1691, Sor Juana's *villancicos* in honor of St. Catherine of Alexandria were sung in the cathedral in Oaxaca.[5] In 1692, the second volume of her *Works* was published in Seville, including her critique of Vieira's sermons the *Carta Athenagórica*, now given a new title.[6] By 1693 things seemed to have changed, however, as in that year Sor Juana signed a general confession, the first half of which is traditional and formulaic, but the second half of which reads as a personal confession; she writes: "God knows that for many years I have lived in religion without religion, if not worse than a pagan might live. ...It is my will to renew my vows and pass a year seeking your approval."[7] This has been called her "renunciation." Paz notes two themes at work here: first, "the admission that during her twenty-five years of convent life she has lived outside religion, that is, devoted to secular, even pagan, occupations and affairs," and second, "her jubilee: Sor Juana had taken her vows in 1669, and in 1694 she was completing her 25th year as a nun; now, as a symbolic act, she was to take her vows for a second time."[8] This year of "jubilee" is a year of repentance and penitence, and Sor Juana is said to have turned to self-mortification at this time.[9] On 17 February 1694, Sor Juana signed

[4] Ibid.

[5] These verses are considered some of the most "feminist" written by Sor Juana. See Arenal and Powell, 160–63, for the Spanish text and translation of Poem 317, Carol VI, an excellent example of the strong message in support of women's intelligence in these carols. *The Answer/La Respuesta, Including a Selection of Poems*, trans. Electa Arenal and Amanda Powell (New York: The Feminist Press at the City University of New York, 1994).

[6] "Critique of a Sermon by an Orator Great among the Finest…" Paz notes of this second volume that the dedication asks that "Orve y Arbieto not defend her works against 'the detractions of the vulgar,' not 'curtail the freedom of readers' opinions,'" a request from Sor Juana very much in line with concerns at the heart of her work (Paz, 431). This second edition of her works was also introduced with praises for Sor Juana written by illustrious poets and writers of her day, including seven esteemed theologians. Paz calls the "seven texts of the seven theologians" "seven vindications" (433).

[7] 1693 is the date of her general confession, which "probably lasted several weeks" (Paz, 460). Her year of "jubilee" and penance began in 1694.

[8] Ibid., 461.

[9] According to her earliest biographers, she began mortifying her flesh after her series of confessions, "endeavoring in her undertakings to crucify her appetites and

a document declaring her belief in the doctrine of the Immaculate Conception (with her blood, according to her early biographer Calleja, but the text itself makes no mention of it). On 5 March 1694, Sor Juana signed a document, which at the time of its publication in 1700, after her death, was given the title: "Profession That, Signed with Her Blood, Sister Juana Inés de la Cruz Made of Her Faith and Her Love to God, at the Time of Abandoning Humane Studies in Order, Released from That Attachment, to Follow the Road of Perfection."[10] However, nowhere in the text of the document itself does Sor Juana actually state she will give up "humane studies," nor does the document even mention Sor Juana's studies at all. The document declares her belief in the doctrines of the Roman Catholic Church, asks for forgiveness, and asks for the intercession of the Virgin. In the same year, Sor Juana sold most, if not all, of her library and musical and scientific equipment and gave the proceeds to charity. Barely a year had passed when Sor Juana contracted the plague while caring for her sisters in the convent who had fallen ill, and she died on 17 April 1695. Dorothy Schons describes the end of Sor Juana's career rather dramatically, saying that two years after her "renunciation," Sor Juana's "penitence reached the heights of the heroic when, during the plague that invaded the convent of St. Jerome, Juana labored night and day nursing the sick, comforting the dying, and laying out the dead. Her fragile spirit, broken by the storms that had once beaten around her, gave up the unequal struggle."[11]

Much has been made of this change in Sor Juana's activity from writing and publication to silence, her move from study to service. In the introduction I highlighted a few of the views taken on this shift in Sor Juana's life and work. Some view it as a true and fortunate conversion to a faith she did not previously demonstrate, which is the image given by her early biographers. Calleja, in 1700, for example, says that "in the year 1693 the divine grace of God found in the heart of Sister Juana its dwelling place and abode."[12] However, this view has been difficult to uphold since the discovery of documents indicating that Sor Juana began re-amassing books and writings almost as soon as she donated

passions" (Paz, 462, quoting Oviedo). Paz writes, "It is difficult to believe that the self-confident and defiant person of 1691 and 1692 had turned into the raving penitent of 1694. But we have no reason to believe that Oviedo and Calleja were lying" (462). This view will be challenged later in the chapter.

[10] Ibid., 462–63.

[11] Schons, 57.

[12] Quoted in Paz, 459.

them and that she had begun writing again. It has also been suggested that these hagiographic biographies of her life, published quickly after her death, and giving us the only account of her last years, were directed by church authorities to sanctify the memory of this popular figure for the church's purposes, minimizing her secular interests and creating the image of a dutiful, saintly nun, abiding by the expectations of her gender and station in sincere repentance of any previous activity to the contrary.[13]

Others have formed the opinion that the documents and change in focus were due to a renewal of her vows after twenty-five years with the convent, and what action she would take at the end of the time of renewal can be speculated with the discovery of the books and writing in her cell at her death.[14] Others consider it an unfortunate capitulation to ecclesiastical authorities due to a change in the power dynamics in New Spain leaving her without the strong allies she once enjoyed. Elías Trabulse argues that church authorities secretly brought a case against Sor Juana in 1693, the year of her first penitential document, indicating that she renounced, confessed, and gave away her books and instruments because she was intimidated and coerced by religious authorities to do so.[15] They did not officially charge her with heresy, however, and kept the proceedings quiet, possibly because of her great popularity and

---

[13] This biography was likely commissioned by the Archbishop of Mexico, Aguiar y Seijas, and included in the edition of her work published after her death, *Fama y Obras Póstumas*. He is the archbishop called "fiercely misogynistic" by Paz and is generally accepted to be an enemy of Sor Juana in her lifetime. Elías Trabulse argues that Aguiar y Seijas orchestrated the edition and biography, reframing the popular Sor Juana into a religious, repentant, and submissive woman at her death, as he desired her to be. This rewriting of her life and reputation corresponds with the control authorities were attempting to master in this age of change and challenge as they strove to reinstate order and preserve their power. See Stephanie Merrim in *Early Modern Women's Writing* on these methods of control, particularly over women, in the seventeenth century.

[14] This position is argued by both Pamela Kirk and Michelle Gonzáles, *Sor Juana: Beauty and Justice in the Americas* (Maryknoll NY: Orbis Books, 2003).

[15] Trabulse argues that these charges were brought against her by misogynistic Archbishop Aguiar y Seijas. He also suggests that the case against her was not so much about her secular studies as it was about her theological positions on the *finezas* and the Immaculate Conception. *Los Años Finales de Sor Juana: Una Interpretación (1688–1695)* (Mexico City: Centro de Estudios de Historia de México Condumex, 1995).

significant support in Spain.[16] It could very well be a combination of many of these factors. Octavio Paz sums it up thus:

> The change was precipitated by three circumstances. The first, external in nature, was the riot; in a few days the balance of power was radically altered, the Viceroy weakened, and the influence of Aguiar y Seijas expanded. Thus, when the second volume of her *Works* arrived in New Spain with laudatory opinions of the seven Spanish theologians, the effect must have been just the opposite of what was desired: the book was seen not as a refutation but as a challenge. The second circumstance was the wave of religious superstition that swept over New Spain following the natural and political disasters that were seen as punishment from God. Third, although by temperament Sor Juana was reasonable, even a rationalist, it is difficult to imagine that she would not have attributed to her past attitudes a part, however minimal, of the calamities suffered by New Spain.[17]

I argued in chapter 2 that Sor Juana indicated a turn to silence in her *Respuesta* written in 1691. I do not interpret this change from written communication to silence as an absolute departure from the trajectory on which she showed herself to be in earlier works. She spoke of her desire and intention to turn to silence from written communication to silence, and regularly stressed the limits of knowledge and language for expressing the divine. Electa Arenal and Amanda Powell also provide a reading of Sor Juana's silence informed by the intension she expresses in her *Respuesta*:

> By its end, Sor Juana's document declares the likelihood of her future silence, unless she receives support from her former ally, Bishop Fernández: "Unless your instructions intervene, I shall never in my own defense take up the pen again" (par. 43). Therefore, she is careful at the outset to define the meaning of the absence of speech: "I had nearly resolved to leave the matter in silence: yet although silence explains much by the emphasis of leaving all unexplained, because it is a negative thing, one must name the silence, so that what it signifies may be understood" (par. 4). With both seriousness and humor she stresses that, in order to be understood, she must indicate what her silence will say. Playing on saying/not saying and knowing/not knowing, she skirts direct contention with the powers that be and posits alternative "female" viewpoints. Throughout, she plumbs another silence, the "silence of treachery"—that of those who did not defend Christ, of those who would not speak up for her. Sor Juana inverts and reassigns the usual gender attributions with regard to the issue of silence. As we have remarked, the *Answer* gives notice of her decision to silence herself. She

[16] See Elías Trabulse and Frederick Luciani.

[17] Paz, 447.

was intent when writing it, however, on speech: on proving the sanctity of her lifelong pursuit of knowledge. Even St. Paul, she shows, encouraged desirable silence for both sexes.[18]

In the spirit of Sor Juana, I will not claim my interpretation of her silence to be the one true explanation of her motives, but I will offer it as a possible way to read and understand her action.[19] It could be that the authorities silenced her, that she was forced to give up writing to a certain degree against her will, but it cannot be denied that she gave pretext to her silence such that whether or not she ultimately chose it for herself, her silence would have meaning and content; her silence would communicate. Could it be the silence of protest, signifying the result of male dominance in church and society, and against the silencing of women and women's voices? Could it also signify the position in which such a passionate quest for theological knowledge ultimately ends: at the limits of language, and hence in silence?

Interestingly, Kierkegaard also intended to end his publication with his great treatise on indirect communication, *Concluding Unscientific Postscript.* He, too, had planned to end in silence.[20] Kierkegaard, however, was pushed through a series of provocations in print to respond, and he ultimately continued to publish, eventually authoring works in his own name and advocating a form of discourse he called "bearing witness."[21] Yet, the evidence in his journals suggests that he had intended to "conclude" his public writing with *Postscript,* a work in which he gives a reading of his entire pseudonymous corpus as indirect communication through another pseudonym and encourages the communicator of Christianity to withdraw herself from the communication so as not to gain adherents, but to truly encourage the reader or hearer to undertake the way herself.

Kierkegaard disguises himself in pseudonyms, much the way Bakhtin suggests the novelist must disguise herself, a form of dissembling Bakhtin

[18] Arenal and Powell, 32–33.

[19] See also Mabel Moraña, "La Retórica del Silencio en Sor Juana Inés de la Cruz," in *Viaje al Silencio: Exploraciones del Discurso Barroco* (Mexico: UNAM, 1998).

[20] See Hong and Hong, "Historical Introduction," in *Concluding Unscientific Postscript,* vol. 2 (Princeton: Princeton University Press, 1992) xi.

[21] This is known as the "*Corsair* Affair," which made *Postscript* not a conclusion to, but rather a "turning point" in, Kierkegaard's authorship.

likens to silence. [22] Bakhtin subjected himself to authorial silence as well, whether by choice or as with Sor Juana, through a combination of intention and political powers and pressures. His theoretical reasons for assuming and promoting forms of silence include his belief in the failure of direct discourse to communicate authentic knowledge, the lie of certain knowledge, and the corruption of discourse itself. [23] His conception of discourse includes his belief that the word can be violent as it impinges upon the word of another and that discourse is prompted by self-interest.[24]

Ruth Coates develops the argument of her book *Christianity in Bakhtin* around the themes of silence and exile. She says these metaphors "may be applied to Bakhtin himself, who was forced into silence at a young age by political circumstances over which he had no control."[25] She identifies two ways in which he fell silent. One is quite literal in that Bakhtin "fell silent by ceasing to publish almost immediately after he started. Following the Tolstoy Prefaces of 1929 and 1930 there followed a period of thirty-three years during which…his voice was not heard in the scholarly dialogue."[26] These years

---

[22] R. Coates explains: "It is possible to speak of the silencing, or exile, of a third subject, God Himself, whose supremely authoritative discourse has been squeezed out of the world of culture as a result of the same paradigmatic shift which, if Bakhtin is correct, forced the writer of prose fiction to hide his or her true self. Bakhtin closely associates God with author in his early and late work" (R. Coates 23). Bakhtin takes such a notion even further as he develops a concept in which "the non-monologic writer of fiction…is obliged to hide his or her true face, to become discourse's fool, a master of indirect speech, which for Bakhtin ('Notes of 1970–1971,' 352–53) is a form of silence" (R. Coates, 23), and so Coates talks about Bakhtin's "theory of the silenced author." Ruth Coates, *Christianity in Bakhtin* (Cambridge: Cambridge University Press, 1998).

[23] It is interesting to note that perhaps the most famous systematic theologian of all, the scholastic writer of *Summa Theologiae*, Thomas Aquinas himself, ceased writing because of a theological breakthrough of sorts. It is said that Thomas never wrote again after a religious experience during mass in 1273, saying that compared to what was revealed to him, everything he has written seems like straw.

[24] Coates comments: "The possibility of ideological plurality is guaranteed by the incarnation of ideologies in discourse. On another level, in this period Bakhtin comes to suspect that all forms of discourse have pretensions of grandeur: this is inherent in every, essentially violent, act of self-assertion, on whatever level. Thus the novelist goes into exile, refraining from the direct speech which would implicate him (or her) in violence and deceit" (R. Coates, 125).

[25] Ibid., 22.

[26] Ibid.

roughly correspond to his years in exile. The second way in which Bakhtin was silent involved the form in which he was able to communicate the themes he wanted to discuss. Because of the political climate, "he became unable to write philosophy and was forced to channel his ideas through literary criticism."[27] In the cases of Bakhtin and Sor Juana, we encounter two thinkers and writers who choose forms of silence in the midst of various pressures and political oppression, but take forms of silence that continue to communicate, that bear the content of the message their corpus conveyed.

In conclusion we will: (1) examine Sor Juana's silence and the relation it has to epistemic and linguistic limits, (2) interpret Sor Juana's silence as an active decision and consider her works of service outside public discourse as a form of communication in the embodiment of one's ideas and beliefs, and (3) consider the corruption of discourse, utilizing Bakhtin's life and thought, and interpretations of Sor Juana's silence. I interpret Sor Juan's silence as an act of resistance against the corruption of discourse and the dominance and control of the realm of speech by the powerful, as Josephine Ludmer asserts: "Silence constitutes Juana's space of resistance vis-á-vis others' power."[28]

The Form of the Incarnate

Throughout this project, I have worked from an understanding of the Christian faith as something that is lived, embodied, or thus incarnated. One does not simply hold beliefs about God within one's intellect, but pursues a life that reflects our understanding of God in space and time, as Christ himself demonstrated.[29] We saw in Kierkegaard an emphasis upon religion as such a living of one's ideas; it is also true of the philosophy of Socrates. However, it is particularly true of the Christian religion, according to Kierkegaard; he finds the active life to be at the core of the religion, evidenced in Christ:

> *Christian dogmatics...must grow out of Christ's activity, and all the more so* because Christ did not establish any doctrine; he acted. He *did not teach* that there was redemption for men, but *he redeemed men*.... [A] Christian dogmatics grows out of Christ's activity. Through Christ's activity (which actually was the

[27] Ibid., 22–23.

[28] Josefina Ludmer, "Tricks of the Weak," in *Feminist Perspectives on Sor Juana Inés de la Cruz*, ed. and trans. Stephanie Merrim (Detroit: Wayne State University Press, 1991) 89.

[29] Bakhtin says, "A point of view is chronotopic, that is, it includes both the spatial and temporal aspects" ("Notes from 1970–1971," 134).

main thing) his nature also was given; Christ's relationship to God, man, nature, and the human situation *was conditioned by his activity.*[30]

This emphasis on one's activity as the best conveyer of Christian knowledge is also found in Bakhtin's work and is demonstrated by Sor Juana in her last year. She prepares us for this reading of her final form of communication, and writes in conclusion to her *Carta Athenagórica*, published three years before her general confession in 1693: "May his Majesty give us the grace to recognize his benefits, and to respond to them, which shows a greater understanding. May he grant that when we consider benefits we do not remain at the level of speculative argument but go on to practical service."[31]

Robert Solomon observes of Kierkegaard: "He had little tolerance for abstract ideas, for categories that one could only think about and not live in."[32] Solomon goes on to explain that Kierkegaard attacked "the Kantian vision at its very foundation, he rejected the 'anonymous' transcendental self of knowledge, and insisted that the only self that was of any significance whatever was the acting, 'ethical' self."[33] And perhaps most importantly, he clarifies that this ethical or religious life is such that it is not certain that "what is most important" in it "can ever be *said.*"[34] Such a perspective is similar to that of Bakhtin, who "lays great emphasis on the necessity for theoretical truth to be incorporated into spatiotemporal reality if it is to become living and binding upon individuals."[35] Bakhtin has a highly incarnational understanding of being and knowledge, writing in "Philosophy of Act" that an "unincarnated thought" leads to an "impersonal, rootless being."[36] Coates comments: "A living truth is an embodied truth, a word made flesh."[37] And we see a similar idea in Sor Juana's *loa* to *Divino Narciso*, in which she communicates the idea that the dramatic demonstration of Christian teaching to follow in the *auto* is a better form for

---

[30] Søren Kierkegaard, *Søren Kierkegaard's Journals and Papers,* vol. 1, A–E, ed. and trans. Howard V. Hong and Edna H. Hong (Bloomington and London: Indiana University Press, 1967) 168, entry no. 412.

[31] *Carta Athenagórica,* Kirk, 249.

[32] Robert C. Solomon, *Continental Philosophy since 1750: The Rise and Fall of the Self* (Oxford: Oxford University Press, 1988) 89.

[33] Ibid., 90.

[34] Ibid., 91.

[35] R. Coates, 35.

[36] Bakhtin, "Toward a Philosophy of Act," 114. Translated by R. Coates, 35.

[37] R. Coates, 35.

teaching than direct instruction, because through the drama, one can see the ideas demonstrated to the eyes. Although it seems her *auto sacramentales* were never performed, the form itself is significant. It is textual, but its essence is in the performance; actors embody [encarnar] particular identities within the colonial context.[38] It is not only words, but it is enacted. And finally in Sor Juana's work, as she pauses in her prolific writing career and dedicates herself to the physical care of those in need, we are instructed to look to her life itself and not only her words. Sor Juana's life exemplifies a continued, rigorous search for knowledge, all the while exhibiting a full recognition that the completion of this will not be possible and will only be realized through the life itself, in action as she attends to the physical needs of those in her community.

If Christianity is of the nature we have described, that is, a religion that seeks the transformation of the individual and society, and if Christian knowledge is found in undergoing and engaging in this process in community, it is a religion to be lived. As noted, the lived life is not static, and thus it resists direct expression; language cannot fully convey it. So, at last Sor Juana lives in service, giving up public discourse for silent action, not to the detriment of the words she left behind her, but in fuller expression of her religious understanding and in reflection of Christ's ministry as she cared for the poor and the sick. Her previous words give content to the silence, so that we know this move expresses more than surrender to powers and pressure or that, even in the silencing, she still communicates theologically despite their efforts. She says of silence in her *Respuesta*: "Although it explains a great deal by its insistence on not explaining, some brief label is needed to enable one to understand what it is intended to mean. Otherwise, silence will say nothing, since its function is precisely that: to say nothing."[39]

As also noted in chapter 4, Bakhtin contrasts authoritative discourse with that which internally persuades, as that which through a dialogue with the discourse of another, one forges a discourse of one's own. One's moral, religious, and ethical consciousness is not formed by direct acceptance of imposed thought, but it is constituted in dialogue with the ideas of others and one's own response, appropriation, and assimilation. One's consciousness becomes a conglomeration, formed under a diversity of influences: discourses, ideas, people, experience, history, and communities. Authentic truth is of this sort, particularly to the extent that it is concretized, or incarnated in the life of

---

[38] Martínez-San Miguel, 173.

[39] *Respuesta,* OC 4:442.

the one holding it. Bakhtin says in "Discourse in the Novel" that "Truth is restored by reducing the lie to an absurdity, but truth itself does not seek words; she is afraid to entangle herself in the word, to soil herself in verbal pathos."[40] For Bakhtin truth seeks such incarnation rather than verbal expression, and he lifts the statement from Tyutchev that "the spoken thought is a lie."[41] Ideas, thought, or beliefs must be lived or made real in time and space. And for Bakhtin, as for Kierkegaard, life is defined by committed action, as one "constantly actualizes, concretizes abstract truths by incarnating them in the deed and thus bringing them into the historical process," which stems from a life that is "a vital, open, unique process charged with values and proceeding from specific spatial and temporal locatedness."[42]

Just as a person is situated, incarnate in time and space, so must thought be incarnate in space and time, or must therefore be expressed in action. This emphasis on the chronotope, embeddedness in both space and time, is a feature of Bakhtin's thought we have not dealt with explicitly in this project, but it not only corresponds with the emphasis throughout on temporality and location, it also relates to the ongoing stress that ideas are to be lived and embodied. Coates draws out the implications of Bakhtin's chronotope for Christianity:

> Indeed, Christianity, at its inception, may be viewed as nothing other than a materialisation of God, and a degradation, a debasement of the entire Jewish/Old Testament world-view, a literal turning of its subject into flesh in order to overthrow its elitism, with respect both to the common Jew and to the Gentile, once and for all. In the Incarnation, heaven is brought down to earth; ahistorical, metaphysical truths enter into the realm of chronotopic (spatial and temporal) limitation and possibility and are thereby divested of their power to distance and to terrify the believer.[43]

And she continues:

> [Bakhtin] saw Christ as the means by which God ceases to be an abstract principle: "even God had to be incarnated in order to show mercy, to suffer and forgive, to come down, as it were, from the abstract viewpoint of justice" ("Author and Hero," 113). Many aspects of Jesus' ministry reflect and carry forward the materialising and familiarising principle inherent in the act of Incarnation itself. It may be suggested that the materialising principle that

[40] Bakhtin, "Discourse in the Novel," 309.

[41] Bakhtin, "Author and Hero," quoted and translated by R. Coates, 117.

[42] R. Coates, 162.

[43] Ibid., 133.

> informs the gospels and is epitomised by the Incarnation overthrows a religion based on absence and fear in favour of a familiar God expressed in material terms in Christ's teaching and paradigmatically, in his physical person. The "high, spiritual, ideal, abstract" philosophy of late Temple Judaism is transformed by Christ into a carnivalesque experiential philosophy.[44]

Sor Juana hinted in her writing and communicated in her concluding silence that the quest for knowledge of God eventually pushes beyond language entirely, and it seems for Sor Juana this reality pushes to action: she gave her possessions to provide for the poor, and lived her last years in active service. She critiqued the authoritarian, patriarchal, dogmatic forms that theology took during her day, asserting that such bold claims of achieved knowledge were false. At last she provides an even higher example of theological form: the embodiment of faith in action. And the writing preceding this step communicates the theological and philosophical meaning of this move. Her admission of lack of knowledge, her Socratic ignorance, is parody, mocking those pseudo-intelligences that claim full or achieved knowledge. This "ignorance" functions much like the clown in the novel, which, according to Bakhtin, is a form of silence. Sor Juana utilizes it in all three genres here discussed: in her letters explicitly; in her poem *Primero sueño,* through her acknowledged failure to understand or gain full knowledge; and in her *loas,* especially through her illustration of arrogant claims of achievement later surpassed or *Plus Ultra*. The irony of her claims of ignorance, as well as the diversity of genres utilized by Sor Juana, possess limited means to express religious truth. The most appropriate form is the life itself, embodied in time and space, in action.

Discourse, Power, and Corruption

In chapter 1, I asserted that direct speech is not the most appropriate form for communicating Christianity, and I expounded Kierkegaard's theory of indirect communication. Here, in conclusion, we consider the limits of language even when it exists in the diversity of indirect forms of discourse we have discussed throughout. For Bakhtin, not only can a non-fiction prose author not "allow him or herself the luxury of direct speech," but further: "The authoritative, direct authorial word becomes suspect precisely because discourse itself becomes suspect in Bakhtin's view, corrupted by violence and falsehood, that is to say, by the effects of the Fall on language and, behind it, language users. Silence in

[44] Ibid.

Bakhtin, on all levels so far discussed, is at once the result of and the response to the Fall."[45] Not only is indirect discourse necessary because of the nature of knowledge and embodied truth, but because all discourse is implicated in falsehood and violence, leading Bakhtin to consider forms of silence as the alternative. In "Notes from 1943," he expounds: "This word-violence (and lie) is linked up with thousands of personal motives in the creator, muddying the purity of his thirst for success, influence, recognition (not of the word, but of the creator), with the striving to become an oppressing and consuming force."[46] Discourse is so linked with self-assertion, violence, and falsehood that Bakhtin says "the genuinely good, impartial and loving person has not yet spoken, he has realized himself in the spheres of everyday life, he has not touched the official word." He says such a person "does not become a writer."[47] From Bakhtin, one comes to understand that the corruption of language actually begins within the human before the word is even formed on one's lips; the corruption begins with ambition, the desire to impress others, the drive toward self-promotion. The implications this has for a reading of Sor Juana's silence is clear: throughout her work she criticized claims of ultimate theological knowledge, competitive rhetoric, and the arrogant self-seeking behind such theological pursuits and discourse, finally removing herself from the public discourse altogether.

Coates draws the link "between discourse and corruption, on the one hand, and silence and truth, on the other," and writes: "By the end of Bakhtin's work Christ most demonstrates his authority in silence, since speech has been impossible."[48] She goes on to piece together Bakhtin's understanding of Christ as he hints at it in his fragmented "Notes of 1970–1971," where he ponders the role of Christ in Dostoevsky's *Brother's Karamazov*. Bakhtin writes: "The word as something personal. Christ as truth. …The unuttered truth of Dostoevsky (Christ's kiss). The problem of silence."[49] And somewhat more coherently, he says: "The denial of (failure to understand) the sphere of necessity through which freedom must pass (both on the historical and the individual-personal plane), that intermediate sphere that lies between the Grand Inquisitor (with his

[45] Ibid., 23.

[46] Bakhtin, "From Draft Exercise Books," 153, trans. by R. Coates in *Christianity in Bakhtin*, 118.

[47] Ibid., 154, trans. by R. Coates in *Christianity in Bakhtin,* 118.

[48] R. Coates, 173.

[49] Bakhtin, "Notes Made in 1970–1971," 148.

state power, rhetoric, and authority) and Christ (with his silence and his kiss)."[50] Coates makes this assessment:

> In the light of Bakhtin's increasing concern with the corruption of discourse we are justified in hazarding how he might have understood this phenomenon: in a world where a lie in the interest of power occupies the ideological center (the Grand Inquisitor's lie to the people) Christ's only alternative is to refrain from speech, since to speak would be to participate in the conspiracy.[51]

Josefina Ludmer also notes the relationship between discourse, power, and violence, writing that, for Sor Juana, "public saying is a space occupied by authority and violence," as it is the one in power who "grants and retracts the word," and "Juana, as a woman, says that rather than she being its mistress, the word is granted, retracted, and demanded."[52] She goes on to note the coercive nature of public discourse and Sor Juana's response of silence:

> Juana progressively disabuses herself of the public word, a zone that becomes associated with the mechanisms of discipline.... Juana thus decides that to *publish,* the highest form of saying, does not interest her. That space the culture posits as its valued and dominant zone is precisely where Juana says, "I don't know," I won't say, I abstain, underscoring yet again that saying, writing, publishing (the three now forming a series) are demands originating from others and associated with violence, with coercion:... "And, in truth, I have written nothing except when coerced and constrained, and then only to give pleasure to others; not alone without pleasure of my own, but with absolute repugnance."[53]

Ruth Coates calls Bakhtin's problem with discourse one "of living with integrity if every act of self-assertion, including every discursive act, is necessarily an act of violence and deceit, and thus a threat to the right of others to their own word."[54] Sounding not unlike Bakhtin and his concern that discourse is inherently so corrupt and self-promoting that it cannot be innocent as one's rhetoric impinges upon the voice of another, Ludmer notes Sor Juana's response to the various power dynamics in rhetoric that threaten one's authentic word. Observing not only that those in power "grant" Sor Juana the word, but also that Sor Juana commits something similar herself, Ludmer writes of the artificial and fictitious gesture that is "granting the word to those defined by

---

[50] Ibid., 151.

[51] R. Coates, 121.

[52] Ludmer, 90.

[53] Ibid., quoting from Sor Juana's *Respuesta*, trans. Stephanie Merrim.

[54] R. Coates, 119.

their lacks (lacking land, lacking writing) and of bringing their particular language to light."[55] She goes on to describe the way in which this gesture is the work of the "superior culture" and of the educated, those "who disguise and mute their own voices in the fiction of transcription to propose an alliance to the weak and subordinate against the common enemy."[56] However, this move, both in "granting the word" and in "identifying oneself with the other," bears "the same imperative: the weak must accept the superior's project."[57] Ludmer notes that Sor Juana not only finds herself as the one being "granted" the word by superiors, but also as a perpetrator of the violence in an attempt to "give voice" to the *indios*. As a *criolla,* she is one with some power and with enough means to live the privileged existence of a nun, enjoying outstanding connections; through her publications, she represents the *indios* in her dramas and writes poems in their native tongue, Nahuatl.

Silent Resistance

We have found that one theme running throughout Sor Juana's works is a concern that the pursuit of religious knowledge and the communication of it not be a matter of arrogance or self-promotion. In *Primero sueño,* she challenges the attitude of those, like Phaethon, who would seek knowledge of the Absolute in pursuit of fame; in her letters she critiques this attitude in the sermon of Vieira, and in her *loa* to *El Mártir del Sacramento,* she compares claims of knowledge to be like the vain and false claims of Hercules. She questions the way religious discourse has traditionally proceeded because it lends itself to such arrogance and abuse of power, to acts of violence and coercion.

Although Sor Juana does not display a fully developed theory of discourse and its corruption in perfect correspondence to that found in the writings of Bakhtin, she certainly does show evidence of an awareness of a link between rhetoric and violence and discourse and arrogant self-promotion; she demonstrates a belief that discourse, and specifically knowledge claims, are not innocent. As Josefina Ludmer argues, Sor Juana grapples with the relationship between public discourse and power, and she does so both as one under the power of others (bishop, Holy Office, mother), as well as one who holds power as a *criolla* depicting the *indios* in her writing. Ludmer details the three powers provoking Sor Juana's resistant response: "We thus have three cases of

[55] Ludmer, 90.

[56] Ibid.

[57] Ibid.

superiority: the mother, the bishop, and the Holy Office. All three command fear and generate not saying: not saying that one knows (to the mother), saying that one doesn't know how to say (to the bishop), not saying because one doesn't know (the realm of theology)."[58] Ludmer correctly points out that Sor Juana does not claim to write for her pleasure, but at the request or demand of her "superiors," those in political and ecclesiastical power. Her works are commissioned, requested, and expected. These people in positions of power grant her voice and demand her speech.[59] In turn, Sor Juana supports her position with the voices of the powerful, those of the highest authorities: "Saint Thomas…had not spoken because he knew no words worthy of Albertus…[and] speech deserted the mother of John the Baptist when she was visited by 'la Madre del Verbo' (the Mother of the Word)."[60] One option Sor Juana has is to endeavor to resist the force of those present authorities with the word of past authorities, pitting historical power against current powers. But the time comes when Sor Juana removes herself from this wielding of authority and power altogether. She releases herself, even if temporarily, from the hold of the word and the violence and corruption of the discourse itself.

We may want her to have continued writing because we consider that the stronger form of protest, but as recent feminist scholars in sociology and linguistics and postcolonial theorists have argued, requiring articulate speech according to the dictates of the dominant group is another way of imposing the standards of the dominant group upon the "muted" group.[61] Sociolinguist Susan

---

[58] Ibid., 89.

[59] Ibid., 90.

[60] From Sor Juana, *Respuesta*, trans. Stephanie Merrim in Ludmer's article, "Tricks of the Weak."

[61] "Dominant" and "muted" or "silent" are the terms used by E. Ardener in 1975 in his important work noting the silence of women in anthropological studies due to the methods and expectations of the interviewer/researcher. It is to ignore the form of protest and resistance behind the silence. "The 'muted group' thesis usefully draws attention to the importance of the symbolic language, the form, of dominant and subordinate discourse. However, as I will demonstrate with a series of examples, the Ardeners' formulation is flawed in several respects. First, it assumes that 'mutedness' is a static reflex of women's structural position. In contrast, when viewed in terms of broader theories of gender and symbolic domination, 'mutedness' becomes only one of many theoretically possible outcomes of gender relations" [Susan Gal, "Between Speech and Silence: The Problematics of Research on Language and Gender," in *Gender at the*

Gal discusses the complexity of silence, particularly through differences between imposed and self-chosen silence. She recognizes that in most feminist scholarship, "silence is generally deplored, because it is taken to be a result and a symbol of passivity and powerlessness: those who are denied speech cannot make their experience known and thus cannot influence the course of their lives or of history."[62] However, she finds that other studies emphasize "the paradoxical power of silence, especially in certain institutional settings. In religious confession, modern psychotherapy, bureaucratic interviews, and in police interrogation, the relations of coercion are reversed: where self-exposure is required, it is the silent listener who judges, and who thereby exerts power over the one who speaks."[63]

Gal notes a variety of places and ways silence is used across cultures and genders. She writes of the strategic use of silence as a defense against those in power, and she gives the example of the Apaches who utilized silence in battle to confuse and disconcert the white soldiers. Another example she offers is the seventeenth-century English Quakers. She says that both male and female Quakers refused to speak when it was expected of them by others, and that this "marked an ideological commitment. It was the opposite of passivity, indeed a form of political protest."[64] She also gives the example of the Nigerian Woman's War of 1929 to demonstrate how "women sometimes produce a cultural commentary of gesture and ritual that may be called inarticulate because it rejects words altogether."[65] She says: "Contemporary witnesses of the Women's War report that women's protests included marching nude, lying on the ground kicking their legs in the air, and making obscene gestures."[66] Studies of this resistance noted that "these gestures were mysterious and alarming to European observers but, for the women and men involved, they constituted an eloquent protest against the male political control and government taxation that women saw as a violation of their rights."[67] Silence can be ambiguous, but Gal's "examples of silence as subversive defense and

---

Crossroads of Knowledge: Feminist Anthropology in the Postmodern Era, ed. M. di Leonardo (Berkeley: University of California Press, 1991) 189].

[62] Gal, 175.

[63] Ibid.

[64] Ibid.

[65] Ibid., 193.

[66] Ibid.

[67] Ibid.

even political protest suggest that linguistic forms, even the most apparently quiescent, are strategic actions, created as responses to cultural and institutional contexts."[68]

In Sor Juana's context, her refusal to speak can be understood as an act of resistance. Ludmer calls Sor Juana's play between saying and not saying, knowing and not knowing, a "trick of the weak," utilized also by others without significant power. Ludmer writes that it serves to separate "the field of saying (the law of the other) from the field of knowing (my law), combines, as in all tactics of resistance, submission to and acceptance of the place assigned to one by the other, with antagonism and confrontation, retreat from collaboration."[69] The discovery of her reassembled library at the time of her death suggests such a resisting, and even a rebelling against, the domination of those in power.

Both her *Respuesta,* and the one thing she claims to have written for her own gratification, *Primero sueño,* give silence autobiographical significance. Ludmer even identifies the space within which Sor Juana places herself to be one of silence: "she fills the space of knowing with silence: books are mute.... Her readings begin with St. Ambrose, St. Augustine's teacher, and progress in silence. It is from this other web, no longer the space of not saying but of its praxis, that Sor Juana writes about women's silence."[70] Here Ludmer asserts an interpretation of Sor Juana's silence as one of praxis. Ludmer sees it primarily as a resistant form of communicating about the silencing of women. Her silence speaks of the injustice of women barred from theological study and dialogue. It pronounces judgment on the silencing of voices at the margins—the colonial subject, the subaltern. It signals a protest of the theological "tables" that do not listen to the voices of the other, of those from the southern hemisphere, from those educated in styles different than those of the West, of women. Sor Juana's ultimate decision to cease the struggle to participate in the discourse, after rebuff and probably quiet threats against her, remains similar to the decision faced by many marginalized by the theological institutions of today. We have seen groups leave the table and begin conversations of their own in other locations and publishing houses. When "to speak would be to participate in the conspiracy," the only alternative is to refrain from speech, as Christ did in "The

[68] Ibid., 176.
[69] Ludmer, 91.
[70] Ibid.

Grand Inquisitor."[71] Does there come a time when the best option available is to remove oneself from the discourse as it is implicated in violence?

In addition to this protest, Sor Juana's action may also be a demonstration of that which she previously communicated regarding theological pursuits, discourse, and knowledge. It is a theological praxis. The form in which to communicate the Christian faith, then, is ultimately that of a life in time, space, and community engaged in the process of transformation and action. The form of communication cannot simply refer to a genre in which one expresses ideas, but the actual life demonstrating it. Christian knowledge, then, as a matter of action and not of intellect is best communicated in non-static, non-propositional form. Commenting on the final sentence of Wittgenstein's *Tractus*: "Whereof one cannot speak, thereof one should be silent," Solomon says, "What cannot be said can nevertheless be *shown*."[72] Sor Juana spent her career explaining what could be known and said, ultimately focusing on what cannot be fully known or truly said, and her last years were spent showing it.

Conclusion: Theology within the Limits of the Inconclusive

Since the time of Kant theology has had to deal explicitly with the limits of human knowing, particularly metaphysical knowing. But even before Kant articulated these ideas critically, theologians have confronted this complication to their assertions of knowledge of the divine. The apophatic theologians were certainly aware of the limits on their knowing. And even before Christian apophatic theologians, like Pseudo-Dionysius, was Socrates, who recognized the limits of human knowledge, claiming ignorance, and the author of Job, who asserted that God's ways are hidden. Likewise, theologians have dealt with the limits of knowledge and human language, like Augustine and Aquinas, turning to the use of analogy in an attempt to describe what is beyond the reach of definition in words.

Even the most well conceived doctrine of revelation cannot avoid the darkness confronted by the apophaticists. A simultaneous veiling occurs with the unveiling; what is revealed can run counter to human experience, leaving some in dark despair. And although revelation may be said to have an objective side, most theologians do not deny the other side, the subjective, that which requires appropriation by the individual in community; revelation is never revelation when it is only the one or the other, but must include both.

---

[71] R. Coates, 121.

[72] Solomon, 148.

Knowledge of God is something gained only in the encounter and subjective appropriation of it, and such an encounter cannot be expressed in direct speech. Theologians and philosophers have attempted different strategies to deal with the inconclusive and subjective nature of such knowledge. Socrates taught through a maeutic form. Plato used analogies and metaphors. Both used the dialogue. Luther retained a rather stark conception of the hiddenness of God. Kierkegaard used indirect communication through his pseudonymous authorship. Sor Juana Inés de la Cruz used a variety of genres.

Because we experience such limits in knowledge due to the subjectivity of religious truth, theology must foster ways of communicating that take these limitations into account instead of distorting them through direct forms of discourse that suggest a conclusiveness we do not have. Theology must incorporate forms of discourse that reflect these limitations, which in their very form communicate something of the nature of religious knowledge and faith. If the task of theology is to communicate religious knowledge in a way that is internally persuasive, then the discourse needs to be such that it invites response, participation, self-evaluation, interpretation, and appropriation. This is likely to include a step away from the posture of authoritative discourse, and instead is more likely to be that of unofficial discourse, or in a form of indirect communication as Kierkegaard describes it. Theological discourse ought not speak only in the language of those in power, nor attempt to persuade based solely on an authoritative voice or position, but should invite the reader to consider and appropriate it to her own life.

I have argued for discourse that is open to multiple perspectives, which corresponds with the multiplicity of Christianity as it relates to people and communities of faith located in time and space. Authoritative discourse, in contrast, is that form which is imposed using coercion and violence (either physical or rhetorical) and takes the propositional form of discourse aligned with the powerful. This style of discourse is often symbolized by the sword because the forms of dominant and authoritative discourse often insist upon a similar structure (linear) in order for the discourse to be judged acceptable, rigorous, or even rational. Alternately, I have here promoted discourses that allow for the variety of Christian opinions, that do not impose themselves upon the individual but actually invite the listener or reader to consider the message, challenge it, alter it, appropriate it, and make it her own. As I have shown in Sor Juana's dramas, such an internal response and acceptance do not occur at the end of a point, but through an invitation to consider, discuss, and respond. The straight discourse of the sword, that which is used to force a point at the expense of the other and threaten the rational freedom of the other, then, is not the appropriate form for the task. A discourse that does not take the shape of the sword cannot easily be brought into the competitive battle that is theology, however. And a curved or open discourse does not stand in a defensive position. It does, however, as Sor Juana demonstrates, welcome critique and questions, which constitutes dialogue. The motion of a curved discourse moves in contrast to the thrust of the sword, as it functions to gather in the welcoming motion of the sweeping sickle.

The rhetorical forms I have discussed all possess a "spirit of process and inconclusiveness," which correspond to authentic human life and the appropriation of Christ's life and benefits. The discourse is infused with the concrete (temporality, contemporaneity, contextuality, and embodiment), and with movement as it relates to the person in the present with all of its uncertainty, pointed to an open future. These forms break open the closed discourse and concluded dialectic of totality systems; they are non-canonical. Yet the forms discussed here are a more fitting means for communicating the subjective nature of Christian knowledge, while they are also an effective means to resist unitary, systematic tendencies in traditional Christian discourse that work to counter the very appropriation of Christian teaching. Yet at the end, it is silence, and a lived embodiment of the beliefs themselves, which may best communicate the Christian knowledge as it stands at the relation between Christ and living people and communities, as it stands dynamically at that rift between revelation and lived experience. The Christian faith upon which theology reflects is found at that encounter between the eternal divine and the temporal human, between the metaphysical and the corporeal. As Christ himself lived at that encounter, so the Christian faith is found in the incarnation of its belief, which, proceeding in time and space, is inconclusive and lacking the eternal, distanced perspective necessary for a comprehensive, concluded, and total account. It is action, not words, then, that ultimately conveys the Christian message.

Bibliography

Primary Texts by Sor Juana Inés de la Cruz

Juana Inés de la Cruz. *The Answer/La Respuesta, Including a Selection of Poems*. Translated by Electa Arenal and Amanda Powell. New York: The Feminist Press at the City University of New York, 1994.

———. *The Divine Narcissus/El Divino Narciso. Translated by Patricia A. Peters and* Renée Domeier, O.S.B. Albuquerque NM: University of New Mexico Press, 1998.

———. *Joseph's Scepter*. In *The Story of Joseph in Spanish Golden Age Drama*, translated by Michael McGaha. Lewisburg: Bucknell University Press, 1998.

———. *Obras Completas de Sor Juana Inés de la Cruz*. Volumes 1–4. Edited by Alfonso Méndez Plancarte and Alberto Salceda. México-Buenos Aires: Fondo de Cultura Económica, 1951–1957.

———. *A Sor Juana Anthology*. Translated by Alan S. Trueblood. Cambridge MA: Harvard University Press, 1988.

———. *Sor Juana Inés de la Cruz, Selected Writings*. Translated by Pamela Kirk. New York: Paulist Press, 2005.

———. *Sor Juana's Dream*. Translated by Luis Harss. New York: Lumen Books, 1986.

Secondary Literature on Sor Juana

Alatorre, Antonio. "La Carta de Sor Juana al P. Núñez (1682)." *Nueva Revista de Filología Hispánica* 35, no. 2 (1987): 591–673.

Arenal, Electa. "Where Woman Is Creator of the Wor(l)d. Or, Sor Juana's Discourses on Method." In *Feminist Perspectives on Sor Juana Inés de la Cruz*, edited by Stephanie Merrim, 124–41. Detroit: Wayne State University Press, 1991.

Arenal, Electa, and Amanda Powell. "Introduction." In *The Answer/La Respuesta, Including a Selection of Poems*. Translated by Electa Arenal and Amanda Powell, 1–37. New York: The Feminist Press at the City University of New York, 1994.

Arenal, Electa, and Stacy Schlau. *Untold Sisters: Hispanic Nuns in Their Own Words*. Albuquerque: University of New Mexico Press, 1989.

Bénassy, Marie-Cécile. "Hipótesis Sobre la 'Conversion' Final de Sor Juana Inés de la Cruz." *Revista de la Universidad de México* 30, no. 3 (Noviembre 1975): 21–24.

Benoist, Valerie. "El Escribirlo No Parte de la Osadía: Tradición y Mímica en la Loa para *El Divino Narciso* de Sor Juana Inés de la Cruz." *Latin American Theatre Review* 33, no. 1 (Fall 1999): 73–84.

Castro López, Octavio. *Sor Juana y el Primero Sueño.* Mexico: Centro de Investigaciones Lingüístico-Literarias. Instituto de Investigaciones Humanísticas, Universidad Veracruzana, 1982.

Cevallos, Francisco Javier. "La Alegoria del Deseo. La 'Loa para el Auto *El Mártir del Sacramento, San Hermenegildo,*' de Sor Juana Inés de la Cruz." *Teatro y America* (1992): 43–52.

Checa, Jorge. "Los Caracteres del Estrago: Babel en *Primero Sueño*." In *Mujer y Cultura en la Colonia Hispanoamericana*, edited by Mabel Moraña, 257–71. Pittsburgh: Biblioteca de América, 1996.

Daniel, Lee A. "The *Loas* of Sor Juana Inés de la Cruz." *Letras Femeninas* 11, no. 1 (1985): 42–48.

———. "Sor Juana's Baroque Martyr—*Auto, El Mártir del Sacramento, San Hermenegildo*." *Latin American Theater Review* 28, no.1 (Fall 1994): 101–12.

Feder, Elena. "Sor Juana Inés de la Cruz; or, The Snares of (Con)(tra)di(c)tion." In *Amerindian Images and the Legacy of Columbus*, edited by René Jara and Nicholas Spadaccini, 473–529. Minneapolis: University of Minnesota Press, 1992.

Fiol-Matta, Licia. "Visions of Gender: Sor Juana and the *First Dream*." In *Nepantla: Views from the South* 4.2. 2003.

Franco, Jean. *Plotting Women: Gender and Representation in Mexico*. New York: Columbia University Press, 1989.

Gaos, José. "El Sueño de un Sueño." *Historia Mexicana* 10, no. 1 (1960): 54–71.

Glantz, Margo. *Borrones y Borradores. Reflexiones Sobre el Ejercicio de la Escritura (Ensayos de Literature Colonial, de Bernal Díaz del Castillo a SorJuana)*. Mexico: Coordinación de Difusión Cultural Dirección de Literatura, UNAM, Ediciones del Equilibrista, 1992.

Godzich, Wlad, and Nicholas Spadaccini. "Popular Culture and Spanish Literary History." In *Literature Among Discourses: The Spanish Golden Age*, edited by Wlad Godzich and Nicholas Spadaccini. Minneapolis: University of Minnesota Press, 1986.

Gonzáles, Michelle A. "Seeing Beauty within Torment: Sor Juana Inés de la Cruz and the Baroque in New Spain." In *A Reader in Latina Feminist Theology: Religion and Justice,* edited by María Pilar Aquino, Daisy L. Machado, and Jeannette Rodríguez. Austin TX: University of Texas Press, 2002.

———. *Sor Juana: Beauty and Justice in the Americas*. Maryknoll NY: Orbis Books, 2003.

Haraway, Donna. "Situated Knowledge: The Science Question in Feminism as a Site of Discourse on the Priviledge of Partial Perspective." *Feminist Studies* 14.3 (1988): 575–99.

Harss, Luis. "Introduction." In *Sor Juana's Dream*, translated by Luis Harss. New York: Lumen Books, 1986.

Kennet, Frances. "The Theology of *The Divine Narcissus*." *Feminist Theology* 9.25 (September 2000): 56–83.

Kirk, Pamela. "Introduction." In *Sor Juana Inés de la Cruz, Selected Writings*, translated by Pamela Kirk, 5–42. New York: Paulist Press, 2005.

———. "Sor Juana Inés de la Cruz: Precursor of Latin American Feminism." *JHLT* 5, no. 3 (1998): 16–38.

———. *Sor Juana Inés de la Cruz: Religion, Art, and Feminism*. New York: Continuum Publishing Company, 1999.

Lavrin, Asunción. "In Search of the Colonial Women in Mexico: The Seventeenth and Eighteenth Centuries." In *Latin American Women: Historical Perspectives*, edited by Asunción Lavrin. Westport CT: Greenwood Press, 1978.

Leonard, Irving A. *Baroque Times in Old Mexico: Seventeeth-Century Persons, Places, and Practices.* Ann Arbor: The University of Michigan Press, 1959.

Luciani, Frederick. *Literary Self-Fashioning in Sor Juana Inés de la Cruz.* Lewisburg: Bucknell University Press, 2004.

Ludmer, Josefina. "Tricks of the Weak." In *Feminist Perspectives on Sor Juana Inés de la Cruz*, translated and edited by Stephanie Merrim, 86–93. Detroit: Wayne State University Press, 1991.

Marcus, Leah S. "Renaissance/Early Modern Studies." In *Redrawing the Boundaries: The Transformation of English and American Literary Studies,* edited by Stephen Greenblatt and Giles Gun. New York: Modern Language Association of America, 1992.

Martinez-San Miguel, Yolanda. *Saberes Americanos: Subalternidad y Epistemología en los Escritos de Sor Juana.* Pittsburgh: Instituto Internacional de Literatura Iberoamericana, University of Pittsburgh, 1999.

Marvall, José Antonio. *Culture of the Baroque: Analysis of a Historical Structure.* Translated by Terry Cochran. Minneapolis: University of Minneapolis Press, 1986.

———. "From the Renassaince to the Baroque: The Diphasic Schema of a Social Crisis." In *Literature Among Discourses: The Spanish Golden Age*, edited by Wlad Godzich and Nicholas Spadaccini, 3–40. Minneapolis: University of Minnesota Press, 1986.

Mazzotti, José Antonio. "Resentimiento Criollo y Nación Étnica: Él Papel de la Épica Novohispana." In *Agencias Ciollas. La Ambigüedad "Colonial" in Letras Hispanoamerican,* edited by José Antonio Mazzotti, 143–60. Pittsburgh: Instituto Internactional de Literatura Iberoamericana, 2000.

McKendrick, Melveena. *Theater in Spain 1490–1700.* Cambridge: Cambridge University Press, 1989.

McKenna, Susan M. "Rational Thought and Female Poetics in Sor Juana's 'Primero Sueño': The Circumvention of Two Traditions." In *Hispanic Review* 68, no. 1 (Winter 2000) 37–52.

Merrim, Stephanie. *Early Modern Women's Writing and Sor Juana Inés de la Cruz.* Nashville: Vanderbilt University Press, 1999.

———. "Toward a Feminist Reading of Sor Juana Inés de la Cruz: Past, Present, and Future Directions in Sor Juana Criticism." In *Feminist Perspectives on Sor Juana Inés de la Cruz*, edited by Stephanie Merrim, 11–37. Detroit: Wayne State University Press, 1991.

Montross, Constance M. *Virtue or Vice? Sor Juana's Use of Thomistic Thought.* Washington DC: University Press of America, Inc., 1981.

Moraña, Mabel. "Poder, Raza, y Lengua: La Construcción Étnica del Otro en los Villancicos de Sor Juana." *Colonial Latin American Review* 4, no. 2 (1995): 139–54.

———. "La Retórica del Silencio en Sor Juana Inés de la Cruz." In *Viaje al Silencio: Exploraciones del Discurso Barroco*. Mexico: UNAM, 1998.

———. *Viaje al Silencio: Exploraciones del Discurso Barroco.* México: UNAM, 1998.

Myscofski, Carole A. "Review Symposium on *Sor Juana Inés de la Cruz: Religion, Art, and Feminism* by Pamela Kirk (New York: Continuum, 1998)." *Horizons* 25, no. 2 (1998): 303–306.

Parker, A. A. *The Allegorical Drama of Calderón: An Introduction to the "Auto Sacramentales."* Oxford: The Dolphin Book Co. Ltd., 1968.

Pasquariello, Anthony. "The Evolution of the *Loa* in Spanish America." *Latin American Theater Review* 3, no. 2 (Spring 1970): 5–19.

Paz, Octavio. *Sor Juana or, Traps of Faith.* Translated by Margaret Sayers Peden. Cambridge MA: Harvard University Press, 1988.

Perelmuter Pérez, Rosa. "La Estructurea Retórica de la *Respuesta a Sor Fioleta.*" *Hispanic Review* 51, no. 2 (Spring 1983): 147–58.

———. *Noche Intellectual: La Oscuridad Idiomática en el Primero Sueño.* Mexico: UNAM, Instituto de Investigaciones Filológicas, Centro de Estudios Literarios, 1982.

Pérez, María E. *Lo Americano en el Teatro de Sor Juana Inés de la Cruz.* New York: Eliseo Torres, 1975.

Peters, Patricia A., and Renée Domeier, O.S.B. "Introduction." In *The Divine Narcissus/El Divino Narciso,* translated by Patricia A. Peters and Renée Domeier, O.S.B. Albuquerque NM: University of New Mexico Press, 1998.

Picon-Salas, Mariano. *A Cultural History of Spanish America.* Translated by Irving A. Leonard. Wesport CN: Greenwood Press, 1982.

Rabb, Theodore K. *The Struggle for Stability in Early Modern Europe.* New York: Oxford University Press, 1975.

Sabat-Rivers, Georgina. "Apologia de America y del Mundo Azteca en Tres Loas de Sor Juana." *Revista de Estudios Hispanicos* (1992): 267–91. ———. "A Feminist Rereading of Sor Juana's *Dream.*" In *Feminist Perspectives on Sor Juana Inés de la Cruz*, edited by Stephanie Merrim, 142–61. Detroit: Wayne State University Press, 1991.

———. "Loa del Auto a San Hermenegildo: Sor Juana Frente a la Autoridad de la Sabiduría Antigua." *En Busca de Sor Juana.* Alicante: Biblioteca Virtual Miguel de Cervantes, 2005.

———. *El "Sueno" de Sor Juana Inés de la Cruz: Tradiciones Literarias y Originalidad.* London: Tamesis Books Ltd, 1976.

Schons, Dorothy. "Some Obscure Points in the Life of Sor Juana Inés de la Cruz." In *Feminist Perspectives on Sor Juana Inés de la Cruz*, edited by Stephanie Merrim, 38–60. Detroit: Wayne State University Press, 1991.

Scott, Nina M. "*La Gran Turba de las Que Nombres:* Sor Juana's Foremothers in *La Respuesta a Sor Fioleta.*" In *Coded Encounters: Race, Gender, and Ethnicity in Colonial Latin America*, edited by Javier Cevallos-Candau, 206–23. Amherst MA: University of Massachusetts Press, 1994.

———. "'If you are not pleased to favor me, put me out of your mind…': Gender and Authority in Sor Juana Inés de la Cruz: And the Translation of Her Letter to the Reverend Father Maestro Antonio Núñez of the Society of Jesus."*Women's Studies International Forum* 11/5 (1988): 429–38.

———. "Sor Juana and Her World." *Latin American Research Review* 29, no. 1 (1994): 143–54.

———. "Sor Juana Inés de la Cruz: 'Let Your Women Keep Silence in the Churches.'" *Women's Studies International Forum* 8, no. 5 (1985): 511–19.

Tavard, George T. *Juana Inés de la Cruz and the Theology of Beauty: The First Mexican Theology*. Notre Dame: University of Notre Dame Press, 1991.

Trabulse, Elías. *Los Años Finales de Sor Juana: Una Interpretación (1688–1695)*. Mexico City: Centro de Estudios de Historia de México Condumex, 1995.

———. *Ciencia y Religion en el Siglo XVII.* Mexico: El Colegio de México, 1974.

———. *El Enigma de Serafina de Cristo: Acerca de un Manuscrito Inédito de Sor Juana Inés de la Cruz (1691)*. Toluca: Instituto Mexiquense de Cultura, 1995.

———. "La Guerra del las Finezas. La Otra Respuesta a Sor Fioleta en un Manuscrito Inédito de 1691." In *Mujer y Cultura en la Colonia Hispanoamericana*, edited by Mabel Moraña, 203–15. Pittsburgh: Biblioteca de América, 1996.

———. "El Silencio Final de Sor Juana." In *Sor Juana & Vieira, Trescientos Años Después,* edited by K. Josu Bijuesca and Pablo A. J. Brescia. Santa Barbara: Center for Portuguese Studies, Department of Spanish and Portuguese, University of California, Santa Barbara, 1998.

Trueblood, Alan S. "Introduction." In *A Sor Juana Anthology,* translated by Alan S. Trueblood. Cambridge MA: Harvard University Press, 1988.

Vuola, Elina. "Sor Juana Inés de la Cruz: Rationality, Gender, and Power." *JHLT* 9, no. 1 (2001): 27–45.

Wardropper, Bruce W., editor. *Critical Essays on the Theatre of Calderón*. New York: New York University Press, 1965.

Weber, Alison. *Teresa of Avila and the Rhetoric of Femininity*. Princeton: Princeton University Press, 1990.

Wilson, Katharina M., and Frank J. Warnke. "Introduction." In *Women Writers of the Seventeenth Century*. Athens GA: University of Georgia Press, 1989.

Other Works Cited

Allen, Diogenes. *Philosophy for Understanding Theology*. Atlanta: John Knox Press, 1973.

Altman, Janet Gurkin. *Epistolarity: Approaches to a Form*. Columbus: Ohio State University Press, 1982.

Anderson, Thomas C. "Kierkegaard and Approximation Knowledge." In *International Kierkegaard Commentary, Vol. 12. Concluding Unscientific Postscript to "Philosophical Fragments,"* edited by Robert L. Perkins, 187–203. Macon GA: Mercer University Press, 1997.

Bakhtin, M. M. "Discourse in the Novel." In *Dialogic Imagination,* translated by Caryl Emerson and Michael Holquist and edited by Michael Holquist, 259–422. Austin TX: University of Texas Press, 1981.

———. "Epic and Novel." In *Dialogic Imagination,* translated by Caryl Emerson and Michael Holquist and edited by Michael Holquist, 3–40. Austin TX: University of Texas Press, 1981.

———. "Forms of Time and the Chronotope in the Novel." In *Dialogic Imagination,* translated by Caryl Emerson and Michael Holquist and edited by Michael Holquist, 84–258. Austin TX: University of Texas Press, 1981.

———. "From Notes Made in 1970–1971." In *Speech Genres and Other Late Essays*, translated by Vern W. McGee and edited by Caryl Emerson and Michael Holquist, 132–58. Austin TX: University of Texas Press, 1986.

———. "From the Prehistory of Novelistic Discourse." In *Dialogic Imagination,* translated by Caryl Emerson and Michael Holquist and edited by Michael Holquist, 41–83. Austin TX: University of Texas Press, 1981.

———. *Problems of Dostoevsky's Poetics*. Edited and translated by Caryl Emerson. Minneapolis: University of Minnesota Press, 1984.

———. *Toward a Philosophy of Act.* Translated and notes by Vadim Liapunov and edited by Vadim Liapunov and Michael Holquist. Austin: University of Texas Press, 1993.

Bernstein, Richard J. *Beyond Objectivism and Relativism: Science, Hermeneutics, and Praxis*. Philadelphia: University of Pennsylvania Press, 1983.

Bonaventure. *The Soul's Journey into God.* In *The Classics of Western Sprituality*, translated by Ewert Cousins. Mahway NJ: Paulist Press, 1978.

Bornkamm, Heinrich. *Luther's World of Thought.* Translated by Martin H. Bertram. St. Louis: Concordia Publishing House, 1958.

Brown, James. *Subject and Object in Modern Theology.* New York: Macmillian Company, 1955.

Brown, Penelope, and Stephen Levinson. "Universals in Language Usage: Politeness Phenomena." In *Questions and Politeness*, edited by Ester N. Goody. Cambridge: Cambridge University Press, 1978.

Bruns, Gerald L. *Heidegger's Estrangements: Language, Truth, and Poetry in the Later Writings*. New Haven: Yale University Press, 1989.

Burrell, David B. *Analogy and Philosophical Language.* New Haven: Yale University Press, 1973.

Cameron, Deborah. *Feminism and Linguistic Theory*. 2nd edition. London: Routledge, 1992.

Carnell, Edward John. *The Burden of Kierkegaard.* Grand Rapids MI: William B. Eerdmans Publishing Company, 1965.

Cixous, Héléne. "The Laugh of the Medusa." In *The Critical Tradition: Classic Texts and Contemporary Trends*, edited by David H. Richter, 1090–102. New York: St. Martin's Press, 1989.

Coates, Jennifer, editor. *Language and Gender: A Reader*. London: Routledge, 1998.

———. *Women, Men, and Language: A Sociolinguistic Account of Gender Differences in Language*. 2nd edition. London: Longman, 1993.

Coates, Ruth. *Christianity in Bakhtin: God and the Exiled Author.* Cambridge: Cambridge University Press, 1998.

Connor, Steven. *Postmodernist Culture: an Introduction to Theories of the Contemporary.* 2nd edition. Cambridge MA: Blackwell, 1997.

Corngold, Stanley. "*Sein und Zeit:* Implications for Poetics." In *Martin Heidegger and the Question of Literature*, edited by William Spanos, 99–114. Bloomington: Indiana University Press, 1979.

Dahlstrom, Daniel O. *Heidegger's Concept of Truth*. Cambridge: Cambridge University Press, 2001.

Deleuze, Gilles. *Difference and Repetition*. Translated by Paul Patton. New York: Columbia University Press, 1994.

Demos, Raphael. "Introduction." In *The Dialogues of Plato,* volumes 1–2, translated by B. Jowett, M.A. New York: Random House, 1937.

Dillenberger, John. *God Hidden and Revealed: The Interpretation of Luther's* Deus Absconditus *and Its Significance for Religious Thought*. Philadelphia: Muhlenberg Press, 1953.

Drake, H. A. *Constantine and the Bishops: The Politics of Intolerance*. Baltimore: The Johns Hopkins University Press, 2000.

Dunning, Stephen N. "The Illusory Grandeur of Doubt: The Dialectic of Subjectivity in *Johannes Climacus*." In *International Kierkegaard Commentary, Vol. 7: Philosophical Fragments and Johannes Climacus*, edited by Robert L. Perkins, 203–22. Macon GA: Mercer University Press.

Evans, C. Stephen. *Kierkegaard's "Fragments" and "Postscript": The Religious Philosophy of Johannes Climacus*. Atlantic Highlands NJ: Humanities Press, 1983.

Foucault, *Discipline and Punish: The Birth of the Prison*. Translated by Alan Sheridan. New York: Vintage Books, 1977.

Fraser, Nancy, and Linda J. Nicholson. "Social Criticism without Philosophy: An Encounter between Feminism and Postmodernism." In *Feminism/Postmodernism*, edited by Linda J. Nicholson, 19–38. New York: Routledge, 1990.

Gal, Susan. "Between Speech and Silence: The Problematics of Research on Language and Gender." In *Gender at the Crossroads of Knowledge: Feminist Anthropology in the Postmodern Era,* edited by M. di Leonardo, 175–203. Berkeley: University of California Press, 1991.

Gerrish, B. A. "'To the Unknown God': Luther and Calvin on the Hiddeness of God." *Journal of Religion* 53 (1973): 263–92.

Gilbert, Sandra M., and Susan Gubar. *The Madwoman in the Attic: The Women Writer and the Nineteenth Century Literary Imagination*. New Haven: Yale University Press, 1984.

Gill, Jerry H. "Kant, Kierkegaard, and Religious Knowledge." In *Essays on Kierkegaard*, edited by Jerry Gill, 58–73. Minneapolis: Burgess Publishing Company, 1969.

Gilligan, Carol. *In a Different Voice*: *Psychological Theory and Women's Development*. Cambridge MA: Harvard University Press, 1982.

Goioechea, David. "Kierkegaard's Leap Out of the Hermeneutical Circle." In *Søren Kierkegaard and the Word(s): Essays on Hermeneutics and Communication*, edited by Paul Houe and Gordon D. Marino, 39–48. Copenhagen: C.A. Reitzel, 2003.

Green, Ronald M. "Kierkegaard's *Philosophical Fragments*: A Kantian Commentary." In *International Kierkegaard Commentary, Vol. 7 Philosophical Fragments and Johannes*

Climacus, edited by Robert L. Perkins, 169–202. Macon GA: Mercer University Press, 1994.

Gregory of Nyssa, "An Address on Religious Instruction." In *Christology of the Later Fathers*, edited by Edward Hardy and translated by C. Richardson. Philadelphia: Westminster Press, 1954.

Grenz, Stanley J. *A Primer on Postmodernism*. Grand Rapids: William B. Eerdmans Publishing Company, 1996.

Griffin, David Ray. *God and Religion in Postmodern Theology: Essays in Postmodern Theology*. Albany: State University of New York Press, 1989.

Grislis, Egil. "Martin Luther's View of the Hidden God: The Problem of the *Deus Absconditus* in Luther's Treatise *De Servo Arbitrio*." *McCormick Quartlery* 21, no. 1 (November 1967): 81–94.

Hall, John. *Lighten Our Darkness: Toward an Indigenous Theology of the Cross*. Philadelphia: Westminster Press, 1976.

Hannay, Alastair. "Kierkegaard, Hermeneutics, and indirect communication." In *Søren Kierkegaard and the Word(s): Essays on Hermeneutics and Communication*, edited by Paul Houe and Gordon D. Marino, 11–27. Copenhagen: C.A. Reitzel, 2003.

Harries, Karsten. "Language and Silence: Heidegger's Dialogue with Georg Trakl." In *Martin Heidegger and the Question of Literature*, edited by William Spanos, 155–72. Bloomington: Indiana University Press, 1979.

Heidegger, Martin. *On the Way to Language*. Translated by Peter D. Hertz. New York: Harper & Row, 1971.

———. "The Origin of the Work of Art." In *Poetry, Language, Thought*, translated by Albert Hofstadter, 15–88. New York: Harper & Row, 1971.

———. "The Thinker as Poet." In *Poetry, Language, Thought*, translated by Albert Hofstadterm, 1–14. New York: Harper & Row, 1971.

———. "What Are Poets For?" In *Poetry, Language, Thought*, translated by Albert Hofstadter, 89–142. New York: Harper & Row, 1971.

Heywood, Thomas, J. "Revelation, Knowledge, and Proof." In *International Kierkegaard Commentary, Vol. 7: Philosophical Fragments and Johannes Climacus*, edited by Robert L. Perkins, 147–68. Macon GA: Mercer University Press, 1994.

Hirsch, Edward. *The Demon and the Angel: Searching for the Source of Artistic Inspiration*. New York: Harcourt, 2001.

———. "The Work of Lyric: Night and Day." *Georgia Review* 57, no. 2 (Summer 2003): 368–80.

Hofstadter, Albert. "Introduction" and "Notes." In *Poetry, Language, and Thought,* translated by Albert Hofstadterm. New York: Harper & Row, 1971.

Holmer, Paul. "Kierkegaard and Religious Propositions." *Journal of Religion* 35, no. 3 (July 1955): 135–46.

———. "Kierkegaard and Theology." *Union Seminary Quarterly Review* 12 (1957): 23–31.

———. "On Understanding Kierkegaard." In *A Kierkegaard Critique,* edited by Howard A. Johnson and Niels Thulstrup, 40–53. New York: Harper and Brothers, 1962.

Holquist, Michael. "Introduction." In *Dialogic Imagination,* translated by Caryl Emerson and Michael Holquist and edited by Michael Holquist, xv–xxxiii. Austin TX: University of Texas Press, 1981.

Hong, Howard V., and Edna H. Hong. "Historical Introduction." In *Concluding Postscript to "Philosophical Fragments,"* volume 2, translated and edited by Howard V. Hong and Edna H. Hong. Princeton: Princeton University Press, 1992.

Horsley, Richard A. *Jesus and Empire: The Kingdom of God and the New World Disorder.* Minneapolis: Fortress Press, 2003.

Houe, Paul. "Between the Word and the Words: Hermeneutics and Communication in Kierkegaard after All?" In *Søren Kierkegaard and the Word(s): Essays on Hermeneutics and Communication*, edited by Paul Houe and Gordon D. Marino, 284–95. Copenhagen: C.A. Reitzel, 2003.

Hultgren, A. "The *Pistis Christou* Formulations in Paul." *Novum Testamentum* 22 (1980): 248–63.

Irenaeus. *Against the Heresies.* In *Irenaeus of Lyons,* translated by Robert M. Grant. New York: Routledge, 1997.

Jansen, Nerina. "Deception in Service of the Truth: Magister Kierkegaard and the Problem of Communication." In *International Kierkegaard Commentary, Vol. 12. Concluding Unscientific Postscript to "Philosophical Fragments,"* edited by Robert L. Perkins, 115–28. Macon GA: Mercer University Press, 1997.

Jantzen, Grace M. *Power, Gender, and Christian Mysticism.* Cambridge: Cambridge University Press, 1995.

Johnson, Luke Timothy. "Romans 3:21–26 and Faith of Jesus." *Catholic Biblical Quarterly* 44 (1982): 77–90.

Jule, Allyson. "Silence as Femininity? A Look at Performances of Gender in Theology College Classrooms." In *Being Feminist, Being Christian: Essays from Academia*, edited by Allyson Jule and Bettina Tate Pedersen, 35–58. New York: Palgrave Macmillan, 2006.

Kattenbusch, Ferdinand. "*Deus Absconditus* bei Luther," in *Festagabe f'r D. Dr. Julius Kaften zu seinem 70.* Geburtstag, Tübingen: J.C.B. Mohr, 1920, 170-214. Quoted by Egil Grislis, "Martin Luther's View of the Hidden God: The Problem of the *Deus Absconditus* in Luther's Treatise *De Servo Arbitrio*," *McCormick Quarterly* 21, no. 1 (November 1967): 85.

Kellenberger, J. "Kierkegaard, indirect communication, and Religious Truth." *International Journal of the Philosophy of Religion* 16 (1984): 153–60.

Kierkegaard, Søren. [Johannes Climacus, psued.] *Concluding Unscientific Postscript to "Philosophical Fragments."* Translated and edited by Howard V. Hong and Edna H. Hong. Princeton: Princeton University Press, 1992.

———. [Johannes Climacus, psued.] *Philosophical Fragments.* Translated and edited by Howard V. Hong and Edna H. Hong. Princeton: Princeton University Press, 1985.

———. [Anti-Climacus, psued.] *Practice in Christianity.* Edited and translated by Howard V. Hong and Edna H. Hong. Princeton: Princeton University Press, 1991.

———. *Søren Kierkegaard's Journals and Papers.* Volume 1, A–E. Edited and translated by Howard V. Hong and Edna H. Hong. Bloomington and London: Indiana University Press, 1967.

———. *Søren Kierkegaard's Journals and Papers.* Volume 2, F–K. Edited and translated by Howard V. Hong and Edna H. Hong. Bloomington and London: Indiana University Press, 1970.

———. *Søren Kierkegaard's Journals and Papers.* Volume 3, L–R. Edited and translated by Howard V. Hong and Edna H. Hong. Bloomington and London: Indiana University Press, 1995.

Krell, David Farrell. "Art and Truth in Raging Discord: Heidegger and Nietzsche on the Will to Power." In *Martin Heidegger and the Question of Literature*, edited by William Spanos, 39–52. Bloomington: Indiana University Press, 1979.

Kristeva, Julia. *Powers of Horror: An Essay on Abjection.* Translated by Leon S. Roudiez. New York: Columbia University Press, 1982.

———. *Time and Sense: Proust and the Experience of Literature.* Translated by Ross Guberman. New York: Columbia University Press, 1996.

Lakoff, Robin. *Language and Woman's Place.* New York: Harper and Row, 1975.

Lindstrom, Valter. "The Problem of Objectivity and Subjectivity in Kierkegaard." In *Kierkegaard Critique*, translated from the Swedish by Niels Erik Enkvist, 228–43. New York: Harper and Brothers, 1962.

Longenecker, Bruce W. "Pistis in Romans 3:25: Neglected Evidence for the 'Faithfulness of Christ.'" *New Testament Studies* 39 (1993): 478–80.

Lorca, Federíco Garcia. "Deep Song." In *Deep Song and Other Prose*, translated and edited by Christopher Maurer, 23–41. New York: Marion Boyars, 1991.

———. *In Search of the Duende.* Edited and translated (prose) Christopher Maurer and translated (poem) by Norman di Giovanni, Edwin Honig, Langston Hughes, et al. New York: New Directions, 1998.

———. "Lecture: A Poet in New York." In *A Poet in New York,* translated by Greg Simon and Steven F. White and edited by Christopher Mauer, 183–201. New York: Farrar, Straus and Giroux, 1988.

Löwith, Karl. "On the Historical Understanding of Kierkegaard." *Review of Religion* 7 (March 1943): 227–41.

Lubcke, Poul. "indirect communication and Kierkegaard's Transcendental Existential Perspectivism." In *Søren Kierkegaard and the Word(s): Essays on Hermeneutics and Communication*, edited by Paul Houe and Gordon D. Marino, 28–38. Copenhagen: C.A. Reitzel, 2003.

Lukács, Georg. *The Theory of the Novel: A Historico-Philosophical Essay on the Forms of Great Epic Literature.* Translated by Anna Bostock. Cambridge MA: The MIT Press, 1977.

Luther, Martin. *Lectures on Galatians* (1535), Chapters 1–4. In *Luther's Works*, volume 26, translated by Jaroslav Pelikan, edited by Jaroslav Pelikan, and associate edited by Walter A. Hansen. St. Louis: Concordia Publishing House, 1963.

———. *Table Talk*. In *Luther's Works*, volume 54, edited and translated by Theodore G. Tappert and general edited by Helmut T. Lehmann. Philadelphia: Fortress Press, 1967.

Lyotard, Jean Francois. *The Postmodern Condition: A Report on Knowledge*. Translated by Geoff Bennington and Brian Massumi. Minneapolis: University of Minnesota Press, 1991.

———. *The Postmodern Explained*. Translated by Don Barry, Bernadette Maher, Julian Pefanis, Virginia Spate, and Morgan Thomas. Minneapolis: University of Minnesota Press, 1992.

Marcus, George E. *Anthropology as Cultural Critique: An Experimental Moment in the Human Sciences*. Chicago: University of Chicago Press, 1986.

Maximus the Confessor. *The Classics of Western Spirituality*. Translated and notes by George C. Berthold and introduction by Jaroslav Pelikan. New York: Paulist Press, 1985.

Mehl, Peter J. "Edifying Hermeneutics: Kierkegaard's Existential 'Method' and Its Limits." In *Søren Kierkegaard and the Word(s): Essays on Hermeneutics and Communication*, edited by Paul Houe and Gordon D. Marino, 49–59. Copenhagen: C.A. Reitzel, 2003.

Mihailovic, Alexandar. *Corporeal Words: Mikhail Bakhtin's Theology of Discourse*. Evanston IL: Northwestern University Press, 1997.

Miller, Ronald H. *Dialogue and Disagreement: Franz Rosenzweig's Relevance to Contemporary Jewish-Christian Understanding*. New York: University Press of America, 1989.

Mooney, Edward F. "Exemplars, Inwardness, and Belief: Kierkegaard on Indirect Communication." In *International Kierkegaard Commentary, Vol. 12. Concluding Unscientific Postscript to "Philosophical Fragments,"* edited by Robert L. Perkins, 129–48. Macon GA: Mercer University Press, 1997.

Mosés, Stéphane. *System and Revelation: The Philosophy of Franz Rosenzweig*. Translated by Catherine Tihanyi. Detroit: Wayne State University Press, 1992.

Nicholson, Linda J. "Introduction." In *Feminism/Postmodernism*, edited by Linda J. Nicholson, 1–16. New York: Routledge, 1990.

Nussbaum, Martha C. *Love's Knowledge: Essays on Philosophy and Literature*. New York: Oxford University Press, 1990.

Oberman, Heiko A. *Luther: Man between God and the Devil*. Translated by Eileen Walliser-Schwarzbart. New Haven: Yale University Press, 1989.

Oppenheim, Michael D. "Taking Time Seriously: An Inquiry into the Methods of Communication of Søren Kierkegaard and Franz Rosenzweig." *Studies in Religion* 7, no. 1 (Winter 1978): 53–60.

Otto, Rudolph. *The Idea of the Holy: An Inquiry into the Non-Rational Factor in the Idea of the Divine and Its Relation to the Rational*. Translated by John W. Harvey. London: Oxford University Press, 1950.

Palmer, Richard E. "The Postmodernity of Heidegger." In *Martin Heidegger and the Question of Literature*, edited by William Spanos, 71–92. Bloomington: Indiana University Press, 1979.

Piety, M. G. "A Little Light Music: The Subversion of Objectivity in Kierkegaard's *Philosophical Fragments*." In *International Kierkegaard Commentary, Vol. 7:*

Philosophical Fragments and Johannes Climacus, edited by Robert L. Perkins, 47–62. Macon GA: Mercer University Press, 1994.

———. "The Reality of the World in Kierkegaard's *Postscript.*" In *International Kierkegaard Commentary, Vol. 12. Concluding Unscientific Postscript to "Philosophical Fragments,"* edited by Robert L. Perkins, 169–86. Macon GA: Mercer University Press, 1997.

Plato. *The Dialogues of Plato.* Volumes 1–2. Translated by B. Jowett, M.A. New York: Random House, 1937.

———. "Theaeteus." In *The Loeb Classical Library*, edited by G. P. Goold, *Plato* VII, translated by Harold North Fowler. Cambridge MA: Harvard University Press, 1996.

Pojman, Luis P. *The Logic of Subjectivity: Kierkegaard's Philosophy of Religion.* (University, AL): The University of Alabama Press, 1984.

Polka, Brayton. "Aesthetics and Religion: Kierkegaard and the Offence of Indirect Communication." In *Kierkegaard on Art and Communication,* edited by George Pattison, 23–54. New York: St. Martin's Press, 1992.

Poole, Roger. *Kierkegaard: The indirect communication.* Charlottesville: University Press of Virginia, 1993.

Pseudo-Dionysius, *Pseudo-Dionysius: The Complete Works.* The Classics of Western Spirituality. Translated by Colm Luibheid and Paul Rorem. New York: Paulist Press, 1987.

Rendtorff, Trutz. "The Modern Age as a Chapter in the History of Christianity; or, The Legacy of Historical Consciousness in Present Theology." *Journal of Religion* #65 (1985): 478–99.

Rosenfeld, Alvin H. "'The Being of Language and the Language of Being': Heidegger and Modern Poetics." In *Martin Heidegger and the Question of Literature*, edited by William Spanos, 195–213. Bloomington: Indiana University Press, 1979.

Rosenzweig, Franz. *Franz Rosenzweig: His Life and Thought.* Presented by Nahum N. Glatzer. New York: Schocken Books, 1961.

———. *Philosophical and Theological Writings.* Translated and edited by Paul W. Franks and Michael L. Morgan. Indianapolis: Hackett Publishing Company, Inc., 2000.

Rosenzweig, Franz, and Eugen Rosenstock-Huessy. *Judaism Despite Christianity: The "Letters on Christianity and Judiasm" between Eugen Rosenstock-Huessy and Franz Rosenzweig*. Edited by Eugen Rosenstock-Huessy. University, AL: University of Alabama, 1969.

Royer, Fanchón. *The Tenth Muse: Sor Juana Inés de la Cruz*. Paterson NJ: St. Anthony Guild Press, 1952.

Seaman, Donna. "A Conversation with Edward Hirsch." *Triquarterly* (Fall 2003): 61–76.

Showalter, Elaine. "Toward a Feminist Poetics." In *The New Feminist Criticism: Essays on Women, Literature, and Theory,* edited by Elaine Showalter. New York: Pantheon, 1985.

Simpson, Christopher. "A Way Between Freeplay and Totality: Kierkegaard on Faith and the Other." In *Søren Kierkegaard and the Word(s): Essays on Hermeneutics and*

Communication, edited by Paul Houe and Gordon D. Marino, 60–70. Copenhagen: C.A. Reitzel, 2003.

Smith, James K. A. "Alterity, Transcendence, and the Violence of the Concept: Kierkegaard and Heidegger." *International Philosophical Quarterly* 38, no. 4, issue 152 (December 1998): 369–81.

Solberg, Mary M. *Compelling Knowledge: A Feminist Proposal for an Epistemology of the Cross*. New York: State University of New York Press, 1997.

Solomon, Robert C. *Continental Philosophy since 1750: The Rise and Fall of the Self.* Oxford: Oxford University Press, 1988.

Spanos, William. "Heidegger, Kierkegaard, and the Hermeneutic Circle: Towards a Postmodern Theory of Interpretation as Dis-closure." In *Martin Heidegger and the Question of Literature*, edited by William Spanos, 115–48. Bloomington: Indiana University Press, 1979.

———. "Martin Heidegger and the Question of Literature: A Preface." In *Martin Heidegger and the Question of Literature*, edited by William Spanos, ix–xix. Bloomington: Indiana University Press, 1979.

Spender, Dale. *Man Made Language*. 2nd edition. London: Routledge Kegan Paul, 1980.

Tanner, Kathryn. *Jesus, Humanity, and the Trinity: A Brief Systematic Theology*. Edinburgh: T&T Clark, 2001.

Taylor, Mark C. *Kierkegaard's Pseudonymous Authorship: A Study of Time and the Self.* Princeton: Princeton University Press, 1975.

Thomas, John Heywood. "indirect communication: Hegelian Aesthetic and Kierkegaard's Literary Art." In *Kierkegaard on Art and Communication,* edited by George Pattison, 114–23. New York: St. Martin's Press, 1992.

Thulstrup, Niels. *Kierkegaard's Relation to Hegel.* Translated by George L. Stengren. Princeton: Princeton University Press, 1980.

van Huyssteen, J. Wentzel. *The Shaping of Rationality: Toward Interdisciplinarity in Theology and Science.* Grand Rapids: William B. Eerdmans Publishing Company, 1999.

Walsh, Sylvia. "Kierkegaard: Poet of the Religious." In *Kierkegaard on Art and Communication*, edited by George Pattison, 1–22. New York: St. Martin's Press, 1992.

———. "Subjectivity verses Objectivity: Kierkegaard's *Postscript* and Feminist Epistemology." In *International Kierkegaard Commentary, Vol. 12. Concluding Unscientific Postscript to "Philosophical Fragments,"* edited by Robert L. Perkins, 11–31. Macon GA: Mercer University Press, 1997.

Watkin, Julia. "Boom! The Earth is Round!—On the Impossibility of an Existential System." In *International Kierkegaard Commentary, Vol. 12. Concluding Unscientific Postscript to "Philosophical Fragments,"* edited by Robert L. Perkins, 95–113. Macon GA: Mercer University Press, 1997.

Westphal, Merold. *Becoming a Self: A Reading of Kierkegaard's "Concluding Unscientific Postscript."* West Lafayette IN: Purdue University Press, 1996.

———. "Kierkegaard's Climacus—a Kind of Postmodernist." In *International Kierkegaard Commentary, Vol. 12. Concluding Unscientific Postscript to "Philosophical*

Fragments," edited by Robert L. Perkins, 53–71. Macon GA: Mercer University Press, 1997.

Index